David Baer is Principal and Lecturer in Old Testament and Biblical Languages, Seminario ESEPA, San José, Costa Rica.

JOURNAL FOR THE STUDY OF THE OLD TESTAMENT
SUPPLEMENT SERIES
318

THE HEBREW BIBLE AND ITS VERSIONS
1

Sheffield Academic Press

When We All Go Home

Translation and Theology in LXX Isaiah 56–66

David A. Baer

Journal for the Study of the Old Testament
Supplement Series 318

The Hebrew Bible and its Versions 1

Copyright © 2001 Sheffield Academic Press

Published by
Sheffield Academic Press Ltd
Mansion House
19 Kingfield Road
Sheffield S11 9AS
England

http://www.SheffieldAcademicPress.com

Typeset by Sheffield Academic Press
and
Printed on acid-free paper in Great Britain
by Bookcraft Ltd,
Midsomer Norton, Bath

British Library Cataloguing-in-Publication Data

A catalogue record for this book is available
from the British Library

ISBN 1 84127 180 2

CONTENTS

PREFACE

Already in Jerome's day, the variance between the Hebrew and Greek texts of the book of Isaiah had come in for comment. Having 'sweated in the learning of a foreign language', Jerome well earned his right to opine that the Septuagintal translators 'were unwilling at that time to expose the solemn truths of their faith to the gaze of Gentiles, in case they should give what is holy to dogs or pearls to swine'. It is not difficult to admire the perspiring learner of foreign tongues and to honour his translational exertions. Indeed, Jerome's observation of Jewish nationalism in the Greek Isaiah looks acute in the light of the present study, even if one must question the motives and tactics that he remarked. Though Jerome and others similarly inclined have been this way before, one dares hope to have exposed here and there a 'solemn truth' heretofore concealed or, if not, to have stumbled upon one or two dusty pearls.

My own research into the Septuagint began on the day I sat down over tea in Cambridge with Professor Robert Gordon and has continued since then, profoundly shaped by its genesis under a targumist's careful eye. During my years as a postgraduate student, Robert proved himself an exceptional mentor and friend. His counsel as the editor of the series to which this volume contributes now provides yet another motive for expressing that appreciation which does not fade.

The Revd Dr Andrew Macintosh is an unstinting encourager, his enthusiasm seeming never to ebb. Dr Graham Davies and Professor William Horbury, each in his own way, have been interested in this project and most kind. Corpus Christi College distinguished itself in my case, as in countless others, by providing the ambience and care that cultivate both scholarship and family life.

It would not have been possible for my family to spend three and a half of the best years of our lives in Cambridge and then for me to continue this research elsewhere without financial support from several sources. I am especially grateful to all those who stand behind the work of Seminario ESEPA (San José, Costa Rica) and the Latin America Mission. Dick and Marilyn Lauber have understood what it takes. I owe thanks as well to the managers and electors of the Purvis Fund, the Crosse Studentship and the Hort Fund. My colleagues at Seminario ESEPA are to be thanked for tolerating my absences, not always conveniently scheduled.

If somewhere there exists a more exceptional locale for biblical research than Desk Four of Cambridge's Tyndale House Library, I cannot imagine it. Though that institution's helpful staff doubtless celebrated the return to order of that space upon my evacuation of it, I am grateful for their tolerance during its long descent into chaos. Dr Karen Croot, of Sydney University's School of Communication Sciences and Disorders read these chapters and offered invaluable advice without once surrendering to the urge to offer a diagnosis. Dr Tim Laniak knows the virtues and vices of North and South, and the adventure of living with one foot in each. There are indeed friends who stand closer than brothers.

Finally, my Linda, Christopher and Johnny are a gift in praise of which words fail utterly. In dedicating this book to my wife, I join our two boys in rising to honour their mother, my praise mingling with their blessing.

ללינדא

קמו בניה ויאשרוה בעלה ויהללה

(Proverbs 31.28)

ABBREVIATIONS

AB	Anchor Bible
ABD	David Noel Freedman (ed.), *The Anchor Bible Dictionary* (New York: Doubleday, 1992)
ANE	Ancient Near East(ern)
BDB	Francis Brown, S.R. Driver and Charles A. Briggs, *A Hebrew and English Lexicon of the Old Testament* (Oxford: Clarendon Press, 1907)
BDF	Friedrich Blass, A. Debrunner and Robert W. Funk, *A Greek Grammar of the New Testament and Other Early Christian Literature* (Cambridge: Cambridge University Press, 1961)
BH	Biblical Hebrew
BHS	*Biblia Hebraica Stuttgartensia*
BibInt	*Biblical Interpretation: A Journal of Contemporary Approaches*
Bijdragen	*Bijdragen: Tijdschrift voor Filosofie en Theologie* 40 (1979), pp. 12-14.
BIOSCS	*Bulletin of the International Organization for Septuagint and Cognate Studies*
BO	*Bibliotheca orientalis*
BZAW	Beihefte zur *ZAW*
CBQ	*Catholic Biblical Quarterly*
CChr	Corpus Christianorum
DJD	Discoveries in the Judaean Desert
editio	Joseph Ziegler, *Isaias* (Septuagint Vetus Testamentum Graecum, Auctoritate Academiae Scientiarium Gottingensis editum, 14; Göttingen: Vandenhoeck & Ruprecht, 3rd edn, 1983).
EJ	*Encyclopaedia Judaica*
GKC	*Gesenius' Hebrew Grammar* (ed. E. Kautzsch, revised and trans. A.E. Cowley; Oxford: Clarendon Press, 1910)
HR	*History of Religions*
HUB	Moshe H. Goshen-Gottstein (ed.), *The Book of Isaiah* (The Hebrew University Bible; Jerusalem: Magnes Press, 1995).
HUCA	*Hebrew Union College Annual*
ICC	International Critical Commentary
JBL	*Journal of Biblical Literature*

JNSL	*Journal of Northwest Semitic Languages*
JSOT	*Journal for the Study of the Old Testament*
JSOTSup	*Journal for the Study of the Old Testament*, Supplement Series
JSP	*Journal for the Study of the Pseudepigrapha*
JTS	*Journal of Theological Studies*
KB	Ludwig Koehler and Walter Baumgartner (eds.), *Lexicon in Veteris Testamenti libros* (Leiden: E.J. Brill, 1953)
LSJ	H.G. Liddell, Robert Scott and H. Stuart Jones, *Greek–English Lexicon* (Oxford: Clarendon Press, 9th edn, 1968)
LXX	Septuagint
Mekilta	*Mekilta de-Rabbi Ishmael* (trans. Jacob Z. Lauterbach; 3 vols.; Philadelphia: Jewish Publication Society 1961 [1933]).
MT	Massoretic Text
NCB	New Century Bible
NH	New (Late) Hebrew
NovTSup	*Novum Testamentum*, Supplements
NRSV	New Revised Standard Version
OBO	Orbis biblicus et orientalis
OG	Old Greek
OTL	Old Testament Library
SBLDS	Society of Biblical Literature Dissertation Series
SBLSCS	Society of Biblical Literature Septuagint and Cognate Studies
SBT	Studies in Biblical Theology
Tanakh	*Tanakh: A New Translation of the Holy Scriptures According to the Traditional Hebrew Text* (Philadelphia: Jewish Publication Society of American, 1985).
TJ	Targum Jonathan
TO	Targum Ongelos
VT	*Vetus Testamentum*
VTSup	*Vetus Testamentum*, Supplements
ZAW	*Zeitschrift für die alttestamentliche Wissenschaft*

Chapter 1

INTRODUCTION

The State of LXX Isaiah Studies

Conquest and Opportunity

This book explores matters of translation technique and theology as these are to be glimpsed in the Greek translation of the Hebrew biblical book of Isaiah. Four large ships have plied these waters already in this century. R.R. Ottley,[1] Joseph Ziegler,[2] I.L. Seeligmann[3] and Arie van der Kooij have each made dominant, though very different, contributions to this field of study. The convenience that the labours of the first three have recently been evaluated by the fourth[4] renders further discussion along those lines unnecessary at the moment, though interaction with each of them in this work will be frequent.

Insofar as LXX Isaiah studies are concerned, the legacies of Ottley, Ziegler and Seeligmann are centred around one or two major monographs on the Greek Isaiah, complemented by smaller articles that touch some detail of the subdiscipline or by substantial works that bear tangentially upon it.[5] Van der Kooij's monograph, on the other hand, does

---

1. *The Book of Isaiah According to the LXX (Codex Alexandrinus)* (2 vols.; Cambridge: Cambridge University Press, 2nd edn, 1909 [1904, 1906]).

2. *Untersuchungen zur LXX des Buches Isaias* (Münster: Aschendorffschen, 1934), and his masterful contribution on this prophet to the Göttingen Septuagint, *Isaias*, III (Göttingen: Vandenhoeck & Ruprecht, 1983; first published, 1939); hereafter, *editio*.

3. *The LXX Version of Isaiah: A Discussion of its Problems* (Leiden: E.J. Brill, 1948).

4. Cf. A. van der Kooij, 'Isaiah in the Septuagint', in C.G. Broyles and C.A. Evans (eds.), *Writing and Reading the Scroll of Isaiah*, Studies of Interpretation Tradition II (Leiden: E.J. Brill, 1997), pp. 513-29. Cf. further, in the same volume, S.E. Porter and B.W.R. Pearson, 'Isaiah through Greek Eyes: The Septuagint of Isaiah', pp. 531-46, esp. the comments on van der Kooij.

5. Cf., for example, R.R. Ottley, 'On the LXX of Isaiah v: 14, 17, 18', *JTS* 4

not concern LXX Isaiah exclusively.[6] However, he has supplemented
this work by a steadily growing series of articles that analyse discrete
textual units in LXX Isaiah and issues that are directly pertinent to it.[7]
Van der Kooij accepts Seeligmann's suggestion that a contemporising
reading of Isaiah explains many of the differences between the Hebrew
and Greek texts of the book. However, somewhat in contrast with
Seeligmann's view that the Isaiah translator's novelties are most easily
to be found in 'isolated free renderings', van der Kooij is concerned to
discern the 'coherence' of entire pericopes.[8] Van der Kooij takes LXX
Isaiah seriously *as a translation*. However, he does not wish to neglect
the further step of reading the Greek text *as a coherent work on its own*.[9]
Taken as a whole, van der Kooij's *oeuvre* represents an approach to the

(1903), pp. 269-70, and *A Handbook to the Septuagint* (London: Methuen, 1920),
the title page of which promotes its writer as 'Author of "Isaiah According to the
Septuagint"'. Cf. Ziegler's formidable productivity within the Göttingen Septuagint
project as well as articles that straddle LXX Isaiah and another subdiscipline, such
as 'Die Vorlage der Isaias-LXX und die erste Isaias-Rolle von Qumran (IQIsa)',
JBL 78 (1959), pp. 34-59. Whereas Ziegler's efforts produced a large number of
editions and text-critical studies, Seeligmann's efforts were directed to more
broadly interpretive ends. Cf. 'Voraussetzungen der Midraschexegese', in G.W.
Anderson (ed.), *Congress Volume* (Leiden: E.J. Brill, 1953), pp. 150-81; 'Indications of Editorial Alteration and Adaptation in the Massoretic Text and the Septuagint', *VT* 11 (1961), pp. 201-221; and 'Problems and Perspectives in Modern
Septuagint Research', *Textus* 15 (1990), pp. 169-232 [trans. of 1940 Dutch
original]. Ziegler remained ever the text critic, Seeligmann the student of Jewish
exegesis. 'Problems and Perspectives'—the latter's most lengthy work apart from
his *LXX Version*—is introduced, characteristically, by a quotation from the Tosefta.
    6.   *Die alten Textzeugen des Jesajabuches* (Göttingen: Vandenhoeck &
Ruprecht, 1981).
    7.   Cf. bibliography under Kooij, Arie van der.
    8.   Seeligmann, *LXX Version*, p. 41; A. van der Kooij, 'A Short Commentary on
Some Verses of the Old Greek of Isaiah 23', *BIOSCS* 15 (1982), pp. 26-37, and
'Isaiah in the Septuagint', in Broyles and Evans (eds.), *Writing and Reading the
Scroll of Isaiah*, pp. 513-29 (516). The former study has now been greatly expanded
as *The Oracle of Tyre: The Septuagint of Isaiah 23 as Version and Vision* (VT Sup,
71; Leiden: E.J. Brill, 1998). Seeligmann recognizes more coherence in the Greek
Isaiah than his stated methodology would lead one to anticipate, a happy tension
between theory and practice that surfaces at several points in his *LXX Version*.
    9.   Van der Kooij sketches his five-step method in 'Accident or Method? On
"Analogical" Interpretation in the Old Greek of Isaiah and in 1QIs[a]', *BO* 43 (1986),
pp. 368-69.

study of LXX Isaiah that is similar to the assumptions and methodology employed in this work.

If one does not expend words here on behalf of the many scholars who have shaped and steered the broader discipline of Septuagintal studies, this silence is tribute payable to the summaries, handbooks and survey articles that are readily available.[10] The same economy will be practised with regard to those scholars who have dealt with one or another aspect of the Greek Isaiah in particular, though we will meet a number of these *en route*. The maritime imagery obligates us to recognize the ice-breaking labours of such early scholars as Anton Scholz, even if his discernment of a *Vorlage* that differs widely from the MT has not persuaded many.[11] Specific words or topics in LXX Isaiah have been clarified in this century by a large number of short studies that have filled in the picture presented by the works referred to above.[12] These have been supplemented by numerous text-critical and exegetical analyses of discrete textual units.[13]

10. Cf. esp. S. Jellicoe, *The Septuagint and Modern Study* (Oxford: Oxford University Press, 1968); M.K.H. Peters, 'Septuagint', in D.N. Freedman (ed.), *ABD*, V, pp. 1093-104; E. Tov, *Textual Criticism of the Hebrew Bible* (Philadelphia: Fortress Press, 1992), *The Text-Critical Use of the Septuagint in Biblical Research* (Jerusalem: Simor, 1997); 'The Septuagint', in M.J. Mulder (ed.), *Mikra* (Assen: Van Gorcum, 1990), pp. 161-88; and K.H. Jobes and M. Silva, *Invitation to the Septuagint* (Carlisle: Paternoster, 2000).

11. *Die alexandrinische Uebersetzung des Buches Jesaias* (Würzburg: Leo Woerl, 1880). Scholz provides many useful lists of MT/LXX divergences. They are best viewed as illustrative—rather than exhaustive—of the phenomena they mean to identify. Cf. also F. Wutz, *Die Transkriptionen von der Septuaginta bis zu Hieronymus* (Stuttgart: W. Kohlhammer, 1925). Wutz's transcription theory is discussed (and largely dismissed) in the relevant surveys. Mention is due here because of his utilization of large numbers of examples from Isaiah to support his argument.

12. E.g. R.L. Troxel, 'ΕΣΧΑΤΟΣ and Eschatology in LXX-Isaiah', *BIOSCS* 25 (1992), pp. 18-27; J.W. Olley, 'The Translator of the Septuagint of Isaiah and "Righteousness"', *BIOSCS* 13 (1980), pp. 58-74 (cf. bibliography for Olley's larger work on this topic); J. Lust, 'The Demonic Character of Jahweh and the Septuagint of Isaiah', *Bijdragen* 40 (1979), pp. 2-14.

13. E.g. P.W. Flint, 'The Septuagint Version of Isaiah 23.1-14 and the Massoretic Text', *BIOSCS* 21 (1988), pp. 35-54; H.G.M. Williamson, 'Isaiah 1.11 and the Septuagint of Isaiah', in A.G. Auld (ed.), *Understanding Poets and Prophets* (Sheffield: JSOT Press, 1993), pp. 401-12; J.A. Emerton, 'A Note on the Alleged Septuagintal Evidence for the Restoration of the Hebrew Text of Isaiah

The stately voyage of this diverse flotilla has been disturbed, if not endangered, by the work of a French scholar who cuts aggressively— some would say recklessly—to and fro across the path of even the largest vessels. In his *L'herméneutique analogique du judaïsme antique d'après les témoins textuels d'Isaïe*,[14] Jean Koenig attempts to rehabilitate the reputation of the translator of LXX Isaiah (as well as the scribe[s] responsible for 1QIsaᵃ), crediting him with an exegetical mastery that contrasts with the preference of previous scholars for attri-buting many MT–LXX divergences to accident and incomprehension.

Koenig wastes no words in reverence of his scholarly predecessors. It is difficult not to conclude that he has overstated the alleged sins of the 'empiricist' fathers, who hardly refused to admit theological exegesis. Furthermore, van der Kooij has rightly criticized the 'fragmentary character' of Koenig's method.[15] Nevertheless, in granting the prob-ability of scribal intelligence and in situating the translator's labours squarely within the realm of ancient Jewish (and other Near Eastern) exegetical tradition, Koenig's monograph makes a welcome and unset-tling contribution to LXX Isaiah studies.

Invaluable as these studies—large and small—have proved to be, they collectively leave tracts of open sea for further exploration. Ex-cluding Ottley's commentary format, even the larger works discussed above do not attempt to treat large sections of text, much less to describe exhaustively matters of translation technique or exegetical practice. Indeed, the later chapters of LXX Isaiah have been left virtu-ally untouched, except insofar as some interesting detail has here or there provided illustrative material for a work whose principal focus lies elsewhere.[16] (This may be a peculiarly modern version of a scribal

34.11-12', *Eretz-Israel*: 16 (1982; Harry M. Orlinsky volume), pp. 34-36; A.A. Macintosh, *Isaiah xxi: A Palimpsest* (Cambridge: Cambridge University Press, 1980).

14. VTSup, 33; Leiden: E.J. Brill, 1982.

15. 'Accident or Method', p. 36, and 'Isaiah in the Septuagint', in Broyles and Evans (eds.), *Writing and Reading the Scroll of Isaiah*, pp. 513-29 (517). Koenig's method is at points the virtual antithesis of van der Kooij's search for coherence within the Greek text and, furthermore, his treatment analyses only a small number of examples.

16. One exception is A. Zillessen's 'Bemerkungen zur alexandrinischen Übersetzung des Jesaja (c. 40–66)', *ZAW* 22 (1902), pp. 238-63, an article that pays special attention to influence between *Paralelstellen*. Even here, examples from chs. 40–55 strongly outnumber those from 56–66.

tendency to concentrate on the *beginnings* of a work, one that is old
enough to be known by Targumists!)[17] Indeed, it is symptomatic of LXX
Isaiah studies that one of the most useful insights into this translator's
approach surfaces and is then passed over virtually without comment in
an article that is only incidentally concerned with the Greek Isaiah.[18]

In short, the attempt to understand LXX Isaiah and its translator has
produced considerable effort and admirable achievement. There
remains, however, much mapping to be done.

The Translator's 'Freedom' and Competence
The issue of freedom versus conservatism figures prominently in this
volume. It is a commonplace that LXX Isaiah is a 'free' translation.
While this is undoubtedly the case if the poles of reference are 'freedom' and word-for-word 'literalism',[19] it will be argued that reference
to the Isaiah translator's 'freedom' must be strongly qualified in two

---

17. Cf. S.A. Kaufman and Y. Maori, 'The Targumim to Exodus 20: Recon-
structing the Palestinian Targum', *Textus* 16 (1991), pp. 13-78, esp. p. 64 ('Addendum: Of Beginnings and Ends'): 'The end of a text is subject to fewer scribal
improvements than its beginning... Scribes, like readers, generally began their
work of transmission and "correction" at the beginning of the text... The result is
that the earlier chapters of a heavily tradited text are subjected to a much greater
degree of intentional modification than are later portions of the same text.'

18. Cf. J. Lust, 'Exegesis and Theology in the Septuagint of Ezekiel. The
Longer 'Pluses' and Ezek 43:1-9', C.E. Cox (ed.), *VI Congress of the International
Organization for Septuagint and Cognate Studies, Jerusalem 1986* (Atlanta:
Scholars Press, 1987), pp. 201-232 (204). The presentation of the 'long' and 'short'
pluses of LXX Isaiah, Jeremiah and Ezekiel in Lust's article shows with astonishing
clarity the degree to which the LXX translator—despite his celebrated 'freedom'
vis-à-vis his source text—holds tight to that very text. Though this translator
produces roughly twice the number of pluses than the other translators who were
surveyed, nearly *all* of these are 'short' (four words or less) (more than 98 per
cent). On the minus side, the translator produces fewer minuses than the other
translator. Again, the percentage of these which are 'short' (95.2 per cent) is far
higher than in the other books. Compare Ziegler's (*Untersuchungen*, p. 47) much
more general observation: 'Größere Textausfälle sind selten. Ganze Verse fehlen
nur 2, 22 und 56, 12.'

19. Cf. J. Barr, *The Typology of Literalism in Ancient Biblical Translations*
(Mitteilungen des Septuagints-Unternehmems, Göttingen: Vandenhoeck & Ruprecht,
1979), for the paradigmatic work on this topic. Barr points out that particular kinds
of 'freedom' routinely coexist with expressions of 'literalism'.

ways. First, he is certainly not free from 'commitment to the *Vorlage*'.[20] On the contrary, his much-observed paraphrastic and even midrashic tendencies have almost entirely concealed from scholarly view a pronounced conservatism that binds him, first, to the immediate text of his own *Vorlage* (flights of fancy are virtually absent, most divergences being limited to one to three words) and, then, to other biblical texts in Isaiah and elsewhere.

In the second place, his alleged liberty does not make him an existential lone cowboy, whose solitary figure—unsheltered and unloved— roams the translational plains. Rather, he is a representative of wider Jewish interpretative tradition. He is best appreciated when allowed to stand among his peers. His values, motivations and annoyances, it will be argued throughout this work, are shared by Targumists and interpreters elsewhere. Far from being independent of attested Jewish exegetical tradition or free of its influence, he is both shaped by it and one of many shapers of it. Presumably, he laboured on behalf of a community that would not find his product odd, nor care to embrace it if it had.

With regard to the translator's competence, it is not necessary to labour the point that he (and other Septuagint translators) struggled to understand their Hebrew source text, an experience that will inspire sympathy in modern students of Hebrew Isaiah. One unfortunate tendency has been to allow this difficulty to explain too many LXX deviations (Ottley and, occasionally, Ziegler) or too few (Koenig). It seems quite likely that the Isaiah translator was capable of 'fertile misinterpretation'[21] and frankly barren mistakes at the same time that he is to be credited with some complex and premeditated exegetical feats. Though Koenig envisages the space between himself and the 'empiricists' (Ottley, Ziegler *et al.*) in terms of whether the scribe/translator was active or passive, one senses that the issue of intellectual competence is not wholly absent from their conflicting appraisals. If Ziegler's translator was occasionally too dim, Koenig's is almost certainly too bright.

In terms of conscious *exegetical* prowess, one might speak of a continuum upon which the translator's modern examiners place him. At

20. Cf. Seeligmann, 'Problems', p. 223: 'The LXX itself is a conglomeration of translations by many and varied an author. Its commitment to the *Vorlage*, which no translation can ever repudiate, will always, somewhat, disqualify it as a document of an independent theology.'
21. Sadly, one must cede to Seeligmann credit for this delightful description ('Alteration and Adaptation', p. 203).

one extreme, Ottley is likely to explain a given LXX deviation as a misunderstanding, or tacitly to imply that no explanation exists. Ziegler gives careful attention to intertextual influence but, on balance, knows a largely passive scribe who is prone to lose his way. Seeligmann allows more room for ideology, though this is understood to show its face furtively rather than in the development of a sustained exegesis of the Hebrew book. Van der Kooij echoes Seeligmann's approach in many respects, but finds 'well-reasoned interpretation' along lines known to ancient Jewish exegesis.[22] Koenig reads LXX Isaiah as the interpretative *tour de force* of a master exegete.

The present study is developed along lines that are compatible with the works of Seeligmann and van der Kooij. Mistakes and a not quite victorious struggle with the book's difficult Hebrew appear to lie at the root of many of the LXX deviations. These coexist, however, with theological concerns and exegetical practice that produce a work that can only be fully appreciated when allowed *bona fide* status as ancient Jewish biblical interpretation.

The Translator's Homiletical Motivation
More than any other student of LXX Isaiah, Seeligmann repeatedly acknowledges the 'homiletical' origins and character of the translation.[23] He appears to come to this conclusion almost entirely upon grounds of *content* rather than *style*. That is, the translator interacts with other biblical passages and actualizes his text in a way that shows his homiletical intentions. Curiously, Seeligmann seems never to have pursued the support for the preached character of the book that is to be found in its *style*. In Chapters 2 and 3, the homiletical implications of the book's style—specifically of its grammatical deviations from the MT—will come in for analysis.

The Translator's Ideological Profile
This book will argue, against such scholars as H.M. Orlinsky, that the translator's own ideology and understanding of the book are accessible to careful analysis of his translation technique. With Orlinsky and some exponents of the 'Scandinavian school',[24] however, it will be argued

---

22. Cf. 'Short Commentary', p. 46, and *Textzeugen*, pp. 66-69; cf. also J. Schaper, *Eschatology in the Greek Psalter* (Tübingen: J.C.B. Mohr [Paul Siebeck], 1995), p. 21.

23. Cf. 'Alteration and Adaptation', p. 207 n. 1; 'Problems', pp. 195, 232.

24. Taken as a whole, Scandinavian Septuagintalists have made valuable contri-

that the LXX translators (of Isaiah, in the present instance) did not proceed so as to create a *systematic* exposition of their own theology. This
can be illustrated, for example, from the indifferent way in which the
LXX translator deals with references to the divine eye(s) or hand(s),
sometimes representing these literally and sometimes paraphrasing. No
case for a consistent *theological programme* can be constructed upon
such evidence.

This study reproduces neither the scepticism of the Orlinsky/ Scandinavian school nor the optimism, as reported in Chapter 4, of the work
of C.T. Fritsch and others. Rather, it notices recurrent patterns of translation within LXX Isaiah, and continuities with less restrained exegetical
treatments of Hebrew Isaiah (chiefly, Targum Jonathan), in order to
argue for a *tendency* on the part of the translator to display his theological understanding of the text.

The translator's understanding of his source text—which is brought
to expression in smooth Hellenistic Greek—repeatedly displays a tendency (a) to ameliorate the source text's least circumspect statements
about God (Chapter 4); (b) to tone down and otherwise ameliorate sexual, cultic and other potentially awkward language (Chapter 5); and (c)
to move the text in a nationalistic direction that also reflects the Diaspora
situation of the translator and his community (Chapters 6 and 7).

Methodological Considerations

Terminology and Assumptions
I will use the neutral terms 'deviation'[25] and 'divergence' to refer to
those features of the LXX that do not correspond to a straightforward

---

butions to issues of LXX grammar and syntax while remaining sceptical with regard
to attempts to identify the translators' theological assumptions. One mentions two
collections of essays and a recent monograph that are representative of this
undistracted focus: I. Soisalon-Soininen, *Studien zur Septuaginta-Syntax* (Helsinki:
Suomalainen Tiedeakatemia, 1987); A. Aejmelaeus, *On the Trail of the Septuagint
Translators* (Kampen: Kok, 1993); and R. Sollamo, *Repetition of the Possessive
Pronouns in the Septuagint* (Atlanta: Scholars Press, 1995). Chapter 4 of this
volume interacts with the similarly minded Swedish scholar Staffan Olofsson, who
nonetheless ventures somewhat further into the area of theological exegesis in *God
Is my Rock: A Study of Translation Technique and Theological Exegesis in the
Septuagint* (Stockholm: Almqvist & Wiksell, 1990).

25. So E. Tov, *The Text-Critical Use of the Septuagint in Biblical Research*.
Second Edition, Revised and Enlarged (Jerusalem: Simor, 1997), p. 39.

translation of the MT. Nothing in the research that undergirds this monograph disturbs the consensus view that the *Vorlage* of LXX Isaiah was similar to the MT.[26] Nevertheless, it is impossible to attain certainty in this regard. I do not wish to prejudice the argument by using a more biased term for individual MT–LXX differences.

That the translation is the work of just one author will be assumed in the discussion that follows. This has become a widely held view.[27] The close analysis of a wide variety of translational patterns that stands behind this book confirms the essential unity of LXX Isaiah.[28]

With regard to the date of the translation, the modern consensus places the genesis of LXX Isaiah somewhere near the middle of the second century BCE.[29] Nothing in the present analysis requires that this approximation be revised.[30] The present research identifies numerous lexical and stylistic similarities between LXX Isaiah and other Septuagint books that are presumed to be late (e.g. Proverbs, Job and the originally Greek works). Though these results fall beyond the margins of the present work, they may serve further to solidify the consensus (usually argued on internal grounds) for a mid-second-century Greek Isaiah. I hope to present these parallels as well as some conclusions based upon them in a future study.[31]

---

26. Cf. A. van der Kooij, ' "The Servant of the Lord": A Particular Group of Jews in Egypt According to the Old Greek of Isaiah. Some Comments on LXX Isa 49, 1-6 and Related Passages', in J. van Ruiten and M. Vervenne (eds.), *Studies in the Book of Isaiah: Festschrift William A.M. Beuken* (BETL, 132; Leuven: Peeters, 1997), pp. 383-96 (395), and 'Isaiah in the Septuagint', p. 517. One reckons with a moderate degree of textual fluidity among the MT, the Qumran texts, and the presumed *LXX Vorlage* without indications of a strong relationship between any two or more witnesses. This situation has often been described. Cf., for example, van der Kooij, 'Isaiah in the Septuagint', pp. 517-18.

27. Cf. Fischer, Ziegler, Seeligmann, *passim*.

28. I leave the question of chs. 36–39 to one side, though in my view the claim that these are the work of a different translator is open to challenge. In a future study, I hope to deal with the separate possibility, hinted at but not pursued by Ziegler (*Untersuchungen*, pp. 42-44), that ch. 66 stands somewhat apart from LXX Isaiah chs. 1–65.

29. See below, Chapter 2, n. 10.

30. The same is true of his presumed location in Hellenistic Alexandria. Cf. Ziegler, *Untersuchungen*, p. 1.

31. Seeligmann ('Alteration and Adaptation', p. 186) is one of the few scholars who articulates—albeit briefly—the tension between the well-known rule of de Lagarde that identifies free translation as a mark of *early* translation, on the one

Texts and Citation

The Hebrew and Greek texts of Isaiah are quoted as found in, respectively, *Biblia Hebraica Stuttgartensia*[32] and Ziegler's *editio*, except where indicated otherwise. Although the English translations of both texts are my own, I have where possible used the vocabulary of the *New Revised Standard Version* for the Hebrew text, occasionally citing this translation without change. Frequently, however, I have offered a more literal translation for ease of comparison with the Hebrew text itself. English translations of the Greek text are my own, with occasional concessions to Ottley's English translation in order to facilitate discussion.

Lexical and Semantic Analysis

This study is in the first instance the result of an analysis of the translation of all Greek 'content words/elements'[33] that appear in Isaiah 56–66, as well as the clauses, sentences and pericopes in which these lexemes occur. This attempt exhaustively to survey the book's last 11 chapters has been balanced by the application of the same method to the bulk of the material in chs. 1–55.

As each Greek content word has been placed on a lexical 'map', continuities and discontinuities between the translator of Isaiah and those of the other books become clearer. At the same time, from the Hebrew side, 250 Hebrew lexemes that appear in Isaiah 56–66 have been placed on a more detailed map that classifies every occurrence of such words in the Hebrew Bible according to its Greek translation.

Thus, the complex translational phenomenon that we know as Septuagint Isaiah is viewed through two grids. One works from the

---

hand, and the existence of remarkable fluidity in books that are unanimously accepted as late translations, on the other. Compare Sebastian Brock, 'The Phenomenon of Biblical Translation in Antiquity', in Sidney Jellicoe (ed.), *Studies in the Septuagint: Origins, Recensions, and Interpretations. Selected Essays with a Prolegomena by Sidney Jellicoe* (New York: Ktav, 1974), pp. 541-71 (550-552). Tov (*TCU*, p. 27) uncouples the matter of freedom from the issue of chronological order by asking a question: 'Some translations are free and even paraphrastic, e.g., Isaiah, Job, Proverbs, Esther and Daniel... Do free (paraphrastic) translations imply an intensive exegetical interest in these books?'

32. Stuttgart: Deutsche Bibelgesellschaft, 1967/77.

33. Cf. Tov, *TCU*, p. 59, for the distinction between 'content words/elements' and 'grammatical words/elements' (essentially prepositions, conjunctions and particles).

Greek text back to its corresponding Hebrew text.[34] The other begins, as the historical process itself did, with the Hebrew text and maps the corresponding Greek equivalents. Despite the non-mechanical and unsystematic labour in which human translators engage, this method allows one to discern significant patterns and even, when working from the Hebrew text, to achieve a degree of predictive insight with regard to the Greek translation that will emerge. Perhaps more importantly for the attempt to penetrate the translator's exegetical method and theological biases, *exceptions* to translational norms stand out more crisply and occasionally call attention to an underlying exegetical manoeuvre.[35]

Grammatical and Syntactical Analysis
The research represented here also seeks to catalogue the kinds of grammatical and syntactical habits that characterise this translator. At the most basic level, to cite a few examples, he prefers to make singular nouns and adjectives plural, demonstrating a particular resistance to the representative singular. He consistently inserts conjunctions where the Hebrew text is asyndetic, and he is particularly given to using the postpositive particles δέ and γάρ. Although he often collapses the details of Hebrew poetry, he is just as likely to correct the ellipsis that is a feature of much nuanced Hebrew parallelism.

As with the lexical data, this purely descriptive information seldom thrills. However, the establishing of translational patterns proves its worth at the exegetical level, as time and again a preference *against the norm* reveals exegetical motivation.

Describing the Purpose and Meaning of the Greek Text
Neither the abundant data that such a method produces nor a global attempt to characterize the Isaiah translator's 'translation technique' will figure explicitly in this book. Rather, building upon the empirical data that such research produces, this study seeks to articulate the translator's homiletical motivation and several points of ideological inclination more clearly than has heretofore been possible, at least insofar as chs. 56–66 are concerned.

The results are from time to time compared with Targum Jonathan (and, occasionally, with other works of ancient Jewish exegesis). Frequently, the same concerns with regard to the Hebrew text that animate

34. Taking into account the inherent limitations of such a quest for the *Vorlagen*.
35. Cf. van der Kooij, 'Accident or Method', p. 369.

the LXX translator appear to have inspired the work of the *meturge-manim* as well. Usually, however, the two translations achieve their respective solutions by different means.

In the pages that follow, I argue upon grammatical and syntactical grounds what Seeligmann suggested years ago from a different angle, namely that this translator is a preacher whose homiletical purpose is to be glimpsed with remarkable frequency. The 'midrashic' appearance of his text ought not to be mistaken for a loose grip on his Hebrew source. Rather, he is a contemporizing expositor of his source, a text from which he does not feel himself at liberty widely to diverge. His concerns for the dignity of God—together with a number of attendant modesties—motivate him to express the *sense* of that text in ways that seem appropriately reverential, and he accomplishes this when possible with minimal violence to the details of the Hebrew text. Such careful language, together with his expressions of Diaspora nationalism, make him an early exponent of the type of Jewish interpretative traditions that are seen in more developed form in the Targumim, Midrashim and Talmudim.

Chapter 2

'IMPERATIVIZATION' IN LXX ISAIAH

The size of the book of Isaiah and its importance within the interpretative traditions might suggest that its translation into Greek would have been entrusted to a particularly able craftsman.[1] One might expect to find in Septuagint Isaiah evidence of a skilled linguist, a master of both source and target languages, a careful and accurate scholar whose attention to the details of the sacred text would put him in good stead before this daunting task.

On the surface, however, the translator of LXX Isaiah seems to wear little of the expected scholarly garb. While his Greek is supple, it appears that he reads Hebrew only as a learned language.[2] As to scholarly care,

---

1. The preface of an ambitious collection of essays on Isaiah begins with these words: 'No other book outside of the Torah itself had a greater impact on the theology of early Judaism and Christianity than the book of Isaiah. Isaiah, along with Deuteronomy and the Psalms, is one of the most frequently quoted and interpreted books of the Bible in the literature of late antiquity. Isaiah also had a major impact on the literature of the first Temple, exilic, and second Temple periods'; Broyles and Evans (eds.), *Writing and Reading the Scroll of Isaiah*, p. ix.

2. That is, he is not a fluent native reader of Hebrew. Scholars have written generally about the limited command of Hebrew evidenced by some LXX translators. Cf. Seeligmann, *LXX Version*, p. 54, 'Problems', p. 208. More generally, H.B. Swete, *An Introduction to the Old Testament in Greek* (Cambridge: Cambridge University Press, 1914), p. 319; J. Barr, *Comparative Philology and the Text of the Old Testament* (Oxford: Oxford University Press, 1968); reprinted with additions and corrections, Winona Lake, Indiana, USA: Eisenbrauns, 1987), pp. 267-69; Olofsson, *God Is my Rock*, p. 21. H. St J. Thackeray has low and high regard, respectively, for the translator's Hebrew and Greek: 'The translator is, moreover, *less competent on the whole* than the translator or translators of the Jeremiah group, though *he tries to hide his ignorance by paraphrase or abbreviation*, occasionally giving the general sense of a passage, while omitting to render the difficult words... On the other hand, the Isaiah translator, while *careless* about producing a literal rendering, *employs a Greek which much more nearly approaches the classical style*

When We All Go Home

he seems more interested in straining out the essential message of the text before him than in reproducing its artistry. He routinely discards the intricate parallelism that he discovers in Hebrew Isaiah, collapsing poetic structures into an abbreviated prose that usually says much the same thing, but without the poetic balance or repetition of his source.[3] On the other hand, we shall see that this disregard for the norms of Hebrew poetry is not confined to abridgement. With roughly the same frequency, he expands the text vis-à-vis the MT in order to 'correct' poetic ellipsis.[4] Such expansion is almost always restricted to a word or a short clause.

However, this translator is no dullard schoolboy, churning out translation exercises with a view only to finishing. Rather, he is a preacher, or at least a preacher's aide. His text has moved him, but not in the direction of literary appreciation. Rather, he is moved by homiletical

---

than the Greek of the more painstaking translators of the other prophetical books.' Cf. 'The Greek Translators of the Prophetical Books', *JTS* 4 (1903), pp. 578-85. Thackeray cannot be accused of overrating any hermeneutical prowess that the translator may have displayed, and so might have remained sceptical of some of the claims made in this book. While I am in general agreement with Thackeray's appraisal of the translator's linguistic skills, I think that these characteristics are complemented by far more hermeneutical dexterity than Thackeray's words suggest.

3. Cf. J. Fischer, *In welcher Schrift lag das Buch Isaias den LXX vor?* (BZAW, 56; Giessen: Alfred Töpelman, 1930), p. 7. Fischer describes 'die Zusammenziehung von Texten durch den Ü.r. Es schien unserem Ü.r manchmal durch abgekürzte Wiedergabe der Sinn genügend ausgedrückt; für den Parallelismus hatte er wenig Empfinden'. Cf. also A. van der Kooij, 'Servant of the Lord', p. 385; and Ziegler, *Untersuchungen*, pp. 46-56. Some of Ziegler's examples of LXX minuses conform to this pattern.

4. This is seldom recognized when describing the 'shorter' text of the LXX: Fischer's remarks are typical of many scholars: 'Vor allem fällt auf, daß die Is. LXX gegenüber M sehr oft ein Defizit aufweist, das allerdings über den Umfang eines Verses kaum hinausgeht, sondern meist geringer ist' (*Schrift*, p. 6). Fischer is preparing to argue—correctly I think—that the LXX *Vorlage* ≈ MT. However, he tacitly ignores the presence of numerous LXX additions by 'corrected' ellipsis, which counterbalances the translator's simultaneous habit of 'collapsing'.

Cf. for example, Isa 40.30, where the unbalanced parallelism of the Hebrew text is given a more precise equilibrium in the Greek, even though this requires the addition of a substantive and considerable restatement of the syntax: // ויעפו נערים וֹיגעו // וֹבחורים כשול יכשלו = πεινάσουσιν γὰρ νεώτεροι // καὶ κοπιάσουσιν νεανίσκοι // καὶ ἐκλεκτοὶ ἀνίσχυες ἔσονται.

intentions towards proclamation of the book's essential message—as he perceives this to be—to his own community.[5]

This is a feature of the Isaiah translator that has not received sufficient attention either by text critics like Joseph Ziegler—whose instinct was to propose a variant *Vorlage* when the LXX diverged from the MT—or by more recent scholars like Jean Koenig, who envisages a sort of scholarly scribe practising a wide-ranging hermeneutical agenda upon his text.[6]

This translator is also a biblical theologian of sorts. He knows the book of Isaiah well, often introducing into the verse that lies before him elements of an Isaiah passage from elsewhere in the book.[7] He leaves evidence that his translation did not proceed systematically from front to back. On at least one occasion, translation of a given text is carried out in a manner that suggests that a Greek translation of a similar passage *later* in the book already existed and lay before him. He knows the Greek Pentateuch and alludes to it regularly.[8] He may also know the

---

5. Cf. Fischer, *Schrift*, pp. 8-9: 'Es liegt ihm keineswegs daran eine genaue, wortwörtliche Ü.g. herzustellen, sondern sein Streben ist vorzüglich darauf gerichtet, den Sinn zum Ausdruck zu bringen.'

6. For a proposed methodology for the study of LXX translation technique, which includes a helpful critique of Ziegler's tendency to conjecture a hypothetical *Vorlage* against the full weight of the Greek manuscript tradition, cf. M.H. Goshen-Gottstein, 'Theory and Practice of Textual Criticism. The Text-Critical Use of the Septuagint', *Textus* 3 (1963), pp. 130-58. Cf., generally, Ziegler, *Untersuchungen*, and Seeligmann, *LXX Version*.

7. The same can be said of the scribe responsible for 1QIsaᵃ. For example, the plus at the end of 1.15 is taken from a similar phrase at 59.3; cf. Tov on 'harmonization', *Textual Criticism*, p. 261. J. Koenig finds ideological consequence in the borrowing, chiefly because the grammatical awkwardness that it creates at 1QIsaᵃ 1.15 suggests that it is more than a mere literary harmonization; cf. *L'herméneutique analogique*, pp. 221-28. On the need to approach individual readings in LXX Isaiah with an eye to their 'coherence' with similar passages elsewhere in the book, cf. the various publications of Arie van der Kooij, e.g. 'Servant of the Lord', p. 395 and 'Short Commentary', p. 37. For the shared (by LXX and 1QIsaᵃ) tendency towards fulfilment-interpretation, cf. van der Kooij, *Textzeugen*, pp. 83-94, and 'Short Commentary', p. 45.

8. One mentions just a few examples among many: גבור = γίγαντα at 3.2, a selection that Ziegler understands to be occasioned by the same equivalence in Gen 6.4; cf. *Untersuchungen*, p. 61; also p. 103, where Ziegler mentions several other examples. R.R. Ottley notes similar reliance, but upon Gen. 10.8-10; cf. *The Book of Isaiah According to the Septuagint (Codex Alexandrinus)*. II. *Text and Notes*

Torah in Hebrew and/or Aramaic. He is familiar with Jeremiah, Ezekiel and the Minor Prophets.[9] He has probably reflected upon the Greek Psalms as well.[10]

(Cambridge: Cambridge University Press, 1906), p. 115. Cf. also Ziegler, *Unter-suchungen*, pp. 108-109, with regard to שׁכם = ἐπαξύνθη at Deut. 32.15 and Isa. 6.10: 'Der Übers. hat viell. an Dt 32, 15 gedacht.' Cf. also Seeligmann, *LXX Version*, pp. 45-49, for a substantial discussion. Cf. also L.H. Brockington, 'Septuagint and Targum', *ZAW* 66 (1954), pp. 80-86 (84): 'The translators of Exodus and Isaiah have many usages in common, and, more particularly, there are many reminiscences in Isaiah of the song in Exod. 15. It is easy to see how the translator might be familiar with the Greek form of the song which was likely to be used frequently in worship. It is not so easy to determine why the rest of Exodus should also be drawn upon but we may suppose that the translator had heard it frequently in public worship, and, if it was already in written form, had a copy.'

9.   Cf. Olofsson, *God Is my Rock*, 89. Olofsson explains an unusual translation at 1.24 by offering that 'the reason for the translation...is probably that the translator was so imbued with the ideas preached by the prophets that he naturally understood...' Olofsson's comments are most likely to be understood with reference to the prophetic corpus *in Hebrew*. On the other hand, I.L. Seeligmann suggests that the *Greek* Micah predates the Isaiah translation; cf. *LXX Version*, p. 103 n. 24. H. St J. Thackeray thinks the 'germ or nucleus of the Greek versions of some of the Prophets' may have been short selections translated earlier for liturgical purposes: 'Primitive Lectionary Notes in the Psalm of Habakkuk', *JTS* 12 (1911), pp. 191-213 (210).

10.   This apparent dependence upon other Greek texts appears to justify the modern consensus—suggested by Ziegler and developed by Seeligmann—that Isaiah was translated relatively late. The possible prior existence of portions of Isaiah in Greek may explain why it was not until later that what I call the 'LXX Isaiah project' became a matter of necessity. Ziegler and Seeligmann counter the view from earlier in this century—represented by Thackeray, Redpath and Ottley—that Isaiah was translated after the Pentateuch or Hexateuch and *before* the other Prophetical books. The literature displays a marked reluctance to set absolute dates. Most would now speak of a period in or not far from the first half of the second century BCE. Cf. H.A. Redpath, 'A Contribution towards Settling the Dates of the Translation of the Various Books of the Septuagint', *JTS* 7 (1906), pp. 606-15; H. St J. Thackeray, 'Greek translators', and 'Review of R.R. Ottley, *The Book of Isaiah According to the Septuagint*', *JTS* 10 (1909), pp. 299-304; Seeligmann, *LXX Version*, pp. 70-94; 'Problems', p. 200. Fischer's dating links him to the earlier consensus. In *Schrift*, p. 6, he finds a *terminus ad quem* in 146, since the translator at 23.14 shows he did not know of the destruction of Carthage in that year; he then works his way back to an earlier period (250-201 BCE), when Carthage ruled Spain, as the likely period of the Isaiah translation.

Several features recur with sufficient regularity to justify their inclusion within a description of the 'translation technique' that has produced LXX Isaiah.

I have alluded to what I perceive to be the homiletical intentions of our translator. It is, of course, not surprising that a translation of the Hebrew Bible made by Diaspora Jews should utilize a 'lectionary mode', with modest adjustments made to the biblical text in order to make it suitable for liturgical reading.[11] While it has remained impossible to determine exactly when and how the Torah and the Prophets were read in Second Temple synagogue worship, it is to be expected that they did play an important role in that context.[12]

For a Greek Isaiah that may postdate the Greek Psalms, cf. Olofsson, *God Is my Rock*, p. 23.

11. It is Thackeray whose name is usually attached to the 'liturgical' theory of LXX origins. Thackeray believed that the 'Later Prophets' were translated in two stages: first, 'a rendering of select passages appointed as lessons for the festivals and special sabbaths; secondly a complete version'; cf. *The Septuagint and Jewish Worship: A Study in Origins* (The Schweich Lectures, 1920; Oxford: Oxford University Press, 1921), p. 28. However, as far as I can see, Thackeray did not address indications of homiletical conversions in the text of the LXX. For a summary, cf. Jellicoe, *Septuagint*, pp. 64-70. Cf. also S. Brock, 'The Phenomenon of Biblical Translation in Antiquity', *Alta: The University of Birmingham Review* 2.8 (1969), pp. 96-102; reprinted in S. Jellicoe (ed.), *Studies in the Septuagint: Origins, Recensions, and Interpretations. Selected Essays with a Prolegomenon by Sidney Jellicoe* (New York: Ktav, 1974), pp. 549-50. Brock locates the genesis of the LXX in 'the combination of these two needs...the liturgical and the educational'. He also posits a Diaspora practice of oral translation into Greek, which ad hoc translations were later standardized when a written translation was undertaken, p. 552. Cf., similarly, Seeligmann, 'Problems', pp. 196-99.

L.H. Brockington finds in LXX Isaiah 'just the kind of expository interpretation that one might expect a reader to offer his hearers at a service of worship where it would be fitting to dwell on the deliverance wrought by God for his people'; 'Septuagint and Targum', (p. 82). Brockington is correct, it seems to me, that there is expository interpretation in the Greek Isaiah. However, the evidence upon which he bases this conclusion is not always compelling. The use of σώζειν to translate words like פליטה is the essence of salvation-oriented exposition he discerns. However, the Isaiah translator is actually *less* apt to treat פליטה in this way than is the LXX as a whole.

12. A recent description of the 'state of the question' is found in C. Perrot, 'The Reading of the Bible in the Ancient Synagogue', in M.J. Mulder (ed.), *Mikra: Text, Translation, Reading and Interpretation of the Hebrew Bible in Ancient Judaism and Early Christianity* (CRINT, 1; Assen: Van Gorcum, 1990), pp. 161-88.

It would be no less expected that the use of a biblical text like Isaiah in synagogue settings should lead to contemporizing application of the text, and that such a use should exercise some influence upon the form of its translation. If the translator was a participant in synagogue liturgy, then it would be natural for him to have in mind a reading or hearing public as he set about translating his Hebrew text. What is surprising about LXX Isaiah is the extent to which the translation takes on a hortatory—one might dare say even a homiletical—tone. This is accomplished, in part, by a frequent recurrence to imperatival forms of Greek verbs.[13]

Imperativization as a Feature of LXX Isaiah

In this chapter, I will first illustrate the scope of imperativizing alterations that LXX Isaiah exhibits by referring to examples from the first 55 chapters of the book. I will then attempt to catalogue all such changes as they occur in chs. 56–66.

With regard to the relationship of such imperativized translations to the Hebrew source text, there appear to be three principal categories of imperativization: *authorized, semi-authorized* and *unauthorized.* In practice, this differentiation often looks more like a spectrum that reflects degrees of authorization rather than three discrete categories.

Functionally, there also appear to be three classes of imperativization. When the translator directs an imperative towards his audience, it produces a *homiletical exhortation.* When its recipient is an individual protagonist—or a group of these—in the text, it results in a *heightened rhetorical effect.* Finally, the imperativization is sometimes directed to God in prayer. Insofar as any net effect can be discerned, the result is *intensified prayer.*

In the following analysis, instances of LXX imperativisation will be

13. Students of LXX Isaiah from time to time mention isolated cases of imperativization. Cf., for example, Seeligmann on Isa 21.2 (*LXX Version,* p. 57). As far as I am aware, however, no one has noticed its frequency in this translation, nor attempted to link it to a homiletic purpose.

More frequently hortatory intention is observed on non-grammatical grounds. Cf., for example, Seeligmann's comment on 10.20: 'It is precisely through the transposition of מכבוד into ἀδικήσαντας (sic) that the whole of this verse—which, thus, warns against fraternization with the oppressors of Israel, and calls upon the people to have faith in the God of Israel—impresses one as being exclusively an exhortation to Alexandrian Jewry of the period' (*LXX Version,* p. 111).

classified according to their form, with comment upon their function added where appropriate. In the examples from chs. 1–55 I will group the phenomena of authorized and semi-authorized forms together under the rubric of 'Imperativization with substantial authorization', then introduce those that lack such authorization. However, when I turn to examine the specific cases in chs. 56–66, I will discuss them according to all three formal types that I have mentioned above: authorized, semi-authorized, and unauthorized imperativizations.

Imperativization with Substantial Authorisation as a
Feature of LXX Isaiah
In most cases imperativization is carried out with a degree of authorization from the consonantal text. I refer to those instances that require only an alternative vocalization of the existing consonants as *authorized*.[14] I will use the term *semi-authorized* for those instances of imperativisation which reflect a vocalization that is divergent from the MT *and* some element of consonantal alteration. This term seeks to take into account the fact that the resulting translation utilises the elements afforded by the consonantal text as its point of departure and its essential components. Nevertheless, it deviates in its configuration of these features by discarding or supplementing one or more elements of the source text. Finally, *unauthorized* translations are those which are carried out with no apparent basis in the Hebrew text.

Isaiah 26.9. In a context that is remarkably similar to sapiential psalmody, the prophet at MT Isa. 26.9 feels the assurance that 'when your judgements are upon the earth, the inhabitants of the world learn righteousness'. The LXX, however, understands the MT's צֶדֶק לָמְדוּ ישְׁבֵי תֵבֵל as though the verb were vocalized as לִמְדוּ and produces δικαιοσύνην μάθετε οἱ ἐνοικοῦντες ἐπὶ τῆς γῆς. This requires the secondary alteration that construes ישְׁבֵי תֵבֵל as a vocative, thus producing a hortatory tone which is entirely lacking in the prayer of the MT. Because this transformation has required no consonantal changes, it is an *authorized imperativization*.

The conversion does not appear to be the result of atomistic

14. For example, an unpointed verb for which the context intends an indicative mood is read as though it were an imperative. בָּתְבוּ or קָטְלוּ is read as בִּתְבוּ or קִטְלוּ. These examples are chosen for the sake of simplicity. Imperativization in LXX Isaiah is by no means confined to the qal conjugation.

translation that pays no heed to the context. It seems that the translator has neither missed those contextual features of the Hebrew text that are sapiential nor those that correspond to psalmic prayer. Indeed, the LXX *adds* the assertion φῶς τὰ προστάγματά σου ἐπὶ τῆς γῆς, an affirmation that would be quite at home in wisdom literature.[15] Furthermore, there are indications in the details of LXX Isa 26.9 that the translator is influenced by the vocabulary of psalmody. He may allude to Ps. 37(36)[16] and perhaps also to Ps. 63(62).[17] Rather than alter or misunderstand the tone of MT Isaiah 26, the translator seems to *extend* the genre of sapiential prayer in a hortatory direction by briefly emerging to address a certain public. The resumption of reference to God in the vocative in LXX 26.11-18 demonstrates that his emergence from prayer to exhortation has been only a brief outburst rather than a naive erasure of the purpose and *genre* of his Hebrew text.

Isaiah 21.7–10[18]. Both *authorized* and *semi-authorized* imperativization are particularly common with hiphil verbal forms, possibly because the consonants of הַקְטִילוּ forms lend themselves to reformulation as הַקְטִילוּ imperatives.[19] However, one should not assume that those consonantal features that *facilitate* our translator's frequent imperativizing habit are an adequate explanation for them, as if they were mere accidents of translation.

In Isa. 21.7 one reads of a sentry's attentive listening in these terms: וְהִקְשִׁיב קֶשֶׁב רַב־קָשֶׁב.[20] The LXX changes this third-person prediction to an imperative: ἀκρόασαι ἀκρόασιν πολλὴν, as though reading

15. On the addition of φῶς, cf. 'G Is 26, 9, G Jer 10, 13-14 et le Thème de la Lumière', in Koenig, *L'herméneutique analogique*, pp. 136-41. Koenig speaks of 'la conversion de la phrase en parénèse légaliste', p. 137.

16. καὶ ἐξοίσει ὡς φῶς τὴν δικαιοσύνην σου.

17. Cf. especially the Isaiah translator's otherwise unprecedented use of ὀρθρίζειν for שָׁחַר—an equivalency that appears elsewhere only in Ps. 63(62), 78(77), and twice in Job—and the unauthorized addition of πρὸς σέ ὁ θεός.

18. For an exacting analysis of the Hebrew text and versions of Isa. 21, as well as rabbinic commentary upon the same, cf. Macintosh, *Palimpsest*.

19. As we shall see, the translator does not require *full* consonantal authorization of this kind. The example that follows, in 21.7, demonstrates this: הַקְשֵׁב / הִקְשִׁיב = ἀκρόασαι. The unsuffixed 2ms hiphil imperative normally requires loss of the *yod*.

20. *Tanakh: A New Translation of the Holy Scriptures According to the Traditional Hebrew Text* (Philadelphia: Jewish Publication Society of America, 1985), Isa. 21.7: 'He will see mounted men, / Horsemen in pairs— / Riders on asses, /Riders on camels— /*And he will listen closely, / Most attentively*' (emphasis added).

הַקְשֵׁב for the MT's וְהִקְשִׁיב. It is unclear whether the translator considers the imperative to be directed towards the sentry—as it is the sentry who will hear in the MT—or towards the reader. At first glance, the former seems more likely.

However, it would be a mistake to conclude that such imperativization reflects simply an isolated choice from the options presented by an unpointed text, one which happens to be different from the alternative chosen by the reading tradition reflected in the MT. Against such an assumption, one observes that the context surrounding LXX 21.7 also shows a marked imperatival tendency. This inclination manifests itself where the authorization afforded by the Hebrew text is less convenient than it is in the case of hiphil verbal forms, and even when such authorization is entirely absent.

The context comprises Isaiah's 'oracle concerning the wilderness of the sea'.[21] In it there are three loci of imperativization in addition to the one at 21.7. In 21.5 the translator has exercised his options upon the verbs which the Massoretic tradition understands to be infinitives absolute. He has levelled all the translated verbs found in the verbal chain עָרֹךְ הַשֻּׁלְחָן צָפֹה הַצָּפִית אָכוֹל שָׁתֹה קוּמוּ הַשָּׂרִים מִשְׁחוּ מָגֵן to the imperatival mood, which the MT allows only to מִשְׁחוּ and קוּמוּ.[22] The result is not hortatory, for the readers are not being addressed. It may, however, heighten the dramatic urgency of the verse.

The same dramatic function may apply to 21.8, where וַיִּקְרָא אַרְיֵה[23]

21. So 21.1a, as a heading for 21.1b-10.

22. The first instance requires only alternative vocalization: עֲרֹךְ/עָרֹךְ = ἑτοίμασον; the second verbal construction (צָפֹה הַצָּפִית) is omitted altogether, a common result of the translator's tendency to collapse lists and poetic parallelism; the third verb in the MT requires only revocalization, the assumption of a less common *plene* spelling (אֲכוֹל/אָכוֹל), and pluralization (the latter is exceedingly common in LXX Isaiah) or a revocalization and consonantal metathesis (אֲכֹל/הֹאכֵל), which is also common in this translated text; שָׁתֹה requires only to be vocalised as שְׁתֵה and then made plural. On metathesis in Jewish exegesis and translational accident, cf. van der Kooij, 'Short Commentary', p. 41, and *Textzeugen*, p. 68; C. McCarthy, *The Tiqqune Sopherim and Other Theological Corrections in the Masoretic Text* (OBO, 36; Göttingen: Vandenhoeck & Ruprecht, 1981), pp. 141-42; Scholz, *Uebersetzung*, p. 43; D.P. O'Brien, '"Is This the Time to Accept...?" (2 Kings V 26B): Simply Moralizing (LXX) or an Ominous Foreboding of Yahweh's Rejection of Israel (MT)', *VT* 46 (1996), pp. 448-57 (452); Tov, *TCU*, pp. 142-43.

23. *Tanakh*, 'And like a lion he called out.' NRSV emends: 'Then the watcher called out'; cf. 1QIsaᵃ וַיִּקְרָא רֹאֶה, ‎ܠܘܦ ܪܐܘ.

is curiously translated as though it were וּקְרָא אֶל(וֹ)רִיה: καὶ κάλεσον
Οὐρίαν.[24] The intended meaning is at best unclear.

However, in 21.10 the imperatival inclination of this entire LXX passage begins to suggest hortatory intent as well: מְדֻשָׁתִי וּבֶן־גָּרְנִי אֲשֶׁר
שָׁמַעְתִּי מֵאֵת יהוה צְבָאוֹת אֱלֹהֵי יִשְׂרָאֵל הִגַּדְתִּי לָכֶם is rendered as
ἀκούσατε, οἱ καταλελειμμένοι καὶ οἱ ὀδυνώμενοι, ἀκούσατε ἃ
ἤκουσα παρὰ κυρίου σαβαωθ· ὁ θεὸς τοῦ Ἰσραηλ ἀνήγγειλεν ἡμῖν.
It is possible that the unauthorized imperatives (ἀκούσατε, twice) are
meant to be the sentry's words.[25] However, the LXX has also transferred
the immediate source of the report from the sentry (הִגַּדְתִּי) to the God
of Israel (ἀνήγγειλεν). Furthermore, לָכֶם has unexpectedly been
translated inclusively, as ἡμῖν. Finally, the addressees have been demetaphorized and made plural: מְדֻשָׁתִי וּבֶן־גָּרְנִי = οἱ καταλελειμμένοι
καὶ οἱ ὀδυνώμενοι. It becomes increasingly evident that this verse is
perhaps best understood in translation as a homiletical contemporization addressed to Diaspora readers or listeners: '*Hear*, you who are left
and you who are aggrieved! *Hear* the things which I have heard from
the Lord of Hosts! The God of Israel has announced (them) *to us*!'[26]

When such contextual details have been taken into account, it is possible to return to the hiphil verbal construction in 21.7 (וְהִקְשִׁיב קֶשֶׁב
רַב־קָשֶׁב) and to speculate that its imperativizing translation (ἀκρόασαι
ἀκρόασιν πολλὴν) is not wholly to be explained as an accident caused
by orthographic confusion. At the very least, it is an example of a widespread tendency to insert imperatival exchanges into the text. It is also

---

24. Cf. R.R. Ottley, *The Book of Isaiah According to the LXX (Codex
Alexandrinus). I. Introduction and Translation with a Parallel Version from the
Hebrew* (Cambridge: Cambridge University Press, 1909), Isa. 21.8: 'And call Uriah
to the watchtower of the Lord' (!); LSJ defines οὐρία as *a water-bird*, which might
at least make *something* comprehensible of this LXX command. It is possible to
imagine the summoning of a bird to the Lord's watchtower, though it is difficult to
imagine what *for*.

25. Or, alternatively, those of the prophet.

26. Seeligmann has anticipated this particular observation. Cf. *LXX Version*,
p. 109: 'Prophesying occurs in the translation of 21.10 in the sense of a revelation
by God. The Hebrew text is, here, somewhat obscure... [In the LXX] those who are
exhorted to listen to these words of the prophet are: those who are left over, and
those who are harassed; we shall see further on that the translator, in choosing this
wording, which is practically independent of the Hebrew text, must have had in
mind his exiled compatriots. God Himself—the Greek text continues—has revealed
this to us; surely a remarkable departure from the Hebrew "to you", possibly
intended as a contemporization.'

possible that it is directed at this translator's intended readership or audience, as a homiletical summons to careful listening.

Isaiah 44.21. This verse affords us an example of imperativization of a niphal form which at the same time involves transformation of the verb from a passive to an active form.[27] In the MT, לֹא תִנָּשֵׁנִי is a word of assurance to Israel that she will not be forgotten by God. It appears to serve as the fourth consecutive reassuring statement by God in this verse: (1) '...for you are my servant'; (2) 'I formed you'; (3) 'you are my servant'; (4) '*You will not be forgotten by me*'.

However, the translator has not read the sentence in this way. Rather, he sees it as an imperative[28] that is parallel to the command that initiates the verse: 'Remember these things, O Jacob'.

Μνήσθητι ταῦτα, Ιακωβ καὶ Ισραηλ, ὅτι παῖς μου εἶ σύ· ἔπλασά σε παῖδά μου, καὶ σύ, Ισραηλ, μὴ ἐπιλανθάνου μου.

Remember these things, Jacob and Israel, because you are my servant. I formed you (to be) my servant; and you, Israel, <u>do not forget me</u>.

The pronominal suffix on the end of this weak *and* passive verb (לֹא) תִנָּשֵׁנִי may have presented sufficient difficulty as to explain by itself the transformation that has occurred.[29] Additionally, the imperative at the beginning of the verse offers an imperatival precedent.

In addition to these orthographic and grammatical features, an ideological motive may also figure in the imperatival translation of תִנָּשֵׁנִי. As we shall see, the Isaiah translator finds the bare possibility of divine imperception—even if the purpose is to deny it—distasteful. This by itself might have accounted for the alteration, even if he was not challenged by the grammar. Regardless of the causes, an imperativization has ensued, one that could effortlessly be pressed into the service of homiletical exhortation: *And you, Israel, do not forget me!*

Isaiah 24.11. Imperativization is also practised upon words other than verbs. For example, in Isa. 24.11, a noun has been translated as an imperative, perhaps with the 'assistance' of some orthographic con-

---

27. Together with the subject-complement inversion that such a transformation often requires.

28. I.e. לֹא + the imperfect functioning as a (negating) imperative.

29. Instead of תִנָּשֵׁנִי he appears to have read תִנְשֵׁנִי, which is also the suggested reading of the verb in GK §117x.

fusion.[30] The substantive צְוָחָה has been translated as ὀλολύζετε, as though the translator read צוחו.[31] Instead of the MT's, 'There is *an outcry* in the streets for lack of wine,' the LXX offers, '*Wail* because of the wine, everywhere!' Clearly, this outcome produces a heightened dramatic effect rather than a homiletical exhortation.

It should be noted that there are instances that change an imperative in the MT to a declarative statement in the LXX. However, these are far less frequent and can usually be explained individually without recourse to the kind of widespread inclination that appears to produce LXX imperativizations.

Imperativization Lacking Authorization as a Feature of LXX Isaiah
The apparently haphazard nature of some of the conversions we have seen may suggest nothing more than a translator who is in over his head, furiously struggling to keep his nose above water by translating atomistically. However, those examples of imperativization that we have seen—all of which enjoy at least some authorization from the text—are only part of the evidence. When they are placed within the wider context of hortatory remarks that have no such authorization, then the case can be made that this translator has exhortation on his mind, and is going to practise it by hook or by crook. For example, there are numerous brief exclamations and homiletical exhortations scattered throughout LXX Isaiah that appear to be contributions of the translator with no underlying Hebrew to explain them.

---

30. One would not want to create the impression that imperativizations are unusually common either in verses that were particularly difficult for the translator or in those which have undergone more widespread alteration in translation. However, 24.11 *does* show evidence of broader reconfiguration. The parallel clauses נלה מְשׂוֹשׂ הָאָרֶץ // ערבה כל־שׂמחה have lost the underlined words in a fairly typical (for this translator) case of 'collapsing'.

31. The verb read by the translator, צוח, is attested in the HB only at Isa. 42.11. However, it is not at all uncommon in Aramaic and Syriac. This may attach itself to evidence gathered elsewhere that suggests that the translator read the Hebrew of his source text through a grid that was more attuned to later Hebrew (cf. Aramaic). Cf. M. Jastrow, *A Dictionary of the Targumim, the Talmud Babli and Yerushalmi, and the Midrashic Literature* (New York: Judaica Press, 1996 [1950]), 1266.

Renderings that appear to read ו or ה for some other letter are common in this translation, though the interchange of one of these with the other is not. The same two letters are often identified in variant readings in the wider practice of biblical text criticism; cf. Tov, *TCU*, p. 73.

Isaiah 26.10. At 26.10, in the midst of a series of clauses that discuss the determination of the ungodly to remain so, the LXX translator appears to insert his own exclamation, ἀρθήτω ὁ ἀσεβής!: *May the ungodly be taken away!*[32] One can imagine how the stubborn description of the ungodly in the context might provoke such an exasperated cry.

Isaiah 44.20. This verse offers at least one and perhaps two 'didactic exhortations'.[33] In the first instance, רעה אפר[34] has been translated by γνῶτε ὅτι σπόδος...In the second, ἴδετε stems from no obvious Hebrew equivalent. While the first of these is semi-authorized, the second may have appeared without any such prompting from the Hebrew text.

This verse challenges one to distinguish between our translator's capacity for alluding to other biblical books and the by-products of his long battle with the orthographic features of his text or manuscript. It is often difficult to discern which of the two has more strongly influenced his translation at any given point. One or the other has produced an unauthorized imperativization in 44.20.

At the beginning of the verse, the translator has read רעה as either רדעה[35] or ד-ע—which has then been rendered as plural—or as דעו. In either case, he has produced γνῶτε as the opening word of the verse. Ἴδετε then occurs near the end of the verse, apparently without authorization from the Hebrew text. Two possible explanations for this LXX plus deserve attention. The first rests upon a rhetorical structure that appears commonly in the Former Prophets.[36] The imperatives דעו and ראו are juxtaposed in those verses to form a twin (and presumably intensified) summons to attention. The Isaiah translator may display his knowledge of this repeated feature by adding a second call to what a

32. Alternatively, the MT may barely conceal a degree of authorization for this exclamation. נכחות יעול is clearly responsible for generating ἀλήθειαν οὐ μὴ ποιήσῃ. It may also be the source of ἀρθήτω ὁ ἀσεβής, if one can reasonably conjecture that a translator saw something like יִלָּבַח עַוָּל (understanding לקח for לכה). Though this takes us on to admittedly speculative ground, the substantive עול does correspond to ἀσεβής 4x in Job.

33. I refer by this term to imperatives that summon the attention of the audience, but are otherwise devoid of content: e.g. 'Listen!', 'Look!', etc.

34. 'He feeds on ashes...'

35. Cf. Prov. 24.14.

36. Cf. 1 Sam. 12.17; 14.38; 23.23; 24.12; 25.17; 2 Sam. 24.13; 1 Kgs 20.7; 20.22; 2 Kgs 5.7.

ר/ד orthographic interchange has already convinced him is an imperatival context. With or without such a precedent from biblical rhetoric, he has apparently produced an unauthorized imperativization.

A second explanation for the problematic ἴδετε relies solely on the orthographic elements of the Hebrew text. It allows for some degree of authorization for ἴδετε from within v. 20 itself. According to this approach, ולא has been translated twice. Clearly, οὐκ answers to ולא. Already, however, the absence of the copula in Greek might alert us to the possibility that the translator struggled with his text at this point, for he far more commonly *adds* a prosaicizing copula than he omits one.[37] Orthographic confusion elsewhere in this book suggests that it would not have been impossible for him to read ולא as ראו.[38] The moderate graphic similarity of ל and ד brings this conjecture into the arena of the conceivable. If this latter process accounts for the LXX plus, then we have also a doublet, for ולא has then been translated twice.[39]

---

37. The ratio of copulas added/copulas omitted is 2.59/1 in chs. 56–66 and similar elsewhere in LXX Isaiah.

R.A. Martin attempted to isolate syntactical features that would provide criteria by which to distinguish translation Greek from native Greek on empirical grounds; cf. *Syntactical Evidence of Semitic Sources in Greek Documents* (Septuagint and Cognate Studies, 3; Missoula, MT: SBL, 1974), pp. 19-20; cf. also K.H. Jobes, *The Alpha-Text of Esther: Its Character and Relationship to the Masoretic Text* (SBLDS, 153; Missoula, MT: SBL, 1996), pp. 10, 17. One of the criteria used by both Martin and Jobes is the ratio of copulative καί to postpositive δέ. When judged by this measure, LXX Isaiah falls within 'translation Greek' proportions, but among the translated books of the LXX it is in line with those whose style is closest to 'composition Greek'. For our purposes, it is worth noting that LXX Isaiah is intolerant of asyndeton, introducing *both* καί *and* δέ with abandon.

On the problem of copulative waw in Hebrew mss. and in the Versions, cf. M.H. Gottstein, 'Die Jesaia-Rolle im Lichte von Peschitta und Targum', *Biblica* 35 (1954), pp. 51-71 (54 n. 4), and—by the same author—'Die Jesaiah-Rolle und das Problem der hebräischen Bibelhandschriften', *Biblica* 35 (1954), pp. 429-42 (437).

38. This by way of the process that forms a new word using two out of three available Hebrew radicals and the liberty to reorder two or more of these.

39. There is an additional imperatival element in the translation of ולא יאמר ('*And he does not say*, "Is not this thing in my right hand a fraud?"'). The translator has turned this phrase towards some second person plural audience. The future negation that results (οὐκ ἐρεῖτε, 'You will/shall not say...') appears more likely to function imperatively than as a simple negative report regarding future speech. Quite likely the translator is preaching to his own generation of 'Jacob/Israel' (cf. 44.1, 2, 21).

Thus, it is not always a simple matter to determine whether or not an imperativization has been authorized by the local details of the Hebrew text. The explanation of ἴδετε which sees it as an unauthorized interjection does not stand alone. When we examine LXX Isa 57.1, below, we shall encounter fresh encouragement for concluding that the translator's hortatory instinct is strong enough for him to interject such 'didactic imperatives' even when an orthographic basis for this does not exist. Though such additions may not require us to imagine an oral forum in order to make sense of them, they do suggest that the translator has certain kinds of behaviour that he expects to elicit from his audience or readership by explicitly urging it upon them.[40]

Isaiah 40.27; 43.10. If the above examples leave any doubt that our translator is persuaded of the existential relevance of these texts for his community or that he is possessed of a hortatory agenda, two further instances might prove convincing. At 40.27, the rhetorical question, 'Why do you say, O Jacob...' is converted to a command: '*Do not* say, O Jacob...'[41] With regard to the available features of the Hebrew text,

40. Brockington applied the thesis of P. Kahle to the Isaiah translator's interest in 'salvation'; cf. 'Septuagint and Targum'. In speaking of 'the two targumists (Greek and Aramaic)' (p. 80), he writes, 'This is just the kind of expository interpretation that one might expect a reader to offer his hearers at a service of worship where it would be fitting to dwell on the deliverance wrought by God for his people' (p. 82). 'This seems to call for a re-consideration of the relation of the LXX to the Targum from this point of view, namely, that the one is not dependent on the other, but both exhibit evidence of a common tradition which, for the most part, may well have been oral' (pp. 82-83).

In my view, there is little in this material that would call into question the Lagardian hypothesis of a Greek Ur-text in favour of Kahle's assertion that the project witnessed to in the Letter of Aristeas was a revision of multiple Greek translations into an 'authorized' LXX. However, the evidence of homiletical intention that LXX Isaiah provides does suggest that the translator himself had purposes with which the Aramaic *meturgeman* might easily have sympathized. For a helpful summary of Lagarde versus Kahle, cf. Jellicoe, *Septuagint*, pp. 59-73; also Tov, *TCU*, pp. 6-8, 12-15.

41. למה תאמר יעקב = Μὴ γὰρ εἴπῃς, Ιακωβ. The parallel rhetorical question—ותדבר ישראל—remains a question in translation: καὶ τί ἐλάλησας, Ισραηλ...Indeed, it preserves the interrogative elements (למה = καὶ τί) that are absent via ellipsis in the second stich in the Hebrew and absent via imperativization in the first stich of the Greek. 'Corrected ellipsis'—whereby the elided portion of two parallel structures is restored in the Greek translation—is exceedingly common in LXX Isaiah.

such a transformation is substantial enough to be considered largely *unauthorized.*

Moreover, the declarative statement that introduces 43.10, 'You are my witnesses...', becomes in the hands of our translator, '*Be* my witnesses'. This last example is all the more striking, in that it requires the provision of an imperative verb meaning 'Be...!' where the Hebrew has only a verbless clause.[42]

There are nearly one hundred cases of imperativization in LXX Isaiah. While one occasionally notices the reverse—Hebrew imperatives which are turned into declarative statements in Greek—these are far less common and, it seems, accidental. One observes, then, a tendency to *preach* the book while *translating* it. This characteristic of the translator's technique occurs throughout this long book, as is the case with all the features I will discuss in this volume. The even distribution of these translational idiosyncrasies across the 66 chapters of the book persuades me that we are reading the work of just one translator.

Imperativization in LXX Isaiah 56–66

Authorized imperativization in chs. 56–66

Isaiah 56.10. In Isa 56.10, צֹפָו[43] עֹרִים כֻּלָּם = ἴδετε ὅτι πάντες ἐκτετύφλωνται. The translator has read the text as though it were vocalized צְפוּ. The resulting rhetorical summons to '*see that*' or '*see*

It is possible that the translator's creative contribution to this verse is minimal. C.R. North writes, 'To this Yahweh's answer is "*Why* (a note of reproach here) do you *keep saying* so?"' The LXX may have expressed such 'reproach' by turning this into a prohibition. Cf. *The Second Isaiah: Introduction, Translation and Commentary to Chapters XL–LV* (Oxford: Oxford University Press, 1964), p. 89.

The LXX is not unique among similar literature in its resolution of a rhetorical question to an imperative. M.L. Klein discusses 'Resolution of the Rhetorical Question' as one common feature of Targumic technique. Cf. 'Converse Translation: A Targumic Technique', *Biblica* 57 (1976), pp. 515-37 (532). Klein's analysis covers the Pentateuch only. Cf. also R. Hayward, *The Targum of Jeremiah: Translated, with a Critical Introduction, Apparatus, and Notes* (The Aramaic Bible, 12; Edinburgh: T. & T. Clark, 1987), p. 25. R.P. Gordon, referring to Klein's article, notes that the Targumists not only *resolved* rhetorical questions when facing dissident texts. They were also known to *create* such questions as a way of bringing 'such texts into line'. Cf. 'The Targumists as Eschatologists', in J.A. Emerton (ed.), *Congress Volume, Göttingen, 1977* (VTSup, 29; Leiden: E.J. Brill, 1978), p. 114.

42. אַתֶּם עֵדִי נְאֻם־יְהוָה = γένεσθέ μοι μάρτυρες...

43. Qere צְפוּ.

how' requires a semantic shift as well, for צָפָה normally has connotations of stealthy observation, whether carried out behind enemy lines or from a watch-tower. Ἰδεῖν lacks this meaning and is never generated by צָפָה elsewhere in the LXX.[44] Thus, it is only upon weak semantic grounds that the LXX produces ἴδετε ὅτι to announce Israel's blindness. The translator's affection for this word is clear, for he uses it with the slenderest of justification. The employment of ἴδετε in this verse is unexpected and may speak eloquently of the translator's homiletical bias.[45]

Isaiah 61.10. In the rendering by which תגל נפשׁי becomes ἀγαλλιάσθω ἡ ψυχή μου, the 3ms imperative ἀγαλλιάσθω is arguably a literal translation of the apparently jussive תגל.[46] Nevertheless, it should be noted that the translator has seized upon an imperatival option despite the 'indicative' parallel that אׁשׁישׂ represents and the possibility of reading תגל as a defective rendering of non-jussive תָּגֵל. The result may be a slightly heightened dramatic tone vis-à-vis the MT.

Isaiah 63.16. In 63.16, אתה יהוה אבינו גֹּאֲלֵנוּ מעולם שׁמך = ἀλλὰ σύ κύριε πατὴρ ἡμῶν ῥῦσαι ἡμᾶς ἀπ᾽ ἀρχῆς τὸ ὄνομά σου ἐφ᾽ ἡμᾶς εστιν. The translation reflects vocalization as an imperative: גְּאָלֵנוּ[47] rather than the substantivized participle גֹּאֲלֵנוּ. The choice is understandable in the light of the vocative addresses to God that begin at 64.14[48] and recur immediately prior to the appearance of גֹּאֲלֵנוּ.[49]

---

44. צָפָה produces a strong standard translation pattern of -σκοπ- lexemes. Only Ps. 5.4—where וַאֲצַפֶּה = καὶ ἐπόψομαι—and Jer. 48(31).19—where עמדי וצפי is rendered στῆθι καὶ ἔπιδε—offer any analogy.

45. He rounds out his treatment of this half-verse by providing φρονῆσαι as a complement for לֹא ידע = οὐκ ἔγνωσαν. This kind of added complement is entirely in concord with his general discontent with allusive poetics.

46. By comparison with the 'indicative' form of this verb (תגיל), the MT's תָּגֵל has lost the medial *yod* but has not suffered the retraction of the tone that is common to jussive forms. Curiously, nearly all modern translations and commentators render this verb 'indicatively' (with 'rejoices', 'shall rejoice' or some equivalent of these), perhaps because of the parallel with the non-cohortative אׁשׁישׂ. NEB/REB are exceptional: 'let me exult...'

47. Cf. GK §64b.

48. Though at a later point in the verse in LXX.

49. אתה יהוה אבינו.

Isaiah 26.13 provides a remarkable parallel. In that verse, יהוה
אלהינו בעלונו is rendered κύριε ὁ θεὸς ἡμῶν κτῆσαι ἡμᾶς. As opposed
to 63.16, the imperativization of *this* prayer is only *semi*-authorized, for
a waw must be omitted from בעלונו in order to 'read' בְּעָלֵנוּ.

Though Seeligmann refers to 63.16 only to illustrate the translator's
'lack of mastery of the Hebrew language', the conversion found there is
just as helpfully understood in light of his own view that 'certain
passages...have been formulated under the influence of the liturgy in
the Jewish–Alexandrian milieu'.[50]

This is the first case of imperativization directed *towards God* in LXX
Isaiah 56–66. However, it is not surprising that our translator, whose
urge to contemporize a text produces both a dramatic intensification and
a tendency towards exhortation, might also intuitively lead his audience
in prayer when his source text presents such an option.[51] If one were to
postulate for this translator a liturgical preoccupation, this might well
be understood to include the tendency to move texts towards both
exhortation and prayer. The examples we are canvassing support at
numerous points the hypothesis that such a background and motivation
indeed existed.[52]

---

50. For the translator's alleged difficulties with Hebrew language and style, cf.
LXX Version, pp. 57-58; for liturgical influence, pp. 101-103. Seeligmann's survey
of the data is suggestive rather than systematic.

On p. 114, Seeligmann notices the very rich contemporization of a prayer in the
two verses which follow 63.16. Curiously, however, he chooses not to explore the
possibilities: 'In 63.17/18, a certain degree of contemporization is obtained by a
divergence from the Massoretic text... Whereas the Hebrew text constitutes a
complaint of the violence of the enemy, the translator causes *either the prophet or
the exiles to pray to God*: 'Turn Thou to us that we may soon take possession of
Thy Holy Mountain'... *No great importance should be attached to the use of the
first person, since the translator always takes considerable liberty in changing
persons and number*...' (emphases added). One would want to ask whether those
who pray this prayer might not now include the Diaspora Jews who used this
translation. Additionally, Seeligmann appears to assume that *frequent* changes must
be *insignificant* changes, an approach that would not seem in this instance to lead to
a deeper understanding of this translator. For more on the substantial adaptation of
63.15-19, see Chapter 5.

51. To be precise, his text is *already* a prayer. What he has done with גאלנו is to
put a request on the lips of his pray-er. For the possibility that the interpolated first-
person plurals of the LXX in surrounding verses mean that the translator understood
this as a prayer to be voiced by his own generation, see the preceding note.

52. I do not find all of Seeligmann's proofs for a 'liturgical setting' to be

Isaiah 66.5. In 66.5, אָמְרוּ אֲחֵיכֶם שֹׂנְאֵיכֶם מְנַדֵּיכֶם = εἴπατε ἀδελφοὶ ἡμῶν τοῖς μισοῦσιν ἡμᾶς καὶ βδελυσσομένοις ἡμᾶς. The imperative εἴπατε—created by vocalizing the MT's אָמְרוּ as אִמְרוּ—is part of a wide-ranging transformation of this verse.

The substantial personalization which this verse has undergone[53] raises the question of contemporization once again. It appears that the translator has understood this sentence as a command to speak to some outside group that holds his community[54] in low esteem. If there has been a thoroughgoing contemporisation of chapter 66,[55] then one is drawn to think in the first instance of the translator's own Diaspora community as those despised ones who are here urged to speak out in some way.[56]

Semi-Authorized Imperativization in chs. 56–66
Isaiah 56.9. In Isa. 56.9, כֹּל חַיְתוֹ שָׂדַי אֵתָיוּ לֶאֱכֹל = πάντα τὰ θηρία τὰ ἄγρια δεῦτε φάγετε. At times the translator produces an imperatival Greek form that merely makes explicit an imperatival function that already existed in the Hebrew text. This is accomplished here by interrupting the semantic link between the two verbs. Each now is independently imperative. There may be a slight rhetorical intensification.

Isaiah 58.5-6. Verse 58.5, הֲלָזֶה תִקְרָא־צוֹם וְיוֹם רָצוֹן לַיהוה = οὐδ' οὕτως καλέσετε νηστείαν δεκτήν and 58.6, הַתֵּר...פַּתֵּחַ חַרְצֻבּוֹת. אֲגֻדּוֹת מוֹטָה...וְשַׁלַּח רְצוּצִים חָפְשִׁים וְכָל־מוֹטָה תְּנַתֵּקוּ = ἀλλὰ λῦε

convincing. For example, it is not clear to me, in the case of Isa 26.13, that בְּעָלוּנוּ became κτῆσαι ἡμᾶς under the influence of 'some liturgical association' (*LXX Version*, p. 57). Might not a familiarity with prayer and an instinct for engaging in it be enough?

I would want to define 'liturgical setting' sufficiently loosely so that it does not demand much more than a heightened sensitivity to the use that this translation would have in the worship of Alexandrian Jewry. Evidence for such a concern is to be found in the contemporizations that abound in the translated text, without necessarily locating this or that phrase as a set piece from some specific liturgical moment.

53. Cf. below, Chapter 7.
54. I.e. 'us'.
55. See below, Chapter 7 for an elaboration upon this possibility.
56. Seeligmann's comments on LXX Isa. 21.10—a verse that figured in our introduction to 'imperativization' early in this chapter—may be relevant to the details of Isa. 66.5 as well. Perhaps in dealing with the hated and rejected of this verse—as Seeligmann suggested for 21.10—the translator might 'have had in mind his exiled compatriots' (cf. *LXX Version*, p. 109).

πάντα σύνδεσμον ἀδικίας...<u>διάλυε</u> στραγγαλιὰς βιαίων συναλλαγμάτων...<u>ἀπόστελλε</u> τεθραυσμένους ἐν ἀφέσει... καὶ πᾶσαν συγγραφὴν ἄδικον <u>διάσπα</u>.[57] This series of imperatives begins with the resolution of a rhetorical question into a plural imperative.[58] The passage contains a mixture of authorized and semi-authorized imperativizations. In 58.6 the translator has successfully preserved the consonants of three of the four verbs.[59] In conformity with this chain of imperatives, the final imperfect verb is also levelled to a semi-authorized imperative.

The rhetorical questions continue in 58.7: הֲלוֹא <u>פָרֹס</u> לָרָעֵב לַחְמֶךָ וַעֲנִיִּים מְרוּדִים <u>תָּבִיא</u> בָיִת כִּי־תִרְאֶה עָרֹם <u>וְכִסִּיתוֹ</u> וּמִבְּשָׂרְךָ <u>לֹא תִתְעַלָּם</u>. The LXX, for its part, continues to resolve the varied verbal forms as imperatives: <u>διάθρυπτε</u> πεινῶντι τὸν ἄρτον σου καὶ πτωχοὺς ἀστέγους <u>εἴσαγε</u> εἰς τὸν οἶκόν σου· ἐὰν ἴδῃς γυμνόν, <u>περίβαλε</u>, καὶ ἀπὸ τῶν οἰκείων τοῦ σπέρματός σου <u>οὐχ ὑπερόψῃ</u>.[60]

The LXX is not entirely creative here, for the translator is merely making explicit an imperatival intent that is already implicit in the Hebrew text. On balance, however, he appears to have made a palpable contribution to the tone of the passage. His intervention heightens the dramatic effect and perhaps also brings out a hortatory nuance vis-à-vis the audience more strongly than is accomplished in the parent text.

Unauthorized Imperativization in chs. 56–66
Isaiah 57.1 and Other Homiletical uses of ἴδετε *in LXX Isaiah.* Imperativizations that lack any precedent in the Hebrew text are rare.[61] One of them—at LXX Isa. 57.1—requires extended treatment. In the Septuagint, Isaiah ch. 57 begins with a curious imperative.

---

57. TJ also renders the four verbs of 58.6 imperativally (in one case, as a jussive).

58. In function, though not in form.

59. Indeed, even the vowels can be read as in the MT, for the (apparent) infinitives absolute פָרֹס, הָבֵא, and וְשַׁלַּח are formally identical to the corresponding singular imperatives.

60. As at the beginning of 58.5, the future indicative is employed in a (negative) imperatival role.

61. This is as one would expect given that this translator's 'freedom' does not cut him loose from his parent text. As we shall observe in some detail, he is 'free' with regard to LXX precedent. However, this freedom is conditioned by his text and his interpretative tradition.

ἴδετε ὡς ὁ δίκαιος ἀπώλετο καὶ οὐδεὶς ἐκδέχεται τῇ καρδίᾳ

<u>See how</u> the righteous person[62] has perished, yet no one takes it to heart!

In the MT, this apparent homiletical tone is missing:

הצדיק אבד ואין איש שם על־לב

The righteous perish, and no one takes it to heart…

In this chapter and the following one, I provide evidence of the Isaiah translator's tendency to imperativize and personalize,[63] and argue that such transformations serve homiletical ends. Until now this argument has rested upon grammatical grounds, and will continue largely to do so. However, in the intrusion of this imperatival exclamation at 57.1a we may now have evidence from a new and non-grammatical quarter that corroborates the homiletical character of this translation.

62. Curiously, the translator defies his own habit of pluralizing collective or representative singulars in both occurrences of הצדיק in this verse. Furthermore, he uses the aorist and the perfect to translate the two reports of the righteous man's passing away (אבד and נאסף), while the passing of אנשי־חסד is described in the present as though this latter were the same habitual recurrence that the Hebrew text suggests it to be. While this could be due simply to a correlation of the Hebrew perfect with the Greek aorist and perfect tenses, and of the Hebrew participle with the Greek present tense, it is nonetheless suggestive. Did the translator have in mind some specific righteous person, and his death?

Cf. on the Hebrew text, J. Blenkinsopp, 'The "Servants of the Lord" in Third Isaiah. Profile of a Pietistic Group in the Persian Epoch', *Proceedings of the Irish Biblical Association* 7 (1983), pp. 1-23; reprinted in R.P. Gordon (ed.), *'The Place Is Too Small for Us': The Israelite Prophets in Recent Scholarship* (Winona Lake, IN: Eisenbrauns, 1995), pp. 392-412; cf. esp. p. 395: 'After the opening passage (56.1-8), which adopts a controversially liberal position on the status of eunuchs and aliens, a sustained anti-syncretist diatribe (56.9-57.13) clearly indicates intragroup conflict without requiring the existence of a well-defined sub-group within which the polemic originated. As we read on, however, we become aware that the term "servants of Yahweh", which at the beginning alludes to the entire community (56.6), begins to be restricted to a minority within the province which is experiencing opposition and even persecution at the hands of its opponents.' One wonders whether the LXX might not understand the צידק of 56.1 to refer to a minority of one!

63. I.e. to convert third-person references to the first and second persons. Dr G. I. Davies has suggested the term 'dialogue-ization' for this phenomenon.

Before we arrive at such a conclusion, there are two lines of evidence that must come under review. First, one must establish for the Isaiah translator the uniqueness of such a use of ἴδετε. It may be that a recognizable and more widespread tradition of LXX interpretation lies behind this plus, rather than any homiletical tendency specific to LXX Isaiah. If that were the case, this verse could not be entered as evidence supporting the peculiar 'preached' nature of LXX Isaiah.

Second, one must inquire into the Isaiah translator's use of this term elsewhere. Such an undertaking may uncover a motivation other than a homiletical one for its appearance. One might then transfer such an explanation to the plus at 57.1, perhaps finding in some element of the Hebrew text or context a feature that would explain its presence there. Features *in the Hebrew text* that generate the intrusion of ἴδετε—if these should be found to exist—would diminish its profile as a novelty on the part of our translator. Conversely, one might uncover indications that the homiletical intent I have deemed evident via the intrusion of ἴδετε in 57.1 is more widespread in this document, and that ἴδετε fulfils a role elsewhere in expressing this, thus bolstering the claim that this translation is, in a sense, preached as well as translated.

In the Septuagint, ἴδετε nearly always translates an imperatival form of ראה. This is true even more exclusively than a handful of apparent exceptions might suggest. One of those exceptions, Deut. 32.39, seems at first to provide an unauthorized occurrence of ἴδετε like the exclamation at LXX Isa. 57.1, but this is not the case: ראו עתה כי אני אני הוא = ἴδετε ἴδετε ὅτι ἐγώ εἰμι. The translator seems to have caught the notion of repetition communicated by אני אני. However, he has transposed this from אני to ראו. Such 'misplaced' repetition probably accounts for the otherwise anomalous 'unauthorized' occurrence of ἴδετε.

At 2 Kgs 10.10, we find another unusual source of ἴδετε, though it is hardly a difficult one.

דעו אפוא כי לא יפל מדבר יהוה

Know then that no word of the Lord shall fall...

ἴδετε αφφω ὅτι οὐ πεσεῖται ἀπὸ τοῦ ῥήματος κυρίου...

See, Apho, that no part of the word of the Lord shall fall...

Ὁράω is not an unsatisfactory equivalent for ידע. Nevertheless, it is an uncommon one and deserves explanation. In the Former Prophets imperatival forms of ידע and ראה are frequently juxtaposed to form a twin (and presumably intensified) summons to attention.[64] To the translators of this material, such a construction was no doubt familiar as a stock word-pair. The distinctive nuances of the two words might well have faded slightly before the rhetorical unity that their coupling produced. Since this word-pair occurs chiefly in the Former Prophets,[65] it is perhaps this semantic levelling of the two words that explains the exceptional provision of ἴδετε for דעו at 2 Kgs 10.10.[66]

The Greek Psalms and Job each provide one unusual source for ἴδετε, but both instances are semantically unremarkable. For our purpose, their interest lies in that (a) they honour in the breach a nearly unanimous LXX preference for reserving ἴδετε for imperatival ראה, and (b) the example from the Psalms provides grist for a reconstruction of a similar Isaiah passage, which we will meet below.[67] In Ps. 46(45).9 we read,

לכו־חזו מפעלות יהוה

Come, <u>behold</u> the works of the LORD.

δεῦτε ἴδετε τὰ ἔργα κυρίου.

Come, <u>see</u> the works of the LORD.

This is just a case of a synonym of ראה generating ἴδετε.

In the example from Job[68] we discover a syntactical rearrangement by imperativization and personalization which would be at home in LXX Isaiah. The generation of ἴδετε by נבט is the kind of artistic dissension with which the Job translator approaches almost any LXX standard. But it is not a *semantic* departure of any importance.

---

64. 1 Sam. 12.17; 14.38; 23.23; 24.12; 25.17; 2 Sam. 24.13; 1 Kgs 20.7; 20.22; 2 Kgs 5.7.

65. In Exod. 33.13, Moses' words to the Lord are similar. He says, 'Show me (הודיעני) your ways...consider too (וראה) that this nation is your people.' It will be observed, however, that the suffixed hiphil form of ידע somewhat distances this plea from the standard 'know...and see!' construction that we are discussing. Jeremiah, in his denunciations of Zion, provides the only three true duplications of this construction outside the Former Prophets (2.19; 2.23; 5.1).

66. Alternatively, we may have a divergent *Vorlage* or a divergent reading of the same *Vorlage*. It is not impossible to imagine a scenario whereby ראו / דעו = ἴδετε, based upon a ע/א guttural interchange and the well-known likeness of ד and ר.

67. Cf. the treatment of Isa. 46.5 below, especially the speculation that the translator may have produced ἴδετε as a result of reading the MT consonants as though they represented a form of חזה.

68. Job 6.19.

הביטו ארחות תמא הליכת שבא קוו־למו

The caravans of Tema <u>look</u>, the travellers of Sheba hope.

ἴδετε ὁδοὺς Θαιμανων ἀτραποὺς Χαβων οἱ διορῶντες

<u>See</u> the ways of the people of Tema (and) the paths of the people of Sheba, O you who see clearly.

Forty-nine other occurrences of ἴδετε answer to imperatival ראה. This is the LXX standard equivalence by a wide margin. Only a string of difficulties in Isaiah awaits attention in order to round out the evidence. Thus far, this survey shows that the unauthorized *provision* of ἴδετε does not occur in the LXX outside of the Greek Isaiah. If, therefore, it occurs *there*, it is a feature unique to our translator.

We proceed, then, to a consideration of ἴδετε in Isaiah, a subject that presents us with the smattering of translational anomalies one comes to expect in this book. There are six occurrences of this plural imperative in LXX Isaiah, at 9.1, 40.26a, 44.20, 46.5, 56.10a and 57.1 itself. Most of them are problematical in their respective ways.[69]

The first occurrence is Isa. 9.1:

עם ההלכים בחשך ראו אור גדול
ישבי בארץ צלמות אור נגה עליהם

The people who walked in darkness <u>have seen</u> a great light; those who lived in a land of deep darkness—on them light has shone.

ὁ λαος ὁ πορευόμενος[70] ἐν σκότει, ἴδετε φῶς μέγα οἱ κατοικοῦντες ἐν χώρᾳ καὶ σκιᾷ θανάτου φῶς λάμψει ἐφ᾽ ὑμᾶς.

O people which walks in darkness, <u>see</u> a great light! O you who dwell in a land and in a shadow of death, light shall shine upon you.

This verse exemplifies the imperativization and personalization that is common to LXX Isaiah. The reading tradition crystallized in the MT vocalizes our verb as רָאוּ and the text is consistently descriptive in the third person. The Greek translator has read the initial verb as רְאוּ and

---

69. The singular ἴδέ comports itself according to a strong LXX standard, and does not particularly illuminate the problem of Isa. 57.1.

70. Somewhat atypically, the translator has singularized ההלכים (but see BHS proposal to delete) as ὁ πορευόμενος. As noted above, his standard manoeuvre is to pluralize collective singulars. Probably, this latter habit has been counterbalanced here by his preference for levelling number and other grammatical features. Since עם (ὁ λαὸς) cannot be sensibly made plural, its attendant modifier (ההלכים = ὁ πορευόμενος) has been brought into (numerical) line by being made singular.

has converted the final prepositional phrase from the third to the second person plural. The outcome of these conversions is that the verse now addresses either the readers or the readers as proxy for some original group of hearers. It has been cut loose from its historical moorings and contemporized. One might well conclude that it has been moved in a homiletical direction. If so, the utilization of ἴδετε has played no small part in this transformation.

One must distinguish between the options that the consonantal text *allows* the translator, on the one hand, and the kind of options *that he routinely chooses*, on the other. The first is a matter for discrete analysis on a case-by-case basis. The latter requires a perspective global enough to account for 66 chapters' worth of evidence.

In the verse at hand, the consonantal text *allows* the translator to produce a second-person, imperatival context. It does not compel him to do so. He might have chosen this option in the absence of any larger homiletical agenda, though it must be recognized that this choice will require *consonantal* alteration before he is finished. For our purposes, this discrete observation must then be complemented by our noting that his imperativization in this case has utilized a specific word: ἴδετε. Thus, one will have to be attentive as to whether or not ἴδετε is for the translator a 'homiletically charged' word, one that facilitates a wider urge to speak imperatively. If it is, we should expect it to appear in circumstances where imperativization is not as easily[71] authorized by the consonantal text as it is in Isa. 9.1.

The second occurrence of ἴδετε in LXX Isaiah is unremarkable from a textual point of view. Isaiah 40.26a produces a straightforward translation in which עיניכם = וראו שאו־מרום‎ = ἀναβλέψατε εἰς ὕψος τοὺς ὀφθαλμοὺς ὑμῶν καὶ ἴδετε. Every feature of the Greek sentence is fully authorized by the Hebrew text.

A third example is found at 44.20:

רעה אפר לב הותל הטהו ולא־יציל את־נפשו
ולא יאמר הלוא שקר בימיני

> He feeds on ashes; a deluded mind has led him astray, and he cannot save himself and he does not say, 'Is not this thing in my right hand a fraud?'

71. Though only in relative terms, for—as noted—it does require secondary alteration within the verse.

γνῶτε ὅτι σποδὸς ἡ καρδία αὐτῶν καὶ πλανῶνται καὶ οὐδεὶς
δύναται ἐξελέσθαι τὴν ψυχὴν αὐτοῦ ἴδετε οὐκ ἐρεῖτε ὅτι ψεῦδος ἐν
τῇ δεξιᾷ μου.

<u>Know that</u> their heart is ash(es), and they wander, and no one is able to
save his (own) soul. <u>See!</u> You will not say,[72] 'There is a lie in my right
hand!'

For an analysis of this verse, see 'Isaiah 44.20' above pp. 35-37.
Regardless of the precise mechanics of this verse's translation, it does
come alongside 57.1 to provide our first unambiguous corroboration of
the fact that the Isaiah translator was able to produce ἴδετε with little or
no authorization. Verse 44.20 seems to lie somewhere between 9.1,
where the text merely had to be (re)vocalized as an imperative,[73] and
57.1 (see below), where it appears the Hebrew offers no concrete
authorization at all.

Isaiah 46.5, our fourth occurrence of ἴδετε, is an exceedingly difficult
case:

למי תדמיוני ותשׁוו ותמשׁלוני ונדמה

To whom will you liken me and make me equal, and compare me, as
though we were alike?

The LXX, for its part, renders,

τίνι με ὡμοιώσατε ἴδετε τεχνάσασθε οἱ πλανώμενοι.

To whom have you likened me? <u>Look!</u> Work artfully, O you who are
deceived!

With the appearance of ἴδετε in this verse, the Isaiah translator has
once again stretched our ability to comprehend his intention. The MT
offers a rhetorical question in which למי extends its interrogative force
to three consecutive verbs, the first and third of which have a 1cs suffix
referring to God, who is the speaker.

The translator begins well, but clearly runs into trouble at mid-
sentence. Leaving aside the problematic ἴδετε for the moment, one
observes that ותמשׁלוני apparently becomes τεχνάσασθε.[74] The verb
has lost its syntactical connection to the opening interrogative particle.

72. Or, with more (negative) imperatival content, 'You shall not say...'
73. With the attendant conversion of עליהם to עליכם later in the verse.
74. That the first verb, תדמיוני, is responsible for ὡμοιώσατε seems clear
enough not to warrant discussion here.

Neither has it retained the 1cs suffix. It has become a simple imperative. To his credit, the translator has probably not lost his grip on the mocking character of the passage, for τεχνάζειν, 'to employ art cunningly', is as much at home amidst a satirical discussion of idolatry as any other word might have been.[75] It is difficult to determine what the translator thought he saw here, though it is just conceivable that מֹשֵׁל[76] might be colourfully rendered by τεχνάζειν. As for the final word, the translator seems either to have mistaken ונדמה for נִדָּחִים[77] or to have conjectured some form of רמה.[78]

If I have correctly outlined the Hebrew–Greek equivalencies in this verse, then ἴδετε fills the 'slot' of ותשׁוו, the second of the three Hebrew verbs. The only available orthographic explanations are speculative and can establish—at most—only that the translator may have thought he read a text that is substantially different from what we have in the MT.[79] It can be stated, however, that the slot filled by ותשׁוו has

75. Τεχνάζειν is a *hapax legomenon* in the LXX, though the related τεχνᾶσθαι occurs in Wis. 13.11, a passage strongly reminiscent of this one.

76. The standard lexica attest a hiphil meaning, *to compare*. A truly factitive meaning (*to make like*) seems not to be attested in classical Hebrew, though this does not imply that the translator could not have taken such an etymologizing step if he glimpsed or thought he glimpsed a use of מֹשֵׁל which required it.

77. Niphal participle of נדח, *to be thrust out, banished, outcast*. This would require the two conversions, ה/ח and ו/י, plus a fair amount of dyslexic rearrangement. However, none of these would be unusual for this translator. The notion that apparent LXX Isaiah deviations from a *Vorlage* similar to MT may owe their existence to a sometimes radical reordering of Hebrew consonants in the mind of the translator is not a novelty in the scholarly literature. For an example of this in the work of a classical text critic, cf. Ziegler, *Untersuchungen*, p. 17. Ziegler explains ὄνειδος at 59.18 by stating that the translator read חרון אף as חרפה. Ziegler subjects this verse to a complicated reconstruction, which *BHS* seems to have followed. For our purposes, it is important that Ziegler does *not* insist that the Hebrew text originally had חרפה, though he often seems to rush to such text-reconstructive judgments. Rather, he thinks it had חרון אף, which the LXX translator merely *read* as חרפה. Such a reading would conform to my observations of frequent points where the translator used two of three or more available radicals + a 'dyslexic' reordering of these to 'create' a Hebrew word which he then translated.

78. Only the piel is found in BH, with the meaning *to beguile, deal treacherously with* (pael with the same meaning in Aramaic). This assumes a ד/ר interchange, which is common enough not to be considered problematic.

79. The first suggests that ותשׁוו has been read as חזו, an equivalence that is

not been left empty on the Greek side, but has been dutifully filled by
ἴδετε, regardless of whether or not the translator understood the
Hebrew verb.

Either he wrestled a verb that does not look exactly like anything that
would be expected to generate ἴδετε into a verbal form that does; or
he failed to come to any conclusion about what וּתְשֻׁוּוּ was meant to
say, and supplied ἴδετε instead, rather than leave its slot with no
corresponding Greek word. In either case, he has once again produced
ἴδετε with only the slightest prompting from his Hebrew text.

Neither of these explanations wrests all homiletical or dramatic
'charge' from ἴδετε. Once more, the fact that a given arrangement of
letters *can* be read to produce ἴδετε is one thing. The fact that assorted
collections of consonants—and perhaps none at all—on different
occasions *are* read to produce ἴδετε is quite another. The cumulative
weight of evidence begins to suggest that our translator—whether
consciously or not—*wants* to cry ἴδετε. It encourages the view that he
will say ἴδετε given the slightest authorization, as in 46.5. This path
may lead towards the conclusion that he *has* inserted ἴδετε at 57.1,

---

attested in Ps. 46(45).9. It would have required the reader to supply ה for the MT's
ת, as well as a שׁ/ת interchange (which occasionally occurs among sibilants).
Second, it is possible to imagine that our translator 'read' שִׂיחוּ, which when placed
alongside the MT would require the loss of one ו, a ת/ח conversion, and some
rearrangement of the radicals. שִׂיח, in its verbal and nominal forms, refers to
speaking, conversing, musing upon or meditating. The Greek Psalms twice translate
this verb with μελετάω, a decidedly mental rather than verbal activity. It is these
latter nuances that may have conducted the translator to the idea expressed by
ἴδετε.

As a third possibility, the translator may have read a form of piel (Aramaic pael)
שׁוה (BDB, II: *to set, place*, synonymous with שׂוּם) and supplied the complements
that make it mean *to pay attention to*. In this regard, cf. Isa. 41.20 (למען יראו וידעו
וישימו וישכילו = ἵνα ἴδωσι καὶ γνῶσι καὶ ἐννοηθῶσι καὶ ἐπιστῶνται),
Ps. 16(15).8 (שׁוּיתי יהוה לנגדי = προωρώμην τὸν κύριον) and 1 Sam. 9.20 (MT
אל־תשם את־לבך להם = TJ לא תשוי ית לבך על יהון).
Perhaps the best fit would be provided by the verb שׁוּר (BDB II), *to behold,
regard*. If the translator borrowed the initial *waw* of ותמשלוני (= LXX τεχνάσασθε,
without καὶ), then one has only to posit a reading of the second of three consecutive
waws as ר in order to produce ותשורו.

The thread that unites each of these possibilities is the failure of each of them
unambiguously to produce a Hebrew imperative. Any one of these scenarios may
represent the actual translation process at this point, but none inspires sufficient
confidence to shed the label 'speculative'.

making it the most radically unauthorized example of an homiletical impulse that has bubbled up already on numerous and quite distinct occasions.

The fifth occurrence of ἴδετε in Isaiah occurs in 56.10a, where צֹפוּ = ἴδετε. That verse has been analysed above. We return, then, to the sixth example, the only verse in LXX Isaiah—indeed, the only verse in the entire LXX—where ἴδετε appears with no apparent justification whatsoever in the consonantal text.

Isaiah 57.1 as a unique example of homiletical style. As we have seen, Isaiah 57.1a reads:

הצדיק אבד ואין איש שם על־לב

The righteous person perishes, and no one takes it to heart.

Ἴδετε ὡς ὁ δίκαιος ἀπώλετο, καὶ οὐδεὶς ἐκδέχεται τῇ καρδίᾳ...

See how the righteous person has perished, yet no one takes it to heart!

Our analysis of the Isaiah translator's use of ἴδετε encourages the view that this word is a tool by which he bends texts in imperatival and/or homiletical directions. Isaiah 57.1a, then, finds its place within a broader pattern of 'preached' translation. It stands apart only in that, uniquely here, *no* explanation for the appearance of ἴδετε is forthcoming from the Hebrew text. How is this to be explained?

We have seen that the *creative* use of ἴδετε is unique to the translator of Isaiah, though other LXX translators use the word predictably and consistently to translate ראו. The examples I have discussed in Isaiah show that the translator is willing to provide this verb with only minimal invitation from the consonantal text. I suggest that 57.1a must be seen in continuity with this pattern of translational behaviour. The translator has been preaching from the outset. His principal tools have been grammatical (imperativization and personalization; see also Chapter 3) and orthographic ones. The word ἴδετε has upon five separate occasions been the result. Verse 57.1a furthers this agenda, but this time without any verb that can be conveniently converted to an imperative. In order to fill this lexical vacuum, the translator simply provides the verb. The *provision* of ἴδετε at 57.1—against the backdrop of the previous *utilization* of ἴδετε—illuminates just how far this translator is willing to go in order to bring his text to the attention of his readers.[80]

---

80. LXX Isa. 51.12 may also be relevant to this study. In that verse, the MT

Summary and Conclusion

The LXX Isaiah translator displays a tendency to turn non-imperative forms into imperatives. Such imperativizations are authorized, semi-authorized, or unauthorized by the consonantal text. The result, in most cases is either a heightened dramatic effect or homiletical exhortation.

This grammatical evidence of a homiletical inclination is complemented by the use of 'didactic exhortations' like ἴδετε, sometimes with little or no authorization from the source text.

In the following chapter, we will notice how the translator frequently 'personalizes' his text in a manner that complements the imperativization discussed in this chapter and strengthens the argument that a contemporizing and homiletical purpose lies behind this translation.

offers a rhetorical question: 'Who art thou, that thou fearest man...?' The LXX resolves this to an imperative and supplies a verb of perception: γνῶθι τινα...

Chapter 3

'PERSONALIZATION' IN LXX ISAIAH

In addition to the phenomenon of 'imperativization' that we considered in the previous chapter, a second 'homiletical' ploy recurs throughout the book. It too appears to exercise a contemporizing effect upon the texts to which it is applied. I will refer to it by the not wholly satisfactory term 'personalization', meaning by this the substitution of first- and second-person grammatical forms for third-person forms.[1]

The translator is persuaded that his text speaks as much to and about 'you' and 'us' (i.e. his audience, sometimes including himself) as it does to and about his forebears in ancient Israel. He wants to introduce his readers into the Isaiah text, to massage the links between the original protagonists and the Jewish community of his day.[2] This may be a feature of a text whose genesis lies in oral performance.[3]

1.   The opposite phenomenon occurs as well. However, when the LXX is placed alongside the MT as approximating to the presumed *Vorlage*, it is observable that the translator prefers (a) to *provide* elements of 'dialogue'/'personalization' that are absent from his Hebrew text; (b) to *alter* Hebrew elements in the same direction; and (c) to *omit* elements of the Hebrew (such as suffixes) that do *not* facilitate such dialogue/personalization. When all these features are taken together, the ratio of LXX deviations in a personalizing direction versus LXX deviations in a depersonalizing direction in chs. 56–66 is greater than 1.6 to 1. The ratio is similar in other chapters.

2.   In light of the common pronominal shifts between the first and second persons in Greek textual traditions of both testaments, it is important to note that the examples in this chapter are largely free of such instability.

3.   Such an 'oral genesis' does not necessarily imply a Kahlian view of origins for LXX Isaiah, one which is aptly summarized by the reference of one of his disciples to 'the two targumists (Greek and Aramaic)' (Brockington, 'Septuagint and Targum', p. 80). It need only require that the translator who produced a bona fide *Ur-text* was motivated by homiletical concerns.

L. Boadt attempts to discern indications of orality in the prophetic oracles of the Hebrew Bible. Some of the characteristics that he identifies may be useful in analysing the *translated* text of Isaiah vis-à-vis its Hebrew source text: 'What

The same kind of personalization is to be glimpsed in several New Testament speeches where Old Testament texts are quoted sermonically, which corroborates the suspicion that it is an exegetical–homiletical practice that knows wider use. In Acts 3.22-23, for example, Peter's speech makes a christological application of the 'prophet like Moses' motif in Deut. 18, 15-18.[4] The underlined second-person plural features depart from the details of MT and LXX Deut. 18.15-16, and 18, which appear to be quoted in conflation: Μωυσῆς μέν εἶπεν ὅτι Προφήτην <u>ὑμῖν</u>[5] ἀναστήσει κύριος ὁ θεὸς <u>ὑμῶν</u>[6] ἐκ τῶν ἀδελφῶν <u>ὑμῶν</u>[7] ὡς ἐμέ· αὐτοῦ ἀκούσεσθε κατὰ πάντα ὅσα ἂν λαλήσῃ <u>πρὸς ὑμᾶς</u>.[8] The speech underlines its contemporization three verses later: <u>ὑμεῖς</u> ἐστε οἱ υἱοὶ τῶν προφητῶν καὶ τῆς διαθήκης…(Acts 3.25).

Similarly, Acts 4.11 quotes Ps. 118(117).22 but takes the liberty of identifying 'the builders' of the Hebrew and Greek texts of the psalm—

characteristics would we expect to find in prophetic speeches that are proclaimed aloud? According to the studies of Milman Parry and his disciples, we would expect formulaic language and a definite rhythm in the speech patterns, with a relatively wide variation in their combination and reuse in subsequent lines… Another significant factor would be repetition of words and patterns, even redundancy of thought at times. Repetition and recapping of major points is necessary in oral cultures, because people near the back of a crowd may have trouble hearing the speaker the first time, or may have missed part of the beginning. *Among further techniques is the frequent use of the first and second persons to establish the rapport of speaker and audience as well as a mutual sense of intimacy*' (emphasis added). Cf. 'The Poetry of Prophetic Persuasion: Preserving the Prophet's Persona', *CBQ* 59 (1997), pp. 6-7. Several of the characteristics that Boadt mentions, in addition to the ones I have emphasized, appear frequently in LXX Isaiah where they are not present in the MT.

4.   Similarly, Acts 7.37.

5.   The 2s of Dt 18.15 (לך/σοι) and/or the 3p of 18.18 (להם/αὐτοῖς) are brought into line with the sermonic 2p of Peter's speech.

6.   Cf. Deut. 18.15 (אלהיך/ὁ θεός σου) and prior footnote. In Acts, a considerable number of mss have ἡμῶν.

7.   Cf. Deut. 18.15 (מקרבך מאחיך/ἐκ τῶν ἀδελφῶν σου), 18.18 (מקרב אחיהם/ἐκ τῶν ἀδελφῶν αὐτῶν), and preceding footnotes.

8.   Nothing in the Deuteronomy passage corresponds to the words πρὸς ὑμᾶς. אליו תשמעון/αὐτοῦ ἀκούσεσθε occurs in Deut. 18.15. ככל/κατὰ πάντα occurs in the subsequent clause (18.16), but in the syntax of both MT and LXX this introduces אשר־שאלת/ᾐτήσω). In 18.18, one reads את כל אשר אצונו ודבר אליהם/καὶ λαλήσει <u>αὐτοῖς</u> καθότι ἂν ἐντείλωμαι αὐτῷ. The quotation at the end of Acts 3.22 probably owes its existence to a homiletical conflation of these various elements.

those who have rejected the stone that was destined for greatness—as 'you builders': ὁ λίθος ὁ ἐξουθενηθεὶς ὑφ᾽ ὑμῶν τῶν οἰκοδόμων. In a slightly less creative manner, Paul turns the onus of the third-person references of Deut. 32.21 against his contemporaries: Ἐγὼ παρα-ζηλώσω ὑμας (Deut. אכניאם/παραζηλώσω αὐτοὺς) ἐπ᾽ οὐκ ἔθνει, ἐπ᾽ ἔθνει ἀσυνέτῳ παροργιῶ ὑμᾶς (Deut. אכעיסם/παροργιῶ αὐτούς).[9]

In this chapter, I will discuss instances of personalization occurring in LXX Isaiah as a whole, then in chs. 56–66. The latter discussion will first mention examples achieved with the use of unauthorized first- and second-person elements, then the conversion of grammatical features to first- and second-person forms and, finally, an example in which an abstract Hebrew noun is altered to a substantive that denotes persons.

Personalization as a Feature of LXX Isaiah

Isaiah 26.16

In spite of the tendency to insert nationalistic readings that we will see in Chapters 6 and 7 of this work, the translator does not carry out this 'personalization' as a triumphalist programme. Indeed, he is as apt to address his readers with a stern indictment as with tender consolation.

In 26.16, a personalizing conversion redirects the human piety and divine discipline that are found in the MT towards first-person referents. The plaintive cry, 'O Lord, in distress *they* sought thee, they poured out a prayer when your chastening was upon *them*', becomes the more immediate, 'Lord, in distress *I* remembered thee, in slight affliction was thy correction upon *us*'. Chapter 26—or some portion of it—is introduced at 26.1 as a song that will be sung in the land of Judah. It is difficult to be certain whether this song includes the vocative prayer language that begins at 26.3, or whether this is, instead, a prayerful response to a much briefer song.[10]

In MT 26.15 the prophet speaks gratefully to the Lord of his enlargement of the land, a statement that twice mentions the גוי that has been the beneficiary of this divine generosity.[11] Apparently, this fortunate

9. Rom. 10.19.
10. In which case the song itself would occupy only the first two verses.
11. The translator, on the other hand, deviates radically from the MT by way of a double imperativization that pleads with the Lord to 'add evil(s) to them, O Lord, add evil(s) to all the 'glorious ones' of the land (alternatively, 'earth')'.

people stands over against the dead[12] of 26.14, whose very memory has been exterminated. In MT 26.16, then, those who 'sought you' seem to be the members of the גוי of 26.15, and a description of their piety is carried out in the third-person plural. The translator, however, will not let go of the 'I-thou' vocabulary of the prayer.[13]

He sustains the theme of remembrance/memory,[14] but this now becomes the prophet's testimony of *his own* conduct. Where the MT recalls that God's nation-enlarging mercies began when 'in distress *they* sought you, *they* poured out a prayer', the translator gives us κύριε, ἐν θλίψει ἐμνήσθην σου, ἐν θλίψει μικρᾷ ἡ παιδεία σου ἡμῖν.[15]

12. Who are perhaps identical to—or the human worshippers of—the 'other lords' of 26.13.

13. The majority of the prayer is characterized rather by '*we*-thou' language. However, 26.9, at least, is individual and intimate. Perhaps his continuation of this singular mode here occurs because he has lost the thread of the argument at 26.15; cf. Seeligmann (*LXX Version*, p. 104) on that verse: '[H]e evidently did not understand.'

14. He does this slightly *against* his parent text. פקד does not obviously suggest 'memory' and nowhere else generates μιμνήσκειν. פקד is sometimes paired with זכר, usually as divine activities: cf. Jer. 3.16; 14.10; 15.15; Hos. 8.13; 9.9; Pss. 8.5; 106(105).4; curiously, just two verses earlier in Isa 26.14, verbal פקד is used for the divine destruction of כל־זכר. However, the LXX reads it as *every male* (זָכָר)!

15. The surprising ἐν θλίψει μικρᾷ may result from reading צקון לחש ('They poured out a whispered prayer.') as קטון לחץ, regardless of whatever grammatical clumsiness this insinuates. (This translator is seldom put off by such awkwardness.) It has the amenable effect of ameliorating the force of God's discipline, which is now to be understood as directed *against his own people*. This of course raises the possibility that the reconfiguration was intentional. If so, then the problem presented by the relative orthographic dissimilarity of צ and ט in the Second Temple period (see next paragraph) would be somewhat eased, for it would not require a visual 'accident'.

צקון/קטון requires a צ/ט conversion and the 'dyslexia' that is frequent in this translator's orthographic reconfigurations. לחץ/לחש requires the interchange of sibilants.

On the other hand, the translator may not have strayed so far from the details of the Hebrew text, for he may simply have understood צוק (BDB II, *to pour out*) according to BDB I, *to constrain, bring into straits, press upon*. This would account for ἐν θλίψει, if not for μικρᾷ.

Isaiah 1.4

Even the Lord's stormy opening clauses are turned against some pre-sent body of hearers. In 1.4 the third-person report, עֲזְבוּ אֶת־יְהוָה נִאֲצוּ אֶת־קְדוֹשׁ יִשְׂרָאֵל נָזֹרוּ אָחוֹר becomes a frontal assault: ἐγκατε-λίπατε τὸν κύριον καὶ παρωργίσατε τὸν ἅγιον τοῦ Ισραηλ.[16]

Sometimes this 'personalization' is an explicit clarification of an implicit second-person referent that appears already in the Hebrew text. Far more often, however, it is completely supplied by the translator.

Isaiah 14.21

Occasionally, the fury of the text is turned not against the listening or reading faithful, but against foreign evil-doers themselves, as though they were present to hear their doom declared. This point should be borne in mind as we survey the variously nuanced ways in which homiletical force is brought to bear in LXX Isaiah. In the taunt of the king of Babylon in ch. 14, we read in v. 21 of the MT, *'Prepare* (m.p.) slaughter for *his* sons because of the guilt of their fathers, lest they rise and possess the earth, and fill the face of the world with cities'. Not content to see the force of sarcasm deflected even for a moment[17] from its deserving target, our translator continues to face the fallen monarch himself and writes, '(You) *prepare your* (m.s.) children to be slain for the sins *of your father*, that they might not rise and inherit the earth and fill the earth with cities'. Though this will require a significant

---

16. The breach between the MT and the LXX here may be slightly less than it appears if the translator understood the Hebrew 3mp perfect verbs as a kind of rela-tive clause referring back to the vocative הוֹי (so NRSV, '…who have forsaken… who have despised…'). However, I am inclined to think that this is not the case, on the grounds of two observations: (1) the translator's less than fluent command of Hebrew suggests that he was unlikely to read the clause according to such an uncommon 'relative' function; and (2), elsewhere he translates the vocative objects of הוֹי declarations with a participle. Cf., for example, 5.8: Οὐαὶ οἱ συνάπτοντες …ἐγγίζοντες. This is an especially valuable verse for comparison since the 3mp imperfect יַקְרִיבוּ may in fact have a semi-relative function with respect to the preceding הוֹי. The translator seems to think so and—unlike 1.4—gives us ἐγγίζοντες. Elsewhere, the common construction is הוֹי + a participle. Cf. also 5.11, 18, 20, 21, 22; 10.1, 5; *passim*.

17. The king is addressed in the second person from MT/LXX 14.8-20. At v. 21, where the MT speaks to some listening group, the LXX persists in berating the king to his face.

58   *When We All Go Home*

reconfiguration of the text,[18] the translator chooses this option rather than turn away from the tyrant who has just appeared before his astonished peers in Sheol.

Isaiah 51.3

Even God himself emerges from the shadows of reported deeds to speak directly to Zion for himself. In 51.3 three descriptions of divine activity are turned into first-person accounts. In the first, כי־נחם יהוה ציון is rendered καὶ σὲ νῦν παρακαλέσω Σιων. The sense of dialogue is enhanced not only by the personalizing translation of כי־נחם יהוה as καὶ παρακαλέσω,[19] but also by the addition of the unauthorized pronoun σε. Furthermore, the addition of νῦν and the translation of the Hebrew perfect by the future tense παρακαλέσω[20] raise the possibility that this report has been entirely contemporized, and is being applied in a more directly homiletical fashion to a contemporary audience that has not yet seen Zion comforted in its day.

In the second instance, נחם כל־חרבתיה becomes καὶ παρεκάλεσα πάντα τὰ ἔρημα αὐτῆς. Finally, וישם מדברה כעדן וערבתה גן־יהוה is translated by the somewhat collapsed clause καὶ θήσω τὰ ἔρημα αὐτῆς ὡς παράδεισον κυρίου. As in 51.5, the conversion to the first person in this last example brings in its trail the apparent postponement of the act: *and I shall make her deserted places...*

18. The second plural הכינו לבניו is transformed to the second singular ἑτοίμασον τὰ τέκνα; similarly, the substantive and pronominal suffix of אבותם are each singularized and the suffix becomes second-person: τοῦ πατρός σου.

19. The degree of premeditation that this requires is signalled by the non-translation of the Tetragrammaton.

20. But notice also נחם/[aorist] παρεκάλεσα in the following stich. Παρακαλεῖν in the future tense (always for Hebrew imperfect verbs or participles) is not lacking in Isa. 40–66, so the translation here may be influenced by this contextual feature without being strictly *contemporizing*.

Cf. the subtle possibilities presented at 51.5, where קרוב צדקי יצא ישעי = ἐγγίζει ταχὺ ἡ δικαιοσύνη μου, καὶ ἐξελεύσεται τὸ σωτήριόν μου. This translation may be an accurate re-statement of the Hebrew text, with its expectation of imminent divine intervention. However, the clarification that God's judgment is approaching ταχὺ may—ironically—place it just a bit farther off than the statement that it is קרוב. Additionally, to say that salvation ἐξελεύσεται—whether or not the translator understood his verb to be vocalized as the imperfect יצא—is to say less than יָצָא.

The analysis of these verses indicates that personalization is part of a more widespread levelling tendency on the part of the translator.[21] Even if the first-person speech in MT 51.1[22] were judged to belong to the prophetic *persona* rather than to God, it is unquestionably the divine voice that is heard at 51.4-8. Thus, in 51.3 the translator sustains the first-person discourse that dominates the context—even at the cost of significant reconfiguration of his text—rather than follow that text in its grammatical shifts from one voice to another.

Added to the nearly one hundred examples of imperativization, the roughly two hundred cases of 'personalization' lead me to suspect that our translator brings to his task a heightened dramatic sense, a contemporizing style, and a truly homiletical intention. Although the opposite phenomenon—the conversion of Hebrew first- and second-person references to the third person in Greek—occurs as well, it does so only half as often. Of the two, 'personalization' is by far the dominant trend.

Personalization in LXX Isaiah 56–66

Provision of Unauthorized First- and Second-Person Elements in Isaiah 56–66

The LXX frequently adds lexical elements that accentuate the personal engagement of the protagonists. Often this is accomplished by means of unauthorized complements, usually pronouns.

Isaiah 56.6. In 56.6 the Lord extends assurances to the following category of aliens: כל־שמר שבת מחללו ומחזיקים בבריתי. In the LXX, formal levelling of the underlined substantives allows the Lord to claim personal ownership of the sabbath(s) as well as of his covenant: καὶ πάντας τοὺς φυλασσομένους τὰ σάββατά μου μὴ βεβηλοῦν καὶ ἀντεχομένους τῆς διαθήκης μου.[23]

The pluralization in the Greek of the representative singular is this translator's standard practice,[24] as is his translation of singular שבת by

---

21. The Isaiah translator is exceedingly given to bringing two or more items into conformity. This levelling instinct is observable with great frequency as a phenomenon of semantics (via lexical choice), grammar and syntax.

22. 'Hearken to me...'

23. Cf. 56.4, את־שבתותי/τὰ σάββατά μου. A pair of mediaeval Lucianic manuscripts omit the second μου in 56.6.

24. כל־שמר = (καὶ) πάντας τοὺς φυλασσομένους (cf. 1QIsa[a] ושומרים את השבת; but 1QIsa[b] כל שמר [app.]). This is true even in that majority of cases

plural σάββατα.[25] For our present purposes, the important point is the
addition of the 1cs pronominal suffix.

Isaiah 57.4. Twice in LXX Isa. 57.4, parts of the body are provided with
an unauthorized 2mp possessive pronoun: עַל־מִי תִּתְעַנָּגוּ פֹּה תַּאֲרִיכוּ
לָשׁוֹן = καὶ ἐπὶ τίνα ἠνοίξατε τὸ στόμα ὑμῶν καὶ ἐπὶ τίνα
ἐχαλάσατε τὴν γλῶσσαν ὑμῶν... These LXX additions may have
been motivated as much by the translator's distaste for poetic allusiveness[26] as by his desire to 'personalize' the text.[27] Nevertheless, the net
effect is in line with his general tendency to increase first- and second-
person features.[28]

Isaiah 57.8-11. MT Isa. 57.8-11 is already characterized by intense dialogue. The LXX adds a number of additional first- and second-person elements that link the disputants even more closely. In 57.8 וְאַחַר הַדֶּלֶת
וְהַמְּזוּזָה is represented by καὶ ὀπίσω τῶν σταθμῶν τῆς θύρας σου.

where the construction is not also subjected to the forces of grammatical levelling,
as here by the parallel plural וּמַחֲזִיקִים/καὶ ἀντεχομένους.
25. Even though this obligates him to alter his text by *omitting* or *pluralizing*
the verbal suffix of מְחַלְלוֹ, since it now refers back to the pluralized σάββατά
μου. He chooses to omit it. The translated LXX books divide clearly into a large
group that prefers to render singular שַׁבָּת as a plural, and a smaller group that
prefers a singular. LXX Isaiah belongs to the former, allowing for a double exception in ch. 66 that may have implications for the question of a distinct recension in
that chapter.
26. Here displayed in the reference to '(the) mouth/(the) tongue' rather than the
more prosaic 'your mouth/tongue'.
27. Elsewhere in the LXX, references to organs of the body, both suffixed and
unsuffixed, are translated unremarkably.
28. This verse compactly displays three additional features that are highly
characteristic of this translation as a whole: (a) lexical levelling (57.3, עֹנְנָה =
ἄνομοι; 57.4, שֶׁקֶר = ἄνομον; 57.1, אָבַד = ἀπώλετο; 57.4, פֶּשַׁע = ἀπωλείας); (b)
lexical spontaneity, observable in the presence of four LXX Isaiah *hapax* equivalencies (עֹנֵג = ἐντρυφᾶν [also in 55.2], רָחַב = ἀνοίγειν, פֶּשַׁע = ἀπώλεια, אָרַךְ =
χαλᾶν); and (c) formal levelling by way of 'corrected' ellipsis (עַל־מִי תִּתְעַנָּגוּ = ἐν
τίνι ἐνετρυφήσατε, עַל־מִי תַּאֲרִיכוּ =καὶ ἐπὶ τίνα ἠνοίξατε, תַּאֲרִיכוּ = καὶ ἐπὶ
τίνα ἐχαλάσατε). The simultaneous expression of a lack of inventiveness faced
with lexical and syntactical synonymity, on the one hand, and of an astonishingly
full lexical repertoire (seen in the large number of Greek words that occur nowhere
else in the LXX), on the other, is one of the central components of this translator's
'technique'.

This translator dislikes allusiveness of any kind. His translation of this phrase obliterates the poetic understatement of the Hebrew text by means of two manoeuvres that are highly characteristic of him: the pluralization of the representative singular[29] and the addition of an unauthorized complement.[30]

At 57.9, the Lord accuses Israel of having sent envoys into the unspecified distance represented by עַד־מֵרָחֹק. The LXX brings this expression into a personalized orbit by rendering it as ὑπὲρ τὰ ὅριά σου. It is not only the possessive pronoun that is unique to the LXX, but also the very idea of *borders*, a concept that defines the envoys' destination *in relationship to the people addressed*.

The final accuzation of 57.10[31] is that *you did not weaken* (qal לֹא חָלִית). That is, Israel did not give in to the weariness that would normally have followed such energetic evil-doing. The LXX attributes to the qal verb the derivative meaning *to appease, to entreat the favour of*, elsewhere reserved for the piel.[32] Thus, the metaphor in the Hebrew text is glossed by the more prosaic οὐ κατεδεήθης μου.[33] The expression becomes more clearly *personal* and at the same time less foreign to the standard vocabulary of religious experience. One feature of this transformation is the personalizing addition of μου.

The same augmented emphasis on personal relationship is perhaps to be detected in the following verse, where the Hebrew is elliptical: וְאוֹתִי לֹא זָכַרְתְּ לֹא־שַׂמְתְּ עַל־לִבֵּךְ. LXX 57.11 'corrects' the ellipsis

---

29. הדלת והמזוזה is collapsed into τῶν σταθμῶν τῆς θύρας σου, which requires the suppression of the article ה and the copula ו, as well as the obvious pluralization דלת.

30. σου.

31. It is difficult to explain ὅτι ἔπραξας ταῦτα unless מצאת has been understood as בזאת. Both the interchange of sibilants (here צ/ז) and confusion between מ and ב are found elsewhere in LXX Isaiah. The rest of the verse offers unprecedented equivalencies (three *hapax* equivalencies and one word that appears only here in the LXX); however, each of them is comprehensible.

32. Both חָלִית and חִלִּית can of course be read out of the same consonants. At Isa. 57.10, the latter requires the reader to give precedence to a conventional religious expression over against the metaphorical references to exertion and exhaustion that abound in the context.

33. Perhaps 'you did not entreat me/plead with me'. Piel חלה does not produce καταδεῖσθαι elsewhere, though it does generate such synonyms as δεῖσθαι, ἐξιλάσκειν, ἐκζητεῖν and λατανεύειν.

created by the presence of only *one* direct object[34] for *two* verbs: καὶ οὐκ ἐμνήσθης μου οὐδὲ ἔλαβές με εἰς τὴν διάνοιαν. In so doing, it slightly intensifies the personalistic character of the passage.[35]

In the same verse מחשה ומעל ם[36] appears to have been read entirely at variance with the eventual Massoretic vocalization. מֶחֱזֶה[38] אָעְלַ ם[37] or a similar configuration would make the personalized καγὼ σε ἰδὼν παρορῶ. It is possible that this short phrase has been reshaped in the light of the translator's insistence that God's perceptive powers are absolute, and in view of his high regard for God's judicial activities. The notion that God should simply have remained silent before Israel's rebellion 'from of old' might have seemed odious, let alone at variance with the biblical record that he spoke repeatedly through the prophetic word. The Greek phrase as it now stands can easily be read to state that God in fact *does* see (you), but chooses to overlook sin for the moment.[39]

34. ואותי (ו).

35. Curiously, על־לבך is represented by the double prepositional phrase εἰς τὴν διάνοιαν οὐδὲ εἰς τὴν καρδίαν σου. (There is substantial manuscript evidence for reading σου after διάνοιαν in Ziegler's Origenic and Lucianic *Hauptgruppe*, but *not* in his Alexandrian group; the latter absence appears to have been decisive for his omission of the pronoun.) If εἰς τὴν διάνοιαν is a translation of על־לבך, one is surprised by the *depersonalized* nature of the rendering. Whatever the origin of this Greek phrase, it is quickly followed up by the expected (οὐδὲ) εἰς τὴν καρδίαν σου.

36. MT מֶחְשֶׁה וּמֶעֱלָ ם.

37. The defective hiphil form תַּעְלֵ ם (without י-).

Παριδεῖν/-ορᾶν occurs eight times in the translated books of the LXX and nine in those with a Greek origin. Of the former, עלם is the source twice (three times if my suggestion for this verse is conceded). The link between עלם and the synonymous ὑπεριδεῖν/-ορᾶν is even stronger. Curiously, מעל is responsible for many of the remaining occurrences of both Greek verbs. It shares the same consonants, but its meaning—*to be unfaithful* or *act unfaithfully*—would not have been suitable for use with a divine subject.

38. This conjecture requires the interchange of the sibilants שׁ and ז. The translator is unlikely to have been perturbed by the absence of hiphil forms of this verb in BH.

39. This reconstruction requires that παρορᾶν retain its most common meaning of *to overlook, disregard*. Such a reading may be strengthened by the fact that παρορῶ—alone in a context that recalls past events and is dominated by the aorist verbs—occurs in the present tense. It may serve for this translator as an affirmation of how God *is*, which provides the explanation for his silence in the face of such varied affronts.

If such an interpretative move has been the translator's intention, then he has transformed a two-word clause that could have opened God to charges of impotence or acquiescence or both. In its place, he has managed to underline God's perceptive powers and his benign patience.

Of course, one also reckons with the possibility that this deviation from the reading tradition that would eventually be consolidated by the Massoretes is a naive one. In this respect, our translator only occasionally provides us with certainty. Whichever the case, his reading has intertwined the first and second persons (here God and Israel) to a greater degree than has the MT.

Isaiah 57.16. Later in the same chapter, v. 16 offers us a pair of unauthorized second-person pronouns. The MT's parallel stichs ולא לנצח אקצוף // כי לא לעולם אריב are rendered as οὐκ εἰς τὸν αἰῶνα ἐκδικήσω ὑμᾶς // οὐδὲ διὰ παντὸς ὀργισθήσομαι ὑμῖν. A divine oracle begins at 57.15[40] and continues to the end of 57.21. It consists entirely of a first-person description of God's chastisement of a figure who is identified only as 'he/him' and the promise that God will himself restore this metaphorical figure.[41]

It is all the more significant, then, that the LXX addition is not only a second-person referent, but also a *plural* one.[42] The poetic allusiveness and the rhetorical value of the representative singular are suppressed. The more prosaic account that survives binds the historical chastisement and the promised mercy to some *group* of hearers. The unauthorized pronouns appear to exercise a contemporizing function. It is not clear whether the translator thought of the people represented by ὑμᾶς as the prophet's audience or as his own. Whatever the case, he has removed the logical steps that the MT requires if an oracle about an unnamed 'he/him' is to be applied by its audience or readers to themselves. In its place, he has left a directly personal—and perhaps homiletical—application of what he takes to be the story's enduring point.

---

40. 'For thus says the high and lofty one...'

41. To be precise, the 'one' who is eligible for God's restorative mercies is identified in 57.15 as דכא ושפל־רוח. A brief glimpse of the representative nature of this singular is seen in the following stich, where this representative vocabulary appears to be exegeted as the plural שפלים...נדכאים. Thereafter, the oracle's referent is singular to the very end (there is a plural reference to the wicked in 57.20, but they are hardly the central concern of the oracle).

42. Cf. also לרחוק ולקרוב/τοῖς μακρὰν καὶ τοῖς ἐγγὺς οὖσι and ורפאתיו/ἰάσομαι αὐτούς in 57.20.

Isaiah 58.6-7. MT Isaiah 58.1-5 is an indictment of the community's unethical behaviour and self-assured cult. It is delivered with a mixture of straightforward description and rhetorical questions. After 58.6-7 states the Lord's standards for his 'fast', a long series of conditional promises of blessing and restoration ensues.[43]

The LXX styles this chapter with slightly more emphasis on the second-person *persona(e)*. In some cases there is the mere addition of a pronoun.[44] In others the alteration is more substantial. The translator follows the reference to 'a man' for exactly one stich in 58.5[45] before breaking free and applying the message to a second-person character: הלכף כאגמן ראשו ושׂק ואפר יציע = οὐδ' ἂν κάμψῃς ὡς κρίκον τὸν τράχηλόν σου καὶ σάκκον καὶ σποδὸν ὑποστρώσῃ. The resolution of the rhetorical questions at 58.7 by means of a sustained (second-person) imperativization was noticed in the last chapter.

The translator's tendency to level grammar and syntax has been noted above. When this reflex is brought to bear upon a sophisticated literary text like MT Isaiah, one might conclude that the personalizations are due to levelling alone rather than to any substantive tendency to produce a more personalized translated text. In that case, however, one would expect to find a roughly equal number of 'de-personalizations', since the grammar could just as easily have been levelled in *that* direction.

However, as noted already, this is not what one discovers. For example, amid the numerous examples of personalization that we have observed in chs. 56–59, there are only three moves in the opposite direction, and some of these may be better explained by other factors.[46]

---

43. Cf. especially the logically connected אז (58.8, 9, 14) and אם (59.9, 13) clauses.

44. 58.3, הן ביום צמכם תמצאו־חפץ = ἐν γὰρ ταῖς ἡμέραις τῶν νηστειῶν ὑμῶν εὑρίσκετε τὰ θελήματα ὑμῶν (levelled with וכל־עצביכם/καὶ πάντας τοὺς ὑποχειρίους ὑμῶν of the following phrase; cf. TJ אתון תבעין צורכיכון); 58.7, ועניים מרודים תביא בית = καὶ πτωχοὺς ἀστέγου εἴσαγε εἰς τὸν οἶκόν σου; 58.9, ויהוה יענה = καὶ ὁ θεὸς εἰσακούσεταί σου; 58.12, מוסדי דור־ודור תקומם = καὶ ἔσται σου τὰ θεμέλια αἰώνια γενεῶν γενεαῖς (levelled with ובנו ממך חרבות עולם/καὶ οἰκοδομηθήσονταί σου αἱ ἔρημοι αἰώνιοι of the previous phrase); 58.13, וקראת לשבת ענג לקדוש יהוה = καὶ καλέσεις τὰ σάββατα τρυφερὰ ἅγια τῷ θεῷ σου.

45. יום ענות אדם נפשׂו/καὶ ἡμέραν ταπεινοῦν ἄνθρωπον τὴν ψυχὴν αὐτοῦ.

46. (a) 57.21, אמר אלהי = κύριος ὁ θεός. אלהי and אלהינו lose their suffix and are thus depersonalized on 7 of the 22 occasions when the Hebrew forms occur.

The net deviation is strongly in the direction of an intensified first- and second-person perspective.

Isaiah 60.17. In ch. 60, one reads that the wealth of nations will make its way to Zion. While this procession travels on its own in 60.3-14, the Lord takes responsibility for the entire scene from v. 15 to the end of the chapter.[47] In 60.17, the Lord makes a statement that could be understood to be his own contribution to the tribute-bearing procession to the Holy City: תחת הנחשת אָבִיא זהב ותחת הברזל אָבִיא כסף ותחת העצים נחשת. The LXX expands the use of the verb from the two occurrences in the Hebrew text to three in the Greek. [48] In addition, the translator adds an unauthorized personal pronoun to each of the three verbs: καὶ ἀντὶ χαλκοῦ <u>οἴσω σοι</u> χρυσίον ἀντὶ δὲ σιδήρου <u>οἴσω σοι</u> ἀργύριον ἀντὶ δὲ ξύλων <u>οἴσω σοι</u> χαλκόν. These deviations from the parent text do not materially alter the actual activity of the procession.

On another 2 occasions (55.7 and 61.2), the word in question is simply not translated. In the latter case, parallel occurrences of ליהוה and לאלהינו are collapsed into a single impersonal expression, κυρίου. This array of data suggests a fairly pronounced tendency to depersonalize such references to God. This might be due to the graphic similarity of אלהים and אלהינו, though this would not explain the three depersonalized *singular* forms (אלהי). Perhaps the tendency to remove possessive suffixes from divine titles shows an ameliorative instinct that proceeds from the translator's reverence for God's name; (b) 58.13, ביום קדשי וקראת לשבת ענג = ἐν τῇ ἡμέρᾳ τῇ ἁγίᾳ καὶ καλέσεις τὰ σάββατα τρυφερά. It is possible that this deviation is due to the proximity and similarity of the *yod* of קדשי and the *waw* of וקראת; (c) והרכבתיך = καὶ ἀναβιβάσει σε; cf. the prior stich: אז תתענג על־יהוה = καὶ ἔσῃ πεποιθὼς ἐπὶ κύριον. Cf. H.M. Erwin's observation that the rendering of divine titles 'is characterized by reverence and restraint', in 'Theological Aspects of the Septuagint of the Book of Psalms' (unpublished dissertation, Princeton Theological Seminary, 1966), p. 56; quoted in Olofsson, *God Is my Rock*, p. 14.

47. Cf. especially 60.15, 'I will make you majestic forever'; 60.16, 'and you shall know that I, the Lord, am your Saviour'; 60.19-20, 'the Lord will be your everlasting light'; 60.21, 'Your people...are the shoot that I planted...so that I might be glorified'; and, climactically in 60.22, 'I am the Lord; in its time I will accomplish it quickly.'

48. This addition is consistent with his tendency to 'correct ellipsis'. However, the details of his source text are a sufficient restraint so that he does *not* correct the final elliptical phrase. Rather, ותחת האבנים ברזל remains untouched in translation: ἀντὶ δὲ λίθων σίδηρον.

However, they ensure that the Lord's self-described activity is understood *with personal reference to Zion* rather than as mere participation in an event, viewed in the abstract.[49]

Isaiah 61.10. In MT 61.10b, the Lord's mercies are depicted as clothing. In the first and second stichs of this metaphor, the speaker announces what the Lord has done for him: '...for he has clothed me with the garments of salvation // he has covered me with the robe of righteousness'. In the third and fourth stichs, the imagery is sustained, but with three changes: (a) metaphor gives way to simile; (b) the Lord is no longer an explicit protagonist; and (c) the verbs become reflexive in function, since each protagonist now dresses himself or herself. We read, '...as a bridegroom decks himself with a garland, and as a bride adorns herself with her jewels'.

This second half of the verse has undergone reconfiguration in the LXX text, which reads, ἐνέδυσεν γάρ με ἱμάτιον σωτηρίου καὶ χιτῶνα εὐφροσύνης ὡς νυμφίῳ περιέθηκέν μοι μίτραν καὶ ὡς νύμφην κατεκόσμησέν με κόσμῳ. First, the verbs have been collapsed from the four of the MT into just three in the Greek text.[50] Second, in the Greek God is the subject of all three remaining verbal clauses rather than just the two of the MT. Third, the final two clauses are still similes,

---

49. The translation of וּפֶחַד וְרָחַב לְבָבֶךָ by καὶ φοβηθήσῃ καὶ ἐκστήσῃ τῇ καρδίᾳ in 60.5 should probably be classified as a demetaphorizing assignment to the unembellished second person of the activities that the MT assigns to 'your heart'. This case is best left outside my collection of substantive personalizations.

50. הִלְבִּישַׁנִי...יְעַטָנִי...יְכַהֵן...תַּעְדֶּה = ἐνέδυσεν...περιέθηκέν μοι...κατεκόσμησέν με. The associations of פְּאֵר with priestly head-dress were probably sufficiently strong so that the non-translation of יְכַהֵן could be tolerated without sacrificing the priestly referent. That is, to wrap someone's head with a פְּאֵר/μίτρα was—without the need to say more—to dress him *as a priest*. If so, then περιέθηκέν μοι corresponds to יְעַטָנִי, with which it is a close semantic match.

פְּאֵר probably refers to the priest-prophet Ezekiel's head-dress in Ezek 24.17 (or his arranged hair, cf. LXX τὸ τρίχωμά σου) and again in Ezek. 44.18 (LXX κίδαρις). In Exod. 39.28 (LXX 36.35) וְאֶת־פַּאֲרֵי הַמִּגְבָּעֹת clearly indicates the priestly head-dress of Aaron and his sons, and is translated καὶ τὴν μίτραν. In Exodus and Leviticus, מִצְנֶפֶת—an article of priestly clothing—is the standard source of μίτρα.

Nevertheless, פְּאֵר does not always imply a priestly connotation. In Ezek. 24.23 it seems to be a more general masculine head-dress (cf. LXX κόμη, *hair*). In Isa. 3.20 it may signify a woman's head-dress, though the LXX does not understand it this way.

but they are now syntactically independent rather than referring back, as comparisons, to God's activity in the prior two stichs.[51]

Finally, the last two stichs no longer refer to two third persons who clothe himself and herself, respectively. Rather, they are personalized and come to speak of how God 'has placed the priestly head-dress *upon me*, as upon a bridegroom' and how he has 'adorned *me* with ornaments, as (one adorns) a bride'. Thus, the LXX maintains a personal reference that has by this stage disappeared from the source text.[52] The first-person statement may have been retained because it is homiletically or religiously useful.

Isaiah 62.8-11. A series of minute additions in Isa. 62.8-11 add to the personalization of that context. In 62.8, the Lord is heard to swear אִם־אֶתֵּן אֶת־דְּגָנֵךְ עוֹד מַאֲכָל לְאֹיְבַיִךְ.[53] MT's מַאֲכָל is to be understood adverbially with reference to the *mode* of the Lord's hypothetical gift of the people's grain: *as food*. However, the LXX translator tidies up the verse by adding a 2ms pronominal suffix to *this* substantive, as to the surrounding ones.[54] His reconfigured result, εἰ ἔτι δώσω τὸν σῖτόν

---

51. In the MT they refer back to the first two stichs in question. God 'dressed me and wrapped me *as a bridegroom puts on his priestly head-dress // and as a bride adorns herself with her jewels*'. These two comparative clauses do not stand alone in the Hebrew text, but are dependent upon the prior assertions about *God's* activities.

52. There may be evidence of the translator's care in the details of the final clause. Such an observation would be important in the light of the tendency of scholars to explain the deviations in a verse like this one exclusively in terms of the translator's *carelessness*. If a kind of translational precision can be discerned in a place like this, then other details that seem like mishap may require a more measured and perhaps positive evaluation.

The fine assonance of the MT text (וְכַכַּלָּה תַּעְדֶּה כֵלֶיהָ) is impossible to produce in translation, since the Greek words that might be used for 'bride' and 'jewellery' do not share the similarity that the author of the Hebrew text has employed so pleasingly. However, the translator finds a suitable imitation of the assonant Hebrew phrase by laying hold of similarities between two *other* words, this time the verb that represents תַּעְדֶּה and the noun that stands in for כֵלֶיהָ. Thus, he is able to produce the assonant κατεκόσμησέν με κόσμῳ.

53. The following oath clause is equally concerned with *your* possessions: וְאִם־יִשְׁתּוּ בְנֵי־נֵכָר תִּירוֹשֵׁךְ אֲשֶׁר יָגַעְתְּ בּוֹ.

54. The addition of a second ἔτι in the second oath clause balances the עוֹד/ἔτι of the first oath clause. The levelling of אֶת־דְּגָנֵךְ...מַאֲכָל to τὸν σῖτόν σου καὶ τὰ βρώματά σου (as though the MT had a *waw* and a second accusative marker) in turn

σου καὶ τὰ βρώματά σου τοῖς ἐχθροῖς σου, slightly increases the personalized tone of the verse.

Two verses later, in a passage that has suffered considerable collapsing,[55] a divine 1cs pronoun is nonetheless added to each of two substantives. עברו עברו בשערים is rendered as πορεύεσθε διὰ τῶν πυλῶν μου and פנו דרך העם as καὶ ὁδοποιήσατε τῷ λαῷ μου. By these means the Lord explicitly claims ownership of Zion and its returning people. At the same time, the translator achieves for these imperatives a certain divine sanction. In the preceding and following verses, the Lord is spoken of in the third person, a feature that might tend to characterize the commands of 62.10 as *the prophet's* words. With his personal pronouns, however, the translator unambiguously places these words upon *divine* lips, thus salvaging a personalistic tone for this verse.

In LXX Isa. 62.11, a pronoun is not *added*, but rather *relocated*. The announcement הנה ישעך בא—'behold, your Saviour comes'—is somewhat modified in translation. Ἰδού σοι ὁ σωτὴρ παραγίνεται produces one and possibly as many as three significant deviations from the MT. In the first instance, the abstract ישעך has become the very concrete ὁ σωτήρ, which appears to mean God himself.

In the second instance—and here the evidence is less conclusive—the 2ms element represented by the suffix of ישעך is now assigned adverbially to בא: 'Behold, the Saviour comes *to you*'. The result may have been homiletically convenient and probably slightly heightens the personalistic character of the verse.

Finally, the use of παραγίνεται—and this for a subject that has now become not only personal but also divine—tempts one to query whether this is not an anti-anthropomorphic translation that subtly evades the notion of divine *locomotion*, though not necessarily that of God's *motion*.[56] A positive reply may be encouraged by the translator's handling

---

/תירושך...אשר יגעת בו brings this entire clause nicely into line with the cadence of τὸν οἶνόν σου...ἐφ'...ᾧ ἐμόχθησας. Considerable care has been applied to this verse in order to level all those features that could be balanced.

55. The five imperatival elements have been reduced to four...פנו...עברו עברו הרימו...סלו סלו סקלו...דרך is translated by the four-member series πορεύεσθε... ὁδοποιήσατε...διαρρίψατε...ἐξάρατε. In addition, the two twin imperatives (עברו עברו and סלו סלו) leave only single imperatives on the Greek side. It is likely that סלו סלו is the one imperatival element that is left untranslated altogether.

56. The verb appears only three times in LXX Isaiah: 56.1, כי־קרובה ישועתי לבוא/ἤγγισεν γὰρ τὸ σωτήριόν μου παραγίνεσθαι; the verse at hand; and the stridently anthropomorphic expression at 63.1, מי־זה בא מאדום/τίς οὗτος ὁ

of anthropomorphic language just two verses later, at 63.1. In that verse, too, *the one who comes from Edom* (בָּא מֵאֱדוֹם) is expressed by ὁ παραγινόμενος ἐξ Εδωμ. Perhaps more importantly, the military bearing of this figure is expressed by צָעָה,[57] a word that the LXX fails entirely to translate. If so—and if LXX 62.11 can be understood to mean, 'Behold, the Saviour *comes to you*', or even '…is *present with you*'—then the contemporizing and homiletic possibilities become immediately obvious.

Isaiah 65.1, 12 and 14. Three pronominal additions to the divine complaint in ch. 65 fill out Hebrew ellipsis without substantially altering the meaning. In 65.1 parallel statements are levelled to form a more precise synonymity: נִדְרַשְׁתִּי לְלוֹא שָׁאָלוּ // נִמְצֵאתִי לְלֹא בִקְשֻׁנִי = ἐμφανὴς ἐγενόμην τοῖς ἐμὲ μὴ ζητοῦσιν // εὑρέθην τοῖς ἐμὲ μὴ ἐπερωτῶσιν.

Later in the chapter the speaker makes clear that the rich promises of vv. 8-10 are not available unconditionally to all claimants. Those who continue to forsake the Lord (v. 11) will receive only the sword. In 65.12 the stubborn deafness of some is offered as justification for the coming slaughter: יַעַן קָרָאתִי וְלֹא עֲנִיתֶם דִּבַּרְתִּי וְלֹא שְׁמַעְתֶּם. The LXX removes any tendency to deflect the light from the faces of the guilty: ὅτι ἐκάλεσα ὑμᾶς καὶ οὐχ ὑπηκούσατε ἐλάλησα καὶ παρηκούσατε.[58]

Similarly, LXX 65.14 avoids any ambiguity when it describes the noisy grief of those whom God has shattered: וְאַתֶּם תִּצְעֲקוּ מִכְּאֵב לֵב = ὑμεῖς δὲ κεκράξεσθε διὰ τὸν πόνον τῆς καρδίας ὑμῶν.[59]

παραγινόμενος ἐξ Εδωμ. Translation of בּוֹא by παραγινέσθαι is in sharp contrast to the Isaiah translator's normal handling of this frequently occurring Hebrew verb.

57. BDB *to stoop, bend, incline*; *one stooping (under a burden)*; the BHS *propositum*, צָעַד, connotes stepping or marching and thus does not escape the burden of anthropomorphism.

58. In this case the personalizing addition is not matched in the second stich. Nevertheless, the translator's tendency to tidy up parallel features of the Hebrew text *does* manifest itself here, this time in the lexical sphere. וְלֹא עֲנִיתֶם/καὶ οὐχ ὑπηκούσατε is paralleled by וְלֹא שְׁמַעְתֶּם/καὶ παρηκούσατε. The translator appears willing to tolerate the loss of the parallel negations in order to lay side by side two verbs that differ only in their respective prefixes. I am not suggesting that this kind of manoeuvre necessarily reflects a planned or even a fully conscious strategy. However, it does require some originality on the translator's part. Παρακούειν—a word that occurs elsewhere only in the 'late' LXX books (1 Esdras, Tob. and Est.)—corresponds nowhere else to לֹא שָׁמַע.

59. But see the following stich: וּמִשֵּׁבֶר רוּחַ תְּיֵלִילוּ = καὶ ἀπὸ συντριβῆς πνεύματος ὀλολύξετε.

70   *When We All Go Home*

Isaiah 66.1-5, 20. The final chapter of LXX Isaiah is peppered with personalizing readings, several of which rely upon the provision of un-authorized pronominal elements. (See below for those which rely upon the conversion of third-person forms.) In vv. 2-5 the Lord's involvement with persons and events is made more explicit in the LXX than in the MT. The Hebrew text of Isa. 66.1-2 appears to affirm the Lord's unique and exclusive role in the creation of all things: השמים כסאי והארץ הדם רגלי... ואת־כל־אלה ידי עשתה ויהיו כל־אלה.[60] If this is indeed its intention, then ויהיו כל־אלה may be a knowing allusion to the ויהי...יהי pattern of the first chapter of Genesis. The LXX converts this expression into a personalized statement of divine *possession*: καὶ ἔστιν ἐμὰ πάντα ταῦτα.

In 66.3 cultic practice in the absence of ethical righteousness suffers a levelling of its own, as dignified patterns of Israelite worship are equated with the most abhorrent acts. The list begins with שוחט השור מכה־איש. The translator, by means of an added pronoun, leaves no ambiguity as to who is the offended party. Collapsing together elements from several members of the list, he has the Lord say ὁ δὲ ἄνομος ὁ θύων μοι μόσχον ὡς ὁ ἀποκτέννων κύνα.

In 66.4 the Lord repeats a complaint regarding the people's culpable deafness that one first encountered in the previous chapter: קראתי ואין עונה דברתי ולא שמעו. As before, the LXX adds a personalising pro-noun to one of the two members of the parallelism: ἐκάλεσα αὐτοὺς καὶ οὐκ ὑπήκουσάν μου.[61]

For the thoroughgoing personalization that occurs in 66.5, see Chapter 2, p. 41.

In 66.20 the Lord regards the eschatological offerings of Israel as explicitly offered *to me*.[62] In the following verse, his selection of Levitical priests is also articulated as a selection *for me*.[63] Both these additions may bear nationalistic import. They are treated in detail in Chapter 7, below.

---

60. The BHS apparatus appears to suggest that 1QIsaᵃ differs from the MT in the direction of the LXX ἐμὰ (ל'). However, it does not.

61. In 65.12 the personalizing element explicitly directs God's call *to the people* (ὑμᾶς). Conversely the extra feature in 66.4 clarifies that the people's disobedience pertained *to God* (μου).

62. יביאו בני ישראל את־המנחה = ἐνέγκαισαν οἱ υἱοὶ Ισραηλ ἐμοὶ τὰς θυσίας αὐτῶν.

63. אקח לכהנים ללוים = λήμψομαι ἐμοὶ ἱερεῖς καὶ Λευίτας.

Conversion to First- and Second-Person Forms in Isaiah 56–66
A stronger hand is applied to the text in those instances of personalization where one kind of grammatical person is converted to another. In
Isa. 59.12 the community acknowledges the consequence of its sin: 'For
our transgressions before you are many, and our sins testify against us.
Our transgressions indeed are with us, and we know our iniquities'. MT
59.13 then provides the details of this rebellion with a series of
infinitives absolute: פָּשֹׁעַ וְכַחֵשׁ בַּיהוה וְנָסוֹג מֵאַחַר אֱלֹהֵינוּ דַּבֶּר־עֹשֶׁק
וְסָרָה הֹרוֹ וְהֹגוֹ מִלֵּב דִּבְרֵי־שָׁקֶר. The LXX translates this sequence in
the light of the 1cp features in the context. The implied subject of the
infinitives absolute is made explicit, a clarification that is extended even
to a substantive!: ἠσεβήσαμεν καὶ ἐψευσάμεθα καὶ ἀπέστημεν ἀπὸ
ὄπισθεν τοῦ θεοῦ ἡμῶν ἐλαλήσαμεν ἄδικα καὶ ἠπειθήσαμεν[64]
ἐκύομεν καὶ ἐμελετήσαμεν ἀπὸ καρδίας ἡμῶν λόγους ἀδίκους.[65]
The adverbial expression מִלֵּב is also given a first-person complement.[66]

When the text at 59.14 returns to speak in an impersonal manner of
the consequences of such corporate apostasy,[67] the LXX deviates in a
personalizing direction by assigning this to the list as one further aspect
of the people's rebellion: καὶ ἀπεστήσαμεν ὀπίσω τὴν κρίσιν.[68]

Isaiah 62.1, with Reference to 57.12
In MT 62.1 the speaker announces that he[69] will not, on account of
Zion/Jerusalem, remain silent 'until *her* righteousness[70] shines out like
the dawn, and *her* salvation like a burning torch'. The LXX, however,

---

64. Subject to the forces applied by this chain of infinitives absolute, וְסָרָה is
translated as though it has been read as either (a) a conjectured verbal form related
to the noun סָרָה; (b) the infinitive absolute of סָרַר; or (c) מָרֹה or מָרוֹ (cf. Lam.
1.20), the infinitive absolute of מָרָה. This would require a ס/מ interchange, which
is not uncommon.

65. TJ also begins the verse with 1cp finite verbs: מְרִידְנָא וּכַדִּיבְנָא...
וְאִסְתַּחַרְנָא...וַהֲוֵינָא מְמַלְלִין.

66. ἀπὸ καρδίας ἡμῶν.

67. This by means of the 3ms hophal imperfect verb and its complements:
וְהֻסַּג אָחוֹר מִשְׁפָּט וּצְדָקָה.

68. TJ is more literal than the LXX vis-à-vis the MT: וְאִסְתַּחַר לַאֲחָרָא דִינָא.

69. Cf. C. Westermann: 'Daß in diesen Worten der Prophet spricht, wird jetzt
von den meisten Auslegern gefaßt', in *Das Buch Jesaia, Kapitel 40-66* (ATD, 19;
Göttingen: Vandenhoeck & Ruprecht, 1966), p. 297.

70. NRSV, 'her vindication' (emphases added).

replaces the 3fs suffixes with 1cs suffixes: ἕως ἂν ἐξέλθῃ ὡς φῶς ἡ δικαιοσύνη μου τὸ δὲ σωτήριόν μου λαμπὰς καυθήσεται.

The translator probably viewed these as the Lord's words.[71] Apparently, he felt at liberty to assign Zion's long-awaited righteousness and salvation to God himself. A curiously similar conversion occurs at Isa 57.12. In contrast to the positive promises of ch. 62, Isaiah 57 brings an indictment against its audience, who are charged with cultic aberrations that include idolatry.

In MT 57.12 one reads, 'I will proclaim your "righteousness" and your works, but they will not help you'. The MT appears to use צִדְקָתֵךְ ironically, since the context makes clear that 'righteousness' is prominent only by its absence! However, the LXX seems to miss this nuanced use of the word. As a result, the translator is virtually compelled to exegete the phrase in a way that draws a clear line between the righteous God and the evil people: צִדְקָתֵךְ וְאֶת־מַעֲשַׂיִךְ as τὴν δικαιοσύνην μου καὶ τὰ κακά σου.

It may be that the memory of this verse exercised some influence over the translation of 62.1, in spite of the vastly different contexts. Whether or not this is the case, LXX 62.1 produces a personalized statement that sustains a first-person (divine) mode of speech after the parent text has reverted to the third person.

Isaiah 62.7. A prudent evasion of one difficulty ends up producing a remarkably daring conversion at Isa. 62.7, where the translator redirects a statement about God to Zionist ends. It was probably motivated by the spirited role that is urged upon Jerusalem's watchmen in 62.6-7.

In those verses the Lord announces, 'Upon your walls, O Jerusalem, I have posted sentinels; all day and all night they shall never be silent. *You who remind the Lord*, take no rest, (7) *and give him no rest* until he establishes and until he makes Jerusalem a praise on the earth'. The italicized phrases might well have caused offence.

In the light of the context, the hiphil participle in הַמַּזְכִּרִים אֶת־יְהוָה suggests those who *remind* the Lord rather than those who *remember* him. The translator, however, has exploited the sliver of ambiguity that this construction allows and has taken some liberties with the syntax in order to bind this phrase to the preceding one. This allows him to create

71. It is difficult to imagine that he would envisage ἡ δικαιοσύνη μου τὸ δὲ σωτήριόν μου as the *prophet's* righteousness and salvation.

the less provocative reading, οὐ σιωπήσονται μιμνῃσκόμενοι κυρίου.[72]

Additionally, אַל־דֳמִי לכם at the end of 62.6 and ואל־תתנו דמי לו at the beginning of 62.7 seem to have collapsed together to produce οὐκ ἔστιν γὰρ ὑμῖν ὅμοιος.[73] Against the force of the context, the translator has chosen to read the one occurrence of דמה that he reproduces in Greek according to the meaning *to be like, resemble* rather than *to cease*.[74]

The two phrases are sufficiently different to cause us to seek an explanation other than parablepsis. We may find it in ideology instead. Elsewhere, the identical phrase is used in prayer: Ps. 83.2, אֱלֹהִים אַל־דֳמִי־לָךְ אַל־תֶּחֱרֵשׁ וְאַל־תִּשְׁקֹט אֵל. However, such a command might have bordered on being offensive for the Isaiah translator, not least because of its implication that God is capable of remaining silently idle whilst Israel is in danger.[75] It would seem that the translator cannot escape his dilemma by means of the unaltered consonantal text, but help lies not far away. It arrives in the form of the more amenable homonym that means *to be like*.

The result is a bold elevation of Zion and her children, to whom the plural ὑμῖν must now refer: *for there will be no one like you* (pl.)[76] *when he establishes and makes Jerusalem a praise in the earth.*[77] It seems

72. 'They shall not cease *remembering/making mention of* the Lord.'

73. The alternative to this is that the phrase in 62.7 has simply been omitted. However, the LXX expression seems to contain features of *both* Hebrew clauses: from 62.6, ὑμῖν = לכם and ἔστιν = the verbless clause (rather than תתנו); from 62.7, γὰρ = ו.

74. I.e. according to BDB I rather than BDB II.

75. In MT 62.6 God's 'remembrancers'—who are probably the same as the Lord's appointed שֹׁמְרִים—are warned against idle silence. In MT 62.7, the same injunction is without pause applied to *him* (i.e. the Lord, whom the remembrancers address).

76. Ottley's 'for ye have none (other) like' is difficult to understand (his parentheses and the word within them indicate this) and neglects the more natural meaning. Ottley may have been more loyal to the phraseology of the HB than was our translator. Cf. L.C.L. Brenton, *The Septuagint with Apocrypha: Greek and English* (London: Samuel Bagster, 1851; reprinted in Peabody, MA: Hendrickson, 1986): 'For there is none like you.'

77. The choice of διορθοῦν to render כון is curious. Elsewhere it tends to mean *to set right, restore to order* (cf. LSJ, p. 434). Indeed the LXX usage leans heavily in a moralistic direction: outside Isaiah it is always used with reference to setting right one's *ways*. Cf. Jer. 7.3, 5; Prov. 16.9(1); Wis. 9.18. (In the difficult passage at Isa. 16.5—where διορθοῦν also translates כון—the reference is to the restoration of

likely that the second-person plural reading in a reference to a future restoration of Zion would have had a contemporizing resonance among Diaspora readers in the centuries before the Common Era. Indeed, it may have sounded to them like a future that included *them* among the *you* of Zion's children. It remains impossible to determine whether the translator intended it so.

Isaiah 63.7. The Lord's blood-splattered arrival from Edom in ch. 63 is interrupted in MT 63.7 by the first-person statement: 'The gracious deeds of the Lord shall I recount, the praiseworthy acts of the Lord according to all *that the Lord recompensed to us* and the great goodness to the house of Israel *that he recompensed to them...*'[78] The passage brings together the experience of Israel past with that of the speaker's own generation.[79]

In the LXX this actualization process seems to have travelled several steps further. This is evident in the first instance via the translation of the Hebrew perfect verbs by the Greek present tense: גְמָלָנוּ אֲשֶׁר כָּל כְּעַל יְהוָה...אֲשֶׁר־גְּמָלָם = ἐν πᾶσιν οἷς ὁ κύριος ἡμῖν ἀνταποδίδωσιν ὁ κύριος...ἐπάγει ἡμῖν. Secondly, the pronominal suffixes of the two verbs are levelled to the first person plural. In the MT this detail was the key to the actualizing purpose of this passage, whereby the speaker's own generation was urged to seek and to see the solidarity between God's dealings with them (גְמָלָנוּ) and his interaction with generations past (גְמָלָם). In the LXX this historical perspective has disappeared. Indeed, Israel's ancient history itself seems to have faded from view. What is left is a general statement about God's dealings with some present community: 'in all that the Lord *repays to us...brings upon us*'.[80]

Davidic rule over Moab. The Greek word may or may not share this nuance there.) One wonders whether a hint of Diaspora pique about the 'old country' might just rise to the surface in the use of this uncommon verb. Jerusalem is there, one might surmise, but not quite what she ought to be.

78. חַסְדֵי יְהוָה אַזְכִּיר תְּהִלֹּת יְהוָה כְּעַל כֹּל אֲשֶׁר־גְּמָלָנוּ יְהוָה וְרַב־טוּב לְבֵית יִשְׂרָאֵל אֲשֶׁר־גְּמָלָם.

79. Cf. Westermann, *Jesaja 40-66*, p. 307: 'Der diese Worte spricht, will die Taten Gottes ins Gedächtnis rufen. Das ist nicht nur ein theoretisches Erinnern an Gewesenes; indem die Gnadentaten Gottes vergegenwärtigt werden, wird an den Gnadenwillen appelliert, der einmal diese Taten vollbracht, und von dem sie jetzt wieder erfleht werden.'

80. That his text restricts *unfettered* contemporization is seen by the translator's return to narrative of the past in 63.9-14.

It is not clear that this is a pleasurable thought. The translation of גמל by ἀνταποδιδόναι—a word which far more often than not has nega-tive connotations—may well link this recompense with the vengeful ἡμέρα ἀνταποδόσεως of 63.4.[81] It is worth noting that the Lord's 'redeemed ones' do not feature in the Greek text of that verse.[82] Furthermore, the second occurrence of גמל is translated by ἐπάγειν, the only time it is so rendered in the LXX. Ἐπάγειν, even more than ἀνταποδιδόναι, acquires in the LXX a very strong presumption of judicial calamity.

It may be that this translator has understood all too well the nature of this passage as a community lament and has expunged virtually all potential hope from it. Perhaps contemporization and the homiletical impulse merge in the appropriation of this text for the translator's pre-sent moment. If so, his result may reflect what Seeligmann has called the twin conceptions that the Diaspora is at once 'God's just punish-ment' and 'an injustice visited on Israel because of the superior might of other peoples'.[83]

Isaiah 63.15. An anti-anthropomorphic translation is probably respon-sible for a personalized reading at LXX Isa. 63.15. In classic lament style, the speaker in the MT queries God with regard to his apparent absence: 'Where are your zeal and your might? The turmoil of your bowels and your compassion are withheld from me!'[84] The LXX reconfigures this verse by means of both a lexical choice[85] and a grammatical/syntactical reassessment. It is the latter that concerns us here.

---

81. The negative associations that usually accompany this Greek verb are evident in (a) the vast majority of the LXX occurrences of αυταποδ- lexemes that are associated with requiting evil, and (b) its use in antithesis to mercy (cf. Pss. 31(30)24; 41(40)11). Of course, this does not mean that the verb cannot be used in a positive sense, only that ambiguous cases are perhaps to be suspected of negative connotations.

82. The translator has understood the abstract plural noun גְּאוּלִים rather than the concrete passive participle that would refer to the Lord's *redeemed ones*.

83. *LXX Version*, p. 111. Seeligmann continues, 'Both these views may occur side by side (in LXX Isaiah), and with less inner conflict than might seem, to us, unavoidable.'

84. איה קנאתך וגבורתך המון מעיך ורחמיך אלי התאפקו. Alternatively, '... The turmoil of your bowels and your compassion? They are withheld from me!'

85. מעיך = ἐλέους σου, an LXX *hapax* equivalency. Cf. C.T. Fritsch, 'Concept of God', in the Greek Translation of Isaiah', in J.M. Myers, O. Reimherr and H.N.

The translator seems to have understood המון מעיך ורחמיך as referring back elliptically to the rhetorical plea...אֵיֵה. Such a reading then
leaves אלי התאפקו as an independent sentence, with קנאתך וגבורתך
המון מעיך ורחמיך as its composite subject. True to his custom when
dealing with ellipsis, however, he has 'corrected' the elliptical silence
by repeating the interrogative ποῦ ἐστιν before the second pair of
divine qualities.

When he turns to the words which remain (אל יהתאפקו), the translator does not follow the Hebrew text in poetically assigning will and
intelligence to abstract divine qualities. Rather, he substitutes God himself as the subject and pluralizes the object. The result is the personalized
reading, ὅτι ἀνέσχου ἡμῶν: 'that you (have) put up with us'.[86]

Isaiah 63.18. MT Isa. 63.18 presents a third-person reference to Israel
(ירשו עם־קדשך) which occurs in a context that is dominated by first-
person forms.[87] After speaking in 63.17 of 'your servants...the tribes
of your inheritance', MT 63.18 appears to explain the community's
dire circumstances by speaking historically: למצער ירשו עם־קדשך
צרינו בוססו מקדשך. The passage is difficult, not least because ירשו
appears not to have an explicit object.[88]

Bream (eds.), *Biblical Studies* in Memory of H.C. Alleman (Locust Valley, NY: J.J.
Augustin, 1960), pp. 155-69 (161): 'The "inward parts, compassion" of God is
translated in the figurative sense in the Greek, thus eliminating the physical concept
in the Hebrew word.'

86. Cf. Ottley, *Isaiah*, I, 'that thou didst bear with us'. Brenton's translation,
'that thou hast withholden thyself from us', appears to make better sense of the
lament context. However, it is difficult to corroborate such a meaning for the
middle voice c. genitive.

D. Barthélemy calls the Greek rendering an 'assimilation facilitante'; cf. *Critique
Textuelle de l'Ancien Testament*. II. *Isaïe, Jérémie, Lamentations* (OBO, 50.2;
Göttingen: Vandenhoeck & Ruprecht, 1986), p. 444. Some modern emendations of
the MT in a personalizing direction seek similar respite from the text's rough edges.
Cf., for example, J.L. McKenzie, *Second Isaiah: Introduction, Translation, and
Notes* (AB; New York: Doubleday, 1968), p. 189: 'MT is emended from
'ēli hit'appāḳû, 'are withheld from me,' to *'al-na' hitappāḳ*, which involves minor
changes and gives much better sense.' But cf. J.N. Oswalt, *The Book of Isaiah.
Chapters 40–66* (Grand Rapids: Eerdmans, 1998), p. 610 n. 70.

87. E.g. למה תתענו יהוה...תקשיח לבנו in 63.17 and היינו in 63.19.

88. Cf. NRSV, 'Your holy people took possession for a little while; but now our
adversaries have trampled down your sanctuary'; *Tanakh*, 'Our foes have trampled

The LXX alters this reference by making it a purpose statement and by personalizing the group that hopes to inherit 'your holy mountain' *in the future*: ἵνα μικρὸν <u>κληρονομήσωμεν</u> τοῦ ὄρους τοῦ ἁγίου σου. This might have been accomplished by reading יִירְשׁוּ (occasionally written defectively as יִרְשׁוּ) rather than MT יְרְשׁוּ, though the syntax of such a reading might have seemed suspect to a native speaker of Hebrew. Additionally, the diminutive expression no longer refers to time—as with MT לְמִצְעָר—but rather to space. The speaker, then, prays that 'we' might inherit 'a small part of' God's mountain.[89]

It is possible to read this as something other than a contemporizing application of the text to Diaspora circumstances. ירְשׁוּ might have been levelled with the surrounding 1cp forms for the sake of smoothness while still remaining solely the words of the biblical prayer. The future reference inherent in κληρονομήσωμεν could be explained on the basis of an alternative and unsurprising vocalization of the consonantal text.

However, it is not difficult to imagine a contemporizing explanation that takes seriously what might have been the Alexandrian community's longing for God's holy mountain. The Isaiah passages that speak of eschatological pilgrimage—chiefly chs. 2 and 66—might have encouraged such hope.[90]

Your Sanctuary, Which Your holy people possessed but a little while.' The latter explicitly understands God's sanctuary as the object of both ירְשׁוּ and בוֹסְסוּ.

89. The translator may have read עַמ־קָדְשְׁךָ and paraphrased it as the 1cp subject of κληρονομήσωμεν while duplicating the קָדְשׁ element in τοῦ ὄρους τοῦ ἁγίου σου. This would be a daring appropriation of an honoured biblical term for one's own community. Alternatively, he may have for unknown reasons understood עַמ־קָדְשְׁךָ as הַר־קָדְשְׁךָ and simply personalized ירְשׁוּ. Some attraction may have been exercised by Isa 57.13 and 65.9. In the former, the Lord promises that 'all who take refuge in me...will inherit my holy mountain'. In the latter, he promises that a seed from Jacob and Judah will inherit 'my mountains', an expression that the translator expands to 'my holy mountain'. These parallels demonstrate that the concept represented by הַר־קָדְשְׁךָ would have been familiar to the translator. They do not, however, diminish the importance of his personalizing/contemporizing translation, κληρονομήσωμεν.

Further personalization occurs in 63.19, where לֹא־מָשַׁלְתָּ בָם = ὅτε οὐκ ἦρξας ἡμῶν and לֹא־נִקְרָא שִׁמְךָ עֲלֵיהֶם = οὐδὲ ἐπεκλήθη τὸ ὄνομά σου ἐφ' ἡμᾶς. These can be understood as idiomatic adjustments that are of little consequence. However, if one grants that a contemporizing kind of personalization has occurred in 63.18, then these alterations may serve an auxiliary function in service of this broader manipulation of the passage.

90. As we shall see, these have been translated in a way that concedes a certain

Isaiah 64.3(4). The lament *genre* continues into ch. 64, and with it the readiness of the translator explicitly to link historical protagonists with a present community that identifies itself in the first person. In 64.4(3) the Lord's uniqueness is spelled out in terms of human perception: וּמֵעוֹלָם לֹא־שָׁמְעוּ לֹא הֶאֱזִינוּ עַיִן לֹא־רָאָתָה אֱלֹהִים זוּלָתְךָ. The opening temporal expression picks up where the same expression left off in 63.16 and 63.19.[91] In each case, the present plight of the community—for better and for worse—is seen in continuity with that of ancestral Israel.

The LXX goes beyond the MT in accentuating this solidarity. When the translator glosses the historical statement לֹא־שָׁמְעוּ with the 1cp οὐκ ἠκούσαμεν, he makes explicit a kind of corporate unity that the MT leaves to the poetic imagination.[92] Indeed, it is possible that he does more, for past figures seem almost to fade completely away before the appropriation of the monolatrous *principle*, and this *by us*. The same move in the direction of a concrete first-person reference recurs several words later when עַיִן לֹא־רָאָתָה is rendered as οὐδὲ οἱ ὀφθαλμοὶ ἡμῶν εἶδον. Creed becomes testimony.[93]

Five verses later, when the speaker attempts to soften God's anger and to dull his judicial memory, the LXX makes explicit what the Hebrew text merely implies with regard to the prayer's beneficiaries. The MT's 'Do not be exceedingly angry, O Lord, and do not remember iniquity forever' is translated, 'Do not be exceedingly angry *with us*, and do not remember *our sins* forever'.[94]

---

priority to Jewish pilgrims vis-à-vis those Gentiles who make the same journey. A marginalized Diaspora community might treasure the anticipation of such a reversal.

91. 63.16, הָיִינוּ מֵעוֹלָם לֹא־מָשַׁלְתָּ. 63.19,...אַתָּה יְהוָה אָבִינוּ גֹּאֲלֵנוּ מֵעוֹלָם שְׁמֶךָ בָּם.

92. לֹא הֶאֱזִינוּ collapses out entirely. Cf. BHS *propositum*.

93. The verse continues to sustain a personalizing approach with יַעֲשֶׂה לִמְחַכֵּה־לוֹ/καὶ τὰ ἔργα σου ἃ ποιήσεις. However, this probably owes as much to the attempt to render idiomatically a Hebrew relative clause that changes the grammatical person of its antecedent as to any personalizing strategy.

94. Is 64.8(9) אַל־תִּקְצֹף יְהוָה עַד־מְאֹד וְאַל־לָעַד תִּזְכֹּר עָוֹן = μὴ ὀργίζου ἡμῖν σφόδρα καὶ μὴ ἐν καιρῷ μνησθῇς ἁμαρτιῶν ἡμῶν. Brenton (*Septuagint*, p. 898) is almost certainly correct that ἐν καιρῷ is a Hebraism. However, this translator generally produces good Greek even when the meaning of the Hebrew is not clear to him. One wonders whether ἐν καιρῷ might just hint at some judicial moment.

Isaiah 66.5. It is difficult to determine whether the complex personalization at 66.5 reflects a naive choice among two options allowed by the unvocalized text or an audacious contemporizing strategy. In the MT, a mocking quote on the lips of some adversarial subgroup of the community is introduced with the words, אָמְרוּ אֲחֵיכֶם שֹׂנְאֵיכֶם מְנַדֵּיכֶם. The LXX translator may have read the first word as the imperative אִמְרוּ, which would have fitted conveniently with the introduction of the oracle in the previous stich, שִׁמְעוּ דְּבַר־יְהוָה הַחֲרֵדִים אֶל־דְּבָרוֹ. However, he would then have been faced with the problem of the 2mp suffixes on the three participles.[95] A solution born of desperation may have been to change the suffixes (Greek object pronouns) to the *first-person plural*,[96] and to differentiate the second and third participles from the first as the audience[97] of the speech that is here urged upon the brethren; thus, εἴπατε, ἀδελφοὶ ἡμῶν, τοῖς μισοῦσιν ἡμᾶς καὶ βδελυσσομένοις.

It seems more likely, however, that this has not been a naive conversion. It is perhaps better explained by ideology. In the first instance, substantial surgery has to be performed in order to make sense of a

95. אֲחֵיכֶם is incoherent, since it illogically posits a third-person entity as the recipients of a (2mp) command. The same is true of שֹׂנְאֵיכֶם and מְנַדֵּיכֶם, with the added difficulty that this party is hostile to the recipients of the command.

96. That is, so to change the first and second suffixes/pronouns, with the second now doing double duty for the second and third participles. These have been semantically linked by the provision of just *one* article (τοῖς) and *one* object pronoun (ἡμᾶς).

Alternatively, βδελυσσομένοις may lack the pronominal object because of its middle voice (מְנַדֵּיכֶם = βδελυσσομένοις, an LXX *hapax* equivalency). The verb can be transitive or intransitive in the middle voice. Piel נדה would mean *to exclude*, sometimes but not often from worship. The translator may have come to the meaning of defilement rather than mere exclusion by relating it to the substantive נִדָּה. Although נִדָּה never equals βδέλυγμα in the LXX, it does denote impurity. Regardless of the specifics of the relationship, we have a purity motif in the LXX that is absent in MT.

It may be that the middle voice, in tandem with the loss of the 2mp suffix, causes βδελυσσομένοις to mean 'defiling themselves'; thus, 'those who hate us and (so) defile themselves', rather than Ottley's 'and hold (us) in abomination' (*Isaiah*, I, p. 325). It may be nationalistic in that it removes the defilement from the speaker's party to some other, perhaps to Gentiles; and in that it may render this a Jew versus Gentile issue (cf. Blenkinsopp, 'Servants of the Lord', pp. 396-97) rather than an internecine Jewish quarrel.

97. Greek datives, functioning as indirect objects of εἴπατε.

translation that vocalizes as אָמְרוּ. If the translator were not committed to the rendering that this understanding produces, he might have looked for an alternative. One lies clearly at hand in the form of אָמְרוּ, but he does not take it.

In the second instance, the subtle but sustained nationalistic content of LXX ch. 66 may suggest that it was impossible for the translator to conceive of a group of 'brethren' who were not only members of the Jewish community, but also haters and defilers of their Diaspora kin.[98] His translation offers the twin conveniences of a hortatory address to the brethren and an identification of the adversary as one who resides 'outside the gates'. The Greek verse allows to those on the inside the status of victims, but not of victimisers.

Isaiah 66.9-12. These verses present yet another case of LXX deviation that *may* be adequately explained on the basis of naive orthographic confusion. However, there is adequate reason for concluding that the Lord has intentionally been distanced from the messy multiple-birth scene of Zion and her children (vv. 7-9). In v. 9, where the Lord's involvement becomes explicit, not one of the four verbs is translated in a straightforward manner.[99] In the LXX the dialogue remains personal, but with an explicit object on the second verb: ולא אוליד = καὶ οὐκ ἐμνήσθης μου. Similarly, the slightest possible deviation in a personalizing direction occurs in 66.10, where כל־המתאבלים עליה— the second of two substantivized participles that are already vocative in function—is translated by a second-person finite verb: πάντες ὅσοι πενθεῖτε ἐπ' αὐτῆς.

---

98. See below for details of this nationalistic bias. Seeligmann (*LXX Version*, p. 112) finds in LXX Isaiah evidence that 'a hypersensitive pusillanimity and vulnerable inferiority complex are characteristic of the Galuth psychology of the Hellenistic diaspora'. Even if Seeligmann's diagnosis comes perilously close to performing long-distance psychoanalysis, there is ample evidence that 'us-versus-them' ethnic presuppositions undergird this translation.

In a private letter dated to the first half of the first century BCE, βδελύσσειν is used to describe loathing of Jews. The letter is likely written by one Jew to another, and seems to request that the recipient consult a certain Egyptian priest about a matter. The writer poignantly urges his reader to make a realistic appraisal of the situation with the words οἶδας γὰρ ὦτι βδελύσ(σ)ονται 'Ιουδαίους. Cf. V.A. Tcherikover (ed.), *Corpus Papyrorum Judaicarum*, I (Cambridge, MA: Harvard University Press, 1957), §141, p. 256.

99. For details, see Chapter 4, 'Isaiah 66.9'.

A more significant personalizing deviation occurs in LXX 66.12. It appears to have nationalistic overtones. In the MT the Lord extends two gifts to Zion: (a) 'peace like a river', and (b) 'the glory of nations like an overflowing stream'.[100] This is consonant with the generally positive picture in which Jews and Gentiles process together to Jerusalem. The LXX, however, views the MT's נטה as an intransitive verb. The Lord himself leans down towards *them*, presumably Zion's children.[101]

This produces a picture of divine involvement with Zion that is in two details more personal than the perspective of the MT. In the first place—as I suggest above—God himself draws close to her, whereas in the MT he extends his generosity to her. In the second—as we will now see—Jews are the beneficiaries of this divine condescension in a way that Gentiles emphatically are not.

In the MT כְּנָהָר שָׁלוֹם means that God extends to Zion *peace*, which is *like a river*.[102] Presumably, the reference is to the force and supply of a full river. The LXX translator, however, has read this as כִּנְהַר שָׁלוֹם and has understood this to mean that the Lord leans down towards Zion *like a river of peace*.[103] The translator must now deal with the parallel clause וּכְנַחַל שׁוֹטֵף כְּבוֹד גּוֹיִם. This clause refers back to נטה and must mean that the Lord extends the glory of nations *to Zion...as an over-flowing stream*.

In the context, כְּבוֹד גּוֹיִם appears to have the positive connotation of wealth. All that is awe-inspiring and bounteous comes in the end to serve God in Zion in a way that is of benefit principally to Jews, but also to the Gentiles, who in this context do not appear to be unwilling pilgrims. The translator, however, appears to give vent to the nationalistic feeling that surfaces at various times throughout LXX Isaiah, but particularly at several points in this final chapter. He seems to read גּוֹיִם כְּבוֹד as the contemptible *hubris* of nations. Rather than serve as tribute in Zion's ecumenical feast, this כְּבוֹד is swept away, for the Lord *bends down...as a stream which overwhelms the hubris of nations*.[104]

100. הנני נטה־אליה כנהר שלום וכנחל שוטף כבוד גוים.

101. Singular אליה = plural εἰς αὐτούς.

102. This is so if the phrase is read adjectivally. It might also be possible to read it adverbially, in which case the Lord extends, river-like, peace to her. The same is true of the second comparative clause of the verse.

103. That is, *like a peaceful river*. Cf. GKC §128p for periphrasis for the adjectival expression of attributes.

104. ἐκκλίνω...ὡς χειμάρρους ἐπικλύζων δόξαν ἐθνῶν. Alternatively, 'as a stream, flooding glory (away) from nations'.

The translator might well have considered that precedent for such a reading was not too far distant. In Isa. 59.19-20, the Lord comes to Zion *as a pent-up river*. Significantly, this event is meant to strike fear in the hearts of nations, but also to redeem the penitent in Zion.[105] One also observes that such waters will move Gentiles to fear the Lord's *glory*. The equation of these two passages in the translator's mind might have occurred effortlessly.

Thus, the LXX offers a personalising move which makes a transitive verb into an intransitive expression of divine presence. This divine condescension will prove welcome to Jews. It appears not to bear good news for Gentiles.

Conversion of Abstract Nouns to Nouns Denoting Persons in Isaiah 56–66

As a minor addendum to this discussion, one observes in LXX Isaiah the occasional assignment to human beings of what the Hebrew text intends abstractly. This is probably best explained as a subset of the translator's habit of frequently rendering an abstract singular by a concrete plural. Nevertheless, its effect in some cases is to *personalize* an abstract statement.

When providing a motivation for the great reversal that the mourners of Zion are promised in ch. 61, the Lord explains in MT 61.8, 'For I the Lord love justice, I hate robbery with burnt offering.[106] I will give their recompense *in truth*, and I will make an everlasting covenant with them'.[107] The statement about truth uses באמת adverbially to characterize

---

Ottley's translation appears to me to be essentially correct: 'Behold, I do incline toward them like a river of peace, and like a torrent overflowing the glory of nations.' Brenton sees a less hostile situation for the Gentiles: 'Behold, I turn toward them (presumably Jews) as a river of peace, and as a tòrrent bringing upon them in a flood the glory of the Gentiles.' It is quite possible to construe the meaning in this way. However, Brenton's understanding of ἐπικλύζειν as a particularly bounteous delivery of riches appears not to do justice to the violent connotation that is often associated with the word, nor to LXX usage. The three LXX occurrences of this verb outside Isa. 66.12 are all associated with the death of foreigners: Deut. 11.4 (Egyptians), Jdt. 2.8 (Assyrians) and *3 Macc.* 2.7 (Egyptians again).

105. ...וייראו ממערב את־שם יהוה וממזרח־שמש את־כבודו כי־יבוא כנהר צר
ובא לציון גואל.

106. Or, as often emended, 'with wrongdoing' (reading בְּעַוְלָה for MT בְּעוֹלָה).

107. The latter half of the verse in the MT reads, ונתתי פעלתם באמת וברית
עולם אכרות להם.

the manner by which the Lord will compensate Zion's afflicted for their suffering. The LXX, for its part, translates באמת as a *dativus ethicus*—logically parallel to להם—and so produces δικαίοις.[108]

The result, whereby the Lord now promises to give *to righteous people* their reward, is achieved only by treating the Hebrew text with some violence. In the first instance, אמת never occurs in the HB as a plural. Secondly, it does not stand alone as a substantive meaning a truthful (or righteous) person. Rather, when it characterizes individuals it occurs in a construct relationship, such as איש אמת,[109] אנשי אמת[110] or עד אמת.[111] Thirdly, the 3mp suffix on the preceding noun—פעלתם—appears to make a reading of אמת as a third-personal plural substantive somewhat clumsy.[112] Finally באמת is a common adverbial phrase that means 'truthfully' and is managed in the LXX by means of only three unimaginative stereotyped expressions.[113]

Thus, δικαίοις appears over against several weighty considerations of grammar and translation precedent. It probably gives evidence of a strong predilection for concrete, plural, and *personal* renderings.

Summary and Conclusion

LXX Isaiah displays a significant tendency to multiply first- and second-person references in the text. Often, though not always, this appears to have a homiletical and contemporizing motivation. Personalization is facilitated by the translator's tendency to level grammatical and

---

108. It should be noted that in his *editio* Ziegler instead reads δικαίως with the eleventh-century codex designated as 544. Ziegler himself cross-references the MT in his apparatus. I find it difficult to favour this reading as anything other than a 'hexaplaric-style' move in the direction of the MT.

109. Neh. 7.2 (ἀνὴρ ἀληθής).

110. Exod. 18.21 (ἄνδρας δικαίους).

111. Jer. 42.5 (μάρτυρα δίκαιον).

112. One can just imagine that ונתתי פעלתם באמת could mean, 'And I will give their recompense to the truthful (to whom it belongs).' But only just.

113. באמת occurs 27 times in the HB. Apart from LXX Isa. 61.8, it is translated by (a) a preposition + δικαιοσύνη (one exception, באמתך ולהשכיל = καὶ διανοηθῆναι τὴν δικαιοσύνην σου in Dan. 9.13, is unremarkable), (b) a preposition + ἀλήθεια (τῇ ἀληθείᾳ alone in Isa. 10.20), or (c) ἐν πίστει. Only LXX Isaiah is eclectic with regard to the three options.

באמת is never translated elsewhere as a concrete plural, as in Isa. 61.8. The fact that it is also never translated as a pure adverb appears to offset what may have been Ziegler's assumption of grammatical precedent for δικαίως.

syntactical features. It is accomplished by (a) provision of first- and second-person features where the source text lacks these, (b) conversion of grammatical features to first- and second-person forms, (c) substitution of a first-person intransitive form for a transitive verb, and (d) the provision of a concrete plural Greek noun referring to human beings for an abstract singular Hebrew noun.

Chapter 4

PROPERLY THEOLOGICAL AMELIORATIVE
TRANSLATIONS IN LXX

Scholars have long debated the extent to which the LXX translators deviate from their presumed *Vorlage* in the interest of safeguarding God's dignity.[1] LXX Isaiah frequently displays non-literal translations of Hebrew passages that depict God in what might be considered unfavourable light. From the point of view of the offence that a straightforward translation might cause, such renderings are *ameliorative* in that they avoid or mitigate the potential scandal.[2]

1. I have already suggested that such a motivation may lie behind several de-personalizing renderings of divine names and titles. Cf. also, *inter alia*, Seeligmann, 'Problems', p. 224 ('characteristic'); Fritsch, 'Concept of God'; Olofsson, *God Is my Rock*, especially the chapter entitled 'Theological Exegesis in the Book of Psalms', pp. 17-33; H.M. Orlinsky, 'The Treatment of Anthropomorphisms and Anthropopathisms in the Septuagint of Isaiah', *HUCA* 27 (1956), pp. 193-200; and A. Soffer, 'The Treatment of Anthropomorphisms and Anthropopathisms in the Septuagint of Psalms', *HUCA* 28 (1957), pp. 85-107; reprinted in Jellicoe (ed.), *Studies in the Septuagint*, pp. 395-417.

When discussing what appear to be ideologically motivated translations, I do not discount *a priori* the possibility that these reflect a *Vorlage* that differs from the MT. Such possibilities must be examined case by case. Cf. Tov, *TCU*, pp. 33-34: 'There certainly was (and still is) a tendency, even among critical scholars, to depreciate the value of the LXX by ascribing most of its deviations to the translators' exegesis and techniques. This was partly influenced by religious and other prejudices, which rejected the possibility that the underlying text of the LXX sometimes differed from MT... Ever since the nineteenth century there have been scholars who, in their evaluation of the LXX, took the middle road between recognizing Hebrew variants and the translators' exegesis.' One hopes that the present work might make some contribution towards mapping out such a 'middle road', not for the sake of moderation but because the evidence points in that direction.

2. Unlike some scholars, I do not restrict my treatment to those ameliorations that are necessarily *conscious* translational acts. This is so for two reasons. In the

This hermeneutical strategy is carried out in four principal ways. First, the translator tends to modify *anthropomorphic* descriptions.[3] Second, he avoids *anthropopathic* descriptions. He is especially attentive to references to God that depict emotional vulnerability. Third, he deals carefully—and at times creatively—with divine descriptions that might suggest *limits to divine perception* or that God is in *less than full control* of a situation. Fourth, he stresses the *dignified remoteness* of God. He seems not to be content with God 'coming down' from heaven.

The dividing line between these categories is at times blurred. This is especially so with the distinction between categories two and three. For example, a description of God in terms of strong emotion might also contain the suggestion that he has been surprised by a turn of events.

Such properly theological ameliorative readings are the subject of this chapter. I will first establish that these are characteristic of the

first place, ameliorative translations that may have depended upon a translator's *unconscious* presuppositions about the subject matter nonetheless produce a text that mitigates potential scandal. Such deviations are a legitimate topic of analysis. In the second, it is in practice frequently impossible to determine the extent to which an ameliorative reading is a conscious act. For a different methodology by a scholar whose basic understanding of the problem is similar to mine, cf. Olofsson, *God Is my Rock*, 2: 'I deliberately restrict myself to the study of conscious theological exegesis reflected in the choice of equivalents, i.e. cases where the translation is more influenced by the theology of the translator than by the meaning of the words in their context. It is of course a complicated task to distinguish between conscious theological exegesis and mere theological influence, since it presupposes discernment of the translator's intentions.' For the simultaneous appearance of 'fully aware' and 'unwitting' alterations in the Targums, cf. M.L. Klein, 'Associative and Complementary Translation in the Targumim', *Eretz-Israel* 16 (1982, Harry M. Orlinsky volume), pp. 134-40 (134).

3.   For a summary of discussion on the inadequacies of this term, cf. Olofsson, *God Is my Rock*, p. 1. Here I adopt Olofsson's approach, which he summarizes as follows: ' "Anthropomorphism" is thus a controversial term in scholarly circles but if no attempt is made to read in any philosophical speculations concerning the corporeality of God it can hardly be discarded. Even though the term is not ideal, "anthropomorphism" has retained its conventional meaning in this dissertation. Thus it is, for example, used for expressions such as "to see Yahweh", for the attribution of human feelings to God, and for the metaphorical employment of parts of the body in connection with God in all kinds of contexts.' I further distinguish between anthropomorphism and anthropopathism, though the distinction is not always a tidy one.

Greek Isaiah, illustrating the various types of theological amelioration
in that work with reference to instances that occur before ch. 56. I will
then canvass those cases that occur in chs. 56–66. We will note in
passing those verses that have received adequate treatment by other
scholars, concentrating instead on those which have been largely overlooked. In the process, continuities between the approach of LXX Isaiah,
the Targums and later rabbinical literature will occasionally surface.
These continuities encourage the view that ameliorative readings in
LXX Isaiah are often theologically motivated and representative of a
hermeneutical method that extends beyond the LXX.[4]

Properly Theological Ameliorative Translations as a Feature of LXX Isaiah

Anthropomorphic Translations as a feature of LXX Isaiah
Isaiah 42.13. The Isaiah translator sometimes draws upon resources
from outside his text in order to avoid anthropomorphic description of
God. Several anomalies in LXX Isa. 42.13 reveal details of the translator's intertextual hermeneutic as he encounters a description of the

---

4.   Olofsson describes the existence of a 'Gehman school' (the term is not
Olofsson's) and an 'Orlinsky school' (*God Is my Rock*, pp. 5-9). The former tends
to identify religious motives behind non-literal Septuagintal translations. The latter,
of which Olofsson declares himself a member, does not (cf. also, *inter alia*, Soffer,
'Anthropomorphisms and Anthropopathisms'). It is true that the eagerness of some
exponents of the Gehman school has resulted in naive statements (see below, where
I discuss the contribution of C.T. Fritsch with regard to LXX Isaiah). However, the
remarkable consistency of the trends within LXX Isaiah—though they are hardly
systematic—combined with the same kinds of tendencies as these appear in other
Jewish literatures that have roots in the Second Temple period, suggests that a
theological explanation is often the only suitable one. Careful scholars, such as
Seeligmann, frequently arrived at this conclusion (e.g. 'Problems', p. 185). One
would now wish to mention J. Koenig's monograph (see below) as an especially
forceful example of the Gehman school, and one that is not completely invulnerable
to the charge of enthusiasm.
    Olofsson's cautionary words, and the warnings offered by his fellows in the
Orlinsky school, are prudent, even if their agnosticism seems occasionally to be
almost credal. It is hoped that the present study will satisfy Orlinsky's disciples by
identifying theologically motivated translations only after sufficient attention has
been given to 'the translation technique in general' (cf. Olofsson, *God Is my Rock*,
p. 7).

Lord in the form of a warrior. These may also support the suggestion
that LXX Isaiah postdates the Greek Minor Prophets.[5] The text reads:

יהוה כגבור יצא כאיש מלחמות יעיר קנאה
יריע אף־יצריח על־איביו יתגבר[6]

> The Lord goes forth like a soldier, like a man of wars he stirs up zeal; he
> cries out, indeed he shouts aloud, he shows himself mighty against his
> foes.

The LXX translates:

> κύριος ὁ θεὸς τῶν δυνάμεων εξελεύσεται καὶ συντρίψει πόλεμον,
> ἐπεγερεῖ ζῆλον καὶ βοήσεται ἐπὶ τοὺς ἐχθροὺς αὐτοῦ μετὰ ἰσχύος

> The Lord, the God of hosts, shall go forth and shall shatter war;
> he shall rouse up passion and shall cry out over his enemies with strength.

LXX Isaiah here circumvents at least two[7] anthropomorphisms.[8] First,
it avoids comparing the Lord's going forth to that of a (human) warrior
by translating יהוה כגבור as κύριος ὁ θεὸς τῶν δυνάμεων. Then it
side-steps comparison of the Lord to a 'man of wars' by rendering
כאיש מלחמות as καὶ συντρίψει πόλεμον.

The latter translation, especially, is inventive. Scholars generally
conclude that it alludes to Exod. 15.3, which reads as follows:

---

5.   Seeligmann suggests the same with reference to (LXX) Micah. Cf. *LXX
Version*, p. 103 n. 24.
6.   The second stich of this verse is the only place in the HB where intransitive
verbal גבר has a divine subject. Thus one is left without data with which to
compare the LXX's μετὰ ἰσχύος. In Zech. 10.6 and 10.12, the Lord strengthens
(גבר) the house of Judah. In each case the translator uses κραταιοῦν. The only
other related case appears at Ps. 103(102).11, where גבר חסדו על־יראיו is given a
divine subject: ἐκραταίωσεν κύριος τὸ ἔλεος αὐτοῦ ἐπὶ τοὺς φοβουμένους
αὐτόν.
7.   A possible third conversion will be discussed below.
8.   Nevertheless, of the major students of LXX Isaiah, Thackeray alone discusses
a possible anti-anthropomorphic motive for the LXX reading; cf. 'Greek Translators', p. 583. Even Thackeray touches only the second of the two anti-anthropomorphic clauses. Koenig dismisses Thackeray's concern. He does not say why;
cf. *L'herméneutique analogique*, p. 59. More recently, Fritsch ('Concept of God',
pp. 163-64) gives brief mention to the ideological turn in the LXX translation of this
verse: 'A clear anti-anthropomorphism is found in 42.13 where the comparison of
God to a man is avoided in the Greek.' TJ also removes all anthropomorphisms
from this verse.

יהוה אישׁ מלחמה יהוה שׁמו

The Lord is a warrior; the Lord is his name.

LXX Exod. 15.3 is also creative, and this in the same direction as LXX Isa. 42.13:

κύριος συντρίβων πολέμους, κύριος ὄνομα αὐτῷ

The connection between the two verses is often recognized. However, in identifying LXX Exod. 15.3 as the principal inspiration for καὶ συντρίψει πόλεμον at Isa. 42.13, the scholarly literature falls prey to four errors.

First, it fails to give due weight to a potential source of inspiration at Hos. 2.20 that is equally compelling.[9] This is probably due to the unexamined assumption that the translation of the Minor Prophets into Greek followed that of Isaiah and, thus, that Hosea—at least *Greek Hosea*—could not have influenced LXX Isaiah.

Second, it tends to view the hermeneutical dynamics at play between Exod. 15.3, Isa. 42.13 and three other relevant verses as operating at the purely verbal level.[10] In fact, there is reason to believe that the translator of Isaiah 42 has taken entire contexts into account.

---

9.   Cf. Thackeray, 'Greek Translators', p. 583: 'Another characteristic of the Isaiah translator, which perhaps also points to an early date, is the agreement which it shows in some of its renderings with the book of Exodus...the anthropomorphism by which Jehovah is called "a man of war" is avoided by the same paraphrase συντρίβων πολέμους in Ex. xv 3, Is. xlii 13.' Ottley follows Thackeray; cf. *Isaiah*, II, p. 308. M.J.J. Menken follows and summarizes Koenig; cf. Menken, *Old Testament Quotations in the Fourth Gospel: Studies in Textual Form* (Kampen: Kok, 1996), pp. 52-53: 'The LXX has, for instance, in Exod. 15.3 by συντρίβων πολέμους, "one who breaks wars". This happened under the influence of the Hebrew text of Ps. 76.4; Hos. 2.20, where it is said that God has broken or will break the war (שׁבר מלחמה); the connecting word which legitimizes the interpretation and translation of one text in accordance with the other, is here מלחמה, "war". *Exod. 15.3 LXX has then in turn influenced Isa. 42.13 LXX, with nearly the same expression...* This procedure is very similar to the later rabbinical hermeneutical rule of גזרה שׁוה, "identical category"; the difference is that what takes place in the former case in the rendering of a text, occurs in the latter case in its explanation' (emphasis added). Koenig and Menken seem to conclude that the Isaiah translator's reference was exclusively verbal and exclusive to Exod. 15.3. It was neither more broadly contextual and theological, nor did it involve reflection upon the verses from Hosea and the Psalms that allegedly supplied the rendering at LXX Exod. 15.3.

10.   So Koenig, for example, who uses LXX Isa. 42.13 as a parade example of *le*

Third, the scholarly literature unnecessarily complicates the textual character of LXX Isa. 42.13 by failing to recognize that the Greek translation of that verse may just as well conform to the standards of the Isaiah translator as to any directly imported borrowing.

Fourth, it does not sufficiently examine the possible ideological motive for the anti-anthropomorphic result which the Isaiah translator produces at 42.13.

With regard to the first and second problems, one observes a certain consensus that LXX Exod. 15.3 has supplied the lexical materials for the conversion at LXX Isa. 42.13. Indeed, that verse was almost certainly *one* source, for it finds its point of departure in the same two Hebrew words—מל חמה שׁ א, 'spoken of the Lord'—which appear to have troubled the Isaiah translator.[11] Further in favour of this direction of influence is the fact that LXX Isaiah does at points rely upon the Greek Pentateuch.[12]

Finally, one can adduce the context of Exod. 15 as a 'bridging' feature that might have drawn the mind of the Isaiah translator in this direction. In terms of the wider context, it goes without saying that the Second Exodus imagery of Deutero-Isaiah finds its source in the first exodus.[13] More narrowly, Isa. 42.10-16 shares with Exodus 15 the

pôle verbal de l'analogie scripturaire as over against *le pôle logique*: 'On se rappelle que le 2e type défini plus haut est caractérisé par *la disparition complète d'un rapport logique* entre la texte emprunteur et le contexte du passage emprunté. Le lien instauré par la méthode consiste alors uniquement en un élément verbal (mot ou formulation)' (*L'herméneutique analogique*, p. 59).

11. This consensus implies an interesting but unarticulated assumption: the Isaiah translator must have known Exod. 15.3 in both Hebrew and Greek. The first would have established the link, via (מל חמה(ות/ה. The second would provide the Greek lexeme συντρίβειν.

12. Cf. Ziegler, *Untersuchungen*, p. 103: 'Es ist schon längst beobachtet worden, daß der Js-Übers. die Pent-LXX gekannt hat und sie öfters als "Wörterbuch" benützt hat, vgl. Thackeray, JThSt 4 (1902/03) 583.'

13. Cf. G.P. Hugenberger, 'The Servant of the Lord in the "Servant Songs" of Isaiah: A Second Moses Figure', in P.E. Satterthwaite, R.S. Hess and G.J. Wenham (eds.), *The Lord's Anointed: Interpretation of Old Testament Messianic Texts* (Carlisle: Paternoster Press, 1995), pp. 105-40 (122-23): 'Although Isaiah 40–55 is extraordinarily rich in its complexity and multifaceted imagery, it is widely recognised that the controlling and sustained theme of these chs. is that of a second exodus. While one should not neglect the importance of the second exodus theme already in chs. 1–39...or its continuing prevalence in chs. 56–66...it is almost omnipresent in chs. 40–55, for which it provides an *inclusio*...With respect to these

character of a song of deliverance.[14]

Nevertheless, this evidence in favour of influence by LXX Exod. 15.3 upon LXX Isa. 42.13 is not conclusive as an argument for *unique* or even *pre-eminent* influence when these texts are placed alongside two similar passages. Both Ps. 76(75).4 and Hos. 2.20(18) have lexical features that are similar to the verses in Greek Exodus and Isaiah that we are examining. The LXX in each case conforms closely to the MT.

Ps 76(75).4 offers:[15]

שמה שבר רשפי־קשת מגן וחרב ומלחמה סלה

There he broke the flames of bow, shield, sword, and war. Selah.

ἐκεῖ συνέτριψεν τὰ κράτη τῶν τόχων, ὅπλον καὶ ῥομφαίαν καὶ πόλεμον. διάψαλμα

There he shattered the power of arrows, shield, sword, and war. Interlude.

Hos 2.20(18) has:

וכרתי להם ברית ביום ההוא
עם־חית השדה ועם־עוף השמים ורמש האדמה
וקשת וחרב ומלחמה אשבור מן־הארץ
והשכבתים לבטח

I will make for them a covenant on that day with the wild animal(s), and with the bird(s) of the sky and the creeping thing(s) of the ground; and I will shatter from upon the land bow, sword, and war; and I will make them lie down in safety.

καὶ διαθήσομαι αὐτοῖς ἐν ἐκείνῃ τῇ ἡμέρᾳ διαθήκην μετὰ τῶν θηρίων τοῦ ἀγροῦ καὶ μετὰ τῶν πετεινῶν τοῦ οὐρανοῦ καὶ μετὰ τῶν ἑρπετῶν τῆς γῆς· καὶ τόχον καὶ ῥομφαίαν καὶ πόλεμον συντρίψω ἀπὸ τῆς γῆς καὶ κατοικιῶ σε ἐπ' ἐλπίδι

chapters which provide the immediate context for the servant songs, B.W. Anderson identifies at least ten texts which make explicit use of second exodus imagery... There are other possible examples, *including 42.13...*' (emphasis added).

14. Exod. 15.1, אז ישיר־משה ובני ישראל את־השירה הזאת ליהוה. Isa. 42.10, שירו ליהוה שיר חדש תהלתו מקצה הארץ.

15. Cf. also Ps. 46(45).10[Eng. 46.9], משבית מלחמות עד־קצה הארץ קשת ישבר וקצץ חנית עגלות ישרף באש = ἀνταταιρῶν πολέμους μέχρι τῶν περάτων τῆς γῆς τόξον συντρίψει καὶ συγκλάσει ὅπλον καὶ θυρεοὺς κατακαύσει ἐν πυρί. References to Ps. 76(75) will assume the reader's familiarity with the vocabulary that is shared by that psalm and Ps. 46(45).

> And I will make for them a covenant on that day with the animals of the
> field and with the birds of the sky and with the creeping things of the
> earth; and arrow and sword and war shall I shatter from upon the earth,
> and I will make you dwell in hope.

It is easy to see how Psalm 76 might have come within the purview
of the Exodus translator. Psalm 76 shares with both Exodus 15 and
Isaiah 42 the character of a שׁיר.[16] The psalm also shares a concern with
the Lord's name.[17] Both texts speak of horse and chariot.[18] If indeed
there is a link between LXX Exod. 15.3 and Ps. 76(75).4, the innovative
nature of the Exodus translation vis-à-vis its source text and the close
conformity between the Hebrew and the Greek versions of the psalm
suggest that the influence runs *from* the psalm *to* LXX Exodus.

Hos. 2.20 might also have inspired the Exodus translator, though this
will likely have been in a supporting role. There are no striking contextual similarities between the two passages, and the lexical parallels
are limited to the presence of שׁבר with the Lord as its subject and
מלחמה as one of its objects.

This leaves only the Hebrew text of Isa. 42.13 among the possible
sources of inspiration for LXX Exod. 15.3.[19] One wonders whether the
plural πολέμους of LXX 15.3[20] may reveal that the Exodus translator
made a connection between his איש מלחמה and the איש מלחמות of
Isa. 42.3. The same plural could of course be an echo of Ps. 46.10,
though this would lack the concrete lexical connection provided by
איש מלחמה.

It appears, then, that the Exodus translator has avoided taking the
anthropomorphism of his text as his own legacy by borrowing a phrase
from one or more of the related texts we have surveyed. This will have
occurred prior to the translation of Isaiah,[21] and may or may not have

---

16. MT 76.1.

17. Exod. 15.3, יהוה שׁמו; Ps. 76.2, בישׂראל גדול שׁמו.

18. Exod. 15.1, סוס ורכבו רמה בים; Ps. 76.7, נרדם ורכב וסוס (or, at least, of
riding a horse; cf. BHS apparatus).

19. Jdt. 9.7 and 16.2, which are brought into the discussion by the HUB
apparatus, are by context and grammatical form clearly allusions to LXX Exod.
15.3. They need not concern us here.

20. Against the singular מלחמה of the Hebrew text of Exodus and of the
arguably influential Ps. 76.4 and Hos. 2.18.

21. Though the relative chronology of the translation of individual books is in
dispute, all agree that the Pentateuch was translated first.

involved the Exodus translator's awareness of a similar Hebrew phrase at Isa. 42.13.[22]

Most scholars, then, trace the origin of συντρίψει πόλεμον at Isa. 42.13 to συντρίβων πολέμους of Exod. 15.3.[23] Ottley writes:

> Scholz gives 'like a man of war' as extra matter in Heb. But Mr Thackeray has pointed out (*Journ. of Theol. Studies*. July 1903) that this phrase is used where Heb. has 'a man of war' also in Exod. xv. 3, the Greek Isaiah and Exodus showing certain affinities. (For the idea expressed by the Greek, cf. Ps. xlvi. 9, lxxvi.3).[24]

Ottley's observation is interesting in that it appears to locate the *real* link between Isa. 42.13 and Exod. 15.3, but to allow that the *idea* expressed by the Greek of the two verses exists independently in the two Psalms.[25] This approach roughly characterizes the way scholars have viewed the relationship (or non-relationship!) among the verses. A common variant is to allow the Exodus translator reference to the Psalms and Hosea passages as well, but to maintain that the Isaiah translator was drawn solely to Exodus. The implication is that he was unaware of any web of relationships that may have interconnected these four or five verses.

However, this appears to sell the Isaiah translator short. He *was* no doubt aware that his text shared (ות/ה)מלחמ(מ איש with Exod. 15.3, and that the latter used the unexpected συντρίβων πολέμους to represent these words. It is this shared *Hebrew* vocabulary that best accounts for his intrusion of συντρίβειν into a verse that has no Hebrew lexeme which might have generated it.

But there is evidence in the singularization of מלחמות to πόλεμον that our translator had in mind another text as well. The Isaiah translator

---

22. J.W. Wevers, unfortunately, does not linger over this verse: 'In the first line the predicate is the participle συντρίβων modified by πολέμους, thus: "The Lord shatters wars (i.e. warfare)," a unique rendering of MT' (sic) מלחמה איש יהוה. Exod interprets the predicate as one who crashes, and so one who is victorious in warfare; cf. Tar⁰ נצחן "victorious"'; cf. *Notes on the Greek Text of Exodus* (SBLSCS, 30; Atlanta: Scholars Press, 1990), p. 228.

23. But not all. Scholz merely includes it among his examples of *freie Übersetzungen*; cf. *Uebersetzung*, pp. 45-46. The HUB apparatus anticipates— albeit only by suggestion—the direction of my argument: 'exeg change (after Hos 2.20) cf. Exod. 15.3 G; note Judith 9.7, 16.2, Roš Haš. §3.8'.

24. Ottley, *Isaiah*, II, p. 308.

25. He might have mentioned Hosea as well.

94

When We All Go Home

displays a strong preference for pluralization. Collective or representative singulars are routinely translated by plurals, though the tendency to render Hebrew singulars with Greek plurals is not restricted to this category alone.

If the singular πόλεμον is merely an idiosyncratic translation, it is a surprising one, for it runs counter to what one expects of this translator. Rather, the fact that the verse already betrays a probable allusion to LXX Exod. 15.3[26] raises the possibility that its intertextual reach extends to other verses as well.

It may well contemplate Hos. 2.20. There are three reasons for supposing so. First, Hos. 2.20 shares imagery and vocabulary which are very similar to Deutero-Isaiah's own.[27] Second, both passages are concerned with the renewal of covenant.[28] Finally, LXX 42.13 hews very close to LXX Hos. 2.18, grammatically speaking. Συντρίψω and συντρίψει differ *only* in grammatical person. Each has accusative singular πόλεμον.[29] The challenge to the MT that LXX Isa. 43.13 executes by singularizing מלחמות to πόλεμον may mark an attempt to bring it into line with LXX Hos. 2.18.

The Isaiah translator, then, may have been aware of the interplay between the Exodus, Hosea, Psalms and Isaiah texts just as modern scholars are. His allusion may not have been a catchword reference to a single text, but a more broadly exegetical nod towards several. It is impossible to determine whether this conceptual inclusion of Hos 2.20(18) in his translational activity—if such it was—utilized the Hebrew or the Greek text of that prophetic book. There is some slight evidence that he referred to the *Greek* Minor Prophets. The Isaiah translator is remarkably eclectic in his renderings of both שבר and מלחמה, yet his Greek at 42.13 exactly matches the equivalents that LXX Hosea uses. This may favour the view that his allusion was in fact to the Greek translation of Hosea.

26. Where, conversely, the singular מלחמה has been pluralized as πολέμους! This may itself be an echo of Hebrew Isa. 42.13, as Koenig thinks, *L'herméneutique analogique*, p. 60. For Koenig, this pluralization is due to both the authorization of H Isa. 42.13 and *une intention de majoration*.

27. Cf., for example, Isa. 42.14-18//Hos. 2.5b(2.3b).

28. Isa. 42.6, ואתנך לברית עם לאור גוים = ἔδωκά σε εἰς διαθήκην γένους, εἰς φῶς ἐθνῶν; Hos. 2.20, וכרתי להם ברית ביום ההוא = LXX 2.18, καὶ διαθήσομαι αὐτοῖς διαθήκην ἐν τῇ ἡμέρᾳ ἐκείνῃ.

29. Both Exod. 15.3 (συντρίβων πολέμους) and Ps. 76(75).4 (συνέτριψεν... πόλεμον) are farther distant.

Still, it must be conceded that the Isaiah translator's preference for rendering these two Hebrew words is συντρίβειν and πόλεμος, respectively, even if he does show a wide variety of equivalencies in addition to these. Thus, he *could have* arrived at his translation under the influence of *Hebrew* Hos. 2.20 alone. At best, therefore, this verse could be entered only as supporting—rather than as primary—evidence for the view that LXX Isaiah came to exist *after* the translation of the Minor Prophets.

The third problem which appears in the scholarly analysis of this text is an unnecessary complication of its text history. Seeligmann writes:

> The rendering of ה צבאות in the Septuagint of Isaiah is the transcription κύριος σαβαωθ; the terms used elsewhere, *i.e.* παντοκράτωρ and κύριος τῶν δυνάμεων appear to have lain beyond the translator's mental horizon. It strikes one, then, as remarkable to read, in 42,13, for ה, כגבור יצא כאיש מלחמות, κύριος ὁ θεὸς τῶν δυνάμεων ἐξελεύσεται καὶ συντρίψει πόλεμον; the more remarkable because a thought expressed here, without any sanction from the Hebrew text, which is also current among translators of other books of the Bible—equally unsupported by the Hebrew original. Evidently the entire formulation συντρίψει πόλεμον, together with the term τῶν δυνάμεων, has its origin in a different stratum of the Alexandrian translations, outside the main body of Isaiah translation.[30]

Seeligmann is correct that κύριος σαβαωθ, rather than κύριος ὁ θεὸς τῶν δυνάμεων, is the Isaiah translator's standard rendering of יהוה צבאות.[31] But יהוה צבאות is not what the translator finds in his *Vorlage*! Instead, he finds the potentially scandalous יהוה כגבור יצא. The route that appeared safest to him may well have been that of converting the first two words to a divine title.[32]

Now גבור is not often used of God, and never (apart from our

30. I.L. Seeligmann, *LXX Version*, p. 37. The idea that συντρίψει πόλεμον has its origin outside the Alexandrian translation is unnecessary and will have been weakened by the discussion above. It will not be evaluated here.

31. צבאות produces σαβαωθ in 47 of its 61 occurrences. Of the remainder, 3 are untranslated because an entire 'oracular' clause is omitted. As this kind of clause-level omission is a recognizable feature of the translator's style, these 3 verses ought not to be considered evidence of how צבאות itself is translated. In the other 12 instances, צבאות is omitted by 'collapse' of a multiword divine title into a simpler one. Thus, when צבאות is explicitly translated, it is *always* rendered σαβαωθ in Isaiah.

32. Or perhaps one divine *name* and one divine *title*.

translator's apparent reading of it as such at Isa. 42.13) as a title. Thus, if our translator found this word in his *Vorlage* in association with God, he would have a limited number of precedents to guide him.[33] In the eight cases where this association is made in the LXX, fully four use some form of -δυνα- to accomplish this, including Isa. 42.13.

Seeligmann's suggestion of multiple textual strata at this point cannot be disproved and may ultimately be accurate.[34] But its speculative character becomes transparent against the backdrop of an alternative explanation that relies upon observations about demonstrable translation technique(s). The translator who was responsible for the substantial form of our LXX text could have independently produced κύριος ὁ θεὸς τῶν δυνάμεων from... יהוה כגבור.[35]

---

33. The word itself does not produce strong preferences across the LXX. The major patterns use -δυνα-, -ισχυ- and γίγας. LXX Isaiah's own management of this word is eclectic, similarly most of the other LXX books where it is found, even those which are more given to predictable standards. Even the unique title אל גבור is translated differently in Isa. 9.5(6) and 10.21, respectively, though this may be due to the special circumstances of 9.5(6).

34. Seeligmann's treatment of this verse is lengthier than the passage cited above. Cf. *LXX Version*, p. 72 n. 2a: 'Is. 42.13 καὶ συντρίφει (sic) πόλεμον for כאיש מל חמות was perhaps influenced by the Greek text of Hos. 2.20 or Ps. 75 (76).4. The words in the Isaiah passage, however, occur in a secondary element in the text, as we try to show elsewhere in this book.' Cf. also p. 118: 'In 42.13, ה כגבור יצא כאיש מל חמות the Septuagint gives κύριος ὁ θεὸς τῶν δυνάμεων ἐξελεύσεται καὶ συντρίψει πόλεμον; similarly, in Exod. 15.3, the phrase איש מל חמה , in contradiction to the Hebrew text, becomes συντρίβων πολέμους. The phrase (completely without parallel in this place in the translation), and again, the literal translation καὶ βοήσεται ἐπὶ τοὺς ἐχθρούς, strongly suggest that an older translation has been ousted by a secondary element. Maybe this betrays the influence of Hos. 2.20 and Ps. 75 (76), where τόξον καὶ ῥομφαίαν καὶ πόλεμον συντρίψω and συνέτριψεν τὰ κράτη τῶν τόξων ὅπλον καὶ ῥομφαίαν καὶ πόλεμον, respectively, form literal translations of a given Hebrew text. Could it be that, at a certain moment, there was some reason for an apologetical text revision, by which a war-cry in the text was replaced by a peace-slogan?' However, *pace* Seeligmann, there is no unusual literalism in the cited clause. In fact the opposite is true: βοάω is a 'stop-gap' (Ottley's term, though Ottley does not include βοάω in his list) word for this translator. As such, it is pressed into service for a large number of Hebrew lexemes. Probably, there is no evidence for a peace slogan either.

35. The presence of ὁ θεός... after κύριος may favour Seeligmann's argument for a double translation. However, the fluidity of translation of divine names and titles in LXX Isaiah (including frequent cases of κύριος for אלהים and θεός for

Finally, the fact that LXX Isa. 42.13 contains not one but two anti-anthropomorphisms vis-à-vis the MT has scarcely ever been taken into account in the scholarly analysis of this text.[36] Indeed, it is possible that there are *three*, for the translation of יתגבר with יהוה as its subject is rendered by the less vigorous expression μετὰ ἰσχύος.[37]

יתגבר is the fifth verb predicated of the Lord in MT Isa. 42.13. In the LXX, it is rendered as an adverb. Together with על־איביו (= ἐπὶ τοὺς ἐχθροὺς αὐτοῦ) it now qualifies either אף־יצריח or יריע (= καὶ βοήσεται).[38]

There are three features of verbal גבר that might have seemed inappropriate in a description of divine activity. First, the translator may have been uncomfortable with the *human* connotations of this verb.[39] Second, there is a consistent element of *becoming* in the biblical usage of verbal גבר.[40] Finally, one notes a persistent *negative* connotation in the contexts where גבר is used. Though the verb itself can be predicated

יהוה as well as expansions and contractions) makes it dangerous to deduce too much from the double substantive here. It is possible that the translator understood the phrase according to the English 'The Lord, the God of ...'

36. Fritsch's brief observation in 'Concept of God', pp. 163-64, is an exception: 'A clear anti-anthropomorphism is found in 42.13 where the comparison of God to a man is avoided in the Greek ...' Fritsch cites the two anti-anthropomorphisms I have discussed, repeating the sole reference to Exod. 15.3 for the first, and adding of the second: 'Here LXX substitutes the words ο θεος τῶν δυναμεων, usually used to translate יהוה צבאות (the Lord of hosts), for the phrase כגבור (like a mighty man) as though to avoid the comparison of God to a man.'

37. It is perhaps conceivable that the translator has understood the first two letters of יתגבר as a preposition ית on analogy with the Hebrew homonym whereby את can represent the accusative marker (= Aramaic ית) or the preposition. Such a scenario would require ignorance or a lapse of concentration on the part of a translator who was not fully fluent in Hebrew and a rearticulation of the remaining letters to produce something like ית גב(ו)רה (= μετὰ ἰσχύος). In the case of this translator, such a process ought not to be ruled out, though it does not commend itself as the most economical explanation.

38. One of these two synonyms has been collapsed out by the Greek translation.

39. As noted above, nowhere else in the HB is the Lord the subject of intransitive גבר. Zech. 10.6 describes the Lord's activity *transitively*: וגברתי את־בית יהודה = καὶ κατισχύσω τὸν οἶκον Ιουδα.

40. For example, previously contained waters *swell*, Gen. 7.18, 19, 20, 24; warriors previously at a disadvantage *prevail*, Exod. 17.11; 2 Sam. 11.23; the weak *become strong*, Zech. 10.6, 12.

of positive subjects,[41] it is more frequently attached to negative actors.[42] This may have made it distasteful for our translator.

Thus, Isa. 42.13 provides the translator with ample motivation for executing an ameliorative reading. It is likely that he achieved this by using exegetical materials not only from Exod. 15.3, but from at least one other verse as well.[43]

Anti-Anthropopathic Translations as a Feature of LXX Isaiah
The Isaiah translator appears to have difficulty with passages that describe God in terms of *human experience*. This is especially true with regard to human emotion. Repeatedly, such depictions are transformed into assertions of God's irrefutable judgment.

When, in the first chapter of Isaiah, the author warms to the task of equating Judah with Sodom and Gomorrah and her cult with a direct offence against God, the prophet goes so far as to suggest that God is wearied by the entire scene. MT 1.14 reads, חדשיכם ומועדיכם שׂנאה נפשׁי היו עלי לטרח נלאיתי נשׂא.[44] The LXX makes the divine diagnosis more severe, for in translation it is the Judaeans themselves—rather than their cult—whom God finds to be offensive.[45]

In having God call Judaean worshippers a πλησμονή (*surfeit, too much*), the translator may take his first step towards depicting an

41. For example, of Saul and Jonathan, 2 Sam. 1.23, of the Lord's חסד, Ps. 103(102).11; 117(116).2; of Judah (but note ambiguity of reference, 1 Chron. 5.2).

42. For example, to the Genesis flood's destructive waters, Gen. 7.18, 19, 20, 24; to wicked people and deeds, 1 Sam. 2.9; Jer. 9.2; Pss. 12(11).5; 65(64).4; Job 21.7; 36.9 (where יתגברו itself seems to mean *evil behaviour*); and to various enemies, 2 Sam. 11.23; Lam. 1.16. Cf. also Dan. 9.27, where it is said of 'the prince who is to come': והגביר ברית לרבים.

43. Another alteration of the picture of the Lord as a 'man of war' occurs in LXX Isa. 13.5. The MT has the Lord come 'with the weapons of his indignation' (וכלי זעמו) to destroy 'the whole earth', a description that seems to imply that he himself uses his own destructive weapons in the battle (in 13.4, he has mustered a 'host of war'). The LXX transforms these 'weapons of his indignation' into warriors (καὶ οἱ ὁπλομάχοι αὐτοῦ), thus edging slightly away from the brute anthropomorphism of the Hebrew text. It may be significant as well that the LXX sees the destruction not of the whole earth but rather of τὴν οἰκουμένην ὅλην (cf. also 13.9, 14).

44. 'Your new moons and your appointed festivals my soul hates. They have become for me a burden. I am weary of bearing (them).'

45. היו לטרח = ἐγενήθετέ μοι εἰς πλησμονήν.

unwearied and judicially clear-sighted deity.[46] That is, the religious crowd divine space with their unrighteous cult, but the Lord himself is not necessarily affected by this. Whether or not this is the case, a decisive step is surely taken in the next clause, where נלאיתי נשׂא is entirely restated. By providing οὐκέτι ἀνήσω τὰς ἁμαρτίας ὑμῶν, the translator dispenses with divine weariness, instead laying hold on the much more comfortable notion of divine judgment (by refusal to forgive). נשׂא can mean *to pardon*, and that is the meaning that the LXX now employs.

The use of נשׂא with this connotation requires a negative sentence, for in the LXX the Lord does *not* forgive. The translator may have simply provided the negative particle, unabetted by any details of the Hebrew text. However, if he sought elements that would facilitate this alteration, his source text was generous in providing some. Strictly speaking, the word נלאיתי remains untranslated, a fact that may suggest that it has been utilized in some less-than-straightforward manner. It is possible that the translator acquired the desired negative by way of the letters לא of נלאיתי.[47] Indeed, his widely recognized tendency to find Aramaic meanings in Hebrew words—and even to reconfigure Hebrew words as distinct Aramaic ones—may have been of some use to him here. In a consonantal text, certain forms of Aramaic לְאִי (*to be tired*) and the negative particle לא/לאו would be identical. Furthermore, the Aramaic negation לֵית (לֵיתָא, לֵית, *there is not*) would account nicely for most

---

46. טרח is rare, appearing elsewhere in the HB only twice (in Deut. and Job). The translator may not have known the word (although this should not be assumed) and thus may have translated *ad sensum*. The idea of cultic fullness (≈ excess) which πλησμονή connotes is certainly not lacking in the context. In 1.11, an unremarkable translation produces τί μοι πλῆθος τῶν θυσιῶν ὑμῶν; λέγει κύριος· πλήρης εἰμὶ ὁλοκαυτωμάτων... The usual source of πλησμονή in the LXX is שׂבע.

47. Cf. Klein, 'Converse Translation', p. 516: 'The most patent examples of converse translation in the targumim are those in which the targumist adds a negative particle לא, לית or אפשר to an otherwise positive statement...' Cf. also pp. 529-30: 'Another method employed by the targumim in order to produce a converse translation is the replacement of the original Biblical verb with another verb of opposite meaning.' Facets of both these types of targumic 'converse translation' appear to have played a role in the formation of LXX Isa. 1.14. Klein's categories are now refined and supplemented with examples from beyond the targums in R.P. Gordon, '"Converse Translation" in the Targums and Beyond', *JSP* 19 (1999), pp. 3-21.

of the consonants of the Hebrew text and provide a meaning (here expressed literalistically) like 'there is not (to me) lifting up...'[48] It is possible, then, that נלאיתי has not been ignored or omitted, but rather disassembled and reused in the interest of producing a judgment text.

Regardless of the precise mechanics by which the translator arrived at the negative statement in the Greek text, there is evidence that this was probably not an accidental and/or insignificant alteration from the point of view of his exegesis. In the first instance, he has supplied both a new meaning and an object for נשא (τὰς ἁμαρτίας ὑμῶν).[49] In the second, renderings on either side of this verse seem burdened to produce the same kind of amelioration.[50] The result is an anti-anthropopathic rendering which allows that the Lord finds the Judaean cult an ugly sight and sound, one to which he will pay no heed. But it is not one that causes him any ill effects.

The Avoidance of Incomplete Divine Perception as a Feature of LXX Isaiah

Isaiah 44.21. The suggestion that God's perception might be less than absolute appears to motivate the translator to strike such language from his text, even when it is meant to deny the very possibility that

48. Like BH אִין, Aramaic לית accepts suffixes. An attested form with the 1cs suffix, ליתנא, would account for all the MT consonants except for one yod. This would yield the (hybrid?) expression ל יתנא נשא, which might have been judged an attractive parallel for 1.15, איננ שמע.

49. Cf. Fritsch, 'Concept of God', p. 165, who merely states that '[t]he objectionable ideas associated with God are euphemized in LXX.' Fritsch does not say what these are.

Ziegler (*Untersuchungen*, p. 60) notes that the translator looks for an object for נשא and finds one via 55.7. Further, 'Die Wendung is bekannt aus Jos 24, 19, vgl auch Js 33.24 ἀφέθη...ἡ ἁμαρτία (= MT).' However, one wonders whether he required explicit textual authorization to create so familiar a phrase.

Ottley (*Isaiah*, II, p. 107) wonders whether the original reading for נשא might have been ἀνοίσω rather than ἀνήσω (as read by a few witnesses). But this seems unnecessary, given that נשא = ἀνιέναι once each in Gen. and Josh and four times in Isa. It is not a difficult equivalence. נשא yields ἀναφέρειν fewer times (once each in Num., Job, Ezek. and Isa.), so that looking for an explanation to a hypothetical inner-Greek corruption offers little advantage over dealing with the extant text.

50. In 1.13, to say οὐκ ἀνέχομαι is arguably to say less than לא־אוכל. The Hebrew expression may connote *inability*, the Greek only *refusal*. Cf. also 1.15, where the prefix on the verb in οὐκ εἰσακούσομαι ὑμῶν (for איננ שמע) may erect the same subtle safeguard (*not to listen to* is not the same as *not to hear*).

the translator himself abhors. For example, MT 44.21 has the Lord say זכר־אלה יעקב וישראל כי עבדי־אתה יצרתיך עבד־לי אתה ישראל לֹא תִנָּשֵׁנִי.[51] God's statement, *You will not be forgotten by me*, rather affirms the durability of divine memory. However, the translator—whether consciously or not—will not have even the notion of forgetfulness associated with a divine subject. The Hebrew, to be sure, is difficult. He reads the statement as an imperative that is directed by God to Israel: Ισραηλ μὴ ἐπιλανθάνου μου.[52]

This is not a radical reconfiguration, since זכר־אלה יעקב וישראל at the beginning of the verse provides a parallel. Likewise, the consonantal text does not require major reworking in order for it to generate this active sense. Nevertheless, it is a rendering that can only result from reading the source text slightly differently from the MT as it stands.[53] It may have been a conscious amelioration.[54]

*Translations that Accentuate God's Remoteness as a
Feature of LXX Isaiah*[55]
Isaiah 35.2. Already in the Hebrew text of Isaiah, God is portrayed as high and exalted. Among humankind, only the arrogant—such as the king of Babylon in ch. 14—aspire to God's heights. They are cast down

---

51. 'Remember these things, O Jacob and Israel, for you are my servant. I formed you (to be) my servant. You, O Israel, will not be forgotten by me.'

52. 'O Israel, do not forget me!'

53. The translator reads a qal verb, rather than this unique niphal form of נשׁה. BHS follows the translator in reading תִנְשֵׁנִי or תִשֵּׁנִי (cf. also *Tanakh*). The second of these *proposita* concedes that the consonantal text cannot *simply* be revocalized, since one expects for the qal imperfect the elision of *nun*. The loss of final ה/י is expected with the suffix, cf. GKC §75 ll-mm.

54. TJ has its own, distinct, amelioration: ישראל לא תתנשׁי דחלתי ('O Israel, you will not forget *my fear*'). Cf. B.D. Chilton, *The Isaiah Targum: Introduction, Apparatus and Notes* (The Aramaic Bible, 11; Edinburgh: T. & T. Clark, 1987), p. 88: 'Even the reflexive form of the verb is retained in the Tg; but the usage is deponent, unlike the case in the MT.'

For the text of TJ Isaiah, cf. A. Sperber, *The Latter Prophets According to Targum Jonathan* (The Aramaic Bible, 3; Leiden: E.J. Brill, 1962), p. 91. Unless otherwise indicated, citations of TJ are taken from this edition.

55. Cf. Seeligmann, 'Problems', p. 225: 'In the tremendous struggle between the image of a God who is exalted and the God who is nearby and familiar, interweaving Jewish history from the Bible through Hassidism, the transformations in the LXX enhance the remoteness.'

in judicial reversal.[56] The Septuagintal translator, like the *meturgeman* on frequent occasions, is happy to accentuate the line that distinguishes God from humankind. This boundary is often articulated in the language of distance, especially on the vertical plane.[57]

It is possible that this tendency to exalt God is to be glimpsed in LXX Isa. 35.2. In the MT of that verse, the blossoming desert is promised הֲדַר הַכַּרְמֶל וְהַשָּׁרוֹן and כְּבוֹד הַלְּבָנוֹן. Presumably, the most attractive features of Lebanon, Carmel and Sharon, are now to characterize the Arabah as well. As a result of this transformation of the landscape, 'they'[58] shall see כְּבוֹד־יהוה הֲדַר אֱלֹהֵינוּ. The salient point for our discussion is the subtle differentiation between the הֲדַר of Carmel and Sharon on the one hand and that of 'our God' on the other. The first of these is translated by ἡ τιμή. When, however, the honour is God's, the translator employs the vocabulary of height, τὸ ὕψος.

A detail of the Greek translation of the throne room vision of ch. 6 hints at the same kind of exegesis. In MT 6.2, the visionary reports that he saw שְׂרָפִים עֹמְדִים מִמַּעַל לוֹ.[59] However, the translator will not have such creatures, no matter how glorious, flying higher than the enthroned deity. His rendering, καὶ σεραφιν εἱστήκεισαν κύκλῳ αὐτοῦ, quietly remedies the awkwardness without much disturbing the general scene.

---

56. Cf. especially 14.14-15, אֶעֱלֶה עַל־בָּמֳתֵי עָב אֶדַּמֶּה לְעֶלְיוֹן אַךְ אֶל־שְׁאוֹל תּוּרָד אֶל־יַרְכְּתֵי־בוֹר.

57. One hastens to add that this manner of speaking does not imply that God was perceived to be absent or inaccessible. Since the tendency to accentuate God's ontological remoteness is a feature that the Septuagint shares with later proto-rabbinical and rabbinical literature, it is appropriate to hear a cautionary word from E.P. Sanders with regard to the earliest rabbinical literature. Cf. *Paul and Palestinian Judaism: A Comparison of Patterns of Religion* (London: SCM Press, 1977), p. 214: 'In 1915, Wicks had already noted the tendency of Christian theologians to find in postbiblical Jewish literature a picture of God as inaccessible, as well as the fact that "modern Jewish theologians take the gravest objection to the idea that this false notion of transcendence was ever held by their people". Wicks proceeded to show that such an idea can hardly be found in the apocalyptic and pseudepigraphic literature. Abelson had previously undertaken to establish that the Rabbinic use of *shekinah* and related terms indicates the Rabbis' view that God was immanent, not remote.'

58. Both LXX and TJ supply a particularized substitute for the pronoun, ὁ λαός μου and בֵּית יִשְׂרָאֵל respectively. Seeligmann, *LXX Version*, p. 97, speaks of 'the addition of a subject' in the LXX, though it is perhaps more likely that the LXX reflects a reading of וִישֻׁרוּן for וְהַשָּׁרוֹן.

59. לוֹ refers unambiguously to the Lord upon his throne.

Since מִמַּעַל does not mean κύκλος, and the two are never equated elsewhere in the LXX, this is almost certainly a conscious retouching.[60]

Properly Theological Ameliorative Translations in LXX Isaiah 56–66

Anti-Anthropomorphic Translations in LXX Isaiah 56-66
Renderings of God's 'face' and/or 'eyes'. Scholars sometimes discern anti-anthropomorphic intent in the translation of complex prepositions that use some form of פָּנִים or עֵינַיִם by Greek expressions that do not utilise πρόσωπον or ὀφθαλμός.[61] This approach has earned justified criticism. In fact, constructions like לִפְנֵי and בְּעֵינֵי might well have been perceived by many readers, writers and speakers of Hebrew as simple adverbs that said nothing at all about a 'face', rather than as anthropomorphisms.[62]

Nevertheless, LXX Isaiah does appear to display a modest *Tendenz* towards anti-anthropomorphism when a passage could be understood to refer to God's face, even if the average reader might not make such a connection. It may be that the Isaiah translator was especially sensitive to such *possibilities*, even if the scandal would not have presented itself to the minds of the majority of his readers.

Isaiah 57.16. In MT 57.16, God promises that his anger will not last forever. If it did, human suffering would prove terminal rather than redemptive: כִּי־רוּחַ מִלְּפָנַי יַעֲטוֹף וּנְשָׁמוֹת אֲנִי עָשִׂיתִי. The Hebrew expression is difficult, but nearly all scholars agree that the רוּחַ in question is the *human* spirit, which grows faint. The translator, however, seems to regard it as God's spirit, or at least that of a celestial being who goes out from God's presence: πνεῦμα γὰρ παρ' ἐμοῦ ἐξελεύσεται.[63]

---

60. Fritsch finds a conceptual parallel; cf. 'Concept of God', p. 166: 'Cf. I Kings 22.19 where the host of heaven is standing "by Him" or "above Him" (עָלָיו). The Greek translator leaves no doubt as to his interpretation of the preposition which he renders περι αυτον, 'around Him'.'

61. Cf., for example, Fritsch, 'Concept of God', pp. 155-69.

62. Cf. M.S. Hurwitz, 'The Septuagint of Isaiah 36-39 in Relation to that of 1-35, 40-66', *HUCA* 28 (1957), pp. 75-83 (76).

Similarly, see Tov, commenting on Num. 12.8 in *TCU*, p. 49: 'Although the translators generally felt free to literally render verses or words in which God is portrayed anthropomorphically, in the present instance, as in others, anthropomorphic expressions were avoided.'

63. In creating the unique equivalency, עָטַף = ἐξέρχεσθαι, the translator might

The MT contains the word מַלְפָנִי, which could easily have been under-stood as a targum-style circumlocution like the familiar...מִן קֳדָם. Indeed, such an understanding probably influenced the translator's comprehension of this verse. He brings this meaning to Greek expression as παρ' ἐμοῦ. This may suggest that even a 'targumistic' expression in the

possibly have thought of BDB I, *to turn aside, incline, bend.* Though cognates are attested in Syriac and Arabic, this lexeme occurs only once in the HB, at Job 23.9. KB combine this lexeme with BDB II, *to envelop oneself*; this meaning is understood in some of the rabbinic citations below. Though suggestive, these meanings still do not come very close to ἐξέρχεσθαι.

It may be that עָטַף has not been translated, rather its 'slot' has been filled with a word chosen *ad sensum*. This might have seemed reasonable once the translator had intuited that the spirit was a heavenly one. (Cf. the suggestively similar wording at Ezek. 30.9: יצאו מלאכים מלפני ביום ההוא / ἐν τῇ ἡμέρᾳ ἐκείνῃ ἐξελεύσονται ἄγγελοι; מלפני is omitted in the LXX.) In the HB, עָטַף far more frequently and quite consistently means 'to be feeble, faint' (BDB III).

Yet another alternative is probably to be preferred. Since a spirit is in view, the possibility that the translator read some form of עוּף suggests itself. In the nearly identical statements at 2 Sam. 22.11 and Ps. 18.11(LXX 17.11), the Lord rides on a cherub and flies (וַיֵּעַף) upon the wings of the wind (עַל־כַּנְפֵי־רוּחַ). Indeed, seraphs fly (עוּף) about the Lord's throne in Isa. 6.6, where עוּף is translated by πετaννύναι and the passive of ἀποστέλλειν, respectively. The latter shows that this translator is capable of a prosaic description (cf. ἐξέρχεσθαι in the verse at hand) of angelic movement.

This verse, together with the notion of the רוּחַ as something other than the divine Spirit, reverberates in rabbinic and early Christian literature. In the former, רוּחַ is generally understood as 'wind' (*Gen. R.* 24.4; *Lev. R.* 15.1.6.1) or as a reference to (unborn) human souls (*Yeb.* 62a, 63b, *'Abod. Zar.* 5a). Curiously, these references are linked to messianic hope. *Yeb.* 62a is representative: 'for R. Assi stated: The Son of David will not come before all the souls in Guf will have been disposed of, since, it is said, *For the spirit that unwrappeth itself is from Me*'; cf. also *Nid.* 13b.

The *Ascension of Isaiah* may take messianic speculation upon this verse one step further. It rehearses the earthly career of Jesus as anticipated in Isaiah's vision with these words, at 3.13: καὶ ὅτι δι' αὐτοῦ ἐφανερώθη ἡ ἐξέλευσις τοῦ ἀγαπητοῦ ἐκ τοῦ ἑβδόμου οὐρανοῦ καὶ ἡ μεταμόρφωσις αὐτοῦ...; P. Bettiolo *et al.* (eds.), *Ascensio Isaiae, Textus* (CChr, Series Apocryphorum, 7; Turnhout: Brepols, 1995), p. 143. Similar language (ἐξέρχεσθαι) is used of the procession of the Holy Spirit in the *Panarion* (or *adversus lxxx haereses*) of the fourth-century writer Ephiphanius Constantiensis (cited in G.W.H. Lampe, *A Patristic Greek Lexicon* [Oxford: Oxford University Press, 1961]). I am indebted to Professor William Horbury for pointing out to me the messianic use of this verse in postbiblical literature.

MT can present the translator with a challenge by referring to God's face.[64] When it does so, the offending matter is deftly excised.

The following verse is translated in a manner that suppresses any possibility of God's emotional vulnerability before human rebellion. MT Isa. 57.17 reads,

בַּעֲוֹן בִּצְעוֹ קָצַפְתִּי וְאַכֵּהוּ הַסְתֵּר וְאֶקְצֹף
וַיֵּלֶךְ שׁוֹבָב בְּדֶרֶךְ לִבּוֹ

> Because of the iniquity of his violent gain I was angry, and I struck him, hiding and being angry, but he kept returning to the way of his heart.

The Greek translation of this verse knows nothing of divine pique, nor of a God who responds to Israel's violent acquisitiveness by simply hiding.[65] δι' ἁμαρτίαν βραχύ τι ἐλύπησα αὐτὸν[66] καὶ ἐπάταξα αὐτὸν καὶ ἀπέστρεψα τὸ πρόσωπόν μου ἀπ' αὐτοῦ καὶ ἐλυπήθη καὶ ἐπορεύθη στυγνὸς ἐν ταῖς ὁδοῖς αὐτοῦ. With the first and third of the three underlined phrases, *God's anger* is transformed into *Israel's grief*. In the case of the second, the Lord's offended self-concealment is replaced by stock prophetic judicial vocabulary that speaks of God turning his face away from sinners.[67]

---

64. This example can only be utilized appropriately if it is viewed together with other examples of a modest bias in LXX Isaiah against the use of πρόσωπον and ὀφθαλμός for the corresponding Hebrew adverbial expressions when these refer to God. This bias is not present when such expressions do not refer to God, though it is not hard to find individual cases which run counter to either trend.

The translation of מִלִּפְנֵי across the whole of the LXX provides an example of this phenomenon. In the five examples where the reference is to humans, πρόσωπον occurs fully four times. Of the nine that refer to God, πρόσωπον appears only three times. Nevertheless, Gen. 23.4 and 23.8 indicate the perils of seeking a system. In those verses Abraham twice refers to his wish to bury his dead מִלְּפָנַי (out of my sight). The first is translated ἀπ' ἐμοῦ, the second ἀπὸ προσώπου μου.

65. The fact that הַסְתֵּר is a hiphil encourages one to look for an object.

66. It appears that the 3ms *persona* in question is Israel/Judah.

67. The standard vocabulary is הסתיר (אֶת) פְּנֵי and ἀποστρέφειν τὸ πρόσωπόν μου.

It is certainly not God's righteous indignation that troubles our translator, but rather the emotional suffering that this might be understood to imply. In 112 occurrences of -λυπ- lexemes in the LXX, God suffers the grief in only 2 (1 Esd. 1.22; Ezek. 16.43). This may imply a certain reservation about applying the terminology to the deity. More important, however, is the shifting of the grief from God (in the Hebrew) to the disobedient human beings whom God now afflicts (for formal parallels, cf. Mic. 6.3; Isa. 40.29).

It will be appreciated that the translator has actually *added* a reference to God's face where the MT has none. However, this is not a haphazard LXX plus that can only be explained as an accident. In the first place, there is reason to suspect that the notion of God absconding when confronted with Israel's rebellion was an infelicitous one to the translator's point of view. Not only is it the case that he is careful to avoid the slightest notion of God's victimization by human disobedience, but there is also a remarkable translation at 45.15 that may well contribute to this discussion. In that verse, God's inscrutability is explained on the Hebrew side in terms of *divine hiddenness*: אכן אתה אל מסתתר. On the Greek side, the same mystery is explained by *human ignorance*: σὺ γὰρ εἶ θεός καὶ οὐκ ἤδειμεν.[68]

In the second place, the additional LXX reference to God's face occurs in the safe form of a very frequent stock phrase for God's judicial action. The total effect, then, is to portray God as unemotionally judicial and Israel as grievously smitten by the divine response to her rebellion. It appears that the tendency of this translator to avoid renderings which speak of God's face can be cancelled out when such a translation makes it possible to negotiate an even more awkward obstacle.

Isaiah 59.15. It may be that the consanguinity of TJ and LXX at Isa. 59.15 evidences a theological amelioration with respect to God's eyes in both versions. In the MT, the Lord's notice of justice's absence is recorded by mentioning his eyes: וירא יהוה וירע בעיניו כי־אין משפט. The LXX negotiates this anthropomorphic expression by producing the more abstract phrase, καὶ οὐκ ἤρεσεν αὐτῷ. Targum Jonathan also moves in an abstract, less anthropomorphic direction: ובאיש קדמוהי.[69]

Some lexical observations appear to support the initial impression of Septuagintal exegesis. First, ἀρέσκειν occurs only here in LXX Isaiah, thus it is not a common way in which to indicate a positive evaluation.[70] Second, each of the four instances in Isaiah where something is described as good or evil in God's eyes is translated in a way that avoids mention of God's face.[71] Thus, ἀρέσκειν is but one member of

---

68. The translator may have exploited the consonants of אל in order to produce οὐκ.

69. '...and it was an evil before him.'

70. Made negative here by οὐκ.

71. In addition to 59.15; cf. 65.12; 66.4, where הרע בעיני = τὸ πονηρὸν ἐναντίον (ἐ)μοῦ; cf. especially 38.3, where Hezekiah reminds the Lord that he has

the translator's inventory of anti-anthropomorphic resources.

However, one must balance against this the observation that ἀρέσκειν occurs frequently elsewhere in the LXX without reference to God, sometimes to render a Hebrew expression that uses בעיני.[72] It seems that the use of ἀρέσκειν and ἀρεστός in LXX Isaiah would not suffice on its own to prove theological exegesis, but that—in the context of clearer anti-anthropomorphism elsewhere—such ameliorative exegesis is probably indicated at 38.3,[73] 59.15, 65.12 and 66.4.

Isaiah 63.16–64.3(4). This passage contains numerous 'correlative ameliorations' in addition to anti-anthropomorphic translations. The reader is referred to Chapter 5 for a discussion of 63.16-19(64.1) that includes reference to the rendering of מפניך as ἀπὸ σοῦ. Any notion that this translator means to stamp out all prepositional and/or adverbial reference to the face of God is belied by verses such as 64.1(2), where מפניך גוים ירגזו is represented by ἀπὸ προσώπου σου ἔθνη ταραχθήσονται.[74] Nevertheless, the allegedly ameliorative translation occurs again in 64.2(3).[75] In the light of the extensive exegetical reworking that 63.15–64.2(3) appears to have undergone, it is likely that the two instances where מפניך is glossed by ἀπὸ προσώπου σου are a reverential touch.[76]

---

done הטוב בעיניך = τὰ ἀρεστὰ ἐνώπιόν σου.

72. For example, Gen. 19.8, of the men of Sodom; Gen. 20.15, of Abraham; etc.

73. In 38.3, both לפניך and בעיניך = ἐνώπιόν σου. Hurwitz follows his teacher, H.M. Orlinsky, in doubting anti-anthropomorphic translation in LXX Isaiah. He explains it in this verse by recourse to the tenuous theory that a different translator is responsible for chs. 36–39. Cf. 'Isaiah 36–39', p. 82.

74. This difficulty is passed over in Fritsch's discussion of the מפניך occurrences just before and after this verse; cf. Chapter 5, note 76.

75. Some scholars suggest that ירדת מפניך הרים נזלו at 64.2(3) is a gloss from 63.19 (cf. BHS and Barthélemy, *Critique Textuelle*, II, p. 445). However, the LXX surely knew these words, as Barthélemy correctly—if partially—points out (p. 446): 'Il n'est pas exact que le *G omette ירדת.'

76. In 64.3(4), the Lord's incomparability is asserted in that only he 'acts in favour of the *one who waits for him*' (יעשה למחכה־לו). The LXX refers to 'your acts (deeds), which you perform *for those who await mercy*' (τὰ ἔργα σου ἃ ποιήσεις τοῖς ὑπομένουσιν ἔλεον). If the argument that this passage is translated in a way that has God perform his wonders while remaining in heaven is judged persuasive, then it is just possible that the unexpected LXX translation of this clause is meant to further such an effort.

Isaiah 65.15-17. For a treatment of references to the divine face and eyes in these verses, see below, 'LXX Isa. 65.16-17', pp. 141-44.

Renderings of God's Mouth and Nose

Isaiah 62.2. Zion is promised a new name in MT 62.2. Its divine origin is assured by the words אֲשֶׁר פִּי יהוה יִקֳבֶנּוּ (which the mouth of the Lord will specify), a phrase that shares the particular anthropomorphism of the more common prophetic sentence, כִּי פִּי יהוה דִּבֵּר. The translator omits the reference to God's mouth, instead describing this name as one ὃ ὁ κύριος ὀνομάσει αὐτό. The Hebraistic inclusion of αὐτό for the verbal suffix of יִקֳבֶנּוּ suggests that the translator is not merely indulging in free paraphrase. Were that the case, he would have omitted αὐτό, which is redundant in Greek, having been adequately represented by the relative pronoun ὅ.

On the grounds sketched out above, it seems more suitable to identify this as an anti-anthropomorphic translation that likely reveals some degree of intentionality. Such a conclusion is encouraged as well by the manner in which the translator handles similar references to God's mouth elsewhere. It must be noted, on the other hand, that in several of the other passages where reference to God's mouth is not translated, a purely orthographic explanation is made possible by the juxtaposition of פִּי and כִּי.

In the Greek Pentateuch there is a strong tendency to use στόμα when speaking of the mouth of a human being or animal, but to avoid this anthropomorphism when speaking of God. In the latter case, the Pentateuch strongly prefers φωνή, ῥῆμα and πρόσταγμα, in that order of frequency. The Septuagint Prophets and Writings do not share this strong inhibition, though even there λόγος stands in for פֶּה on three occasions and θυμός on another two.

When στόμα does occur for God's mouth in the LXX, it is frequently in cases where פֶּה occurs with a third singular suffix referring to God (פִּיו). This use of a suffix may make the reference to God less direct and more tolerable on that account, thus allowing the use of the straightforward στόμα. The Prophets and Writings depart from the Pentateuchal custom by using στόμα often, though many of these cases conform to the 'distancing' conditions that I have mentioned.

LXX Isaiah leans modestly in a direction followed only by Joshua (once). That is, on three of five opportunities, the Isaiah translator renders פִּי יהוה by κύριος, effectively removing the anthropomorphism.

This observation of mildly anti-anthropomorphic results may reduce the possibility that the readings at 34.16 and 40.5—where כִּי פִי appears— are due simply to haplography resulting from the orthographic similarity of the two words.[77]

If contextual exegesis appears more likely than orthographic accident in these 'difficult' cases of LXX Isaiah, it is all the more probable in the verse at hand (62.2), where אֲשֶׁר פִי presents no orthographic stumbling-stone that might have led to the non-translation of פִי. In the case of this anthropomorphism, as with others, it is reasonable to identify a *tendency* to excise the reference to human form, though the translator has no systematic *programme* for doing so.[78]

Isaiah 65.5. When in Isa. 65.5 the Lord says of the practitioners of aberrant cult, אֵלֶּה עָשָׁן בְּאַפִּי,[79] the translator produces οὗτος καπνὸς τοῦ θυμοῦ μου.[80] This rendering requires him to overlook two grammatical details: (a) he must deal with אֵלֶּה as though it were a singular demonstrative pronoun, a movement that runs counter to his strong tendency to pluralize; and (b) he must ignore *beth*, reading עָשָׁן אַפִּי[81] where MT has עָשָׁן בְּאַפִּי.

It is impossible to determine whether this exception to a strong translational preference and violation of grammatical norms was a conscious choice. It seems best to conclude that it represents at least the inability to conceive that this verse should speak of smoke *in the Lord's nose*. By translating אַף according to the derivative meaning 'wrath' rather than the anthropomorphic 'nose' and by rearranging the remaining details, the translator envisages God's judgment upon idolaters rather than their breath-taking ability to irritate the Lord himself.

Renderings of God's hand(s) and feet

Isaiah 59.1. The translator is willing to speak of God's hand, but— *prima facie*—not to sustain the assertion in MT 59.1 with regard to its alleged shortening. The LXX supplies μὴ οὐκ ἰσχύει ἡ χεὶρ κυρίου τοῦ σῶσαι; for the MT's הֵן לֹא־קָצְרָה יַד־יְהוָה מֵהוֹשִׁיעַ. The Greek phras-

---

77. So Fritsch, 'Concept of God', p. 158.

78. The intermittent nature of this tendency becomes evident in the light of 24.3, where the LXX has τὸ γὰρ στόμα κυρίου for the MT's יְהוָה דִבֶּר. Cf. Tov, *TCU*, pp. 62-63.

79. 'These are smoke in my nose (NRSV, 'nostrils').'

80. 'This is (a) smoke of my wrath.'

81. Alternatively, עָשָׁן.

ing remains unabashedly physical and anthropomorphic, though the translator may have considered it more permissible to speak of the *strength* of God's hand rather than its *length*.[82]

The non-systematic nature of the translator's anti-anthropomorphic tendency is evident in the parallel stich, where both the Hebrew and the Greek text speak without flinching of God's *ear* (not) *becoming heavy*. This very inconsistency is sometimes submitted as evidence that non-literal translations, such as the one at hand, do not represent theological exegesis at all. The more adequate explanation would appear to be one that provisionally accepts that there is theological exegesis in 59.1— and that clearer cases elsewhere help to validate this suspicion—but that does not suppose that such exegesis reflects the systematic policy of the translator.

A level of conscious choice with regard to the קצר/ἰσχύειν rendering at 59.1 may be indicated by the fact that the very same conversion occurs at 50.2, as Fritsch observes.[83] Nevertheless, the provisional nature of such a claim is underlined by the remarkable translation at Isa. 23.11. In a chapter where the translator's enthusiasm for -ισχυ- lexemes seems boundless,[84] the MT says of the Lord ידו נטה על־הים הרגיז ממלכות.[85] The translator presents us with an exceedingly ambiguous statement addressed to some second person: ἡ δὲ χείρ σου οὐκέτι ἰσχύει κατὰ θάλασσαν, ἡ παροξύνουσα βασιλεῖς. If this statement follows the MT in speaking of *the Lord's* hand, then it announces the turning of God's wrathful hand from the sea to some other object, perhaps Tyre. In the process, it strengthens the case for seeing ἡ χεὶρ ἰσχύει elsewhere as a piece of anti-anthropomorphic vocabulary.

However, it seems more likely that the translator speaks here of the weakening of some *national* hand, perhaps that of Tyre[86] or of Canaan.[87] If this is the case, then the demetaphorizing translation of acts

---

82. Or, in the still daring terms of the Greek question, its potential *weakness* rather than its potential *shortness*.

83. Cf. 'Concept of God', p. 167: 'In both (50.2 and 59.1) the translator paraphrases the Hebrew *in order to avoid the suggestion* that the Omnipotent's hand could be shortened... So also in Num. 11.23. See Fr 40' (emphasis added).

84. Cf. 23.4, מעוז הים = ἡ δὲ ἰσχὺς τῆς θαλάσσης; 23.8, where המעטירה appears to generate μὴ ἥσσων ἐστὶν ἢ οὐκ ἰσχύει; and 23.11, מעזניה = αὐτῆς τὴν ἰσχύν.

85. 'He has stretched out his hand over the sea. He has shaken kingdoms.'

86. So van der Kooij, *Oracle of Tyre*, pp. 65-66, 82-84.

87. Chapter 23 is an oracle against Tyre. But see the following, parallel, stich:

or characteristics of a hand by the verb ἰσχύειν is not employed uniquely with reference to God. Though it may serve anti-anthropomorphic ends at 59.1 and 50.2, this is not so obvious a conclusion as Fritsch supposed.[88]

Isaiah 60.13-14. In ch. 60 the omission in the LXX of a reference to God's feet in v. 13 might pass as an inadvertence were it not for a similar omission one verse later. The context of MT 60.13 is eschatological reversal:

כבוד הלבנון אליך יבוא ברוש תדהר ותאשור יחדו
לפאר מקום מקדשי ומקום רגלי אכבד

> The glory of Lebanon shall come to you, cypress, plane and pine together, to beautify the place of my sanctuary; and I will glorify the place of my feet.

The LXX omits the verse's final sentence:

> καὶ ἡ δόξα τοῦ Λιβάνου πρὸς σὲ ἥξει ἐν κυπαρίσσῳ καὶ πεύκῃ καὶ κέδρῳ ἅμα δοξάσαι τὸν τόπον τὸν ἅγιόν μου.

The repeated מקום(ו) provides some reason to suspect accidental omission by haplography, even if the presence of just one repeated word does not heartily endorse this explanation.[89] The details of 60.14 tilt the discussion in favour of a premeditated omission, though this is not the necessary conclusion. Zion—where, significantly, the Lord lives—continues to be an eschatological destination:

> κύριος σαβαωθ ἐνετείλατο περὶ Χανααν ἀπολέσαι αὐτῆς τὴν ἰσχύν. Seafaring Tarshish may also be a candidate.

88. One must take into account that the translator is willing to omit references to a hand for reasons that have nothing to do with anthropomorphic reference to God. Cf. 37.14, where Hezekiah receives Rabshekah's message מיד המלאכים/ παρὰ τῶν ἀγγέλων (similarly, 37.24: ביד עבדיך = ὅτι δι᾽ ἀγγέλων). Although the use of such instances as evidence against anti-anthropomorphism elsewhere is conditioned by the tendency of such adverbial expressions to lose concrete reference to their component parts (in this case, to a *hand*), they caution one against hasty conclusions about anti-anthropomorphism when a word like יד is not represented in the translated text.

89. Cf. Fritsch, 'Concept of God', p. 160: 'The whole phrase has been omitted in LXX, maybe by haplography. But this cannot be the explanation for the omission in (60.14)... The omission of (hands in 60.13 and feet in 60.14) is best explained by the anti-anthropomorphic tendencies of the translator.' Fritsch may overvalue the grounds for haplography, even as he refutes them. He appears not to notice that the reference in 60.14 is not to *God's* feet, but to those of *Jerusalem*.

וְהָלְכוּ אֵלַיִךְ שְׁחוֹחַ בְּנֵי מְעַנַּיִךְ וְהִשְׁתַּחֲווּ עַל־כַּפּוֹת רַגְלַיִךְ
כָּל־מְנַאֲצָיִךְ וְקָרְאוּ לָךְ עִיר יְהוָה צִיּוֹן קְדוֹשׁ יִשְׂרָאֵל

The sons of your oppressors shall come bending low to you, and they
shall bow down at the soles of your feet, and they shall call you 'the city
of the Lord', 'Zion of the Holy One of Israel'.

The LXX is once again silent about feet:

καὶ πορεύσονται πρὸς σὲ δεδοικότες υἱοὶ ταπεινωσάντων σε καὶ
παροξυνάντων σε καὶ κληθήσῃ πόλις κυρίου Σιων ἁγίου Ισραηλ.

This appears not to be an accidental omission.[90] Furthermore, the loss
in translation of consecutive statements about feet seems too much to be
attributed to coincidence. It could easily be classed as an anti-anthropomorphism were it not for the fact that the feet of 60.14 belong to Zion
rather than to God.

It is possible to imagine that the translator found such a show of
obeisance before Zion (i.e. bowing at the feet of her inhabitants) to be
offensive, since this is an action that is more commonly directed
towards the Lord. However, his nationalism would seem to argue
against such reserve. One suspects, rather, that the contextual references
to God, who inhabits Jerusalem, placed the *reader* in danger of reading
this anthropomorphic expression about Zion as a description of worship
of God himself. The feet, then, might have seemed like divine ones.
Indeed, the translator *himself* might have understood the expressions in
this way, for καὶ πορεύσονται πρὸς σε...καὶ παροξυνάντων σε
follows without pause upon δοξάσαι τὸν τόπον τὸν ἅγιόν μου,
which *is* a divine reference. Furthermore, his tendency—if he had read
the 2ms references as pertaining to Zion's human inhabitants—might
have been to provide *plural* pronouns.[91]

It seems, then, that at least the first omission at LXX Isa. 60.13-14—

---

90. The missing phrase corresponds to וְהִשְׁתַּחֲווּ עַל־כַּפּוֹת רַגְלַיִךְ (כָּל־מְנַאֲצָיִךְ).
Patterns of lexical equivalencies would suggest that παροξυνάντων σε
corresponds to (כָּל־)מְנַאֲצָיִךְ rather than to some mistaken reading of וְהִשְׁתַּחֲווּ (but
note that תוה = παροξύνειν in Ps. 77[78].41). Because this requires the omission
of כָּל־ (but not of מְנַאֲצָיִךְ, to which it is attached) and the borrowing of ו from
וְהִשְׁתַּחֲווּ (= the second καί of the verse), it appears to be a collapsing together of
two phrases rather than a discrete omission of just one.
91. Elsewhere he very frequently *pluralizes* collective singulars and often
demetaphorizes such images.

and possibly both—are best to be understood as true anti-anthropo-morphisms. It remains an open question as to whether this is a cautious move of the translator in order to avoid a reading of the MT against its intended sense, or whether the translator himself has accepted such a reading (of the feet as belonging to God) and then attempted to avert the potential damage to religious sensitivities.

Other Anti-anthropomorphic Translations
Isaiah 60.16. When in MT Isa. 60.16 the Lord identifies himself as אֲבִיר יַעֲקֹב, the LXX provides the prosaic θεὸς Ισραηλ. This is probably a conscious amelioration. Elsewhere the LXX renderings of אֲבִיר utilize mainly the imagery of animals (ταῦρος, ἵππος) and of human warriors. Fritsch concluded from these observations that the Isaiah translator supplied θεός for אֲבִיר in order to avoid the implicit reference to a bull.[92] Olofsson, however, points out in disputing Fritsch that 'אֲבִיר probably means 'strong' and it is so understood by the LXX translators. Frequently, however, *the reference rather than the meaning of the term is reflected in LXX.'*[93]

Olofsson wonders whether the frequent expression אלהי יעקב together with the use of אֲבִיר in parallel to יהוה has made the term virtually synonymous with θεός in the minds of the Psalms and Isaiah translators.[94] Though Olofsson does not say so, this is plausible in that

92. Cf. Fritsch, 'Concept of God', pp. 161-62: 'Three times in Isaiah God is called אֲבִיר יִשְׂרָאֵל "the Mighty One of Israel" [or Jacob] (1.24, 49.26, 60.16). This designation is taken from Gen. 49.24, where it occurs for the first time in Scripture. It is also foundin (sic) Ps. 132.2, 5. It is suspected thatthe (sic) Masoretes changed the pointing of this term to avoid association with the word אַבִּיר, which means "bull". In the three Isaiah passages the term is not translated literally in the Greek.'

93. *God Is my Rock*, p. 93 (emphasis added). Cf. also the standard lexica. The author continues, 'Thus ταῦρος is a common rendering when the word relates to bulls and once, when it refers to human beings, it is translated by "angels".' Olofsson's discussion of the use of אֲבִיר as a divine name (pp. 87-94) is heavily dependent upon the work of Seeligmann when it deals with the one case in Isaiah. Seeligmann's cautionary words about not hurrying to identify any one of the translator's 'inconsistencies' as evidence of theological exegesis are well advised, though they did not restrain Seeligmann himself from doing so with enthusiasm. However, such wisdom can produce a kind of paralysis in the careful interpreter (Olofsson is among the most virtuously cautious). It can also mask the fact that the Isaiah translator exhibits a number of noteworthy *consistencies*, one of which is his tendency to manipulate the text in order to speak respectfully of God.

94. אֲבִיר = θεός in Ps. 132(131).2, 5 and Isa. 60.16.

it would include אביר (as perhaps צור) with יהוה and אלהים as divine
terminology for which the Isaiah translator appears to find κύριος and
θεός to be interchangeable renderings.[95]

Olofsson concludes that it is 'not probable that theological exegesis
accounts for the rendering of אביר as a designation of God'.[96] His
methodology places the burden of proof upon the shoulders of those
who posit theological exegesis in any given case. His criteria for accepting the probability of theological exegesis seem to reduce in practice to
the impossibility of providing *any other explanation* for the Greek
rendering at hand. This may be an unreasonably rigorous demand.

Whilst Olofsson is correct in dismissing claims (e.g. those of Erwin
and Fritsch) that theological exegesis is *obvious* in a verse like 60.16,
the evidence would appear to shift the burden of proof to the shoulders
of those who would deny the possibility that theology has influenced
the Greek rendering (e.g. Olofsson). First, אביר is not transparently a
term for the deity in the way in which יהוה and אלהים manifestly are.
Second, there is considerable evidence in LXX Isaiah to suggest that this
translator attempts always to speak reverently of God. Third, this latter
tendency also appears in contemporary and later Jewish literature, as a
global comparison of LXX Isaiah with TJ of Isaiah displays. Thus, strict
methodological scepticism with regard to its appearance in the
Septuagint is unwarranted. Fourth, the particular expression at hand—
אביר—has already been associated in the HB and indeed in Isaiah with
human warriors and with animals. It is understandable that the translator might predicate this same term of God only with reluctance. Fifth,
Olofsson's argument that the 'frequent use of the similar phrase 'the
God of Jacob' may have influenced the translator to see אביר יעקב as

---

95. Such an argument might be strengthened by a remarkable translation at
5.13, where the text reads: 'Therefore my people have been exiled' מבלי דעת. The
following clause is a verbless sentence: וכבודו מתי רעב, 'And its (i.e. 'their')
glory (has become) men of famine.' Israel's כבוד is normally understood as her
nobility (so NRSV, 'their nobles') or her amassed population (so *Tanakh*, 'Its
multitude'). However, the LXX appears to have read it with the prior clause as the
(divine) object of דעת: διὰ τὸ μὴ εἰδέναι αὐτοὺς τὸν κύριον. If this analysis is
correct, then the translator has read כבודו as a metaphor for God, perhaps even as a
regal title ('his glory' ≈ 'his majesty'?). For the purpose of our argument, the
striking fact is that he has translated this striking expression by means of the
unremarkable τὸν κύριον.
96. *God Is my Rock*, p. 94.

a virtually identical expression is slightly weakened by the observation that the translator at 60.16 produces θεὸς Ισραηλ rather than θεὸς Ιακωβ.[97]

In the light of these observations, it seems better to conclude that the rendering of אביר יעקב by θεὸς Ισραηλ at LXX Isa. 60.16 is *probably* an ameliorative reading that attempts to avoid speaking of God in the anthropomorphic imagery of the human warrior. The use of the term to speak of animals—not least importantly in the light of Jacob/Israel's religious history, *of a bull*—may also have been a contributing element.

Isaiah 62.11–63.4; 63.10. For the possible evasion of a portrayal of God in terms of *human locomotion* at 62.11–63.1, see Chapter 3, 'Isaiah 62.8-11', p. 67-69. Reconfiguration of the actions of the principal figure in this passage[98] recurs. LXX 63.3, for example, appears to offer several ameliorations. The MT reads:

פורה דרכתי לבדי ומעמים אין־איש אתי
ואדרכם באפי וארמסם בחמתי
ויז נצחם על־בגדי וכל־מלבושי אגאלתי

> I have trodden the wine press alone, and from the peoples no one was with me; I trod on them in my anger and trampled them in my wrath; their juice spattered on my garments and I stained[99] all my clothing (in it).

Remarkable deviations occur in the LXX:

> πλήρης καταπεπατημένης; καὶ τῶν ἐθνῶν οὐκ ἔστιν ἀνὴρ μετ᾽ ἐμου, καὶ κατεπάτησα αὐτοὺς ἐν θυμῷ καὶ κατέθλασα αὐτοὺς ὡς γῆν καὶ κατήγαγον τὸ αἷμα αὐτῶν εἰς γῆν.

---

97. אלהי ישראל is of course even more frequent than אלהי יעקב. However, Olofsson's argument for the virtual identity of אביר יעקב and אלהי יעקב gives special attention to his assertion that יעקב אביר is in itself a variant of the title אלהי יעקב or אל יעקב 'the God of Jacob', one of the ancient Israelite divine names, which is probably a designation from northern Israel' (*God Is my Rock*, p. 90).

98. One is aware that identity of the *persona* who is normally understood as a Divine Warrior in this passage is not unambiguous, and that the tradents of all kinds may have considered him to be someone other than God. For the purpose of the present discussion, however, I assume the more consensual view that this figure is God as Divine Warrior.

99. Alternatively, 'I defiled...'

(Why are you) full of what has been trodden down?[100] Even from the nations no one was with me, and I trod them down in anger, and I crushed them as soil, and I brought their blood down to the ground.

First, אַפִּי—spoken by God—is slightly distanced from him by means of the depersonalized phrase ἐν θυμῷ. Second, divine wrath is expressed in the LXX only once rather than twice. The second Hebrew reference—בחמתי—is replaced by ὡς γῆν. Third, in the LXX God is allowed to execute his violent sentence but he is not stained or defiled by its bloodiness. The two phrases that stain or defile him are replaced by a single sanitized clause, leaving God—so to speak—high and dry: ויז נצחם על־בגדי and וכל־מלבושי אגאלתי are jointly serviced by καὶ κατήγαγον τὸ αἷμα αὐτῶν εἰς γῆν. This Greek sentence appears verbatim in 63.6, where it is authorized by the MT (≈ *Vorlage*).

It appears that the translator has exploited the lexical and formal similarities between 63.3 and 63.6 in order to create an 'acceptable' rendering of the earlier verse.[101] The general picture of 63.6—where the victims' 'juice' *goes down* rather than *up on to God's garments*—overwhelms and replaces the anthropomorphic features of 63.3.

The translator's liberties are exercised at 63.4 as well, in a verse that sets the violence of 63.3 in the context of God's retributive justice:

כי יום נקם בלבי ושנת גאולי באה

For there is a day of vengeance in my heart, and the year of my redemption has come.[102]

The LXX reads:

ἡμέρα γὰρ ἀνταποδόσεως ἐπῆλθεν αὐτοῖς, καὶ ἐνιαυτὸς λυτρώσεως πάρεστι.

---

100. For consistency, I quote and translate according to the (interrogative) punctuation of Ziegler's *editio, pace* Rahlfs, Ottley and Brenton. In this scheme, the Lord's reply to the question that began in 63.1 begins with the words καὶ τῶν ἐθνῶν... Cf., respectively, Ziegler, *editio*, p. 353; A. Rahlfs, *Septuaginta: Idest Vetus Testamentum graece iuxta LXX interpretes, edidit Alfred Rahlfs* (Stuttgart: Deutsche Bibelgesellschaft Stuttgart, 1935, 1979), p. 650; Ottley, *Isaiah*, I, p. 311; and Brenton, *Septuagint*; p. 897.

101. 63.6 is remarkably similar to 63.3 (ואשכרם בחמתי / ואבוס עמים באפי / ואוריד לארץ נצחם/) in three respects: (a) it has two 1cs verbs for trampling/crushing; (b) each of these is qualified by one of the same two adverbial references to anger which occur in 63.3; (c) נצחם is common to both verses.

102. Alternatively, 'of my ransomed ones...'

In the position of בלבי, ἐπῆλθεν αὐτοῖς appears. The LXX effectively removes the reference to God's heart[103] and clarifies that his vengeance is directed *against the nations*. Though the MT makes this point implicitly, since the nations appear in the prior verse, the LXX makes it explicit.

The anti-anthropomorphic bias that seems to orient the translation of these verses may also be present in 63.10, though here one is limited merely to pointing out the possibility without forming firm conclusions. When Israel responded to the Lord's mercy by rebelling against him, he became their adversary: ויהפך להם לאויב. It is possible either that this description of God's enmity with Israel seemed too direct, or that its expression in terms of *an enemy* seemed too anthropomorphic. The translator produces the more abstract statement καὶ ἐστράφη αὐτοῖς εἰς ἔχθραν.[104]

It is important to observe that the following clause is translated in a straightforward manner that avoids neither of the potential irritations that I have mentioned: נלחם־בם הוא = καὶ αὐτὸς ἐπολέμησεν αὐτούς. Any inclination to discern theological reservations in this verse must also be balanced against the translation of 63.8. In that verse, ויהי להם למושיע—which is both *formally similar* and *semantically antithetical* to the phrase in question—is translated by καὶ ἐγένετο αὐτοῖς εἰς σωτηρίαν. Since the Isaiah translator apparently does not hesitate to call God σωτήρ,[105] one ought not to adduce theological reasons for the abstract translation of that sentence. Its formal parallel at 63.10 may have been translated as it has simply by attraction to it.

Thus, LXX 63.10 should not be entered as primary evidence in

103. Cf. Fritsch, 'Concept of God', pp. 160-61: 'The "heart" of God, found only once in Isaiah, is not translated in the Greek text...Ot 375 suggests that the Greek might have read בא להם for בלבי. In any case, the anthropomorphism has been averted in LXX.'

104. TJ distances the statement from God himself in its customary manner: ואתהפיך לבעיל דבב (passive) מימריה (Stenning: להון). However, like the MT, it renders the subsequent phrase literally. Cf. J.F. Stenning, *The Targum of Isaiah* (Oxford: Oxford University Press, 1949), p. 211.

It is just possible that the LXX translator has read the ה of הוא with (ה)לאויב to produce εἰς ἔχθραν καὶ, though this creates problems with the generation of αὐτός. איבה (the translator would need to read וי of MT לאויב as a single yod) would more naturally produce the abstract ἔχθρα (as in Gen. 3.15; Num. 35.22; Ezra 35.5).

105. Cf. Isa. 12.2; 17.10; 45.15; 45.21; 62.11.

support of the translator's anti-anthropomorphic tendency. It may play a small supporting role.

Isaiah 63.15. Scholars have noted two possible anti-anthropomorphisms in LXX 63.15 in addition to the suggestion of divine inactivity that is implicit in the lament form.[106] First, reference to God's inward parts as the locus of compassionate feeling (המון מעיך) is translated by reference to the corresponding *sentiment*: τὸ πλῆθος τοῦ ἐλέους σου.[107] This equivalency does not occur elsewhere in the LXX. It is worth noting that the Greek translator accomplishes his circumlocution by exploiting Greek words that appear elsewhere in the context, a technique that is not limited to this verse.[108]

Second, Fritsch considers the translation of הבט משמים by ἐπίστ–ρεψον ἐκ τοῦ οὐρανοῦ to be anti-anthropomorphic. It may be that in the translator's mind 'turning' is a less alien concept for the deity than 'looking'. However, this is difficult to prove. It would be a merely speculative conclusion were it not for the suggestive precedent which the translator establishes elsewhere when God 'looks'.[109]

106. Cf. J. Skinner, *The Book of the Prophet Isaiah, XL–LXVI* (The Cambridge Bible for Schools and Colleges; Cambridge: Cambridge University Press, 1917), p. 223: 'By a natural anthropomorphism the O.T. attributes the prevalence of evil on the earth to a suspension of Jehovah's watchfulness.'

107. Cf. Fritsch, 'Concept of God', p. 161: 'The "inward parts, compassion" of God is translated in the figurative sense in the Greek, thus eliminating the physical concept in the Hebrew word.'

108. In 63.7, חסדי = τὸν ἔλεον, כרחמיו = κατὰ τὸ ἔλεος αὐτοῦ and ורב חסדיו = καὶ κατὰ τὸ πλῆθος τῆς δικαιοσύνης. In 63.15, המון מעיך = τὸ πλῆθος τοῦ ἐλέους σου.

109. Fischer thinks ἐπίστρεψον was originally επιβλεψον, as in Q and several miniscules; cf. *Schrift*, 13. This is possible. However, the influence of the '2 = 1' phenomenon (cf. 63.17, שוב = ἐπίστρεψον) and the fact that נבט also generates ἐπιστρέφειν in Lamentations make the choice in Ziegler's *editio* seem defensible and probably better.

There is a chance that the הבט // ἐπίστρεψον equivalency is anti-anthropomorphic, if turning is less human than looking. TJ amends the second of the two verbs: וראה = ואתגלי. Cf. Fritsch, 'Concept of God', p. 164: 'It may be that the idea of God's 'looking' was purposely avoided here because the action was associated with a place, "from heaven". So Zi 172. In 64.8(9) the same Hebrew verb form is translated literally.' Ziegler practices the appropriate caution; cf. *Untersuchungen*, p. 172: 'viell. ist ἐπίστρ. absichtlich gewählt, um den Anthropomorphismus zu meiden, weil die örtliche Bestimmung angegeben ist: "aus dem

Isaiah 66.15. We have had occasion to observe that the much-noticed 'freedom' of this translator is not anarchic. Rather, a particular translation that appears to us to embody some libertine exegetical move will often—upon closer analysis—reveal some concrete textual feature that authorized or facilitated the translator's manoeuvre. Conservativism vis-à-vis the translator's *Vorlage* serves as counterpoise to his interpretative instincts.

Conversely, an LXX deviation from the MT (≈ *Vorlage*) that seems unremarkable and which could be attributed to recurrent translational patterns may offer a glimpse into the translator's theological mind. One wonders if this is not the case with Isa. 66.15a, where the anti-anthropomorphic preference that I have attempted to establish elsewhere may show its face, if meekly:

כִּי־הִנֵּה יְהוָה בָּאֵשׁ יָבוֹא וּכַסּוּפָה מַרְכְּבֹתָיו

For behold, the Lord shall come in fire,[110] and his chariots like a whirl-wind...

Ἰδοὺ γὰρ κύριος ὡς πῦρ ἥξει καὶ ὡς καταιγὶς τὰ ἅρματα αὐτου...

For behold, the Lord shall come as a fire, and his chariots as a whirlwind...

Two features in the description of the Lord's eschatological arrival deserve consideration. First, the translator renders בָאֵשׁ not by ἐν πυρί, but by ὡς πῦρ. That this alteration is not due to the opaqueness of the phrase בָאֵשׁ is evident from the following verse, where a syntactical re-shuffling produces ἐν γὰρ τῷ πυρί κυρίου κριθήσεται...from כִּי בָאֵשׁ יְהוָה נִשְׁפָּט.

It is possible to explain the small change of Isa. 66.15 without recourse to ideology. From the angle of orthography, one observes the ease with which בָאֵשׁ might be read as כָּאֵשׁ.[111] Furthermore, one must

---

Himmel"...Es ist aber möglich, daß der Übers. frei wiedergegeben hat, zumal "sich zuwenden" und "hinblicken" eng verwandt sind.'

110. Both אֵשׁ and סוּפָה have the article in this verse. Though our discussion of 66.15-16 will require us to be attentive to the difference between בָאֵשׁ and כָּאֵשׁ, the translations 'in fire' and 'a whirlwind' rather than 'in *the* fire' and 'like *the* whirlwind' reflect the use of the article in Hebrew with the elements of nature. Cf. GKC §126n.

111. Cf. also BHS apparatus: '2 Mss G כָּאֵשׁ.' It is of course possible that this evidence witnesses to an original כָּאֵשׁ. If my attribution of the LXX rendering to ideological concerns is correct, however, the Hebrew manuscripts cited in BHS

reckon with the very frequent levelling of parallel clauses that occurs in LXX Isaiah. It might simply be that וכסופה (= καὶ ὡς καταιγίς) has attracted the previous prepositional phrase in its direction so that both clauses now have ὡς.[112]

Such explanations do not *require* an ideological motivation. However, each of these conversions would *serve* an ideological motivation. For a translator who is concerned to maintain the distance between the divine and the human, it might well seem preferable to have the Lord come *as a fire* rather than *in (the) fire*.[113] The Lord's dignity might seem to be preserved by this one small step away from concreteness and towards abstraction. The conversion of metaphor to simile would certainly not be unique in early Jewish biblical interpretation.[114]

may demonstrate the same kind of movement within the Hebrew text tradition as is evidenced in the LXX.

112. Such lexical levelling is exceedingly common in LXX Isaiah. GKC §119i might seem to suggest the virtual synonymy of ב and כ, as found in this verse, by its comment upon the latter: 'Is 66[15] *with* (i.e. *like*) *fire.*' Nevertheless, as recent studies in Hebrew parallelism have tended to show, the variations between parallel lines of poetry *are* variations. They exist for a reason and can seldom be dissolved into complete identity. Cf., for example, the discussion on pp. 27-28 of A. Berlin, *The Dynamics of Biblical Parallelism* (Bloomington, IN: Indiana University Press, 1985). *Contra* this post-Lowthian understanding of parallelism, the LXX of this verse has made ב and כ identical.

113. The traditional grammatical category of ב *essentiae*—in this case 'consisting of fire'—is another unwelcome reduction of the divine presence that the translator might have glimpsed in באש and then put down with his abstract, comparative translation.

With regard to the use of the comparative sense of the preposition כ to describe God and his accoutrements, one is reminded of the vision of Ezek. ch. 1. כ abounds in that chapter, perhaps to describe what the features of the vision *looked like*, without venturing to assert that such is *what they were*. Description by comparison reaches a kind of zenith in the last verse of the chapter: כמראה הקשת אשר יהיה בענן ביום הגשם כן מראה הנגה סביב הוא מראה דמות כבוד־יהוה = ὡς ὅρασις τόξου, ὅταν ᾖ ἐν τῇ νεφέλῃ ἐν ἡμέρᾳ ὑετοῦ, οὕτως ἡ ὅρασις τοῦ φέγγους κυκλόθεν· αὕτη ἡ ὅρασις ὁμοιώματος δόξης κυρίου.

114. Cf. *inter alia* K.J. Cathcart and R.P. Gordon on TJ of the Minor Prophets, *The Targum of the Minor Prophets: Translated, with a Critical Introduction, Apparatus, and Notes* (The Aramaic Bible, 14; Edinburgh: T. & T. Clark, 1989), p. 2: 'The dictates of simplicity and intelligibility are also responsible for *Tg.*'s habitual conversion of metaphors into similes...' On this phenomenon in the LXX, G. Gerleman (*Studies in the Septuagint. III. Proverbs* [Lund: C.W.K. Gleerup, 1956], p. 26) is representative: 'Unlike Hebrew with its orientally exuberant diction

The possibility of an ideological motivation for this translation may receive additional support from the translation of יבוא by ἥξει. Ἔρχεσθαι is by far the most common equivalent for בוא in the LXX. It appears to be largely synonymous with ἥκειν, the second most common LXX equivalent, since both appear in contexts which are virtually identical. In spite of this general synonymity, however, LXX Isaiah appears to display a distaste for using ἔρχεσθαι of God. Perhaps this verb came too near to connoting a means of (human) locomotion. [115]

The stubborn survival of anthropomorphisms, even in proximity to this verse,[116] need not obviate the possibility of an anti-anthropomorphic turn at this point. According to the description of this translator's technique that I have attempted to establish, his is neither a consistent nor a revolutionary reworking of his text. Rather, he will move a text in one of several directions *when the features of that text*

Greek prose is very restrained in its use of metaphors. A metaphor, while quite natural and proper in Hebrew, will become shocking when clothed in Greek garb, standing out with an almost brutal sharpness. A Greek translator may, of course, transpose in a quite mechanical way the Hebrew metaphors into Greek. But any keenness to Greek style will cause him to moderate or even weed out the metaphors of his original... It is noticeable that the (Proverbs) translator, while frankly accepting even very bold similes, is very cautious as regards metaphorical speech.'

115. Simple or prefixed ἔρχεσθαι renders qal בוא 53 times in LXX Isaiah. Ἥκειν provides this service 30 times, with another 16 occurrences of בוא translated by 10 other lexemes (and 2 non-translations).

However, when God is the subject of בוא—whether as אלהים, יהוה, or an equivalent metaphor—the preferences reverse. Such passages reveal an apparent aversion (though not an absolute one) towards ἔρχεσθαι. In 3.14, יהוה...יבוא = κύριος ἥξει; 19.1, ובא...יהוה = κύριος ἥξει; 35.4, אלהיכם...יבוא = ὁ θεὸς ἡμῶν...ἥξει; 59.19, יבוא = ἥξει; 59.20, ובא = καὶ ἥξει; 60.1(?), בא אורך (אורך // וכבוד יהוה) = ἥκει; 62.11(?), יבא ישעך (ישעך is followed by הנה שכרו) = ὁ σωτὴρ παραγίνεται; and 66.15, יהוה...יבוא = κύριος ἥξει. On the other side, 40.10, אדני יהוה...יבוא = κύριος ἔρχεται; 50.2, באתי = ἦλθον; and 66.18, באה = ἔρχομαι.

In sum, when the deity is the subject of בוא, ἔρχεσθαι cedes its pre-eminence as the translation of choice. It occurs nearly twice as often as its nearest competitor when all occurrences of qal בוא are analysed. When God is the subject of these, it occurs less than half as frequently as ἥκειν.

The evidence is not conclusive, not least because ἔρχεσθαι occurs of God in 66.18. However, the patterns are suggestive of a *tendency*, though not of a *policy*.

116. Cf., for example, 66.14: יד־יהוה = ἡ χεὶρ κυρίου.

allow him to do so without great violence. The Hebrew of Isa. 66.15 provides the necessary elements for accomplishing this.

Anti-anthropopathic Translations in LXX Isaiah 56–66

Isaiah 59.2. The MT follows up the assertion at 59.1 that the Lord's hand has not become too short to save by stating one verse later that human sin has hidden God's face from its perpetrators. This has resulted in God's deafness to their pleas. The words *to their pleas*, however, reflect a reading which derives from the context. The Hebrew sentence itself fails to provide such limitations to this loss of hearing. MT 59.2 reads:

כי אם־עונתיכם היו מבדלים בינכם לבין אלהיכם
וחטאותיכם הסתירו פנים[117] מכם משמוע

> Rather, your iniquities have been barriers between you and your God,
> and your sins have hidden (his) face from you so that he does not hear.

The MT *allows* for the perception that God has been forced into idle passivity, though it is worth repeating that this is hardly the picture that the Hebrew text *requires* of its reader's mind.[118] The actual intention of MT 59.2 seems much closer to a recent description of Hos. 5.15, a verse that has the Lord returning to his place until Ephraim and Judah acknowledge their guilt and seek his face:

---

117. The phrase הסתירו פנים seems odd, since it does not specify to whom the face belongs. BHS notices that the versions add a 3ms suffix and suggests that one read פניו. But cf. Westermann, *Jesaja*, p. 275: 'Es ist aber möglich, daß *pānīm* hier schon wie ein *terminus technicus* für Gottesgegenwart gebraucht wird.' Cf. also O.C. Whitehouse, *Isaiah XL–LXVI* (The Century Bible; Edinburgh: T. & T. Clark, 1905), p. 271 n. 1: 'In the original not "*His* face" but simply "face," as though it were a personal designation of Yahweh... We seem to have a movement—though a nascent tendency only—towards the hypostases of later Judaism (*mêmrâ*, *shechînah*, &c.).'

118. In fact, the burden of the oracle in ch. 65 is to persuade that God is *not* impotent or passive. However, the manner in which this is asserted ('your sins have hidden his face') might have been felt by a later reader to encourage the very idea it was intended to refute. Cf. P.A. Smith, *Rhetoric and Redaction in Trito-Isaiah: The Structure, Growth and Authorship of Isaiah 56–66* (VTSup, 62; Leiden: E.J. Brill, 1995), p. 115: '...the issues of God's ability to hear or to act are clearly implied in the question quoted at 58.3a, a question arising from a situation in which the people think that they have done what they ought, so that the problem must be with God. This is strongly denied by the poet.'

This withdrawal by Yahweh *forms part of his punitive action*; withdrawn, *yet remaining totally in control of events*, he awaits a response from his people. The inexorable doom has been set in motion; behind its workings there lay its cause: the complete rupture of Yahweh's relationship with his people' (emphases added).[119]

The LXX removes any suggestion that sin has the power to turn the divine face. It also transforms a divine deafness that sin has imposed upon God into an implicit divine decision *not to show mercy*:

ἀλλὰ τὰ ἁμαρτήματα ὑμῶν διιστῶσιν ἀνὰ μέσον ὑμῶν καὶ τοῦ θεοῦ καὶ <u>διὰ τὰς ἁμαρτίας ὑμῶν</u> ἀπέστρεψεν τὸ πρόσωπον αὐτοῦ ἀφ' ὑμῶν <u>τοῦ μὴ ἐλεῆσαι</u>.

But your sins stand between you and God, and on account of your sins he has turned his face from you in order not to show mercy.

In the Greek text, God has become an active judge rather than a passive deity who suffers alienation from his people because of sin's active force upon him. The translator accomplishes this by converting the people's sins to the *occasion* of God's judicial turning by means of the inserted preposition διά. This allows him to make God the subject of הסתירו[120] (now singularized as ἀπέστρεψεν), a verb that has now become one member of a stock phrase for divine judicial turning.[121]

119. A.A. Macintosh, *Hosea* (ICC; Edinburgh: T. & T. Clark, 1997), pp. lxviii-lxix.

120. In the light of the graphic similarity of waw and yod in this period—as well as the phenomenon by which יהוה is occasionally abbreviated as י—one wonders whether this conversion might have been facilitated by the possibility of reading הסתיר י פנים. These would be the sort of facilitating elements to which Koenig refers when he observes that, 'Ce qui importait, comme nous l'avons souvent observé, ce n'était pas tant *le degré* de ressemblance formelle des mots mis en relation par la spéculation verbale, c'était le principe de leur participation réciproque, du fait de la ressemblance formelle.' Cf. *L'herméneutique analogique*, p. 371.

Though such facilitating elements might have played a corollary role, they are not strictly necessary. The Greek phrase that the translator uses is common enough, and a passage like Isa. 8.16-18 would have provided a sturdy conceptual parallel.

121. This expression has a distinguished biblical pedigree in both Hebrew and Greek. The HB and the LXX reserve it almost exclusively for the divine retreat from communion with (usually sinful) human beings. In the LXX, a special vocabulary distinguishes those occurrences of the verb סתר that speak of a hiding of the face—usually in the Hebrew Bible an act of God—from those occurrences where something else is being hidden. For God's hiding of his face, only the iconoclastic

Having made God the principal actor, the translator next turns to the possibility allowed by the MT that God is rendered incapable of hearing. With uncharacteristic boldness, he glosses מִשְּׁמֹעַ by τοῦ μὴ ἐλεῆσαι, a pairing of two lexemes that are never brought together elsewhere in the Septuagint.[122]

translator of Job breaks this pattern (cf. 13.24 and 34.29, where the verb κρύπτω is employed). Everywhere else in the translated books of the LXX, הִסְתִיר (אֶת־)פָּנָיו is rendered by ἀποστρέφειν τὸν πρόσωπον αὐτοῦ (cf. Deut. 31.17, 18, 20; Isa. 8.17; 54.8; 59.2; 64.6; Jer. 33(40).5; Ezek. 39.23, 24, 29; Mic. 3.4; Pss. 10.11(9.32); 13(12).2; 27(26).9; 30(29).8; 44(43).25; 51(50).11; 69(68).18; 88(87).15; 102(101).3; 104(103).29; and 143(142).7. Cf. also Exod. 3.6, where the same Hebrew phrase and Greek translation is used of Moses, and Isa. 50.6, where the subject is the Lord's servant.

That this translation is not merely a function of the hiphil is proven by the unanimous LXX pattern of translating hiphil סתר, when the object is not a face, by words other than ἀποστρέφειν. Cf. Isa. 49.2, Pss. 17(16).8, 27(26).9, 64(63).3, σκεπάζειν; Job 14.13, Prov. 25.2, 2 Chron. 22.11, κρύπτειν; Jer. 36(43)26, Ps. 31 (30).21, κατακρύπτειν; Ps. 119(118).19, ἀποκρύπτειν; and Job 3.10, ἀπαλάσσω.

Curiously, the translator of Isaiah takes an unexpected path at two other points where God might seem to be altogether hidden. In 45.15, אָכֵן אַתָּה אֵל מִסְתַּתֵּר ('Truly, you are a God who hides himself...) is translated by σὺ γὰρ εἶ θεός καὶ οὐκ ἤδειμεν ('For you are God, [but] we did not know [it]'). In 57.17, בַּעֲוֹן בִּצְעוֹ קָצַפְתִּי וְאַכֵּהוּ הַסְתֵּר וְאֶקְצֹף ('Because of the wickedness of [their] covetousness, I became angry and I struck [them], hiding and being angry...') cedes to the less radical δι᾽ ἁμαρτίαν βραχύ τι ἐλύπησα αὐτὸν καὶ ἐπάταξα αὐτὸν καὶ ἀπέστρεψα τὸ πρόσωπόν μου ἀπ᾽ αὐτοῦ καὶ ἐλυπήθη ('On account of sin, I grieved him for a little while and I struck him and I turned my face from him and he was grieved...'). In the LXX the grief is all of the people, not of God, and the divine activity is judicial punishment, not enraged and grieving flight.

122. Seeligmann offers the suggestion that the translator knows a verb שׁמם that is synonymous with חמל (= ἐλεεῖν) and that was read in place of MT מִשְּׁמֹעַ; cf. 'מחקרים בתולדות נוסחת המקרא' ('Researches into the Criticism of the Masoretic Text of the Bible' (Chicago: University of Chicago Press, 1961), § 391 *Tarbiz* 25 [1955–56], pp. 118-39 (130-31). Although this possibility is intriguing, it seems more likely that the explanation lies instead along the lines sketched out above. If so, it may be that rendering of מִשְּׁמֹעַ by τοῦ μὴ ἐλεῆσαι has moved the rhetoric from that of *result* to that of *purpose*. The latter would be more amenable to any implicit claim that God remains in control. In the period of the Greek language with which we are dealing, however, the lines drawn between result, consecution and purpose are thin ones (a linguistic development which BDF dare to link to 'Jewish teleology'; R.W. Funk, *A Greek Grammar of the New Testament and Other Early Christian Literature: F. Blass and A. Debrunner* [a translation and revision of the ninth-tenth German edition incorporating supplementary notes of A. Debrunner;

Thus, in a transformation which begins by removing anthropopathic vulnerability to sin's alienation (ἀπέστρεψεν τὸ πρόσωπον), one finds as well an anti-anthropomorphic refusal to speak of God *not* hearing.[123] This is carried out by means of a second evasion of divine vulnerability: rather than suffer the cutting off of his people's voice from his ears, God acts *in order not to show mercy*.

The LXX translator appears once more not to be the only tradent who is perturbed by the anthropopathic qualities of this text. Targum Jonathan has a reading that is remarkably similar to the Septuagint of this verse, though distinct enough to suggest that its similarities are best explained as independent expressions of the same kinds of religious sensitivities. In אלהין חוביכון הוו מפרשין ביניכון לבין אלהכון וחטאיכון גרמו לסלקא אפי שכינתי מנכון מלקבלא צלותכון,[124] the *meturgeman* matches the Greek translator by reducing sin to the occasion or cause[125] of *God's* removal of his presence.[126] Similarly, the MT's משמוע is made concrete in TJ: *so as not to accept your prayer.*[127]

Chicago: University of Chicago Press, 1961], §391[5]). Cf. also BDF §391, p. 400. The classical usage appears to favour purpose, cf. H.W. Smyth, *Greek Grammar* (rev. Gordon M. Messing; Cambridge, MA: Harvard University Press, 1956), §2032d-e, 2744(5). For the Hebrew construction, cf. GKC §114d, 119y; B.K. Waltke and M. O'Connor, *An Introduction to Biblical Hebrew Syntax* (Winona Lake, IN: Eisenbrauns, 1990), p. 36.2.2b.

123. This kind of avoidance of imperfect divine perception is the topic of the section 'The Avoidance of Incomplete Divine Perception', pp. 133-55, where this verse could just as appropriately be discussed.

124. Cf. Chilton, *Isaiah Targum*, p. 114: '[B]ut your *sins* have made a separation between you and your God, and your iniquities have *deserved the removal of the* face *of my Shekhinah* from you, so that he does not *accept your prayer*.' Cf. also Stenning, *Targum*, 196, '...and your sins have become the cause of his removing the presence of the Shekinah from you, that he should not receive your prayer.' For the view that the removal of the Shekinah and consequent cessation of the cult's effectiveness is linked in TJ to the destruction of the Temple in 70 CE, cf. van der Kooij, *Textzeugen*, p. 171.

125. גרם means *to be the* (indirect) *cause of*, or *to engender*, *a thing or action*. Cf. Jastrow, *Dictionary*, p. 270.

126. In TJ, *God's* removal of אפי שכונתי is implied by the syntax. The LXX is slightly more direct, for ἀπέστρεψεν τὸ πρόσωπον αὐτοῦ leaves nothing to ambiguity.

127. There is also anti-anthropo*morphic* concern with the mention of God's face. Cf. B.D. Chilton, *The Glory of Israel: The Theology and Provenience of the Isaiah Targum* (JSOTSup, 23 (Sheffield: JSOT Press, 1983), p. 69, who cites the use of שכינתי as evidence of 'avoidance of anthropomorphism'.

The effect of this complex restructuring is to indicate that the sins of the people have been the occasion of *God's* removal of his Shekinah from the people, so that the cult is rendered ineffective. Clearly, God is in undisputed control of the situation in TJ and LXX, *contra* what could be made of the MT.

Isaiah 59.16 and 63.5. LXX Isaiah occasionally executes an ameliorative reading by means of a careful choice of Greek vocabulary. This appears to be the case in 59.16 and 63.5, where the translator offers us two anti-anthropopathisms. Our translator's theology, it would seem, can embrace divine perception but resists that limitation of it which produces surprise and astonishment.[128]

The prophetic indictment of the people's declension in Isaiah 59 invokes God's view with these words at MT 59.16:

וירא כי־אין איש וישתומם כי אין מפגיע
ותושע לו זרעו וצדקתו היא סמכתהו

> And he saw that there was no one, and was appalled that there was no one who would intervene; and his (own) arm achieved salvation for him, and his righteousness itself upheld him.

The LXX is distinct in several respects that we will examine below:

καὶ εἶδε καὶ οὐκ ἦν ἀνήρ, καὶ κατενόησε καὶ οὐκ ἦν ὁ ἀντιλημψόμενος, καὶ ἠμύνατο αὐτοὺς τῷ βραχίονι αὐτοῦ καὶ τῇ ἐλεημοσύνῃ ἐστηρίσατο.

> And he looked and there was no man, and he perceived and there was no one who would lay hold, and he defended them with his arm and he established (them) in mercy.

I am assuming here that the translator's *Vorlage* ≈ MT. For an alternative view, cf. Whitehouse, *Isaiah*, II, p. 272 n. 1: 'On the other hand, the LXX (cod.Alex.) evidently had a somewhat different text in their original—"on account of your sins he has withdrawn *His* face from you so as not to *have compassion*" (וּמֵחַטּוֹתֵיכֶם הִסְתִּיר פָּנָיו מִכֶּם מֵרַחֵם, where apparently the מ of the opening word has dropped out through the same character that preceded it, viz. [in the LXX copy] of אֱלֹהִים).' Whitehouse assumes two fundamental presuppositions that this study does not: (a) a passive and literal scribe; and (b) a variant *Vorlage* as the primary (and automatic?) explanation of points where the LXX deviates from the MT.

128. Fritsch accurately observes that the major works on LXX Isaiah (Seeligmann, *LXX Version*; Ziegler, *Untersuchungen*; Fischer, *Schrift*; and Ottley, *Isaiah*) do not treat this theme. Cf. 'Concept of God', p. 156.

Dressed for battle, the Lord expresses similar sentiments in 63.5, this time in the first person:

ואביט ואין עזר ואשתומם ואין סומך

ותושע לי זרעי וחמתי היא סמכתני

And I looked, but there was no helper; and I was astonished, and there was no one to sustain (me); so my own arm brought me victory, and my wrath sustained me.

καὶ ἐπέβλεψα, καὶ οὐδεὶς βοηθός· καὶ προσενόησα, καὶ οὐθεὶς ἀντελαμβάνετο· καὶ ἐρρύσατο αὐτοὺς ὁ βραχίων μου, καὶ ὁ θυμός μου ἐπέστη.

And I looked, and there was no helper; and I observed, and no one took part. And my arm rescued them, and my anger stood back.

The verb שׁמם, which is common to both verses, appears 95 times in the Hebrew Bible. BDB lists as its principal meanings *to be desolated* and *to be appalled*.[129] The important lexical context for our purposes is more restrictive. Indeed, it is limited to those fewer than 40 instances in which the verb is *personal*, *active* and *intransitive*. In such passages—where a person *feels* appalled, desolated, or astonished—the Isaiah translator departs from LXX translational norms only in those two instances where God is the subject of such passion. Furthermore, he does so by moving his text in the direction of divine attention rather than divine amazement.

The LXX translators regularly use words of subjective astonishment[130] or injury[131] to render שׁמם inside the parameters I have delineated above. The notion common to all is that the subject has been taken aback, felt an intense revulsion, or suffered some particular injury.[132] It

129. Cf. also Seeligmann, 'Alteration and Adaptation', p. 206 n. 1: 'שׁמ"ם is a stereotyped phrase for astonishment at other people's calamities.'
130. θαυμάζειν, θαῦμα, ἐξιστάναι, ἐκπλήσσειν.
131. χηρεύειν, ἔρημος, ἐρημάζειν, σκυθωπάζειν, ἀναστρέφειν, στενάζειν, στυγνάζειν, ἐκλύειν.
132. Four texts utilize some form of θαυμάζειν (*to wonder, admire, say with astonishment*) or θαῦμα, *wonder, marvel, astonishment*; representative definitions are taken from LSJ. The reader is encouraged to consult the relevant entries in LSJ for full details.): Lev. 26.32; Job 17.8; 21.5; Dan. 4.16; χηρεύειν (*to be widowed, live in widowhood*) appears of Tamar in 2 Sam. 13.20. The LXX translators have recourse six times to ἐξιστάναι (*to be out of one's wits, be distraught; to be astonished, amazed; to lose consciousness*): 1 Kgs 9.8 (cf. 2 Chron. 7.21); Isa. 52.14; Jer 2.12; 18.16. There are three cases in which personal, active, and

is clear both from LXX usage and on wider lexicographical grounds that the personal, active and intransitive use of שׁמם can normally be expected to represent some personal crisis for the subject. Thus, the two instances where the Greek translator of Isaiah assigns a far different meaning to the word are remarkable. They are also probably indicative of an ideologically motivated alteration of the text.

We turn now to a closer analysis of these two passages. In 59.16, κατανοεῖν translates שׁמם, which is predicated of the Lord. Κατανοεῖν[133] is not semantically contiguous with notions of surprise, astonishment or dismay. At most, it might be held to admit some element of novelty or surprise when it means *to learn* or *to apprehend*. However, this does not come near to the normal meaning of שׁמם.

What is more, the translator has applied a syntactical touch to the sentence that is not at all characteristic of his style. Both verbs of perception—וַיַּרְא and וַיִּשְׁתּוֹמֵם—have lost their content in the LXX. We do not find καὶ εἶδε ὅτι and καὶ κατενόησε ὅτι, as we might have expected. Rather, the translator has removed the object from the verb of

___

intransitive שׁמם is translated by ἔρημος (*desolate, lonely, solitary*) or ἐρημάζειν (*to be left lonely, go alone*): Isa. 54.1; Ezra. 9.3; 9.4. The translator of Jeremiah twice interprets שׁמם as a statement of embittered anger against ruined cities by rendering it with σκυθρωπάζειν (*to look angry or sullen, be of a bad countenance*): Jer. 19.8 (of Jerusalem; similarly, cf. 50[27].13, of Babylon; in 49(30).11, a parallel sentence is pronounced against Edom, but the clause containing שׁמ is left untranslated.). Ezekiel describes a reluctant prophet's emotional turmoil with the passive ἀναστρεφόμενος (ἀναστρέφειν = *to turn upside down*): Ezek. 3.15. In the Greek, the same prophet joins Bildad the Shuhite in expressing the troubled emotion of שׁמם by invoking its audible expression. Twice, שׁמם = στενάζειν (*to groan, sigh deeply*): Ezek. 26.16; Job 18.20. Still other texts highlight the *visible manifestation* of surprise, astonishment, injury or loss. Ezekiel provides three translations by στυγνάζειν (*to have a gloomy, lowering look*): 27.35; 28.19; and 32.10. The latter verse is admitted to the discussion because the translator has missed or chosen not to translate the transitive element of וַהֲשִׁמּוֹתִי (assuming that his *Vorlage* ≈ MT). In the process, he has changed the subject from the divine first person to עמים רבים. Thus, this occurrence of שׁמם is—for the Greek translator—personal, active, and intransitive. Possibly, this alteration has taken place under the influence of the two Ezekiel verses cited just prior to 32.10. Eccl. 7.16 offers yet another striking translation of שׁמם, by ἐκπλήσσειν (*to be panic-stricken, amazed, esp. by fear; to be astonished at* a thing). Finally, Dan. 8.27 translates hitpo. אֶשְׁתּוֹמֵם with ἐκλύειν (mid. *to be faint, to fail; to be unserviceable*).

133. *To observe well, understand, apprehend; to perceive, learn, consider; to be in one's right mind, in one's senses.*

perception. Καὶ κατενόησε καὶ οὐκ ἦν ὁ ἀντιλημψόμενος and its parallel sentence in the first line of the verse each appear to comprise *two* statements, rather than one.[134]

This could be seen as an almost archaizing nuance which resembles the manner in which the more literalistic LXX books present *waw copulative* when it introduces causal, temporal, final and other clauses within compound sentences.[135]

Curiously, though, the LXX translator normally does not translate so woodenly as to provide καὶ for such a *waw copulative*, much less for כִּי. The more economical explanation is that which posits an ideological manoeuvre comprised of two steps: First, the translator has substituted a Greek word of perception for a Hebrew verb of surprise, and, secondly, he has removed even the possibility of *unanticipated perception* in each of two parallel lines by syntactical rearrangement. He has separated the content of perception—the two...אֵין כִּי clauses—from their intended verb. Those clauses now become simple statements of fact about human (Judahite?) misery: καὶ εἶδε...καὶ οὐκ ἦν ἀνήρ...καὶ κατενόησε...καὶ οὐκ ἦν ὁ ἀντιλημψόμενος. We shall see shortly that he has not had to invent his materials for this second manoeuvre, but only to import them. The desired *waw copulative* will appear in 63.5, only to find its way back to this earlier verse.

It appears, then, that our translator has not only *softened* a potential blow to God's impassive sovereignty, one that the MT threatened to bring to bear during its condemnation of human evil and rebellion. Rather, he has *reversed* it by demonstrating that God in fact reigned with acute perception over this unholy fracas.

We turn now to Isa. 63.5, the second verse which has undergone a similar transformation.[136] It is possible that significant cross-fertilization

134. Cf. Ottley, *Isaiah*, I, p. 299, 'And he saw, and there was no man, and he perceived, and there was none that would take hold.'

135. Cf. GKC §§ 154-66. There exists the theoretical possibility that the *Vorlage* of LXX Isa. 59.16 twice had ו instead of MT's כִּי, but this is very unlikely.

136. Fritsch ('Concept of God', pp. 156-57) discusses two alleged anthropomorphisms in this chapter, at 63.9 and 63.19(64.1). In both cases, Fritsch bases this judgment upon the apparent avoidance of speaking about God's *face*. However, aspects of his methodology are not beyond suspicion. For example, he finds the translation of בְּעֵינַי (of God) by the 'innocuous phrase εναντιον εμου' at 43.4, 65.12 and 66.4 to be indicative of an anti-anthropomorphic tendency. However, two of the three LXX standard translations for...בְּעֵינַי are 'innocuous', no matter who owns the eyes: ἐναντίον/ἔναντι and ἐνώπιον. Since Isaiah offers us no examples

has occurred between LXX Isa. 59.16 and 63.5, and that this has
influenced the Greek form of one or both of the verses.[137] If so, the
relationship is not one of slavish dependence.

First, שׁמם produces κατανοεῖν in the first instance, προσνοεῖν[138] in
the second, an untidiness that could have been rectified with little fuss.
Over against this disparity, however, the decision to utilize a verb of
acute perception in each case—and a lexically related one at that—is
the far weightier matter.

of...בעיני with a human subject for comparative purposes (excepting 6.10, which is
not really comparable for contextual reasons), it is a questionable procedure simply
to label the (divine) examples that do occur as anti-anthropomorphisms. The trends
outside of Isaiah would suggest the opposite. For a treatment of...בעיני that
concludes that the translator does slightly resist speaking of God's eyes whilst
paying attention to the counter-evidence, see above, 'Rendering of God's "Face"
and/or "Eyes" ', pp. 103-108.

　　Other examples put forward by Fritsch hold up better under scrutiny, for example his suggestion that פי יהוה is translated κύριος because of an anti-anthropomorphic instinct. See above, 'Isaiah 62', pp. 108-109.

　　137. Cf. Ziegler, *Untersuchungen*, p. 172. Ziegler notes (a) the insertion of
וצדקתי at 63.5b in approximately 30 Hebrew mss., by analogy with 59.16; (b) the
similarity of προσνοεῖν and κατανοεῖν, though he does not discuss any implications their presence might have; (c) the appearance in each of αὐτοὺς ('bezieht
sich auf die Israeliten [vgl. V.9]') for לו, since the thought that God might help
himself would be an unusual one; (d) the possible relationship between ἐπέστη and
ἐπεστηρίσατο.

　　138. *To observe, wait attentively for.*

　　In 59.16, the subject of κατανοεῖν is clearly the Lord. In 63.5, it is the warrior
coming from Edom. One wonders whether the distinct prefixes (κατα- in the first
instance, προσ- in the second) might have varied by reason of their subjects'
respective *locations*. That is, the meaning might have been to look *down* and
towards, respectively. Since such a directional meaning for these compound verbs
is unattested in the lexica, this remains speculative.

　　It would become of interest, however, if evidence were to emerge which
suggested that the translator understood the figure coming from Edom as someone
other than God (for example, a messianic or angelic figure). The κατα-/προς-
distinction might then point to a figure other than God—whom this translator is
reluctant to have come down—who *has* come down and who shares on earth the
attentiveness (שׁמם ≈ -νοεῖν) that marks God in heaven. At that point, the sustained
past tense, 1cs narrative for the Hebrew imperfect at 63.7—*the mercy of the Lord
did I call to mind, the excellencies of the Lord...*—might need to be re-examined on
the suspicion that the translator considered it the testimony of a warrior figure who
is distinct from the Lord himself.

Second, מפגיע and סומך are levelled to two forms of ἀντιλαμ–βάνεσθαι, in spite of the attraction that the final word of 63.5 (סמכתני = ἐπέστη) must have exerted upon סומך earlier in the same verse. Still, though the attraction towards 59.16 was strong, it did not result in complete levelling: אין מפגיע and אין סומך could easily have been translated with identical forms once the decision (either conscious or unconscious) to translate them using the same lexeme had been made. They were not.

Third, ותושע לו is handled differently in the two verses in spite of the mutual alteration of לו to αὐτοὺς for contextual reasons.[139] Finally, סמכתהו and סמכתני are handled uniquely in each case.

Thus, the possible relationship should be construed as one of limited, rather than absolute, interaction. For our purposes, the important contribution of the latter verse is syntactical. It appears to provide the *waw copulative* that allows for the notional separation of *perception* and *its content* in both lines of both verses. Though this is a more literal rendering of the *waw* than is customary for this translator, it has served him well in 63.5. Indeed, it has worked *so* well that it has probably been read back into 59.16, where the problematical כי has been brushed aside in its favour.

A further—and in many respects more obvious—anti-anthropomorphism occurs in the evacuation from both verses of any notion that the Lord's arm brought victory *to himself* or that he needed support as he acted. This is clearly visible in 59.16, where the phrase ותושע לו זרעו is entirely rearticulated. In the LXX, the subject of the verb is 'the Lord' rather than 'his arm'. God's arm becomes instead the saving *instrument*. Perhaps it is more significant that God is no longer the beneficiary of salvation or victory, a concept that barely conceals the possibility of scandal. Instead, God protects *them*: καὶ ἠμύνατο αὐτοὺς τῷ βραχίονι.

The same conceptual realignment occurs in the parallel clause, where the LXX finds God to have no need of the support suggested by the MT's וצדקתו היא סמכתהו. In translation, the clause seems implicitly to benefit the same *people* who a few words earlier were identified as the objects of his protection: καὶ τῇ ἐλεημοσύνῃ ἐστηρίσατο. This conversion is underlined by the unexpected translation of צדקה by ἐλεημόσυνη, a tenderness for which the Lord presumably has no need, though hard-pressed human beings certainly do.[140]

139. Cf. Ziegler, *Untersuchungen*, p. 172.
140. Indeed, the pairing of צדקה and ἐλεημόσυνη may suggest that the translator

The same results are achieved at LXX 63.5, though the particulars are quite distinct. Once again, divine self-reference is carefully avoided and the appropriate human objects are supplied. The Hebrew text's ותושע לי זרעי—which the context appears to define as self-vindication of the Divine Warrior, achieved on the battlefield—becomes a merciful rescue of which MT 63.1-6 has nothing to say: καὶ ἐρρύσατο αὐτοὺς ὁ βραχίων μου. The following clause appears to convert the Lord's wrath from the active assistant that made his military exploits possible to a temporarily inert agent that he (in mercy?) has set aside: וחמתי היא סמכתני // καὶ ὁ θυμός μου ἐπέστη.

It is difficult to avoid the impression that ideology has played a determinative role in these similar verses. It has (a) removed any notion of divine imperception (and its corollary, divine surprise), substituting instead an affirmation of divine *perception*; (b) erased the idea that the Lord needs or utilized support; (c) converted two military scenes where mercy was not a feature into images of beneficent rescue.[141]

The Avoidance of Incomplete Divine Perception and/or Divine Passivity in LXX Isaiah 56–66[142]

LXX Isaiah 59.9-15 and 40.27. On occasion, the influence of a passage in Isaiah 56–66 is sufficiently forceful so as to affect the translation of a much earlier verse. This appears to be the case with Isa. 59.9-15a and 40.27, two passages that share an interest in the (in)accessibility of משפט. They seem also to share a resistance to the ideas of divine passivity and/or ignorance of events.

MT 40.27 reads as follows:

> למה תאמר יעקב ותדבר ישראל
> נסתרה דרכי מיהוה ומאלהי משפטי יעבור

> Why do you say, O Jacob, and speak, O Israel, 'My way is hidden from the Lord, and my right is disregarded by my God?'[143]

The LXX varies considerably:

---

understood the word in a way that approximates to *almsgiving*, a meaning that the Hebrew word has frequently in later Hebrew; cf. Jastrow, p. 1263.

141. In both cases, it can be argued that mercy appears *after* battle (cf. 59.20, 63.7-9 and possibly the שנת גאולי of 63.4). However, the importation of these ideas into the verses under analysis is exclusively a feature of the Greek text.

142. For a discussion of this phenomenon in LXX Isa. 57.11, cf. 'Isaiah 57.8-11', pp. 60-63.

143. So NRSV. Alternatively, '...and my right passes my God by.'

μὴ γὰρ εἴπῃς Ιακωβ καὶ τί ἐλάλησας Ισραηλ ἀπεκρύβη ἡ ὁδός μου
ἀπὸ τοῦ θεοῦ καὶ ὁ θεός μου τὴν κρίσιν ἀφεῖλεν καὶ ἀπέστη.

Do not say, O Jacob, and why have you spoken (like this), O Israel?:
'My way has been hidden from God, and my God has taken judgement
away, and stands far off'.[144]

Much could be said about this verse from the perspective of the
established habits of this translator. However, our attention is drawn
particularly to the end of the verse, where ומאלהי משפטי יעבור seems
to have generated καὶ ὁ θεός μου τὴν κρίσιν ἀφεῖλεν καὶ ἀπέστη.

A pair of variations between the two texts is critical for our understanding of this translator: First, the active agent in the MT is 'my
justice', which passes God by. In the LXX, the situation is reversed.
God is now reported to have *taken justice away*. Second, the words καὶ
ἀπέστη are appended in the LXX. These have usually been understood
to describe God's posture following his removal of justice from hapless
Jacob/Israel.[145]

The first variation, which has received little scholarly attention, may
have occurred inadvertently. Indeed, LXX 40.27b(1) follows the word
order of its MT counterpart quite literally: נסתרה דרכי מיהוה =
ἀπεκρύβη ἡ ὁδός μου ἀπὸ τοῦ θεοῦ. The LXX also follows the MT
word order in the following clause: ומאלהי משפטי יעבור is rendered
as καὶ ὁ θεός μου τὴν κρίσιν ἀφεῖλεν, notwithstanding the preposition
מן which is prefixed to the noun in ומאלהי.[146]

---

144. Or, '...and it stands far off.' See below.

145. Cf. Ottley, *Isaiah*, I, p. 223: '...and my God hath taken away my (sic)
judgement, and hath stood aloof!' The addition of a second 'my'—*contra* what the
editions of Rahlfs and Ziegler would eventually suggest—indicates either that
Ottley inadvertently followed the MT or that he was reading a Greek manuscript
that repeated this word (such as those which correspond to Ziegler's second
Hexaplaric *Untergruppe* or to his Lucianic recension). The full title of Ottley's
work would seem to support the former explanation: *The Book of Isaiah According
to the Septuagint (Codex Alexandrinus)*.

Cf. also Brenton, *Septuagint*, p. 875, '...and my God has taken away *my*
judgement, and has departed.'

146. So apparently Ottley, *Isaiah*, II, pp. 300-301: 'ἀφεῖλεν...ἀπέστη] LXX.
have inverted the construction: and apparently duplicated Heb. "will pass away"
with ἀφεῖλεν to parallel the preceding clause, and ἀπέστη. Cf. however ἀφεῖλεν
(diff. Hebrew verb) in vii.17.' It is difficult to locate the value in Ottley's reference
to 7.17. Perhaps he merely cites 7.17 to indicate that God is the subject of ἀφαιρεῖν

However, there may be more here than syntactic rigidity and an invisible mem. Elsewhere we have noted this translator's discomfort with divine ignorance or surprise. In the light of such scruples, the notion of justice passing by the imperceptive deity might have called for closer attention. Already in 40.27, the translator has allowed Jacob/Israel to complain that her way has been hidden from God. That justice itself should pass God by might have seemed one theological bridge too far, even if it comes as a faithless complaint that receives its prophetic comeuppance in this very passage.[147]

If this is the kind of ideological grid that the translator applied to his text, the solution might have lain close at hand. As we have seen when considering the possibility of an *accidental* alteration of the text, MT 40.27 requires very little tampering in order for it to say that God has taken away—rather than failed to take notice of—the justice that Jacob/Israel craves. An overlooked mem joins a reading of יעבור as though it were the hiphil יעביר, thus converting the accused and inattentive deity into one who actively takes away justice from those who do not deserve it. This might have seemed to our translator a less perilous state of affairs.

The second variation—the addition of καὶ ἀπέστη—has been explained on its own terms, though unsatisfactorily. Scholz includes it in his list of 'Synonyme', presumably because ἀφεῖλεν and ἀπέστη are considered to be alternative and synonymous translations of יעבור.[148] However, it is difficult to imagine that ἀπέστη is a translation of

---

elsewhere in LXX Isaiah, then qualifies the relevance of that citation by noting that the Hebrew vocabulary behind ἀφεῖλεν is not what one finds at 40.27. The verb in 7.17 is סור, which may perhaps raise the issue of whether יעבור could have been read as יסור, a standard source of ἀφαιρεῖν. Since the vocabulary and the context of 7.17 are so distinct—the reference is to the day when God removed Ephraim from Judah—it sheds little light on the verse at hand.

147. For the theologically awkward possibilities of this clause, cf. especially Whitehouse, *Isaiah*, II, p. 63: 'The latter clause should be translated "My right passes by unheeded by my God".' Cf. Skinner, *Isaiah*, II, p. 14, where the author suggests the translation 'escapes his notice'.

In 'Isaiah 59.2', pp. 122-27, above, I discuss a similar conversion. There, the sins of the people are allowed the dangerous potential of hiding, or turning away, God's face: וחטאותיכם הסתירו פנים. The LXX makes God the active subject and demotes the people's sins to the status of God's motivation for hiding his own face.

148. Cf. *Uebersetzung*, p. 46.

יעבור.[149] Nor, indeed, is it clear that the two Greek words are synonymous.

Seeligmann cites considerations of word order in suggesting that the extra Greek words (καὶ ἀπέστη) serve as evidence of a separate Greek translation, the shadow of which has been incompletely banished from the present work:

> Here, the question arises whether καὶ ἀπέστη might have its origin in a translation in which κρίσις was the subject, just like משפט in the Hebrew original, and, parallel with the syntax of the preceding clause in the same verse, also in the Greek translation.'[150]

As we shall see, Seeligmann is hinting in a promising direction, for he wishes to see justice rather than God serve as the subject of ἀπέστη. However, in the nature of the case, the existence of a prior Greek translation is an unprovable possibility—among many others—until further evidence for such an alternative translation arises. An explanation which is persuasive upon the grounds of extant evidence would be superior. I suspect that such an explanation can be achieved.

Among students of LXX Isa. 40.27, Ziegler alone notices the influence of Isaiah 59,[151] as well as the orthographic possibilities presented by the verb יעבור. Uniquely in the Hebrew Bible, Isa. 59.9-15a brings together the ideas and vocabulary that are the concern of Jacob/ Israel's complaint in 40.27.

In ch. 59, the text delivers the reasons for which God's justice is not at hand. No longer the complaint of a demoralized community, as in 40.27, the text is now an indictment. The prophet speaks in 59.9-14 as one member of the corrupt people whose behaviour has distanced divine justice from them.[152]

---

149. It would be a *hapax* equivalency.

150. Seeligmann, *LXX Version*, p. 36. It appears that Seeligmann is referring to a non-LXX Greek translation that is known only by the occasional contribution of a variant—here, καὶ ἀπέστη—to the LXX text.

151. Though Seeligmann, without saying so, might have had the influence of ch. 59 in mind when he conjectured a translation in which κρίσις had been the subject of καὶ ἀπέστη. For Ziegler, cf. *Untersuchungen*, p. 71: '40, 27 ἀφεῖλεν + καὶ ἀπέστη + Doppelübers. von יעבור nach 59,9.11.14. Viell. wurde in יעמוד verlesen nach 59, 14 (μακρὰν ἀφέστηκεν = MT).'

152. For this text's recycling of the vocabulary of complaint in the new material of indictment, cf. Smith, *Rhetoric and Redaction*, pp. 120-23; esp. p. 120: 'The poet draws his conclusions from everything he has written so far. In this way he

The following passages illustrate the conceptual and lexical common ground that ch. 59 shares with 40.27. Words with special relevance to 40.27 are underlined:

Isa. 59.9a

על־כן רחק משפט ממנו ולא תשיגנו צדקה

Therefore justice is far from us, and righteousness does not reach us...

διὰ τοῦτο ἀπέστη ἡ κρίσις ἀπ' αὐτῶν, καὶ οὐ μὴ καταλάβῃ αὐτοὺς δικαιοσύνη

On this account, justice stood aloof from them,[153] and righteousness shall certainly not overtake them.

Isa. 59.11b

נקוה למשפט ואין לישועה רחקה ממנו

We wait for justice, but there is none; for salvation, but it is far from us.

ἀνεμείναμεν κρίσιν, καὶ οὐκ ἔστι· σωτηρία μακρὰν ἀφέστηκεν ἀφ' ἡμῶν

We waited for justice, but there is none; salvation has stood at a distance from us.

59.13a

פשע וכחש ביהוה ונסוג מאחר אלהינו

...transgressing and denying the Lord, and turning away from following our God...

ἠσεβήσαμεν καὶ ἐψευσάμεθα καὶ ἀπέστημεν ἀπὸ ὄπισθεν τοῦ θεοῦ ἡμῶν

We have acted profanely and lied and stood back from (following after[?]) our God

responds to *the people's indictment of God* in 58.3a by connecting the people's sins, and not God, with the delay of salvation. *Yahweh is acquitted by the poet's indictment of the people*' (emphasis added). Smith's concern, of course, is restricted to chs. 56–66 of the Hebrew text. But this is precisely the dynamic that appears to link 40.27 with 59.9-14a in the LXX translator's mind.

153. The LXX understands ממנו as 3mp rather than 1cp at 59.9a. From that point until 59.11a, there is a sustained grammatical conversion from the first person to the third person plural. At 59.11b, the LXX reverts to conformity with the MT.

59.14a

והסג אחור משפט וצדקה מרחוק תעמד

And justice has been turned back, and righteousness stands at a distance.

καὶ ἀπεστήσαμεν ὀπίσω τὴν κρίσιν, καὶ ἡ δικαιοσύνη μακρὰν ἀφέστηκεν

And we stood aloof behind justice, and righteousness stood at a distance.

In these verses משפט (= κρίσις) occurs in dense concentration. Furthermore, ἀφιστᾶν becomes the preferred term by which to refer to the figurative distance at which justice,[154] salvation[155] and righteousness[156] stand removed from the people. Additionally, the same vocabulary describes the people's own retreat from God.[157] Indeed, ἀφιστᾶν translates no fewer than three Hebrew verbs in the space of just six verses.[158]

Clearly, Ziegler's abbreviated suggestion that 59.9-14 has inspired the double translation of יעבור has merit. However, Ziegler's treatment can be improved by two considerations. First, Ziegler provides no explanation for how these two chapters might have come into contact in the translator's mind.[159] He has neither entertained the possibility that this is an exegetical move that is initiated by the arousal of theological scruples at 40.27, nor provided any other conceptual link which might have sufficed to link the two contexts, removed as they are by some nineteen chapters.[160] My analysis suggests that ch. 59 came into play at 40.27 because it provided resources that facilitated the conversion of God to the active agent and of משפט to the object of his actions at 40.27. Specifically, it contributes a context in which human sin is clearly the basis of a just distancing of the community from the vindication it craves.[161] It is a short step from the indictment in ch. 59 to

154. 59.9a, 59.14a.
155. In parallel with justice, 59.11b.
156. 59.14a.
157. 59.13.
158. סוג, רחק, and עמד.
159. It is such 'empiricism', in which passive scribal accident is either affirmed or tacitly left as the only viable possibility, that repeatedly provokes Koenig's ire.
160. That is, if one allows oneself the luxury of counting in mediaeval terms what the translator would have gauged by a different—and unknown—unit of measurement.
161. It might reasonably be conjectured as well that the multi-faceted

the assertion in LXX 40.27 that 'God has taken justice away', even if this removes the barb of the complaint voiced in 40.27.

Second, Ziegler has not fully appreciated the strength of the connection between the chapters that the textual evidence supports, though he must be credited for recognizing that a relationship between the two passages exists. Specifically, he has not challenged the notion—found in the translations of Ottley and Brenton—that God is the subject of the added ajpevsth. There is, of course, no sure proof that he is not. However, the link with ch. 59 is appealing at least partially because this chapter speaks of justice 'standing aloof'.[162] It may well be that ἀπέστη at LXX 40.27 does not refer to God at all, but rather to the justice that God has removed. The sentence would then read, 'And my God has removed justice, *so that it stands aloof*.'[163] If such was the translator's

---

phenomenon that Koenig calls *analogies verbales formelles* may have had a hand in the appearance of καὶ ἀπέστη at 40.27. That is, in the light of the conceptual and lexical similarities between 40.27 and 59.9-15, the appearance of העמד and משפט at 59.14 may have facilitated the creative exploitation of the consonants of יעבור at 40.27. It is possible that the translator has given *two* renderings of יעבור at 40.27: (a) ἀφεῖλεν (reading the verb as a hiphil) and (b) καὶ ἀπέστη (exploiting two instances of orthographic likeness to read יעמוד / יעבור = [καὶ] ἀπέστη). On the one hand, this is a less radical solution than the one that posits a direct importation of ἀφιστᾶν from ch. 59, since it allows that the translator worked only with the concrete elements available to him at 40.27, though under the influence of ch. 59. On the other hand, it posits a level of intelligent scribal/translational activity that is impossible to prove. Such inherent 'unprovability' is an abiding weakness of Koenig's approach, though in some degree it adheres as well to any other (including a radically 'empiricist' approach that solves its mysteries by conjecturing fruitful accidents and/or non-extant *Vorlage* and *marginalia*). It does not imply that Koenig's presentation is *implausible*.

162. Using the same Greek verb, ἀφιστᾶν. As we have seen, salvation and righteousness are also the subject of this verb in 59.9-15a.

163. Such a reading would be in essential conformity with Seeligman's brief suggestion that καὶ ἀπέστη 'had its origin' (*LXX Version*, p. 36) in just such a 'translation'.

The use of καί to denote result would be perfectly normal Greek. Cf. H.W. Smyth, *Greek Grammar* (revised by G.M. Messing; Cambridge, MA: Harvard University Press, 1956), §2288 and §2874. Cf. also BDF §442(2), on 'consecutive' καί. BDF note the parallel examples of Mt 5.15 (ἀλλ᾽ ἐπὶ τὴν λυχνίαν [τιθέασιν], καὶ λάμπει), and Lk. 8.16, which reads...ὥστε λάμπειν. Examples in the reference grammars substantiate this use in both Classical and Koine texts. For the view that καί for purpose is a Hebraism, cf. H.S. Gehman, 'Hebraisms of the Old Greek Version of Genesis', *VT* 3 (1953), pp. 141-48 (142). It is easy to imagine that

intention, then this verse is linked more closely with ch. 59 than Ziegler recognized.[164]

The presence of this kind of intertextual hermeneutic in the hands of the translator can be established at many points throughout LXX Isaiah. It permits a satisfactory explanation for 40.27 *within the parameters of the available evidence*. At the same time, it raises the issue of the mechanism by which this later chapter has cast its shadow over the earlier one. It is possible that καὶ ἀπέστη is the work of a reviser rather than the original translator. However, such a post-translation alteration would necessarily have had to occur very early, since the super-numerary words are well established across the textual tradition.

The use of ἀφιστᾶν—the same word which does translational duty for a number of Hebrew verbs in 59.9-15a—may well suggest that it is ch. 59 *in Greek* rather than Hebrew that has influenced LXX 40.27. This is not necessarily the case, for the three words that generate ἀφιστᾶν in ch. 59—רחק, עמד and סוג—do so elsewhere in the LXX, even if infrequently. Thus, the evidence suggests that reflection upon the *Hebrew* of Isaiah 59 might have been enough to produce the inserted καὶ ἀπέστη at 40.27. However, it is tempting to conclude that the multiple occurrence of this particular Greek verb in LXX Isaiah 59 is responsible for its insertion in the contextually similar LXX Isa. 40.27.

We cannot know for certain which of the two texts of ch. 59, Hebrew or Greek, motivated the plus at 40.27, though the argument that one or the other of them has done so seems to be a strong one. If the translator at 40.27 imported the additional pair of words from *Greek* Isaiah 59, one can imagine a range of circumstances by which this might have taken place:

(a)   Our translator may have translated ch. 59 *before* ch. 40.

---

the frequent use of waw to coordinate and subordinate clauses in Hebrew might have increased the frequency of καί with the same function in the LXX, even if it exists independently in non-translation Greek.

164. One concedes that there is precedent in LXX 59.14 for a truly personal protagonist to 'stand aloof'. There ἀπεστήσαμεν ὀπίσω τὴν κρίσιν has the prophetic speaker and his people as its subject. But God himself is not said to 'stand off' in that context, and it seems to me dubious that this is affirmed of him in 40.27. That it *can* be spoken of God in the LXX is evident from Ps. 10.1(LXX 9.22): למה יהוה תעמד ברחוק ="ἵνα τί, κύριε, ἀφέστηκας μακρόθεν. This verse from Psalms is suggestive for the idea, mentioned above in note 161 that a reading of MT's יעבור as יעמוד might have played some role in the appearance of καὶ ἀπέστη.

(b)   An extant Greek translation that included ch. 59—and the word ἀφιστᾶν—might have been known to the translator as he worked on ch. 40.[165]

(c)   An oral translation tradition of the Greek-speaking synagogue may have used ἀφιστᾶν in ch. 59. The translator's familiarity with such a spoken translation might have come into play at the moment of translating 40.27.

(d)   It is conceivable that a translator—having finished ch. 40 at some prior point in time—might have been inspired by ch. 59 to return to the earlier chapter and insert καὶ ἀπέστη. This seems the least likely scenario.

LXX Isa. 62.6-7. For the evasion of a statement that calls upon God not to rest or be silent, see Chapter 3, 'Isaiah 62.7', pp. 72-74.

LXX Isa. 65.16-17 (with Reference to 43.4; 65.3, 12; 66.4, 22 and 23; and Other Biblical and Rabbinical Texts). A curious absence of divine blindness at LXX Isa. 65.16-17 may signal yet another attempt by the translator to soften anthropomorphic descriptions of God and to avoid affirmations of divine limitations. We are concerned especially with the underlined final phrase of 65.16.

אשר המתברך בארץ יתברך באלהי אמן
והנשבע בארץ ישבע באלהי אמן
כי נשכחו הצרות הראשנות וכי נסתרו מעיני
(17) כי־הנני בורא שמים חדשים וארץ חדשה
ולא תזכרנה הראשנות ולא תעלינה על־לב

> Then whoever invokes a blessing in the land shall bless by the God of faithfulness, and whoever takes an oath in the land shall swear by the God of faithfulness; because the former troubles are forgotten <u>and are hidden from my eyes</u>. (17) For behold, I am about to create new heavens and a new earth; and the former things shall not be remembered or come to mind.

The Septuagint has a different rendering:

> ...ὃ εὐλογηθήσεται ἐπὶ τῆς γῆς· εὐλογήσουσι γὰρ τὸν θεὸν τὸν ἀληθινόν, καὶ οἱ ὀμνύοντες ἐπὶ τῆς γῆς ὀμοῦνται τὸν θεὸν τὸν ἀληθινόν· ἐπιλήσονται γὰρ τὴν θλῖψιν αὐτῶν τὴν πρώτην, <u>καὶ οὐκ</u>

---

165. Such an hypothesis could be merged with Seeligman's reading of the evidence. See above.

ἀναβήσεται αὐτῶν ἐπὶ τὴν καρδίαν. (17) ἔσται γὰρ ὁ οὐρανὸς
καινὸς καὶ ἡ γῆ καινή, καὶ οὐ μὴ μνησθῶσι τῶν προτέρων, οὐδ' οὐ
μὴ ἐπέλθῃ αὐτῶν ἐπὶ τὴν καρδίαν.

(But those who serve him shall be called by a new name)...which shall
be blessed upon the earth. For they shall bless the true God, and those
who swear upon the earth shall swear by the true God. For they shall
forget their former distress, and it shall not go up upon their heart. (17)
For heaven shall be new, and the earth new (as well), and they shall not
remember the former things, nor shall they come up upon their heart.

It is immediately apparent that the clause at the end of 65.16—καὶ
οὐκ ἀναβήσεται αὐτῶν ἐπὶ τὴν καρδίαν—bears a striking similarity
to the end of 65.17. It is certainly not a translation of וכי נסתרו מעיני,
the Hebrew phrase that corresponds to the same location in 65.16.

It is conceivable that parablepsis has occurred by way of the word
הראשנות, which is common to the penultimate clauses of vv. 16 and
17. Having taken in the *first* הראשנות—in 65.16—the translator's eye
may then have skipped to the clause that follows the *second* הראשנות
and translated the phrase that follows it. The translator might then have
found his proper place upon returning to the beginning of what we
know as v. 17. It is this scenario of scribal confusion that has
commended itself to Ottley[166] and, apparently, to Ziegler.[167]

However, there are grounds for suspicion that an intentional exegetical
move is responsible for the similarity—for the two Greek phrases are
indeed *similar* rather than *identical*—of the two clauses. First, there are
grounds for *a priori* suspicion that this verse might have represented a
scandal for the translator. It contains two elements that have elsewhere
caused him difficulty: an anthropomorphic reference to the Lord's eyes
and the assertion that something has been hidden from those divine
organs of sight.[168]

166. *Isaiah*, II, p. 382: 'οὐκ ἀναβήσεται κ.τ.λ.] ἐπιλήσονται, active for
passive, has given the verse already an increased likeness to ver. 17; and the final
clause seems now to have been completely confused with it. Heb. 'and because they
are hid from mine eyes'.'

167. *Untersuchungen*, p. 173: 'Durch הראשנות V.16 ist bereits in die LXX-
Vorlage aus V.17b ולא תעל ינה על־לב nach V. 16 eingedrungen; dies geht aus der
abweichenden Form der beiden griech. Sätze hervor.' Ziegler sees the levelling of
the two final clauses as a feature of the Hebrew *Vorlage*, whilst Ottley locates the
confusion at the translator's level.

168. One notes at the same time the curious omission of instrumental beth in at
least the first of the two phrases ישבע באלהי אמן and יתברך באלהי אמן. They are

Second, there are elements within the LXX context that suggest that the changes one observes are the product of *effort* rather than *accident*. For example, the words כי נסתרו מעיני occur in what our translator might have considered to be dangerous proximity to the prior clause, כי נשכחו הצרות הראשנות. By virtue of the parallel arrangement of these phrases, the fact that the eyes belong to the Lord might have suggested that the forgetting was to be of the divine variety as well. It is perhaps no casual fact that the ambiguously passive נשכחו הצרות has been rendered as the active and unmistakably human ἐπιλήσονται γὰρ τὴν θλῖψιν αὐτῶν. In the case of both parallel verbs, the activity has been altogether removed from the divine sphere and planted unambiguously in the human one. Thus, the conversion of נסתרו מעיני under discussion must not be seen in isolation. Rather, it is part of a sustained evacuation of God from the vulnerable pathos of this context.

This evasion of the divine first person reaches into 65.17 as well, where at the outset כי־הנני בורא שמים חדשים is rendered by the impersonal ἔσται γὰρ ὁ οὐρανὸς καινὸς καὶ ἡ γῆ καινή. The following phrase once more assigns a Hebrew passive verb—left ambiguous by the absence of complements—to a Greek third plural active: ולא תזכרנה הראשנות = καὶ οὐ μὴ μνησθῶσι τῶν προτέρων. The result is to reduce the personal protagonists of the narrative from two in the Hebrew—God and the people—to just one in the Greek. The consequence is to distance God not only from anthropomorphic

translated as follows: εὐλογήσουσι γὰρ τὸν θεὸν τὸν ἀληθινόν and ὀμοῦνται τὸν θεὸν τὸν ἀληθινόν. The Hebrew prepositional phrases do not appear to suggest the Greek accusative, yet this is precisely what the translator gives us as the result of his active-for-reflexive conversion.

In the first instance, it may have seemed more prudent to bless God than to invoke a blessing upon oneself (if this is the force of the hithpael) *by God*. If so, then we have a subtle ameliorative reading that may have been facilitated by the details of the second case, that is, the translation of ישבע באלהי אמן.

This second instance is slightly less unusual than the first. Whilst the accusative with ὀμνύειν is rare in the LXX compared with the much more frequent use of the dative for the person or thing *by* which one swears, LSJ provide extrabiblical attestation, 1223. This use of the accusative with ὀμνύειν occurs four times in the LXX outside of this verse: Josh. 2.12, ὀμόσατέ μοι κύριον τὸν θεόν; Prov. 30.9, ὀμόσω τὸν ὄνομα τοῦ θεοῦ; Dan. 12.7, ὤμοσε τὸν ζῶντα εἰς τὸν αἰῶνα θεόν; Bel 7, ὀμνύω δέ σοι κύριον τὸν θεὸν τῶν θεῶν. Such attestation suggests that the accusative in this second, oath-related clause, probably retains an instrumental force. Thus, it is arguably a straightforward translation of the *Vorlage* (≈ MT).

description, but also from the anthropopathic possibility of forgetfulness and/or imperfect perception, even if the Hebrew text employs these
as redemptive metaphors.

Furthermore, one observes with Ziegler that the two Greek clauses are
not identical. In the second one—which is authorized by ולא תעלינה
על־לב —we find οὐδ᾿ οὐ μὴ ἐπέλθῃ αὐτῶν ἐπὶ τὴν καρδίαν. This
bears no surprises.[169]

In the first clause, however, the Greek product reads καὶ οὐκ
ἀναβήσεται αὐτῶν ἐπὶ τὴν καρδίαν. The pronoun αὐτῶν occurs in
the same place as in the authorized phrase in 65.17. However, the verb
itself and the syntax of the future negation[170] are different from what we
find in the latter verse. This does not look like the kind of close
similarity or identity that we would expect upon encountering a simple
case of parablepsis where the translator mistakenly understood two
consecutive verses to end with exactly the same Hebrew phrase.

Targum Jonathan—by· different and less radical means than the
LXX—also cushions the impact. In typical targumistic form, וארי מסתרן
מן קדמי gently inserts the concept of hiddenness 'from before me' in
place of the unmediated Massoretic notion of things which are hidden
'from me'.

Furthermore, there exists a tradition of struggle with the notion of the
divine eye(s) and face across a significant range of biblical passages,
some of them in Isaiah. A brief survey of several cases, first from
beyond the Isaiah translation and then from within it, will establish the
anti-anthropomorphic and anti-anthropopathic alterations that such
descriptions tend to evoke from translators and copyists. LXX Isa. 65.16
may then be seen to fit comfortably within this wider tendency to alter
such anthropomorphic imagery.

A phenomenon that is remarkably similar to Isa. 65.16 is found
within the tradition of the *tiqunne sopherim*, where Zech. 2.12 is given

---

169. This translator frequently appears to intensify a simple Hebrew negation by
rendering it with οὐ μὴ + a subjunctive rather than with οὐ + the indicative. Indeed,
this translation is repeated so often that one begins to doubt whether it represents
any intensification at all. Further, the addition of a possessive pronoun like αὐτῶν
to clarify the relationship of an unspecified Hebrew phrase—as here על־לב—is
quite common to the Isaiah translator.

170. Future, that is, in Greek. In the Hebrew, the time reference of the Hebrew
perfects (נשבחו and נסתרו) is ambiguous, a matter that is reflected in modern Bible
translations.

prominent attention.[171] MT Zech. 2.12[Eng. 2.8] reads as follows:

כי כה אמר יהוה צבאות

אחר כבוד שלחני אל־הגוים השללים אתכם

כי הנגע בכם נגע בבבת עינו

> For thus said the Lord of hosts (after his glory sent me) regarding the
> nations that plundered you: Truly, one who touches you touches the
> apple of his eye.

The scribal and/or exegetical tradition that has issued in the *tiqqune
sopherim* lists the underlined phrase as one of the 18 alleged euphem-
isms that conceal original readings that might have been offensive. In
this case, the original reading is held to have been עֵינִי. That is, the final
stich of this verse was considered by the scribes to have been included
within the divine speech which begins at 2.9[Eng. 2.5]. עֵינִי would then
have referred to the Lord's eye.[172] According to this tradition, an

---

171. Cf. McCarthy, *Tiqqune Sopherim*, p. 61: 'It is logical to begin this
investigation of each of the official *tiqqune sopherim* with Zech. 2.12, *for in the
earliest sources it is this verse which serves as a reminder of the existence of other
similar cases*' (emphasis added).

172. Cf. McCarthy, *Tiqqune Sopherim*, pp. 61-70. Rabbinic tradition appears to
differ as to whether Scripture originally had 'my eye', which the scribes altered to
'his eye' in the interest of religious propriety; or, alternatively, whether Scripture
originally employed 'his eye' as a euphemism, although the clear intention was to
speak of 'my eye'.

Cf. also T. Muraoka, 'Hebrew Hapax Legomena and Septuagint Lexicography',
in C.E. Cox (ed.), *VII Congress of the International Organization for Septuagint
and Cognate Studies, Leuven 1989* (SCS, 31; Atlanta: Scholars Press, 1991), pp.
205-222 (210). Muraoka writes of the translator who produced ἡ κόρη τῆς
ὀφθαλμοῦ αὐτοῦ: 'Thus one's suspicion is aroused whether our translator possibly
deleted the first Bet, reading an apparent synonym עַיְ בַּת [sic; Muraoka must
certainly have intended בַּת עַיְן], which however in its only Old Testament
occurrence in Lam 2.18 is mistranslated as θύγατερ, ἡ ὀφθαλμός σου.' Muraoka is
not here concerned with this verse as one of the *tiqqune sopherim*. Rather, he
wonders whether the translator understood the Hebrew expression. That he includes
αὐτοῦ as part of his translation of a phrase that may have been unintelligible to him
seems to me to argue strongly that the LXX *Vorlage* already contained the present
MT reading. If the translator's *Vorlage* had עֵינִי—which seems to me unlikely—
then the LXX translator has also executed the move from 1cs to 3ms that some
interpretations of the *tiqqune sopherim* suggest for the Masoretic tradition.

The alleged euphemistic change from 'my eye' to 'his eye' must have occurred
very early or not at all. For our purposes, the precise details of the text's history are
not the important concern, but rather the scribal preoccupation with anthropo-

emendation has avoided such an anthropomorphic self-description.[173] The resulting third-person suffix might refer to Israel's enemy or, indeed, to Israel itself.

This brief discussion of Zech. 2.12 has treated exclusively of the Hebrew textual tradition of that verse. The same clause in the best manuscripts of LXX Zech. 2.8 (MT 2.12) reads ὡς ἁπτόμενος τῆς κόρης τοῦ ὀφθαλμοῦ αὐτοῦ, thus agreeing with the 'corrected' MT text.[174] The point of contact with LXX Isa. 65.16 remains solely at the

morphism that either sustains or creates the memory of such changes. The LXX translator at Isa. 65.16 (and elsewhere) may have been party to such preoccupation.

173. In at least one text that has preserved a *tiqqun* list, both the non-euphemistic and the euphemistic readings were considered to be of ongoing importance. Referring to the prologue of the *kinnuyim* (the same 18 instances which are more commonly called *tiqqunim*) of the Baer–Strack edition of the *Diqduqe Hatte'amim* (S. Baer and H. Strack, *Diqduqe Hatte'amim* [Leipzig, 1879; reproduced in Jerusalem, 1970]), McCarthy observes: 'This prologue is particularly interesting because, even though it presents the traditional list and "original" readings, it does so while insisting that they are not genuine emendations, but just "euphemistic" expressions, which, in certain exegetical circles, may be "read" according to their *tiqqun* form for the purposes of interpretation. There is an emphatic denial that these verses were emended, together with the affirmation that they were written in their "euphemistic" form by Moses and the Prophets.' Cf. McCarthy, *Tiqqune Sopherim*, p. 45. This seems to work on analogy with the *kethiv/qere* of standard Massoretic practice.

While the apparatus of *BHS* notes that the *tiqunne sopherim* tradition considers עֵינִי to be the original reading (along with several non-Hebrew authorities), this information does not occur in the *Masora* reproduced in *BHS*. This is so because the best Massoretic manuscripts (e.g. the Leningrad and Aleppo codices) give little or no attention to the *tiqqunim*. Cf. McCarthy, *Tiqqune Sopherim*, p. 51.

174. Several Greek and Latin witnesses understand the eye less ambiguously as belonging to God. This is accomplished either explicitly by means of θεου or κυριου or implicitly by means of μου. One manuscript allows the eye to stand absolutely and anonymously. Cf. Ziegler, *editio*, p. 295. For the inclusion of the more recent evidence from Naḥal Ḥever, cf. D. Barthélemy, *Les devanciers d'Aquila: Première publication intégrale du texte des fragments du Dodécapro-phéton* (VTSup, 10; Leiden: E.J. Brill, 1963), p. 211 (cited in McCarthy, *Tiqqune Sopherim*, p. 66 n. 36), and E. Tov, *The Greek Minor Prophets Scroll from Naḥal Ḥever (8ḤevXIIgr)*, (DJD 8; Oxford: Oxford University Press, 1990).

McCarthy continues, *Tiqqune Sopherim*, p. 67: 'The LXX variants may either represent evidence of recensional activity aimed at bringing the LXX into line with that form of the Hebrew text which the school of Hillel considered normative before the destruction of the Second Temple, or else, they may represent the only *conceptual* level, since I am positing no direct connection between Zech. 2.8(12) and Isa. 65.16. That is, it may be that the Greek translator of Isaiah is possessed of similar religious instincts to those which independently motivated the alleged emendation of the Hebrew text of Zech. 2.12 by its custodians.[175]

In both cases, the alleged offence consists of a divine first-person speech that makes reference to (מ)עֵינִי, whether vocalized as a singular (Zechariah) or a plural (Isaiah). In each case, the solution has been to change the first-person suffix to a third-person suffix, whether this be singular (again, Zechariah) or plural (LXX Isaiah).[176]

Now it must be conceded that the Isaiah translator is willing to speak of God's eyes, and even to allow the Lord to speak directly of 'my eyes'. However, he grants such permission only rarely.[177] The relatively abundant scribal tradition and scholarly discussion that has grown up around Zech. 2.12 may shed some light on the largely unobserved peculiarities at LXX Isa. 65.17.

Also bearing on the argument that the LXX translator desires to avoid any potential limitations of divine perception is further evidence within Isaiah of embarrassment before the notion of God's eyes and face. It is tempting to conclude that the translation of עַל־פָּנַי and לְפָנַי in ch. 65 produces additional evidence of the anti-anthropomorphic instinct that I am suggesting stands behind 65.17.[178] If indeed a certain scandal

surviving direct evidence of the Old Greek, in which case the main-stream of the LXX could represent the text after Origen's recension.'

175. Or, at the very least, which kept alive the tradition that it *had* been emended, and the religious modesty that explained such an allegation.

This concern with the eye of God recurs in the alleged *tiqqun sopherim* at 2 Sam. 16.12: (בעיני Q) אוּלִי יִרְאֶה יהוה בְּעוֹנִי. McCarthy judges the Kethiv to represent the original reading and calls into question the authenticity of the *tiqqune* tradition of this verse. Nevertheless, it is clear from the Targum ('on the tear of my eye') and from the rabbinic tradition that sees here 'a *tiqqun sopherim* for an original anthropomorphic expression, "with his eye/eyes"' that the perceived anthropomorphism with regard to God's eye was problematic at a relatively early stage. The handling of the text at LXX Isa. 65.17 would fit well within this kind of targumic and scribal approach. Cf. McCarthy, *Tiqqune Sopherim*, pp. 81-85.

176. Admittedly, the LXX Isaiah solution is more radical. The MT reference to 'my (i.e. God's) eyes' has now become a reference to 'their *heart*', and this has been embedded in a sentence borrowed—with slight modifications—from 65.17.

177. As far as I can see, only in the two instances in which the Lord speaks of 'my eyes' in 1.15-16.

178. Isa. 65.3 is the only Isaianic use of עַל־פְּנֵי with respect to God. For...לְפְנֵי

attaches to such anthropomorphisms, prepositional phrases like these would provide an easy opportunity for alteration, since non-anthropomorphic translations lay conveniently at hand.[179] In the chapter under discussion, the translator provides ἐναντίον ἐμοῦ for the former in 65.3 and ἐνώπιόν mou for the latter in 65.6, both of which avoid any mention of a *face*.

While the occurrences of -פְנֵי constructions in Isaiah are too scarce for firm conclusions, Fritsch makes a claim for anti-anthropomorphic intent in the translation of the similar expression בְעֵינַי (= ἐναντίον ἐμοῦ) at 65.12.[180] We have already seen that Fritsch's conclusions require important qualifications. For example, he finds the translation of בְעֵינֵי יהוה by the 'innocuous phrase εναντιον εμου' at 43.4, 65.12, and 66.4 to be indicative obviously of an anti-anthropomorphic tendency. However, two of the three exceedingly frequent LXX standard translations for עֵינֵי... are similarly 'innocuous', even when the eyes are not God's. Indeed, ἐναντίον/ἔναντι and ἐνώπιον together account for fully 57 per cent of the translations of this Hebrew construction.[181]

with respect to God, cf. also ἔμπροσθέν μου at 43.10; ἐνώπιόν μου at 48.19, 66.22 and 66.23; and παρ᾽ ἐμοῦ (for מִלְפְנֵי) at 57.16.

179. The translation of occasional statements about God's eyes or face by a fairly straightforward and anthropomorphic Greek rendering would seem not to obviate the argument under development. We have consistently observed that our translator is not anarchic with his Hebrew text. Where certain ideological biases might motivate him to alter his text, he will rarely do so in a radical fashion or without some orthographic or lexical pretext. Rather, he will bring his biases to bear upon those passages *that lend themselves to alteration in the desired direction.* Hebrew anthropomorphic prepositions—such as עַל־פְנֵי and לִפְנֵי—would seem to qualify as 'soft targets' for this technique, for alternatives like ἔμπροσθεν and ἐναντίον lie readily at hand. A reference like those in 1.15-16 where the Lord speaks directly of 'my eyes' might have proved less amenable to alteration.

Koenig makes a similar point when he refers to a problematic anthropomorphism at Isa. 3.8, a passage that we will consider below: 'Sa présence est justement rendue sensible par l'étrangeté de l'attribution des yeux à la Gloire, *dans un texte où il est impossible de réduire la mention de la Gloire à l'équivalence d'une simple qualification adjectivale (hébraïsme de l'état cs pour l'adjectif* (emphasis added; *L'herméneutique analogique*, p. 113).

180. 'Concept of God', p. 157.

181. Of some 339 occurrences of בְּעֵינֵ- in the Hebrew Bible, 24 per cent are translated by ἐναντι- and 23 per cent by ἐνώπιον, both of which carry no risk of connoting physical *eyes*. Translations using ὀφθαλμός—the most common of which is ἐν ὀφθαλμοῖς—comprise the third of three standard translations. This

Since Isaiah offers us few examples of בעיני... with a human referent for comparative purposes, one labels the (divine) examples that do occur as anti-anthropomorphisms only with great caution. One *can* observe that of the six Isaiah occurrences of בעיני with respect to God, none of the LXX renderings refers to *eyes*.[182] By contrast, when the same phrase has reference to human beings, two translations out of three do not hesitate to speak of eyes.[183] Even here, however, qualification is needed, for two of the three phrases in question are *not*

---

kind of constructions is employed for 32 per cent of the occurrences. Ἔναντι- is a strong preference for the translators of the Pentateuch. After that, ἐνώπιον and translations that use ὀφθαλμός become much more popular.

This information is especially relevant since the translational patterns vary according to the book (i.e. the translator), not according to the subject in whose eyes some activity takes place. (Cf. the employment of Greek renderings of בעיני to distinguish the OG and Kaige recension of I-IV Kingdoms, in J.D. Shenkel, *Chronology and Recensional Development in the Greek Text of Kings* [Cambridge, MA: Harvard University Press, 1968], pp. 13-17.) This effectively rules out any theory of anti-anthropomorphic translation of בעיני for the bulk of the LXX. However, as is nearly always the case, the patterns of Greek equivalencies that are apparent in LXX Isaiah are eclectic. Thus, it may in fact be possible to discern an ideological bias in the case of this translator, or, alternatively, to rule this out.

182. 38.3, בעיניך = ἐνώπιόν σου; 43.4, 65.12 and 66.4, בעיני = ἐναντίον μου; 49.5, בעיני יהוה = ἐναντίον κυρίου; and 59.15, וירע בעיניו = καὶ οὐχ ἤρεσεν αὐτῷ.

The last of these is quite suggestive of religious reserve. It is echoed in Prov. 24.18, where rejoicing over fallen enemies is proscribed פן־יראה יהוה ורע בעיניו. The Proverbs translator produces ὅτι ὄψεται κύριος, καὶ οὐκ ἀρέσει αὐτῷ. Cf. also Balaam's words to the angel of the Lord in Num. 22.34: ועתה אם־רע בעיניך אשובה לי = καὶ νῦν εἰ μή σοι ἀρέσκει, ἀποστραφήσομαι.

However, any rush to conclude that such translations *must* be anti-anthropomorphic is restrained by attention to the positive version of this expression, used with reference to human beings. In Gen. 19.8, Lot says of his daughters to the over-heated men of Sodom—whose behaviour is anything but divine—ועשו להן כטוב בעיניכם = καὶ χρήσασθε αὐταῖς καθὰ ἂν ἀρέσκη ὑμῖν. The phrase is also used with a human referent in Gen. 20.15; Lev 10.20; Job 22.30, 33; and four times of Artaxerxes in Est. ch. 1.

183. The three are: 5.21, חכמים בעיניהם = οἱ συνετοὶ ἐν ἑαυτοῖς; 6.10, פן־יראה בעיניו = μήποτε ἴδωσιν τοῖς ὀφθαλμοῖς; 52.8, עין בעין יראו = ὀφθαλμοὶ πρὸς ὀφθαλμούς.

This line of analysis, however, does not produce the clearest imaginable demarcations. Cf., for example, Isa. 18.2, where the inoffensive phrase, על־פני־מים, is translated without a reference to a 'face': ἐπάνω τοῦ ὕδατος.

the very frequent construction that means 'in the sight of', 'in the judgment of' or simply 'before'. Rather, they are somewhat more concrete phrases that, on balance, might be more likely to produce mention of actual eyes.[184]

Still, Fritsch may be correct in asserting that a kind of selective vocabulary is being used when translating this phrase, even if his confidence exceeds defensible bounds. If so, the translation in LXX Isaiah of prepositional phrases[185] that in Hebrew refer to parts of the body at least fails to *contradict* the thesis of anti-anthropomorphic bias on the part of this translator. It may indeed provide mild corroboration of just such an inclination.

Yet another rendering in LXX Isaiah suggests not only that the translator was uncomfortable with the anthropomorphic notion of God's eyes, but that he was willing to take substantial liberties to avoid the scandal which such an idea represented. In MT Isa. 3.8, one reads:

כי כשלה ירושלם ויהודה נפל
כי־לשונם ומעלליהם אל־יהוה למרות עני כבודו

For Jerusalem has stumbled and Judah has fallen, because their speech and their deeds are against the Lord, defying <u>the eyes of his glory</u>.[186]

The LXX differs considerably:

ὅτι ἀνεῖται Ιερουσαλημ, καὶ ἡ Ιουδαία συμπέπτωκε, καὶ αἱ γλῶσσαι αὐτῶν μετὰ ἀνομίας, τὰ πρὸς κύριον ἀπειθοῦντες· διότι <u>νῦν ἐταπεινώθη ἡ δόξα αὐτῶν...</u>

For Jerusalem has been weakened, and Judah has fallen together with (her). And their tongues (speak) with lawlessness, disbelieving (as they do) the things that pertain to the Lord. <u>Therefore, now, their glory has been humiliated.</u>

Because Koenig has dedicated an entire chapter of his monograph to this verse,[187] there is no need to enter into great detail here. For our purposes, it is important to note two innovations carried out by the LXX translator. First, he has read עני as though it were a form of the verb ענה. Second, he has rendered כבודו—of which the 3ms suffix refers to the Lord—as ἡ δόξα αὐτῶν. He thus stamps the glory not as a divine

---

184. The expression at 6.10 is concretely instrumental, while the one at 52.8 has a very specific adverbial function.

185. Fritsch's point touches only בעין־.

186. Cf. NRSV, '...defying his glorious presence.'

187. *L'herméneutique analogique*, pp. 107-17.

quality, but rather as a characteristic of benighted Judah/Jerusalem.

Koenig argues forcefully that these changes—as well as a number of others that have reshaped this verse—are hardly the result of accidental confusion.[188] Rather, the motive is self-consciously one of religious propriety.[189] Indeed, Koenig considers that the reference to divine *eyes* is probably the point of departure for the entire far-reaching restructuring that this verse has undergone.[190]

The thrust of Koenig's argument is persuasive and merits at least tentative acceptance.[191] It places before us an example that appears to

188. Cf., for example, on the influence of Aramaic on the understanding of עוה as 'to be slack', *L'herméneutique analogique*, p. 109: 'L'indication révèle d'emblée le caractère réfléchi de l'exploitation de la source hébraïque. Les indices de 8b vont nous montrer que cette réflexion n'a pas improvisé librement, mais s'est appuyée sur les méthodes de l'herméneutique reçue.' Against Seeligmann's assertion that attribution of such an Aramaic meaning would have been a passive, unconscious move for the translator, cf. pp. 112-13: 'On ne peut sans invraisemblance dénier à G la capacité de reconnaître dans la leçon TM = H la possibilité du substantif de la vocalisation TM. Supposer qu'il a divergé parce qu'il ne comprenait pas l'expression hébraïque à l'état cs., serait méconnaître le champ du possible dans les représentations et imaginations religieuses au sein du Judaïsme.'

189. *L'herméneutique analogique*, p. 113: 'Ce motif c'est l'anthropomorphisme inhérent à la formule de H...Après un vb comme "désobéir à" (proprement "se rebeller contre"), le mot Gloire revêt nécessairement sa pleine valeur théophanique et joue le rôle d'une entité directement représentative de la divinité.'

190. *L'herméneutique analogique*, p. 113 n. 18: 'Il est probable que le traitement de l'anthropomorphisme a été le point de départ de l'adaptation de 3,8 dans G. C'est l'aspect le plus important du texte et les autres éléments lui ont vraisemblablement été subordonnés...'

191. Even if one might have wished for a reckoning with the unexpected appearance of ταπεινοῦν elsewhere in this chapter: In 3.17, ושׂפח = καὶ ταπεινώσει. (BDB query whether verbal ספח/שׂפח) is related to ספחת (*eruption, scab*); KB support this suggestion with their preferred meaning, *to make scabby*, while recognizing that the LXX rendering of this word (special reference is made to Isa. 3.17), 'is already somewhat removed from the original sense'. In 3.26(25), ואנו = καὶ ταπεινωθήσονται (ע/א exchange). Do these two later verses exhibit a knock-on effect from a choice of ταπεινοῦν made for exegetical reasons at 3.8? Or does the translator approach this chapter with a 'humiliation theme' on his mind, thus allowing one to query whether the reading of עוי at 3.8 might be rather more accidental than *réfléchi* (Koenig's term, p. 109)?

Furthermore, Koenig's speculative reconstruction of a *Hebrew* text prior to the MT cannot, in the nature of the case, command absolute credence. However, this

corroborate the view that divine eyes are organs that appear to compel special attention on the part of our translator.[192] Evidence that references to them are problematic not only within wider Second Temple (and later) scribal tradition but also within the work of the LXX Isaiah translator himself begins to accumulate. It appears to corroborate the suspicion that less obvious evasions of anthropomorphic description— such as the one under consideration at LXX 65.16—are not unconscious stumbles after all. Rather, they represent a solution to a religious problem that the text presented to this translator, as other texts would to his fellows.[193]

arguably weaker point is independent of his explanation of how the LXX was derived from its *Vorlage* (≈ MT). The latter is strong and elegantly stated.

192. Divine eyes are not the only problem at Isa. 3.8. When עני is read as a verb of humiliation, כבודו instantly acquires the potential to offend, since the antecedent of the suffix is the Lord himself. The humiliation of the Lord's glory might not expect enthusiastic acceptance in the conceptual world of this translator. Koenig's treatment of the conversion of this 3ms suffix (of God) to the 3mp (of humiliated Jerusalemites/Judahites) is curiously brief (Cf. *L'herméneutique analogique*, pp. 113-17, where this issue is largely dissolved into his treatment of עני as an insertion into a Hebrew text that initially spoke only of 'the Glory'). According to Koenig, this was intended to separate 'the Glory'—that originally stood in as a theophanic reference—from the potentially scandalous verb מרה. Koenig wonders whether this scribal precaution—originally a scrupulous move—might not itself have become scandalous by the time of the LXX project, thus motivating the removal of what had once been inserted.

Regardless of the merits of this query, the rendering ἡ δόξα αὐτῶν—rather than the expected τὴν δόξα αὐτοῦ—might be explained with reference to two established habits of this translator: first, by the technique I call 'formal 2 = 1', as a levelling of this suffix to match the prior לשונם (= αἱ γλῶσσαι αὐτῶν); secondly, by 'pluralization', a technique that is habitually practised upon singulars of all kinds, but especially representative singulars.

However, even these two much-used techniques may not adequately explain the violence done to the text in converting *his glory* to *their glory*. There is, in the scribal traditions attached to other texts, precedent for the execution of this very move on ideological grounds, a parallel that is suggestive for discovering the motive of the Isaiah translator at 3.8. Hos. 4.7, Jer. 2.11 and Ps. 106.20—three verses in which either כבודם or כבודו appear—are found on lists of *tiqqune sopherim*. Cf. McCarthy, *Tiqqune Sopherim*, pp. 97-105. Though in the end McCarthy judges that the MT of these three verses does not conceal different original readings under a veil of euphemism, it is nonetheless illuminating to see how readings similar to MT Isa. 3.8 discomfited scribes at different times and places.

193. If, for the moment, his guild be defined as those who translate, preserve, or pass on biblical texts.

A further example occurs at Isa. 37.17, where the MT reads as follows:

הטה יהוה אזנך ושמע פקח יהוה עינך וראה ושמע
את כל־דברי סנחריב אשר שלח לחרף אלהים חי

Incline your ear, O Lord, and hear; open your eyes, O Lord, and see; and hear all the words of Sennacherib, which he has sent to mock the living God.

The LXX is abbreviated:

εἰσάκουσον, κύριε, εἴσβλεψον, κύριε, ἴδε τοὺς λόγους, οὓς ἀπέστειλε Σενναχηριμ ὀνειδίζειν θεὸν ζῶντα.

Listen, O Lord! Look, O Lord! See the words which Sennacherib has sent to mock the living God!

Fritsch has noticed this anti-anthropomorphic rendering.[194] The collapsing out of the words for organs is conducted in an orderly fashion, though the LXX product is slightly asymmetrical.[195] In spite of this slight variation, it appears that the translator has exercised a degree of care in intentionally removing references to divine organs.[196] Elsewhere, his proclivity for collapsing Hebrew parallelism often leaves a much less balanced result. Thus, the relative attention to structure and

194. Cf. 'Concept of God', p. 158: 'In this passage not only is אזנך omitted, but עינך as well. Anti-anthropomorphism was undoubtedly at work here.' The Hexaplaric manuscripts follow the MT and the synoptic text in 2 Kgs/4 Kgdms.

195. As for auditory perception, הטה יהוה אזנך ושמע is collapsed to εἰσάκουσον, κύριε. With regard to visual perception, פקח יהוה עינך וראה is abbreviated as εἴσβλεψον, κύριε. The alteration comes with the verb that sums up the call to divine attentiveness and provides this with its intended object: the auditory ושמע את כל־דברי סנחריב אשר שלח is rendered as the mixed-sense ἴδε τοὺς λόγους, οὓς ἀπέστειλε Σενναχηριμ, leaving the curious notion of *seeing words*; cf. Isa. 2.1 (הדבר אשר חזה ישעיהו) and Acts 4.29 (καὶ τὰ νῦν, κύριε, ἔπιδε ἐπὶ τὰς ἀπειλὰς αὐτῶν).

196. This excision is all the more remarkable in the light of the occasional characterization of chs. 36–39 as more literal than the rest of LXX Isaiah. Cf., for example, P.K. McCarter, Jr, *Textual Criticism: Recovering the Text of the Hebrew Bible* (Philadelphia: Fortress Press, 1986), p. 90: 'LXX (Isaiah): Very free translation, verging on paraphrase, except in chaps. 36–39, where it is relatively literal.'
As one might have expected, TJ has taken an alternative route towards the same destination. The verse begins, organ-less and non-imperatively, with the words גלי קדמך יוי ודין ושמיע קדמך יוי. The parallel account in 4 Kgdms 19.16 is not similarly modest. It echoes the anthropomorphic language of the MT.

balance that are in evidence here may support the idea that this verse has been *carefully reformulated* rather than *haphazardly collapsed*.[197]

Furthermore, by virtue of the fact that anti-anthropomorphic concerns can be corroborated elsewhere in LXX Isaiah, Fritsch's approach seems superior to the twofold speculative explanation that Seeligmann brings to this verse.[198] Seeligmann assumes that LXX 37.17 exhibits both the survival of elements of a separate Greek translation[199] and the adoption of a 'Hellenic liturgical formula' to express Hezekiah's prayer.[200]

Thus, LXX Isa. 37.17 provides still further corroborating evidence that the Isaiah translator was averse to describing God in terms of the human physique. For our present purposes, the important fact is that this avoidance took place in the case of references to God's *eyes*.

Finally, further evidence that appears to corroborate the observation that this translator creatively reshapes references to the divine eyes, especially when these might suggest less than full perception, is to be found in the analysis of LXX Isa. 59.2, pp. 122-27.

This discussion began by noticing an apparent anti-anthropomorphic translation at 65.16. The subsequent investigation of similar moves within LXX Isaiah and in similar texts throughout the wider scribal and translational tradition encourages the view that such moves are not

197. I choose these latter words advisedly and without intending them as a global characterization of this translator, who can—when it is in his interest to do so—be careful, creative and eloquent.

198. Even if Fritsch merely asserts—in just two sentences—that anti-anthropomorphism is evident here, rather than arguing his case.

199. An idea that recurs repeatedly in Seeligmann's monograph. One must always remain attentive to this possibility, though LXX Isaiah offers only limited evidence upon which to base such an hypothesis.

200. Cf. *LXX Version*, p. 36. Of the abbreviated invocation, Seeligmann writes: 'Evidently the eight words of the Hebrew invocations were summarized in a Hellenic liturgical formula of four words, after which the phrase καὶ ἴδε must have crept in here from some other literal translation from the Hebrew text, and which has ousted the original καὶ ἄκουσον after the introductory formula.' Seeligmann's view seems to rest upon an unknown liturgical formula and an unattested (except for the alleged attestation in this verse) alternative Greek translation. For its part, an anti-anthropomorphic explanation rests upon a recognizable and repeated tendency to squeeze out descriptions of God's physique. This empirical basis makes it preferable.

Careful attention to features of the translator's technique that are repeated (sometimes hundreds of times) does not invalidate more speculative approaches. However, it often provides refreshingly concrete alternatives to them.

accidental and isolated. Rather they appear to result from a religious preference for statements that do not promote anthropomorphic or anthropopathic description of God, divine passivity or divine imperception. Evidence for a final theologically ameliorative strategy on the part of the LXX translator in chs. 56–66 is discussed below.

Translations Which Accentuate God's Remoteness in LXX Isaiah 56–66
Isaiah 57.15. MT Isa. 57.15 asserts a paradox in the Lord's character in that he dwells at two extremes. It reads:

כי כה אמר רם ונשא שכן עד וקדוש שמו
מרום וקדוש אשכון ואת־דכא ושפל־רוח
להחיות רוח שפלים ולהחיות לב נדכאים

> For this is what the one who is high and lifted up has said, who inhabits eternity and whose name is holy: 'I dwell in a high and holy (place), and with the crushed and the lowly of spirit, to revive the spirit of those who are lowly and to revive the heart of those who are crushed...'

On the one hand, he inhabits eternity, a high and holy place. On the other,[201] he lives with the shattered and humbled of spirit. The first statement must have been agreeable to the translator, but it is understandable that he might not have found the second equally palatable.

One factor makes it difficult—though hardly impossible—unquestioningly to assign an ideological motivation to the changes that the translator supplies. It is his difficulty, observable elsewhere, in discerning when unsuffixed את is the preposition rather than the much more common *nota accusativi*.[202] This struggle in recognizing prepositional את might possibly have obliged the translator to rearrange the syntax of this verse, and twice to supply διδούς. It is more likely, however, that the substantial alteration of God's elevation achieved by the LXX is not simply the result of confusion with regard to את, but rather a piece of targum-like theological exegesis that guards the exalted nature of the deity.

Τάδε λέγει κύριος ὁ ὕψιστος ὁ ἐν ὑψηλοῖς κατοικῶν τὸν αἰῶνα,
"Αγιος ἐν ἁγίοις ὄνομα αὐτῷ, κύριος ὕψιστος ἐν ἁγίοις
ἀναπαυόμενος καὶ ὀλιγοψύχοις διδοὺς μακροθυμίαν καὶ διδοὺς
ζωὴν τοῖς συντετριμμένοις τὴν καρδίαν.

---

201. ואת־ relates the following statement syntactically to the same verb, אשכון. The waw seems to serve as an adversative. Therein lies the paradox, for the Lord is both very high and very low.

202. Cf., inter alia, 8.6; 19.23; 45.9; 53.9; 63.11.

> This is what the Lord has said, the Highest among the high, who inhabits eternity, Holy among the holy ones is his name, the Lord, the highest, who takes his rest among the holy ones and gives patience to the faint-hearted and gives life to those who have become shattered of heart.

In the LXX, the participle διδοὺς mediates the relationship of God and humankind. In the MT, God dwells *with* humankind's weaker specimens. In the LXX, he dwells *on high*, but he *gives* patience[203] to the faint-hearted and *gives* life[204] to the broken-hearted.

This verse appears to be translated in a manner that keeps God high—where we might have expected the translator to appreciate his presence—while allowing him a certain generosity towards those who are low. However, in the LXX God does *not* come down among them, let alone live with them.

Isaiah 63.14. A distinction between the divine Spirit and a lesser, commissioned, spirit at 63.14 may carry forward the translator's reluctance to have God *come down*. In rehearsing the Exodus events, MT 63.14a recalls guidance through the desert in these words: כבהמה בבקעה תרד רוח יהוה תניחנו. The translator appears to have read תרד with reference to the adjacent subject, רוח יהוה, rather than with (כ)בהמה. If he has also identified the רוח יהוה with the Lord himself, then his text asks him to speak of divine descent, a movement that he has elsewhere shown signs of disliking.

He appears to have read כבהמה בבקעה with the syntax of 63.13. It is impossible to discern whether this was itself a conscious piece of exegesis that was executed for the purpose of not allowing comparison of the Lord to a beast. At the very least, it can be stated that the elements of scandal are present.[205] Regardless of the precise mental processes involved, the translator's reading leaves תרד as the activity of the Lord's Spirit. Together with the possibly anthropomorphic connotations of God leading Israel through the desert, this might have looked troublesome.

The translator extricates himself from this dilemma by falling back upon an LXX idiom for a lesser wind or spirit that goes out from the

---

203. Μακροθυμία has been altogether supplied, unless it has been derived from the first להחיות.

204. Here the connection to להחיות is easily discerned.

205. The MT applies the simile—כבהמה—to *the people* rather than to God, since it is *they* who, like livestock, go down into a valley and rest.

Lord.[206] He leaves the impression that he has seen this descent not as a movement of God's own spirit, but rather as that of a commissioned, lesser spirit.[207] Presumably, the Lord himself is not directly implicated in the use of תרד/κατέβη. If this *spirit from the Lord* is not to be entirely distinguished from the deity, it may function analogously to the Lord's מימרא. Indeed, it is the מימרא דיוי that leads the people in TJ Isa. 63.14, a verse that omits all mention of a descent.

Isaiah 63.19(64.1). A striking example of the reluctance of the Isaiah translator to have God *come down* from heaven is found in 63.19(64.1), where the prayer in the MT reads, 'Oh that you would tear open the heavens and come down, so that the mountains would tremble at your presence!' The LXX has, 'If you open heaven, trembling shall seize mountains because of you, and (they) shall melt.' For an extensive treatment of this verse in its context, see Chapter 5, 'Isaiah 63.15–63.19 (64.1)', pp. 182-93.

Isaiah 66.9. The imagery of Isaiah 66.9 brings the Lord into the messy urgencies of childbirth. Indeed, the verse's vocabulary allows—even if it does not mean to suggest—his personal involvement in procreation and delivery itself. In commenting upon mother Zion's sudden labour (66.8), MT 66.9 reads:

---

206. This manner of expression is found in 1 Sam. 16.14 (καὶ πνεῦμα κυρίου ἀπέστη ἀπὸ Σαουλ καὶ ἔπνιγεν αὐτὸν πνεῦμα πονηρὸν παρὰ κυρίου) and Num. 11.31 (καὶ πνεῦμα ἐξῆλθεν παρὰ κυρίου καὶ ἐξεπέρασεν ὀρτυγομήτραν ἀπὸ τῆς θαλάσσης).

207. It is possible, though not likely, that the translator does speak here of the divine Spirit itself, though in a respectful, Targumistic way. Cf. Brockington, 'Septuagint and Targum', p. 86: 'Lastly, attention may be drawn to the tendency shown by both LXX and Targum to resolve a construct phrase in which God is the governed word. In the former the preposition παρά is frequently used, e.g. Exod. 14 13 ישועת יהוה—τὴν σωτηρίαν τὴν παρὰ τοῦ θεοῦ and in the latter מן קדם e.g. Gen. 15.4 דבר יהוה—פתגמא מן קדם יהוה.'

The translator of LXX Isaiah utilizes such a 'targumism' to speak of dew (26.19), salvation (46.13), mercy (54.10), covenant (59.21), and even the Lord's Spirit (translated as ἡ ὀργὴ παρὰ κυρίου in 59.19). However, when used of רוח יהוה, it produces an entirely different meaning rather than a mere reverential touching up, which may in part explain why πνεῦμα παρὰ κυρίου was not used at 59.19. It seems the exegetical orientation that I have attempted to sketch out provides a better explanation.

הָאֲנִי אַשְׁבִּיר וְלֹא אוֹלִיד אָמַר יְהוָה
אִם־אֲנִי הַמּוֹלִיד וְעָצַרְתִּי אָמַר אֱלֹהָיִךְ

'Shall I who break (maternal waters) not bring to birth?,' the Lord has
said. 'Shall I—the one who causes birth—shut up (the womb)?,' your
God has said.

At the least, this verse casts the Lord in a midwife's role. The
translator might also have considered that the two hiphil forms of ילד
came perilously close to suggesting procreation, a meaning that the
hiphil of ילד *always* bears outside of Isaiah in the HB and in its Greek
translation.[208] Piel ילד in the HB and forms of the verb in rabbinical
literature *are* used of midwifery.

The LXX deviates remarkably and evacuates the verse of metaphor.[209]

ἐγὼ δὲ ἔδωκα τὴν προσδοκίαν ταύτην, καὶ οὐκ ἐμνήσθης μου, εἶπε
κύριος. οὐκ ἰδοὺ ἐγὼ γεννῶσαν καὶ στεῖραν ἐποίησα; εἶπεν ὁ θεός.

'But I gave this expectation, and you did not remember me,' the Lord
has said. 'Behold, am I not the one who has made (both) the bearing
woman and the barren woman?' God has said.

The major LXX innovations are the following: (a) אשביר was
presumably meant to be read as אַשְׁבִּיר (to break maternal waters), as in
the vocalized MT. However, the LXX has translated אֲשַׂבִּיר (to cause to
hope) in spite of the fact that the hiphil of this verb is unattested in
BH;[210] (b) ולא אוליד (to cause to give birth, beget, bear) is rendered by

208. The hiphil of ילד occurs 176 times in the HB, the majority of these
occurring in the genealogies of Genesis, Ruth and Chronicles. It invariably has a
masculine subject, though the LXX upon occasion translates it with regard to a
feminine subject. It is always translated by γεννᾶν, τεκνοποιεῖν or -τίκτειν and
always denotes paternity or child-bearing. Within Isaiah, the slightest ambiguity
occurs at 55.10, where the metaphorical application of the term to rain and earth
preserves the notion of generation, though not of childbirth. Cf. also Ps. 2.9.

On the tendency of the HB to eschew divine fatherhood as a response to the
fundamental role of 'the physical fatherhood of the gods' in ANE myth, cf.
Westermann, *Jesaja 40–66*, p. 312. Westermann felt the risk that this idea should be
understood in mythological terms had dropped into the background by postexilic
times. The LXX treatment of the verse at hand might suggest that not all were
agreed that the danger had passed.

209. LXX Isaiah frequently demetaphorizes the images of its source text. For the
same phenomenon in TJ Isaiah—applied unsystematically there, as in the Greek
text—cf. van der Kooij, *Textzeugen*, p. 176.

210. There is an Aramaic aphel, which appears sometimes to have a causative
meaning, as in LXX.

καὶ οὐκ ἐμνήσθης μου (you did not remember me), a gloss that seems to have more to do with human (non-)response to the giving of hope than to anything that can be read out of this verb itself; (c) אִם־אֲנִי הַמּוֹלִיד וְעָצַרְתִּי (shall I, who beget, close up [the womb]?) seems connected to the biological details of childbirth. However, LXX glosses this phrase as the more philosophical οὐκ ἰδοὺ ἐγὼ γεννῶσαν καὶ στεῖραν ἐποίησα (Am I not the one who has created [both] the bearing [fertile] woman and the barren woman?).

In sum, הַאֲנִי אַשְׁבִּיר וְלֹא אוֹלִיד suggests imminent fulfilment of a process that, once initiated, cannot be detained. God is intimately involved in it. Its translation—ἐγὼ δὲ ἔδωκα τὴν προσδοκίαν ταύτην—is instead a more general assertion of the Lord's sovereignty over the circumstances that bring Zion's children home. It is possible to conceive that the translator's massive rearticulation of the Hebrew text is simply the child of accident and incomprehension. The אַשְׁבִּיר/אַשְׂבִּיר conversion is easy enough to explain by the absence of diacritical marks in the source text.[211] Similarly, the attribution of a meaning normally linked to the qal feminine of יל"ד to the hiphil masculine might explain γεννῶσαν, though καὶ οὐκ ἐμνήσθης μου is hardly amenable to the same explanation.

Nevertheless, the Hebrew of this verse is simply not difficult enough to produce the level of incomprehension that would push this translator into free paraphrase. Indeed, he competently translates every lexeme in this verse either here or elsewhere. Furthermore, the meaning 'to become the father of' for hiphil יל"ד is exceptionally well established by biblical precedent.

It is more likely, especially in the light of the translator's display of the same tendency elsewhere, that he has executed an ameliorative reading. His achievement is to safeguard God from direct involvement in the bloody details of midwifery. He has also circumvented the notion

A discussion of the new heavens and new earth (as in Isa. 66) in 2 Pet. 3.10-14 employs προσδοκάω three times. It occurs frequently in other New Testament eschatological passages as well. Since Isa. 66.9 contains the *only* Old Testament appearance of the word in an eschatological context, one wonders whether this verse is responsible for the generation of this standard item of New Testament eschatological vocabulary.

211. Ps. 69(68)21 produces the same deviation. Nehemiah does exactly the opposite twice, reading שֵׁבֶר as שֶׁבֶר. Curiously, similar language and vocabulary at Isa. 37.3 produce a free—and perhaps marginally sanitized—rendering: כִּי בָאוּ בָנִים עַד־מַשְׁבֵּר = ὅτι ἥκει ἡ ὠδὶν τῇ τικτούσῃ.

of divine paternity in a context where the imagery of a pregnant woman in labour might have lent itself to connotations that were all too human.

Summary and Conclusion

An examination of the evidence for properly theological ameliorative translations in LXX Isaiah supports neither those scholars who deny that this occurs, nor those who rest the case for such exegesis upon isolated instances. Rather, LXX Isaiah shows an unsystematic tendency to translate creatively in order to deflect descriptions of God that are anthropomorphic or anthropopathic. The same tendency alters statements that could be understood to limit divine perception, even if the Hebrew text displays no such intent. Finally, the translator prefers to keep God high rather than directly to translate MT descriptions of divine descent.

Such ameliorative translations are rarely effected *ex nihilo*. Rather than diverge widely from his source text, the translator prefers to use possibilities that that text affords him, both in the particular context that he is translating and from further afield in Isaiah and the Hebrew Bible. In this sense, his relationship to the Hebrew text displays conservative tendencies. He is anarchic neither with regard to his parent text nor with regard to wider practice in Second Temple and later Judaism. The same religious sensitivities that are on modest display in LXX Isaiah appear in Targum Jonathan and in the scribal tradition which culminates in the *tiqqune sopherim*.

Chapter 5

CORRELATIVE AMELIORATIONS IN LXX ISAIAH 56–66

Correlative Ameliorations as a Feature of LXX Isaiah

The ameliorative translations that were surveyed in the preceding chapters have as their common denominator the transformation of a statement *about God*. In the present chapter, we turn our attention to a number of LXX deviations that do *not* have the deity as their principal referent.

These ameliorations alter the status of non-human beings other than God, remove perceived obscenity or sexual reference, mitigate damage done to creation and avoid direct speech about God. I will first present a broad sampling of such interpretative moves as these occur across the LXX, then focus more exhaustively on those that appear in chs. 56–66.

Correlative Ameliorations That Alter the Identity or Status of Non-human Beings Other than God
Isaiah 2.18–19. Ameliorative readings occur in all sections of the Greek Isaiah.[1] Occasionally, such a conversion serves to protect the Lord's uniqueness by refusing to grant to other potential objects of worship the quality of personality or will.[2] This kind of 'corollary' theological amelioration occurs at Isaiah 2, which describes an elaborate series of reversals that are to take place on the 'day of the Lord'. In 2.18–19, the

---

1. H.M. Orlinsky eloquently describes the dilemma of the Bible translator, ancient or modern: 'He will also realize what it is to be confronted by a Hebrew word or phrase whose meaning…asserts something that he can hardly accept as true, or binding, or dignified, and he must decide whether to produce the unacceptable forthrightly—it is, literally, the word of God!—or paraphrase it, or mistranslate, or even suppress it by benign neglect.' Cf. 'The Septuagint as Holy Writ and the Philosophy of the Translators', *HUCA* 46 (1975), pp. 89-114 (103-104).
2. Cultic practice is a touchy subject in several scribal traditions. Cf., for example, A. Rofé, 'The End of the Book of Joshua According the Septuagint', *Henoch* 4 (1982), pp. 17-35, for an LXX plus about burying of *reliquiae*.

focus changes from human haughtiness to the destiny of false gods. According to one possible reading of the text, these are personified and pictured as beings that can move of their own volition:

והאלילים כליל יחלף³

(19) ובאו במערות צרים ובמחלות עפר

מפני פחד יהוה ומהדר גאונו בקומו לערץ הארץ

> And the idols will utterly pass away and they will enter the caves of the rocks and the holes of the ground, from the terror of the Lord, and from the glory of his majesty, when he rises to terrify the earth.

The LXX appears to read the first word of 2.19 as וּבָאוּ,[4] rather than the imperative בֹּאוּ[5] or the infinitive וּבוֹא. If the verb is read as וּבָאוּ, its subject is ambiguous. It could be either הָאֱלִילִים or the human beings under discussion prior to 2.18. Regardless of the precise form of the word that the LXX translator perceived, it seems likely that he regarded the Hebrew of 2.19 as a further elaboration of the behaviour of *gods* rather than of human beings.[6] The LXX syntax seems to support the MT *as the Hebrew text now stands*, except for the pluralization of יחלף. Thus, both the LXX and one reading of the ambiguous unemended MT[7] extend the comment about gods from 2.18 into the following verse:

καὶ τὰ χειροποίητα πάντα κατακρύψουσιν (19) εἰσενέγκαντες εἰς
τὰ σπήλαια καὶ εἰς τὰς σχισμὰς τῶν πετρῶν καὶ εἰς τὰς

---

3.   The BHS apparatus reads this verb as plural, with 1QIsa[a] and the versions. All seem to take הָאֱלִילִים as the subject. S. Daniel notices Kimchi's alternative: 'On voit que le nom "idoles" devient en grec le complément d'objet du verbe, qui est au pluriel, avec la valeur d'un impersonnel. Kimhi propose le même construction, mais en faisant de Dieu le sujet, non exprimé, du verbe qui est au singulier dans le T.M.' *Recherches sur le vocabulaire du culte dans la Septante* (Études et Commentaires, 61; Paris: Librairie C. Klincksieck, 1966), p. 260 n. 8.

4.   As in the unemended MT. Cf. 1QIsa[a] ובאו. For the UBS committee finding in favour of the MT, cf. Barthélemy, *Critique Textuelle*, II, pp. 19-20.

5.   Which is the BHS *propositum*, on the analogy of 2.10.

6.   The text does not encourage the view that he read יחליפו. Even if he had, hiphil חלף means *to change, to substitute* or *to show newness* rather than *to hide*. ובוא, regardless of any minor changes that it may have suffered in the tradition, does not resemble hiphil forms. The one possible exception, ויביאו, would probably not have led this translator to the syntactically subordinate εἰσενέγκαντες, *pace* HUB, p. ח.: 'יָבָאוּ'. The best explanation appears to be that he *read* the qal imperfect and perfect consecutive that the MT attests, understood them to have הָאֱלִילִים as their subject, and then *altered* them on ideological grounds.

7.   I.e. the one that sees הָאֱלִילִים as the subject of ובאו.

τρώγλας τῆς γῆς⁸ ἀπὸ προσώπου τοῦ φόβου κυρίου καὶ ἀπὸ τῆς
δόξης τῆς ἰσχύος αὐτοῦ, ὅταν ἀναστῇ θραῦσαι τὴν γῆν.

<u>And they will hide all things that are made by hands</u>, <u>carrying them</u> into
the caves and into the crevices of rocks and into the holes in the ground,
because of the fear of the Lord and the glory of his strength, when he
rises to shatter the earth.

By reading the text as he has, the LXX translator has either received
or created for himself the problem of fully personified gods.⁹ It might
not have seemed perilous to have idols חלף in the sense of 'vanish'.¹⁰
To have them 'pass by/away' *and* 'go into' caves, however, might have
breached the translator's threshold of tolerance. Such a momentary
granting to idols of intentionality and mobility in a book that elsewhere
denies them such personal qualities with derisive glee may have proved
embarrassing for the translator.

In order to extricate himself from this dilemma, he executes a subject–complement inversion that makes these idols the *object* of *human*
activity. For the LXX translator, idols will no longer 'pass through' or
'go away',¹¹ nor will they go¹² anywhere on their own. Rather, people
will hide them by carrying them into inaccessible places.

The similarities between the Hebrew texts of 2.10 and 2.19 show
them to function as a type of refrain. This refrain-like character may
encourage the reader to see *both* of the slightly distinct statements as
though dealing with human subjects, as 2.10 clearly does. The LXX
syntax, however, somewhat disrupts this similarity. It does so not only
by linking the syntax of 2.19 to that of 2.18—where the matter of
interest is *gods*, not humans—but also by translating the two forms of
טמן differently, with κρύπτειν at 2.10 and κατακρύπτειν at 2.19.

The subsequent ideological transformation—if, as it seems, ideology
stands behind these details—is therefore accomplished not only by
means of the *grammatical* move already mentioned. It also draws upon
lexical resources.

8. The two prepositional phrases of MT 2.19 have become three in the LXX
under the influence of 2.21. Cf. Ziegler, *Untersuchungen*, p. 61.
9. The works of human hands that are elsewhere said to be 'nothing'.
10. Cf. G.B. Gray, *A Critical and Exegetical Commentary on the Book of Isaiah
I–XXVII* (title page, *I–XXXIX*). I. *Introduction and Commentary on I–XXVII*. (ICC;
Edinburgh: T. & T. Clark, 1912), pp. 50, 56.
11. יחלף.
12. ובאו.

חלף does not mean 'to hide', though κατακρύπτειν certainly does.[13] Once the translator had made the decision to demote the אלילים from the status of actors to that of objects that are acted upon, he may have supplied κατακρύπτειν exclusively by way of the context. That is, if one carries idols into hidden places, the effort is presumably made in order to *hide* them. He also has בוא בצור והטמן בעפר (= καὶ νῦν εἰσέλθατε εἰς τὰς πέτρας καὶ κρύπτεσθε εἰς τὴν γῆν) at 2.10 to guide him. It is possible that this 'local' context was enough to suggest to him the notion of 'hiding' as a substitute for חלף in 2.18.

However, an intriguing and lexically precise parallel in Genesis 35 may suggest that *this* verse supplied the Isaiah translator with the required lexical resources, or at least supplemented those that were available close at hand. In Gen 35.4, the household of Jacob, lately possessed of fresh monotheistic conviction, dispenses with the foreign gods that they had accumulated:

ויתנו אל־יעקב את כל־אלהי הנכר אשר בידם ואת־הנזמים
אשר באזניהם ויטמן אתם יעקב תחת האלה אשר עם־שכם

> So they gave to Jacob <u>all the foreign gods</u> that they had, and the rings that were in their ears; and Jacob <u>hid them</u> under the oak that was near Shechem.

> καὶ ἔδωκαν τῷ Ιακωβ <u>τοὺς θεοὺς τοὺς ἀλλοτρίους</u>, οἳ ἦσαν ἐν ταῖς χερσὶν αὐτῶν, καὶ τὰ ἐνώτια τὰ ἐν τοῖς ὠσὶν αὐτῶν, <u>καὶ κατέκρυψεν αὐτὰ</u> Ιακωβ ὑπὸ τὴν τερέμινθον τὴν ἐν Σικιμοις ...

Now κατακρύπτειν is not a common word in the LXX.[14] Gen. 35.4 and Isa. 2.18 are the only two occurrences where it is used of idols. Its occurrence in these contexts may suggest that the Isaiah translator borrowed the relevant verb from the parallel in Genesis 35.[15] Indeed, if

---

13. חלף//κατακρύπτειν is a *hapax* equivalency, which is not surprising in the light of their clearly different meanings. Scholz and Fischer attempt to reconcile the two words semantically on the grounds of a slight orthographic confusion: 'SCH. denkt an Stamm עלף, aber wohl nur freie Ü.g.: "den Platz ändern" = "verbergen" '; cf. Scholz, *Schrift*, 19. Whilst this possibility cannot be dismissed completely, two observations weaken this approach: (a) ע/ה is not a common confusion in LXX Isaiah and (b), the translator handles עלף competently elsewhere (cf. 21.1; 24.5; 40.31; 41.1).

14. It occurs 18 times in translated books, and once in 2 Macc. If the Isaiah translator needed simply to supply a word that means *to hide* at 2.18, we might have expected the exceedingly frequent κρύπτειν, especially as this occurs nearby at 2.10.

15. The phrase האלילים כליל—the second word of which the translator read

he felt that he needed biblical authorization to effect the desired sub-ordination of the gods at Isa. 2.18–19, Gen. 35.4 may have provided not only a word, but the willpower as well.

Isaiah 24.23. It is frequently difficult to discern whether the translator has achieved a remarkable ideological conversion with the linguistic materials at hand; or whether he has simply made an embarrassing mistake.[16]

Isa. 24.23 is such an occasion:

וחפרה הלבנה ובושה החמה כי־מלך יהוה צבאות
בהר ציון ובירושלם ונגד זקניו כבוד

Then the moon will be abashed, and the sun ashamed; for the Lord of hosts will reign on Mount Zion and in Jerusalem, and before his elders (he will manifest) his glory.

καὶ τακήσεται ἡ πλίνθος καὶ πεσεῖται τὸ τεῖχος ὅτι βασιλεύσει κύριος ἐν Σιων καὶ ἐν Ιερουσαλημ καὶ ἐνώπιον τῶν πρεσβυτέρων δοξασθήσεται

And the brick will crumble,[17] and the wall will fall down, for the Lord will reign in Zion and in Jerusalem, and before the elders will he be glorified.

It is frequently observed that the LXX translator has interpreted the 'apocalypse' of Isaiah 24–27 as a lament over a fallen city. This

as adjectival (πάντα)—might have seemed a particularly appropriate 'trigger' for bringing to mind the words כל־אלהי of Gen. 35.4. Curiously, however, כל remains untranslated in the Gen. verse. Perhaps the Isaiah translator knew a Greek Gen. that had πάντες τοὺς θεοὺς. This possibility must remain at the level of speculation, since the translator's allusion could just as well have been to a Greek text that he knew in Hebrew as well (cf. Chapter 4, note 11); or the contextual similarities without the כל element may have proved sufficient to link the two contexts in his mind. That his allusion was to Hebrew Gen. alone remains conceivable, though the choice of the uncommon κατακρύτειν may favour an explanation via *LXX* Genesis.

16. For the latter option, applied to this verse, cf. Ottley, *Isaiah*, II, p. 224: '… their rendering depends *on their mistake…* Heb. "the moon," לְבָנָה: also, with one change of pointing, לְבֵנָה, has this meaning of "brick": both senses from the root meaning "white." *From this the whole divergence of the verse seems to arise…*' (emphases added). Ottley occupies the 'passive' end of the spectrum, with regard to the possibility of the translator's intelligent purposefulness in such conversions. Koenig, who does not treat this verse, stands scornfully at the other.

17. Or 'dissolve', 'melt'.

understanding of the section comes to light most forcefully in ch. 27. It seems doubtful that the translator has captured the allusion that ch. 27 makes to the vineyard parable of ch. 5,[18] If he *has,* he has expressed this in a highly *demetaphorized* fashion. The restored vineyard has become a city—and a fallen one at that!—with hardly any trace of the viticultural motif that links the two passages in the Hebrew text.[19]

This transformation may be glimpsed already in the passage at hand. The personified heavenly bodies of MT 24.23 have become in the LXX mere brick and wall. Cosmic apocalypse is reduced to urban decay. This is accomplished with minimal alterations to the consonantal MT (≈ *Vorlage*).[20]

TJ also depersonifies the sun and moon, though by a wholly different technique: 'Then *those who serve the moon* will be ashamed and *those who worship the sun* will be humiliated.'[21] TJ's resolution is simpler than that of the LXX because it requires alteration of only the substantives.[22] With regard to the two substantives that the LXX alters, הַלְּבָנָה (moon) is read as הַלְּבֵנָה (brick) and חַחַמָּה (sun)[23] as הַחֹ(וֹ)מָה

18. Cf. H.G.M. Williamson, *The Book Called Isaiah: Deutero-Isaiah's Role in Composition and Redaction* (Oxford: Oxford University Press, 1994), p. 182: 'The allusion to Isa. 5.1-7 at 27: 2-6 is unmistakeable …'

19. Cf., for example, Ziegler, *Untersuchungen*, p. 87: '27,2-5 Aus dem Weinbergslied hat der griech. Übers. etwas ganz anderes gemacht: ein Lied auf die zerstörte Stadt…viell. wird 26,1 auf die Gestaltung von 27,2 ff. eingewirkt haben, wo ebenfalls die Rede ist von dem Liede über eine Stadt: "…man wird singen dieses Lied…siehe ein fest Stadt".'

20. Alternatively, BHS and Tov prefer the vocalized substantives as supported by the LXX: הַלְּבֵנָה and חַחֹמָה; cf. the BHS apparatus; Tov, *TCU*, p. 114; and Tov, *Textual Criticism*, p. 41. In *TCU*, Tov uses this case as an example of a text that can be reliably reconstructed on the basis of the LXX: 'When the content of the reconstructed vocalization differs significantly from that of MT, and when the reconstruction is supported by identical equivalents elsewhere in the LXX, as a rule, the reconstruction is reliable.' However, the context of the 'Isaiah Apocalypse' seems much more amenable to the language of celestial bodies than to that of brick and wall.

21. Emphases added; the Targum has דפלחין לסיהרא and דסגדין לשמשא, respectively.

22. This line of interpretation lives on in the comment of Rashi, who quotes TJ with approval.

23. Cf. J.C.L. Gibson, *Davidson's Introductory Hebrew Grammar~Syntax* (Edinburgh: T. & T. Clark, 1994), §42 Rem. 5: 'The adj. when it expresses the characteristic attribute of a noun is sometimes used instead of it, Is. 24.23 הַלְּבֵנָה

(wall). This much could be accomplished with little effort.[24]

Depersonification of the *verbs* would have presented a heartier challenge, though even here the first half of the task requires only revocalization rather than consonantal reconstruction. With regard to חֻפַּר,[25] the translator probably read a form of פָּרַר, which reflects a modest deviation from the MT.[26] Alternatively, it is just possible that he

the *moon* (*the white*), הַחַמָּה the *sun* (*the hot*).' Cf. also Waltke and O'Connor, *Syntax*, p. 263: 'In some cases the adjective stands where no concrete noun could do duty... The usage may be poetic: in the figure of antimeria (a type of metonymy) an expected noun is replaced by an adjective describing some essential charac-teristic of the elided noun.' Waltke and O'Connor cite Isa. 24.23 as an example of this.

24. The susceptibility of the consonants חמה to multiple vocalizations can be seen as well in Peshitta Isa. 27.4, where the Syriac translator reads the first word of the sentence חֵמָה אֵין לִי (so MT) as חֹמָה and renders it with ܫܘܪܐ. Van der Kooij includes this instance among his *Vokalisationsmöglichkeiten* of Peshitta Isaiah; *Textzeugen*, p. 285. The Peshitta reading appears to be the same as that which is reflected in the LXX. Πεσεῖται τὸ τεῖχος of 27.3 almost certainly results from a reading of the first word of 27.4 (חמה = MT חֵמָה, but LXX understood חֹמָה) with 27.3. This is the same result produced by the LXX reading of the same consonants, differently vocalized (= MT חַמָּה), in 24.23. On this, cf. also Cathcart and Gordon, *Targum of the Minor Prophets*, p. 131 n. 7.

Mekilta de-Rabbi Ishmael applies an אל תקרא exegetical manoeuvre to the occurrence of חמה in Exod. 14.29, one that moves the text in the opposite direction vis-à-vis the MT from the readings we have seen thus far. Exod. 14.29 reads as follows: וּבְנֵי יִשְׂרָאֵל הָלְכוּ בַיַּבָּשָׁה בְּתוֹךְ הַיָּם וְהַמַּיִם לָהֶם חֹמָה מִימִינָם וּמִשְּׂמֹאלָם. In Tractate Beshallah 7.52ff., one reads: 'And whence do we know that the sea also was filled with anger at them? It is said: "And the waters were Ḥmah against them." Do not read Ḥomah, "wall," but Ḥemah "anger."' (וּמִנַּיִן שָׁאַף הַיָּם נתמלא עליהם חמה שנאמר והמים להם חמה אל תקרי חומה אלא חימה). Cf. *Mekilta de-Rabbi Ishmael*, I. (trans. J.Z. Lauterbach; Philadelphia: Jewish Publication Society of America, 1933), pp. 246-47.

MT Isaiah itself probably utilizes the ה/ח consonantal exchange possibility to register a complaint that involves the sun. The MT's עִיר הַהֶרֶס (the city of *destruction*) likely reflects an original עִיר הַחֶרֶס (city of *the sun*), the change coming in response to disapproval of the Jewish temple at Leontopolis (itself seen in relationship to Heliopolis, the centre of Egyptian sun worship); cf. R.P. Gordon, '*Terra Sancta* and the Territorial Doctrine of the Targum to the Prophets', in J.A. Emerton and S.C. Reif (eds.), *Interpreting the Hebrew Bible. Essays in honour of E.I.J. Rosenthal* (Cambridge: Cambridge University Press, 1982), pp. 119-31 (122-23).

25. BDB II, *to be abashed/ashamed*.

26. BDB I, hoph., *to be broken*. Indeed, Isa. 24.19 uses a hithpo. form of פָּרַר

imagined an otherwise unattested pual form of חפר (BDB I) that might suggest the meaning *to be dug* (*to be undermined* >> *to crumble* ≈ τήκω). Such an explanation, whilst speculative in terms of attestation, enjoys the modest virtue of requiring no consonantal alteration.

In contrast to the handling of חפר, the move from ובושה to καὶ πεσεῖται is not facilitated by any observable lexical features. Rather, the new context of brick and wall—which has been established by the three creative vocalizations already discussed—has required an appropriate second verb. Πεσεῖται has met that need without the niceties of graphic similarity or any other authorizing element.[27]

(BDB II), *to be split, cracked, divided* with reference to the earth: פור התפוררה ארץ.

Cf. Joh. Fried. Schleusner, *Novus Thesaurus Philologico-Criticus: Sive, Lexicon in LXX. et Reliquos Interpretes Græcos, ac Scriptores Apocryphos Veteris Testamenti. Editio Altera, Recensita et Locupletata*, III (London: Jacobi Duncan, 1829), p. 264: '*חפר, *erubesco*. Ies. XXIV. 23. Sine dubio derivarunt a פור aut legerunt הפרסה, quæ fuit Grotii sententia.' Schleusner's followers have found the first of his alternatives persuasive enough not to mention the second. Although פרס—which means *to break in two, divide*—is a tolerable semantic match for τήκειν, it suffers the disadvantage of requiring a ה/ח conversion *and* an inserted ס. Scholz writes: 'וחפרה (et erubescet): καὶ τακήσεται d. h. 'וה (Schleus.)...' (*Uebersetzung*, p. 39). Fischer then seems to follow Scholz's distillation of Schleusner: 'וְחָפְרָה > καὶ τακησεται > והפרה (Aram., SCH., S.39), ח in ה w. Sf.' (*Schrift*, p. 40; cf. also pp. 80, 84). Ottley also follows Scholz, apparently without reference to Schleusner: 'Here Scholz, following Schleusner, suggests that LXX. read הפרה (from פרר?) instead of חפרה' (*Isaiah*, II, p. 224). In fact, Schleusner said more, and with less confidence. Ottley's bracketed query betrays some doubt as to what Schleusner was getting at.

27. Cf. Barthélemy, *Critique textuelle*, II, p. 193, with regard to Isa. 27.4(3): 'On notera que le *G aime l'expression πεσεῖται τὸ τεῖχος.' The liking is probably not as strong as Barthélemy suggests, but it is true that the same expression occurs in LXX Isa. 27.3 and 30.13. In the case of 27.4(3), חֵמָה is read as חֹמָה to produce τὸ τεῖχος, just as in 24.23. Barthélemy nods in the direction of intentionality on the part of the translator by describing this as *un parti-pris exégétique* (p. 193). Furthermore, πεσεῖται is supplied with no apparent Hebrew authorization. A similar move seems to take place at 30.13, though in that verse the rudiments necessary for the reconstruction are already present in the mention of a פרץ נפל, and a חומה נשגבה. Still, the verb ἁλίσκειν appears in both 27.3 and 30.13 with reference to the fallen city, enjoying in each case only marginal authorization from the text. This feature belies the intertextual web that enmeshes these verses as well as 24.23. A common interpretative motif appears to link them in the service of furthering the motif of the fallen city/wall.

It is conceivable that an inattentive translator could have accomplished all this by a highly atomistic translation technique. However, he would have had to ignore contextual features that—especially in the immediately preceding verses—compellingly describe the ruin of heaven and earth.

It is also possible that the conversions in this verse are due to the overriding emphasis on the fallen city that permeates chs. 24–27. Raw material like חמה and לבנה may have been translated as they were simply because they could be employed in the exposition of the fallen city theme. This would not have required a negative attitude towards the personification of sun and moon.

It seems more likely, however, that the translator was uncomfortable with his text's personification of the heavenly bodies. Such discomfort may be detectable already in 24.21, where the Lord's visitation upon the צבא המרום במרום utilizes an uncommon and arguably less personal equivalency to produce καὶ ἐπάξει ὁ θεὸς ἐπὶ τὸν κόσμον τοῦ οὐρανοῦ τὴν χεῖρα.[28]

The possibility that the deviations from the MT at 24.23 are intentional is strengthened by the observation that the translator knows how to translate the same substantives in a straightforward manner. At Isa. 30.26—a passage that does not utilize personification of the same bodies—both לְבָנָה and the rare הַחַמָּה[29] survive translation into Greek as selhvnh and ἥλιος, respectively:

Ziegler seems to anticipate Barthélemy's observation that the Isa. translator has an *unexplained* predilection for the idea of a fallen wall: '...oder in nämlichen Vers hat er חֹמָה = Mauer punktiert und dann wegen der öfters sich findenden Wendung: "die Mauer fällt" das Prädikat pesei'tai dazugestellt'; cf. *Untersuchungen*, p. 88. Cf. also p. 89: 'Wie bereits oben gesagt worden ist, wird es aussichtslos sein, das hebr. Äquivalent für πεσεῖται zu suchen...es ist jedoch nur als sinngemäßes Prädikat zu "Mauer" zum Bilde gehören.'

28. Κόσμος renders the exceedingly common צבא in Isa. 24.21 and 49.18, but elsewhere only in Gen. 2.1 (where it is the host *of earth*) and Deut. 4.19 and 17.3 (of *heaven*).

Cf. Ps. 19(18).5, where the MT's שֶׂם־אֹהֶל בהם (i.e. בשמים) לְשִׁמֶשׁ is sometimes read as evidence of solar cult and the אֹהל understood as a religious shrine (e.g. W.O.E. Oesterley, *The Psalms: Translated with Text-Critical and Exegetical Notes* [London: SPCK, 1953], pp. 167-70). The LXX has ἐν τῷ ἡλίῳ ἔθετο τὸ σκήνωμα αὐτοῦ, a rendering that virtually excludes this interpretation.

29. חַמָה occurs only in Isa. 24.23, 30.26(twice) and Cant. 6.10. In the latter verse, it is translated by ὁ ἥλιος.

והיה אור־הלבנה כאור החמה ואור החמה...

καὶ ἔσται τὸ φῶς τῆς σελήνης ὡς τὸ φῶς τοῦ ἡλίου καὶ τὸ φῶς τοῦ ἡλίου...

The worship of the sun—and the prohibition thereof—is a pre-occupation of the biblical literature, not least in the domestication that the celestial bodies undergo in Genesis 1.[30] Indeed, the popularity of the cult of the sun across the ANE is well established.[31] It was certainly well entrenched in Egypt.[32]

This background might well explain an attempt by the LXX translator to depersonify the sun and moon. For these bodies to be ashamed and abashed might seem a sufficient demotion already. However, for a translator such as this one—whose religious sensitivities we have already considered—it might not have been enough.[33]

The lexical details of this verse may have served *two* complementary purposes: to bend the passage into the service of the fallen city theme;

30. Upon its creation in Gen. 1.16, it is merely the nameless המאור הגדל. Cf. 'Sun', in *Encyclopedia Judaica*, XV, p. 517: 'The cult of the sun, very popular in Palestine—as is attested by place names such as Beth-Shemesh, En-Shemesh, Ir-Shemesh—was forbidden in Deuteronomy 4.19 and 17.3. It was, nevertheless, introduced into Judah by Manasseh (II Kings 31.3, 5). King Josiah abolished the cult (II Kings 23.5) and destroyed the horses and chariots of the sun placed "by the kings of Judah at the entrance of the Temple" (23.11).'

31. Cf. K. van der Toorn, 'Sun', *ABD*, VI, pp. 238-39: 'Though they did not speak of the sun in exclusively mythical terms, the peoples of the ANE regarded the sun as a deity... Considering the popularity of the solar cult in the ANE, its absence among the Israelites would have been astonishing... The deification of the sun was severely combatted by the partisans of Yahwism.'

32. Van der Toorn, 'Sun', p. 239: 'In Israel, the Lord fulfilled the role given to...Amon-Re in the Egyptian religion of the New Kingdom.' For a study that finds evidence for solar cult in ancient Israel and 'a rather more direct association between Yahweh and the sun than has often been thought' (p. 256), cf. J.G. Taylor, *Yahweh and the Sun: Biblical and Archaeological Evidence for Sun Worship in Ancient Israel* (JSOTSup, 111; Sheffield: Sheffield Academic Press, 1993). Taylor does not deal with the passage under discussion. Similarly, cf. F. du T. Laubscher, 'Epiphany and Sun Mythology in Zechariah 14', *JNSL* 20 (1994), pp. 125-38.

33. It is possible that the *crux* at Isa. 19.18 shows a parallel struggle with the sun in the *Hebrew* text tradition. The LXX transcription πόλις ασεδεκ may reflect an original עיר הצדק. Seeligmann attempts a reconstruction by which this city was later glossed as עיר החרס (City of the Sun), perhaps with specific reference to the Egyptian city Heliopolis. A later glossator reversed this move with a slight correction to ההרס (City of Ruins) (*LXX Version*, p. 68).

and, simultaneously, to down-grade a religiously suspect personification of the celestial bodies.

If, as appears to be the case, ideology stands behind the complex conversion at LXX Isa. 24.23, then it bears mention that the translator has once again accomplished a far-reaching manoeuvre with fairly *conservative* tactics. He has broken free from the consonantal text only once, by replacing ובושה with καὶ πεσεῖται. Elsewhere, he has chosen to work with the materials that his *Vorlage* handed him, subverting—rather than discarding—these.

Isaiah 51.9–10. LXX Isaiah displays a certain demythologizing tendency that may have influenced the translation of Isa. 51.9–10. These verses follow a passage (51.1–8) in which the Lord invokes the past as an illustration to the readers of what he has been able to accomplish.[34] As though in reply, vv. 9–10 turn back to the Lord in a kind of reverse exhortation: עורי עורי לבשי־עז זרוע יהוה[35] and, again, עורי כימי קדם דרות עולמים. It would seem that the speakers *have* looked to the past—indeed to a primeval day—for they now identify the Lord as he who 'cut Rahab in pieces, who pierced the dragon'. The imagery shifts in 51.10—but does not leave the remote past—for now reference is made to God's mastery over creation in the Exodus.

The exhortations to God's arm to *wake up* and *put on strength* are of the kind that frequently trouble this translator.[36] Furthermore, he might have been uncomfortable with the unapologetic reference to mythological Rahab and the dragon.[37] The first problem is solved by exploiting the presence of second-person imperatives and the fact that very soon the Hebrew text itself will direct such imperatives to Zion. They are feminine because they pertain to the Lord's זרוע, so they can be applied with relative ease to the grammatically feminine city. The Zion-directed context of those commands is brought forward from 51.17[38]

---

34. 51.1, 'Look to the rock from which you were hewn...'; and 51.2, 'Look to Abraham your father, and to Sarah who bore you...' This is interwoven with a call to look to and listen to the Lord himself: 51.1, 4, 7, 'Listen to me...'

35. 'Awake, awake, put on strength, O arm of the Lord!'

36. They are both anthropomorphic and suggestive of divine sleep and temporary weakness.

37. Or, perhaps, to Rahab the dragon.

38. התעוררי התעוררי קומי ירושלם.

and 52.1[39] and explicitly inserted here by the interpolated vocative, Ιερουσαλημ. As an important secondary accommodation, זרוע יהוה is reassigned as τοῦ βραχίονός σου.

As for the verse's cosmological mythology, the remote resonances of כימי קדם דרות עולמים...—which sound as though they refer to the beginning *of time*—become the more subdued ὡς ἐν ἀρχῇ ἡμέρας... ὡς γενεὰ αἰῶνος. The first of the Greek phrases sounds like the beginning *of a day*. The second, though its precise meaning may elude us, seems less awesomely prehistoric than its plural antecedent, דרות עולומים.[40]

The severest anti-mythological manoeuvre, however, comes with the non-translation of הלוא את־היא המחצבת רהב מחוללת תנין.[41] While it is again difficult to prove *intention*, the *result* seems clear. It is simple enough on text-critical grounds to note the possibility of haplography via homoioarkton,[42] and that may be all there is to say about this truncated LXX verse.

However, in the light of the alterations of this verse that have already been discussed, it is at least as likely that the orthographic qualities of these two verses *facilitate* rather than *cause* the omission. Alongside this evidence from the near context, one must place the indications from farther afield that this translator hesitates—when his text allows him to do so—to carry over personifications of idols, nature, or mythic entities such as Sheol.[43] The passage has become an exaltation of Jerusalem rather than a memory of cosmogony. This new theme merges nicely with 51.11 ('and come to Zion with joy'), as though this latter verse were a summary of the outcome that Jerusalem's heroic exertions have achieved.

Correlative Ameliorations That Remove Perceived Obscenity or Sexual Content
Isaiah 13.16. The oft-repeated truism that LXX Isaiah is 'free' in its rendering of the Hebrew text risks making of the translator an

39. עורי עורי לבשי עזך ציון.

40. One wonders, in the light of the following verse, whether the singular γενεά might not in the translator's mind be that of the *exodus*, though the difficulty of associating *Jerusalem* with that event may finally prove fatal to this conjecture.

41. 'Was it not you who cut Rahab in pieces, who pierced the dragon?'

42. הלוא את־היא המחצבת of 51.9 and הלוא את־היא המחרבת of 51.10 are identical at the beginning and differ only by ת/ב at the end.

43. Cf. 38.18 and, possibly, 57.9.

anarchical individualist. In fact, his freedom is conditioned both by a high number of observable consistencies in his translation technique and by religious sensitivities that he appears to share with the custodians of other scribal traditions of his period and later.

Isaiah 13.16, for example, drives home the severity of Babylon's doom with a comment on the fate of the oppressors' families: ועלליהם ירטשו לעיניהם ישסו בתיהם ונשיהם תשגלנה.[44] The Massoretes consider שגל[45] to be obscene, and substitute the euphemism שכב[46] as a Qere on each of its four occurrences.[47] The Isaiah translator—who offers the bland καὶ τὰς γυναῖκας αὐτῶν ἕξουσιν—appears to take Massoretic precaution one step further, as does the translator of Deut. 28.30. The latter verse refers to the unfortunate man who becomes engaged to a woman, 'but another man lies with her' (ואיש אחר ישגלנה). Here the Massoretes substitute ישכבנה. The LXX translator euphemizes still further: καὶ ἀνὴρ ἕτερος ἕξει αὐτήν.[48]

Exactly the same Massoretic and Septuagintal moves occur in Isa. 13.16, creating a three-step evolution from Kethiv ונשיהם תשגלנה to Qere ונשיהם תשכבנה to καὶ τὰς γυναῖκας ἕξουσιν. It appears from 1QIsaᵃ that the euphemistic reading is old.[49] It is impossible to be sure whether our translator knew it. The important fact for our purposes is

44. 'And their infants will be dashed in pieces before their eyes. Their houses will be plundered, and their wives will be raped.'

45. *To violate, rape, ravish.*

46. *To sleep (with).*

47. Deut. 28.30; Isa. 13.16; Zech. 14.2; Jer 3.2.

48. It is clear that the Greek expression in the LXX and later can have sexual implications. However, these are commonly references to 'respectable' sex and sometimes even to the broader state of marriage without direct reference or allusion to sexual relations. Cf., for example, 2 Chron. 11.21; 1 Esd. 9.12, 18; Judg. 10.19; 1 Cor. 7.2, 12, 29.

49. A lacuna in the text has obliterated the second and third letters of the word and sullied the first and fourth. M. Burrows was certain only of הנ..., which is not decisive (*The Dead Sea Scrolls of St. Mark's Monastery*. I. *The Isaiah Manuscript and the Habakkuk Commentary* (Cambridge, MA: American Schools of Oriental Research, 1950), Plate XI. The HUB editors and Tov (*TCU*, p. 73) are confident of ת...בנה, which would support the Qere. The photographs, in their best published edition, suggest to me that HUB and Tov are probably correct; cf. F.M. Cross, D.N. Freedman and J.A. Sanders (eds.), *Three Scrolls from Qumran: The Great Isaiah Scroll, The Order of the Community, The Pesher to Habakkuk* (Jerusalem: Albright Institute of Archaeological Research and Shrine of the Book, 1972).

that he was disturbed by the same offensive language that was later to unsettle the Massoretes.[50]

Correlative Ameliorations That Mitigate Damage Done to Creation
The creation is not subjected to the same grievous damage in LXX Isaiah as it is obliged to absorb in MT Isaiah. Examples of this kind of amelioration are to be found at LXX Isa. 34.4, 40.22, 45.12, 48.13, 51.6 and 54.9-10. In the interest of illuminating the ameliorative reading at 63.19(64.1), these cases are discussed below in 'Correlative Ameliorations Chs. 56–66', pp. 182-93.

Correlative Ameliorations of Cultic Vocabulary and/or
Religious Practice
In early biblical translation and interpretation, cultic vocabulary is sometimes rendered in a way that expresses disdain for practices that are not considered proper. At the same time, certain honoured terminology is safeguarded for use with reference only to approved religion. This is a characteristic that is evident beyond the LXX.[51]

Isaiah 16.12. When Moab, personified, wearies himself upon the high place and comes into his sanctuary, the LXX translator takes the opportunity to register his negative evaluation of the Moabite cult:

והיה כי־נראה כי־נלאה מואב על־הבמה
ובא אל־מקדשו להתפלל ולא יוכל

And when Moab is seen, when he wearies himself upon the high place, he will come into his sanctuary to pray, and he will not be able.[52]

καὶ ἔσται εἰς τὸ ἐντραπῆναί σε, ὅτι ἐκοπίασε Μωαβ ἐπὶ τοῖς βωμοῖς καὶ εἰσελεύσεται εἰς τὰ χειροποίητα αὐτῆς ὥστε προσεύξασθαι, καὶ οὐ μὴ δύνηται ἐξελέσθαι αὐτόν.

50. Alternatively, if he knew only the reading found in the MT Qere and (apparently) 1QIsa[a], then he found difficulty even in the euphemized Hebrew variant.
51. With regard to the LXX, cf. especially Daniel, *Vocabulaire du culte*; cf. also P. Churgin, *Targum Jonathan to the Prophets* (Yale Oriental Series, Researches 14; New Haven: Yale University Press, 1927); reprinted as part of the Library of Biblical Studies (Baltimore: Baltimore Hebrew College, 1983), p. 340: 'Usually מזבח is rendered by the targumist by the Aramic [sic]) parallel מדבחא. But this rendering is applied only to the holy, to God's altar. Whenever it refers to the profane, referring to the idol...it is rendered by אגורא, the pile.'
52. Alternatively, '*...and he will not prevail.*'

And it shall be to your shame, for Moab has become weary at the high
places and (s)he shall come into her hand-wrought (idols) to pray, and
these shall not be able to rescue him.

The MT's description of Moab's entrance—וּבָא אֶל־מִקְדָּשׁוֹ—sounds
like an ironic liturgical summons. It is rendered derisively by the
translator, who registers his evaluation of the help that is (not) to be
found in that place: καὶ εἰσελεύσεται εἰς τὰ χειροποίητα αὐτῆς.[53]
Elsewhere, the word χειροποίητος is a set piece of LXX sarcasm
that uncovers the ironic fact that people request help of things that they
themselves have made. Its polemical use for the gods inside Moab's
sanctuary rather than of the מִקְדָּשׁ itself is carried forward by the
verse's final clause. In the MT, misguided Moab either *cannot pray* or
will not prevail. The LXX, however, appears to make the handcrafted
idols that it has placed inside the sanctuary to be the subject of יוּכָל
rather than Moab personally: καὶ οὐ μὴ δύνηται ἐξελέσθαι αὐτόν.[54]
The provision of the unauthorized words ἐξελέσθαι αὐτόν to complement יוּכָל/δύνηται is reminiscent of Isa. 44.17. In that verse, the
idolmaker who worships his own product is ridiculed in words that link
the two passages:

וּשְׁאֵרִיתוֹ לְאֵל עָשָׂה לְפִסְלוֹ יִסְגּוֹד־לוֹ וְיִשְׁתַּחוּ
וְיִתְפַּלֵּל אֵלָיו וְיֹאמַר הַצִּילֵנִי כִּי אֵלִי אָתָּה

τὸ δὲ λοιπὸν ἐποίησεν εἰς θεὸν γλυπτὸν καὶ προσκυνεῖ αὐτῷ καὶ
προσεύχεται λέγων Ἐξελοῦ με, ὅτι θεός μου εἶ σύ.

Seeligmann considers the apparent influence of Isa. 44.17 upon LXX
Isa. 16.12 to be that of 'an interpretation based on misunderstanding'
that 'led the translator to make free explanatory additions'.[55] However,
there seems to be no reason why this could not have been conscious
exegesis rather than simple misunderstanding. The translator appears to
have borrowed anti-idol satire from 44.17 in order to fill out the picture

---

53. With αὐτῆς, the LXX may follow the standard practice of referring to
nations or peoples in the feminine singular. Ziegler's Lucianic group, as well as
Symmachus (cf. also Eus., οι λ'), have αὐτοῦ. With the masculine αὐτόν at the end
of this verse, the LXX appears to revert to Massoretic form with regard to gender.
The only alternative is to read Moab as both the subject and the reflexive object of
οὐ μὴ δύνηται ἐξελέσθαι αὐτόν, but this seems unlikely.

54. *Pace* Ottley, *Isaiah*, I, but with Brenton, *Septuagint*. The neuter plural τὰ
χειροποίητα would require a singular verb, which both the MT and the LXX have.

55. *LXX Version*, pp. 56-57.

of Moab's fruitless prayers, thus exegeting the cultic reference at 16.12 in a creatively disdainful direction.

Isaiah 45.20. Similar care is taken at Isa. 45.20, a passage dotted with universalistic phrases that bring references to the nations and to their bewildered cults into close proximity to statements about the Lord's uniqueness. MT 45.20 contains a summons either to the nations or to Jews among the nations:

הקבצו ובאו התנגשו יחדו פליטי הגוים
לא ידעו הנשאים את־עץ פסלם
ומתפללים אל־אל לא יושיע

Assemble yourselves and come! Draw near together, (you) survivors of the nations! Those who carry their wooden idol do not know, nor (do) those who pray to a god that does not save.

The LXX deviations are small-scale, but important:

συνάχθητε καὶ ἥκετε βουλεύσασθε ἅμα οἱ σῳζόμενοι ἀπὸ τῶν ἐθνῶν οὐκ ἔγνωσαν οἱ αἴροντες τὸ ξύλον γλύμμα αὐτῶν καὶ προσευχόμενοι ὡς πρὸς θεούς οἳ οὐ σῴζουσιν.

Assemble yourselves and come! Take counsel together, (you) who (have been) saved from the nations.[56] They have not known, those who carry their wooden engraving and who pray, as though to gods that do not save.

Two novelties of the Greek text may represent amelioration of cultic vocabulary. In the first instance, אל־אל לא יושיע may have used the singular noun אל too loosely for the translator's tastes. The context of the Hebrew verse makes it clear that the god in question is of the man-made variety, but the verse and its context utilize vocabulary that is much more commonly used of Israel's God. Indeed, as near as 45.14, it is predicted that the Egyptians will say *of the Lord* and *to Jews*: אך בך אל! In vv. 15, 21 and 22, the Lord is again called אל, a trend that culminates rhetorically in the proclamation, over against the non-saving אל of 45.20: ואין־עוד אלהים מבלעדי אל־צדיק ומושיע אין זולתי.[57]

Under these circumstances, the non-literal glossing of ומתפללים אל־אל לא יושיע in 45.20 by the pluralized καὶ προσευχόμενοι ὡς

---

56. The provision of οἱ σῳζόμενοι ἀπὸ τῶν ἐθνῶν may subtly shift the focus towards an unambiguous reference to *Jews* who have been saved *from (among) the nations*. Cf. the discussion in Chapter 7.

57. 45.21.

πρὸς θεούς, οἳ οὐ σῴζουσιν is probably to be regarded as an exegetical touch that prudently distances *such* gods from the real one.

A second LXX innovation may also seek to separate the true from the false, this time with regard to prayer. In the MT, idol worshippers pray to their helpless god(s). However, the insertion of ὡς assures that idolaters in the Greek text do not. The sentence as it now stands removes idolatrous prayer one step from true communication with deity. In a manner of speaking, such people pray—the text now concedes— but only *as if to gods that do not save.* This is not 'amelioration' in the straightforward sense of softening offensive language. Rather, in down-grading non-Yahwistic prayer to unanswered monologue, he has demonstrated his tendency to reserve for 'orthodox' worship those features of cultic vocabulary that are most to be revered.

Correlative Ameliorations in LXX Isaiah 56–66

Correlative Ameliorations That Alter the Identity or Status of Non-human Beings Other than God in Chs. 56–66
Isaiah 65.3. The word δαιμόνιον is rare in those LXX books that are translated from the Hebrew Bible.[58] For this reason, the four occur-rences in Isaiah stand out disproportionately. Our attention is drawn to LXX Isaiah 65, that describes aberrant cult in a manner that may suggest that the translator has specific contemporary practices in mind.

MT Isa. 65.3 reads as follows:

העם המכעיסים אותי על־פני תמיד
זבחים בגנות ומקטרים על־הלבנים

> ...a people who provoke me to my face, continually, who sacrifice in
> gardens and burn incense upon bricks...

In an unauthorized elaboration upon this cult, the LXX makes two remarkable assertions. In the first place, it asserts that the burning of incense upon bricks—as perhaps sacrifice in gardens—is performed *for the benefit of (the) demons.* The phrase τοῖς δαιμονίοις is wholly without parallel in the Hebrew text. In the second, it immediately

---

58. Once in Deut., three times in Pss. and four times in Isa. Elsewhere, Baruch uses the word twice, this in accordance with the contexts and meaning in LXX Isaiah. Cf. *Bar.* 4.7, where demons receive human worship (cf. LXX Isa. 65.3, poss. 65.11) and *Bar.* 4.35, where they inhabit desolate places (cf. LXX Isa. 13.21, 34.14). Unsurprisingly, the word occurs nine times in Tobit.

describes these demons as figures of the worshippers' deluded imagination: ἃ οὐκ ἔστι.[59]

Isa. 65.11 may also identify a demonic element in aberrant cult, though here there is some motivation in the Hebrew expression הערכים לגד שלחן as well as some textual uncertainty.[60]

It appears that the translator is willing to ascribe the worst motives to these worshippers. For our purpose, the salient point is his simultaneous claim that the demons they mean to worship do not exist at all.

Correlative Ameliorations That Remove Perceived Obscenity or Sexual Content in Chs. 56–66
Isaiah 57.5-10. The indictment of the unfaithful in ch. 57 is carried out in highly charged sexual language, especially in vv. 7-10.[61] Though a

59. Curiously, הישבים—the very next word, in 65.4—appears not to have been translated there. It is conceivable that the translator considered that ἃ οὐκ ἔστι corresponded to these Hebrew letters, though it is difficult to imagine what that connection might have been.

60. Cf. Seeligmann, *LXX Version*, p. 99: 'For δαιμονίῳ, RAHLFS reads—in common with the minority of the tradition—δαίμονι. The circumstance that, elsewhere in the Septuagint, the term δαίμον has been consistently avoided, need not argue against this reading, on the contrary! It is understandable that the Jewish translators of the Bible in Alexandria, where Agathos Dainion was "...nicht bloss der alte Stadtgott...sondern durch all Jahrhunderte Schutzgeist der Stadt", generally had good reason to avoid using δαίμων as the title of an idol. In the passage in question, however, we read, as parallel of the term here discussed, the word τύχη, i.e. the name of the most widely known godhead in Hellenism, who was worshipped also in Egypt and Alexandria. This justifies the supposition that the translation here aims, by means of a very happy transposition, at a daring contemporization; in the place of the ceremony for the ancient Semitic gods of fate גד and מני—probably personifications of good and evil fate and denounced by the prophet—the translation places the Hellenistic cult of these two, set side by side, worshipped as arbiters of fate (Ἀγαθὸς) Δαίμων and Τύχη.' Seeligmann's preferred reading goes against Ziegler's inclusion of τῷ δαιμονίῳ in his text, but it is not impossible. S and two members of Ziegler's *alexandrinische Hauptgruppe* (Q, 26) have δαίμονι.

61. Cf. also 57.5, where the address is directed to הנחמים באלים תחת כל־עץ רענן, 'you that burn with lust among the oaks, under every luxuriant tree'. P.D. Hanson, who thinks the accusation of aberrant cult is a thinly veiled critique of the temple party, summarizes: 'In 57.6-13 the form of address switches from plural to singular. A female prostitute is addressed, her sexual activities described, her professional zeal condemned to futility' (cf. *Isaiah 40–66*). (Interpretation; Atlanta: John Knox Press, 1995), p. 199.

strong case exists for ameliorative translations of erotic vocabulary
beginning at 57.8, it is possible that the translator has made a start
already at 57.5. Reference is made there to הנחמים באלים תחת כל־
עץ רענן, 'You who burn with lust[62] among the oaks, under every green
tree.' The LXX offers the circumspect οἱ παρακαλοῦντες ἐπὶ τὰ
εἴδωλα at the same point in the text where TJ becomes suspiciously
vague: דפלחין לטעותא = '(you) who serve idols...' Whereas the MT
has Eros defiled, these versions subject him to a different ignominy. He
is written out of the story altogether, replaced by garden variety idol
worship.

The English translations of Ottley ('Ye, that call upon your idols...')
and Brenton ('...who call upon idols...') provide a meaning that is
attested for παρακαλεῖν + an object in the accusative, but not for the
verb + ἐπί + an acc. object.[63] It seems plain that the translator has read a
participial form of נחם, *to be sorry, to be consoled*, rather than niphal
הנחמים, from נחם.[64] However, there is no straight path from such a
reading to LXX παρακαλοῦντες ἐπὶ τὰ εἴδωλα. נחם has an active
meaning only in the piel, which is often translated by παρακαλεῖν. In
addition, niphal נחם is often rendered by passive παρακαλεῖν.
However, such expressions mean *to (be) console(d), comfort(ed)* rather
than *to call upon*, as the LXX seems to require in Isa. 57.5.[65]

It appears that the Isaiah translator has deviated from expected norms
in three ways. First, he has read as הַנִּחָמִים the participle that the
Massoretes would eventually vocalize הַנֵּחָמִים. This much requires no

---

62. So NRSV; *Tanakh*, 'You who inflame yourselves...'

63. The lexica appear not to know a use of transitive παρακαλεῖν where the
verb-object relationship is mediated by ἐπί. It is certainly not attested elsewhere in
the LXX.

The details of Greek usage are more accurately reported in J. Lust, E. Eynikel
and K. Hauspie, *A Greek-English Lexicon of the Septuagint, Part II. Κ–Ω*
(Stuttgart: Deutsche Bibelgesellschaft, 1992), pp. 352-53. Observing that the Greek
differs from the Hebrew [*], the entry continues: 'Is 57, 5 οἱ παρακαλοῦντες ἐπί
those who comfort—◊נחם for MT ◊חמם *those who burn with lust*.'

64. All forms of this verb denote *heating* or *warming* of some kind.

65. Piel נחם is never translated by παρακαλεῖν + ἐπί. When niphal נחם is
translated by passive παρακαλεῖν + ἐπί, the preposition ἐπί mediates between the
verb *and its occasion*, not the verb and its direct object. Pass. παρακαλεῖν + ἐπὶ
renders נחם על in 2 Sam. 13.39, Ps. 90(89)13, Isa. 22.4 (act. imperative) and Ezek.
32.31; and נחם אל in 2 Sam. 24.16 (but see על in BHS app.). Cf. also 2 Cor. 1.4,
7.7; 1 Thess. 3.7.

radical reconfiguration, though it does oblige him to ignore the sexual motifs of the context. Second, he has translated this form of נחם by its standard translation-equivalent, παρακαλεῖν. However, he has broken all precedent by providing an active *form* (οἱ παρακαλοῦντες) and, apparently, a *meaning* that corresponds to some occurrences of παρακαλεῖν, but never to the passive Greek forms that often translate נחם, and never to נחם itself. That is, he has exploited the polyvalence of παρακαλεῖν in order to elicit a meaning—*to call upon*—that נחם never has. This meaning suits his purpose, but getting to it requires that he violate the normal relationship of form and meaning. Finally, he has coined what appears to be a neologism (παρακαλεῖν + ἐπὶ + acc.) in order to express the new meaning that he has construed. This latter manoeuvre is all the more surprising for the fact that his dextrous command of Greek does not normally lead him to produce suspect forms.

It is always possible to attribute such a complex manoeuvre to accident or incompetence. However, when such deviations accumulate—as they do in this chapter—and, further, when they appear to share an avoidance of sexually charged vocabulary, an explanation that posits conscious exegesis seems at least as persuasive as one that rests upon a series of similar accidents.

In the second half of 57.8, a sexually profligate woman's misdeeds are narrated: כי מאתי גלית ותעלי הרחבת משכבך ותכרת־לך מהם אהבת משכבם יד חזית.[66] Features of the intended meaning are uncertain, but it is clear that her bed is spread wide to welcome multiple guests. The final clause, יד חזית, is suggestive but hardly transparent. Duhm considered that יד could only refer to the phallus, citing the context and the Talmud's similar use of אֶצְבַּע.[67] Regardless of whether or not this was the author's intended meaning, it is not difficult to imagine that readers could *infer* a sexual meaning.[68]

---

66. 'For from me you have uncovered (NRSV: "For, in deserting me, you have uncovered..."; *Tanakh* translates similarly), and you have gone up. You have made wide your bed and made a pact (NRSV: 'bargain') with them. You love their bed. You have gazed at a "hand".'

67. B. Duhm, *Das Buch Jesaia* (Göttinger Handkommentar zum Alten Testament; Göttingen: Vandenhoeck & Ruprecht, 1922), p. 429.

68. E.J. Kissane notes that many scholars have followed Duhm. However, Kissane prefers a conventional meaning of 'strength' for יד, thus giving to the phrase in question the meaning, 'you have looked for strength'; cf. *The Book of Isaiah: Translated from a Critically Revised Hebrew Text with Commentary (XL–LXVI)*, II (Dublin: Richview Press, 1943), p. 223.

Such a *possible* inference is probably sufficient to explain the LXX's highly prosaic rendering, ᾤου ὅτι ἐὰν ἀπ' ἐμοῦ ἀποστῆς πλεῖόν τι ἕξεις ἠγάπησας τοὺς κοιμωμένους μετὰ σοῦ.[69] Kissane judges that confusion is to blame for the widely divergent LXX reading: '...the Greek translator merely shows that he was just as perplexed as the moderns, and took refuge, as he often does, in a paraphrase.'[70] One cannot rule out such a cause, but Kissane probably sells the translator short. The refuge of paraphrase can be as much sought as fallen into.[71]

The possibility of scandal recurs in 57.9-10, where some scholars discern a disapproving portrayal of aberrant sex, even if this is a metaphor for religious disloyalty. The phrases ותשרי למלך בשמן and חית ידך have each been understood in this way.[72] By beginning the verse with καὶ ἐπλήθυνας τὴν πορνείαν σου μετ' αὐτῶν, the trans-

---

For a variant of the erotic theory, cf. J.D.W. Watts, *Isaiah 34–66* (WBC, 25; Waco, TX: Word Books, 1987), p. 258: 'Then, far removed from Palestine and the lure of Ba'al religions, she still *loved their bed*, in fantasy she *envisioned a hand*, perhaps that of a lover stroking sensuously.'

69. 'You supposed that if you stood aloof from me you would get something (from it). You loved those who slept with you.' TJ's rendering of the verse's final clause may be ameliorative by its own means: אתר בחרת, 'You have chosen a place.'

70. *Isaiah*, II, p. 223.

71. The LXX leaves evidence of a struggle. Of משכבך and משכבם, one seems to have generated τοὺς κοιμωμένους, the other is untranslated. הרחבת seems unaccounted for in LXX 57.8, but may find its match in καὶ ἐπλήθυνας of 57.9 (cf. BHS: 'hi; a שרר = arab *ṭarra* abundavit cf G'; BHS appears to follow the suggestion of P. Wernberg-Møller in 'Two Notes', *VT* 8 [1958], pp. 305-308). מאתי גלית almost certainly corresponds to ἀπ' ἐμοῦ ἀποστῆς, though this is a *hapax* equivalency. The phrase καὶ ἀπέστρεψας in 57.9 seems oddly unaccounted for, but may actually correspond to ותשרי (read as וַתָּסָרִי) from the beginning of the verse, where the Hebrew word appears to lack a Greek equivalent. It is possible to conclude that the translator has worked very hard to put this verse together in an acceptable way, rather than that he escaped his confusion by making up something bland.

72. For ותשרי למלך בשמן, cf. Watts, *Isaiah 34–66*, pp. 254-59. Watts relates ותשרי to שרר (*became raised, excited, be firm*). חית ידך is then read in connection with this sexual meaning. Watts concludes that the reference may be to auto-stimulation, and envisages a pluriform versional effort to get around this: 'LXX ἐπλήθυνας τὴν προνείαν σου "you increased your prostitution" may presuppose a root related to Arab *ṭarra* "abound"...Tg avoids the issue altogether... If the sentence is as erotic as seems possible, it is understandable that translations should tend to soften the sexual imagery.' Cf. also p. 258.

lator indicates his understanding that the reference has not suddenly changed to politics alone. Rather, his rendering is vague, as suits euphemism. As soon as the Hebrew text can be plausibly translated as diplomatic protocol, the LXX becomes quite literal.[73]

Correlative Ameliorations That Mitigate Damage Done to Creation in Chs. 56–66
Isaiah 63.15–19(64.1). This is an anguished lament that in the LXX has been converted into a prayer for the restoration of Jerusalem.[74] In 63.19b(64.1), the LXX deviates in a manner that at first appears to result from a simple misreading of the Hebrew text. Despite appearances, however, this detour may depend more upon ideology than on a careless eye.[75]

לוא־קרעת שמים ירדת מפניך הרים נזלו

Oh that you would tear open the heavens[76] and come down, so that the mountains would quake at your presence!

73. Excepting the unexplained καὶ ἀπέστρεψας. He may have reached back to reclaim ותשרי from the 'risqué' portion of 57.9 for 'safer' use later in the verse (see above, notes 70-71). If Wernberg-Møller is correct that ותשרי corresponds to καὶ ἐπλήθηνας, then it can only refer to καὶ ἀπέστρεψας as one half of a double translation.

74. Cf. Seeligmann, *LXX Version*, p. 114: 'In 63.17/18, a certain degree of contemporization is obtained by a divergence from the Massoretic text... Whereas the Hebrew text constitutes a complaint of the violence of the enemy, the translator causes either the prophet or the exiles to pray to God: "Turn Thou to us that we may soon take possession of Thy Holy Mountain".' This conversion results principally from the LXX reading of גאלנו in 63.16 as the imperative גְּאָלֵנוּ (the MT vocalizes the participle גֹּאֲלֵנוּ) with the resulting secondary adjustment that translates ירשו as ἵνα...κληρονομήσωμεν.

The verses in question are actually one component of a 'long psalm of lamentation' that spans 63.7–64.11; P.R. Ackroyd, *Exile and Restoration: A Study of Hebrew Thought of the Sixth Century BC* (London: SCM Press, 1968), p. 227; cf. also P.D. Hanson, *The Dawn of Apocalyptic* (Philadelphia: Fortress Press, 1975), p. 79.

75. English translations follow the LXX versification.

76. Alternatively, 'Oh that you had...' Cf. J.A. Motyer, *The Prophecy of Isaiah* (Leicester: Inter-Varsity Press, 1993), p. 518: 'The rules governing the particle לוא require a past reference here—not, *Oh that you would*...but 'Oh that you had...' A survey of the usage of similar constructions seems to support Motyer's rendering, though few modern translations take this approach. Cf. also Ottley (*Isaiah*, I, p. 314), who gives us, 'O that thou hadst rent the heavens, that thou hadst come down...' Difference of opinion among modern scholars is reflected in divergent

ἐὰν ἀνοίξῃς τὸν οὐρανόν, τρόμος λήμψεται ἀπὸ σοῦ ὄρη, καὶ τακήσονται.

If you open heaven, trembling will seize mountains because of you, and (they) will melt.

Fritsch alleges anti-anthropomorphic bias as the motivation behind the rendering of מִפָּנֶיךָ by ἀπὸ σοῦ.[77] Though his observation is probably correct, it may be only the beginning of the ideological dynamics that shape the LXX text of this verse.

There are two additional features of the Hebrew text that our translator might have found difficult. First, it is possible that he wished to bypass the notion of a rampaging God doing violence to so fundamental a component of his creation as the שָׁמַיִם.[78] The provision of ἀνοίγειν—'to open'—for the more destructive קָרַע—diminishes the apocalyptic fervour of God's hoped-for dealings with errant humanity.[79] Perhaps

---

translations of a similar construction at Isa. 48.18. For לוּא הִקְשַׁבְתָּ לְמִצְוֹתָי (= καὶ εἰ ἤκουσας τῶν ἐντολῶν μου), NRSV has 'O that you had paid attention to my commandments!' *Tanakh* prefers a present/future perspective: 'If only you would heed My commands!' Cf. also North, *The Second Isaiah: Introduction, Translation and Commentary to Chapters XL–LV* (Oxford: Oxford University Press, 1964), p. 182.

77. 'Concept of God', p. 157: 'The anthropomorphic phrase מִפָּנֶיךָ is rendered freely in the Greek by απο σου. This same clause is found in 64.2(3) by vertical dittography in the Hebrew.' Fritsch does not mention the counter-evidence from 64.1(2), where מִפָּנֶיךָ הָרִים יִרְגָּזוּ = ἀπὸ προσώπου σου ἔθνη ταραχθήσονται.

78. שָׁמַיִם, it will be recalled, is one half of the merism that in biblical tradition represents all of creation: (הַ)שָׁמַיִם וּ(הָ)אָרֶץ.

A similar sensitivity has been discerned in LXX Psalms. In *God Is my Rock*, pp. 19-20, Olofsson writes the following in a section entitled 'The Toning Down of God's Destructive Activities': 'Erwin and Fritsch suggest that there are signs in LXX Psalms of a softening of expressions for God's punishment of man and nature, because such activities were repugnant to the translator's religious outlook.' This assertion is exemplified by the translator's failure to speak of 'the bones you (i.e. the Lord) have crushed' in Ps. 51(50).10. Olofsson's references are to H.M. Erwin's *Theological Aspects* (previously cited) and C.T. Fritsch's 'Studies in the Theology of the Greek Psalter', in B.Z. Luria (ed.), זר לגבורות (Zalman Shazar jubilee volume; Jerusalem: Kiryat Sefer, 1973), pp. 741-29. Olofsson himself remains unconvinced.

One wonders whether the Greek expression might not owe something to the development of 'apocalyptic' in the technical sense of the word. Cf. C. Rowland, *The Open Heaven; A Study of Apocalyptic in Judaism and Early Christianity* (London: SPCK, 1982), p. 11: 'Many (Jews and, later, Christians living in the

the translator imagines the judging deity peering majestically through heaven's window, rather than angrily tearing a hole in one of the two poles of creation itself.[80]

troubled era from 300 BCE–300 CE) would have echoed the cry of the unknown prophet who, in Isaiah 64.1, pleads with God to rend the heavens to solve the many riddles of existence which presented themselves. The answer to this desperate plea is found in apocalyptic.' Cf. also pp. 79-80: 'The proximity which was assumed to exist between heaven and earth in earlier texts is already found to be lacking in one or two exilic texts. For example, the anonymous prophet, whose words we have in Isaiah 64, is looking at a world which seems to him to be devoid of the divine presence. Indeed, he regards the azure firmament above as a barrier which God must cleave in order to redeem his people (Isa. 64.1). By the time we reach the apocalyptic writings of the third and second centuries BC and later, we find that a cosmology has developed in which God is enthroned in glory in heaven, and his activities are carried out among men either by angelic intermediaries or other modes of divine operation like the spirit or *shekinah*.'

It may be that the language of LXX 63.19 (MT 64.1) serves as a halfway house between the conception of God in the Hebrew text (where God dwells in heaven, but the prophet can still plead with him to descend) and the full-blown apocalyptic that Rowland describes.

If one is to seek an explanation for the Greek expression at 63.19 by looking *forward*, towards apocalyptic, one must at the same time take care not to neglect the backwards view. The MT and LXX themselves provide a precedent for the language of 'heaven opened'. In Gen. 6.11, the flood begins when the windows of heaven were opened; God's opening of the heavens is a metaphor for his blessing in Deut. 28.12, Ps. 78.23 and Mal. 3.10. Isa. 24.18, which is part of the so-called 'Isaiah Apocalypse', may provide a certain conceptual parallel: 'Whoever flees at the sound of the terror will fall into the pit; and whoever climbs out of the pit will be caught in the snare. *For the windows of heaven are opened, and the foundations of the earth tremble*' (כי־ארבות ממרום נפתחו ירעשו מוסדי ארץ = ὅτι θυρίδες ἐκ τοῦ οὐρανοῦ ἠνεῴχθησαν καὶ σεισθήσεται τὰ θεμέλια τῆς γῆς). Finally, the book of Ezekiel locates the prophet's initiation as a visionary when, 'as I was among the exiles by the river Chebar, the heavens were opened, and I saw visions of God.'

F. Lentzen-Deis concludes that Isa. 63/64 and the *Taufbericht* of Mk 1.10—where it is said of Jesus that εἶδεν σχιζομένους τοὺς οὐρανοὺς—share *Leitideen* but show little evidence of direct dependence; cf. *Die Taufe Jesu nach den Synoptikern: Literarkritische und gattungsgeschichtliche Untersuchungen* (Frankfurter Theologische Studien, 4; Frankfurt am Main: Josef Knecht, 1970), pp. 101-103.

80. The prayer itself seems more dispassionate in the Greek translation. From the plaintive 'Would that you would tear open...' of the MT, the translator derives the conditional statement, 'If you open...'. (א)לו with a perfect for a future event is either rare or unique (cf. Isa. 48.18 for an ambiguous example that GKC [§151e] regards as referring to a future wish, *contra* many). Such a construction may

Secondly, the LXX syntax is considerably rearranged in a manner that avoids the notion of God's physical descent.[81] The Hebrew text expresses a strong wish that God himself should *come down*. The LXX text, on the other hand, merely reports that, if God should open heaven, *trembling will seize mountains*. This alteration may be merely accidental and based upon orthographic confusion. ירדת might possibly have been read inadvertently as יחרדו, וחרדו,[82] ירעדו or ורעדו.[83] However, the visual resemblance of ירדת to any of these forms is not particularly close.

Fischer offers the intriguing possibility that the translator's eye took in רדת, which he then 'read' as רתת. The latter word occurs only once in the Hebrew Bible,[84] but is common enough in Aramaic as both a noun and a verb.[85] Fischer anticipates the present analysis by suggesting that such a complicated reworking of the text must have been intentional. However, he offers no suggestion as to what might have

intensify the passion of this prayer beyond the norm. In any case, ἐὰν ἀνοίξῃς τὸν οὐρανόν is surprisingly even-tempered. This conditional sentence conforms to the pattern of 'more vivid future conditions' (H.W. Smyth, *Greek Grammar* [revised by G.M. Messing; Cambridge, MA: Harvard University Press, 1956], §§2323, 2336; BDF §§371, 373), *not* to that of a wish. It does not appear that the translator repeats the prayer with particular enthusiasm. The revisers read לוא as a negative; cf. Ziegler, *editio*, p. 357.

81. Or at least his *visible* descent, if a razor can fit between these two ideas. The LXX translator does not tamper with every bellicose divine descent. In 31.4, for example, כן ירד יהוה צבאות לצבא על־הר־ציון is translated in a straightforward manner: οὕτως καταβήσεται κύριος σαβαωθ ἐπιστρατεῦσαι ἐπὶ τὸ ὄρος τὸ Σιων. Perhaps that text did not offer the *exploitable possibilities* that are found in the verse under consideration.

82. Whilst חרד never generates τρόμος, this cannot be held against the possible equivalency in this verse, for חרד produces τρέμειν as near to hand as Isa. 66.2 and 66.5. Furthermore, the use of a noun + λαμβάνειν to render the corresponding Hebrew verb (rather than merely using the corresponding Greek verb itself) is an idiosyncrasy of the Isaiah translator. Cf., for example, 23.5, where יחילו = λήμψεται αὐτοὺς ὀδύνη.

83. רעד produces τρέμειν in Dan. LXX 10.11. (רעד(ה) generates τρόμος in Exod. 15.15; Job 4.14; Pss. 2.11; 48(47).6; 55(54).5; and Isa. 33.14 (אחזה רעדה חנפים = λήμψεται τρόμος τοὺς ἀσεβεῖς!). This possibility is rejected without comment in the HUB apparatus, p. רפב: 'hardly √רעד.'

84. Hos. 13.1, a substantive meaning 'trembling'.

85. Cf. Jastrow, *Dictionary*, p. 1504.

occasioned such a conscious manipulation of the text.[86]

As Fischer hints, the translator may not have failed to understand the Hebrew text. Rather, he may have intentionally employed the technique by which we can observe him using two of the three radicals of a Hebrew word to create a distinct Hebrew lexeme which is then translated.[87] While this often appears not to be premeditated—and simply exhibits his difficulties with the Hebrew—it seems likely that he might also employ it consciously on analogy with the ʾ*al tiqreʾ* exegetical technique of rabbinic tradition.[88]

As we have seen, motivation for such an alteration would not have been lacking in this verse. A manoeuvre along the lines that I have described would allow him to bypass difficulties in 63.19(64.1) that he has elsewhere given us cause to believe might have been theologically problematic for him.

It thus appears to be more than coincidental that divine descent is similarly omitted later in the same passage. MT Isaiah 64.2(3) has the following:

בעשׂותך נוראות לא נקוה ירדת מפניך הרים נזלו

When you performed fearsome acts that we did not expect, you came down, before your face the mountains were shaken.

The LXX is contemporized and—perhaps significantly—abbreviated by one verb:

86. Cf. *Schrift*, p. 66: 'יָרַדְתָּ > τρομος+λήμψεται+ > רֶדֶת = רֶתֶת "das Zittern" ausgelegt (ebenso auch V.2b, LXX 3b, also ד abs. für ת genommen (s. w.) u. Jod abs. ignoriert... Die zweimalige Umwandlung von ירדת zu רדת mit Auslegung רתת kann nicht durch zufällige Verl., sondern nur mit Absicht geschehen sein.' Cf. also p. 83 for the ד/ת interchange. Fischer does not mention the difficulty of the omitted initial י of ירדת. One might presume a preformative י as the first letter of an imperfect verbal form of רתת. However, one then lacks the necessary masculine plural ending of the verb. Such difficulties increase the probability of an intentional alteration that is not stymied by such grammatical niceties.

87. If we allow him such exegetical creativity, it becomes virtually impossible to decide whether חרד, רעד, רתת (so Fischer), or some other Hebrew word served as his lexical bridge *away* from the idea of divine descent and *towards* the notion of trembling mountains. Any one of them might have sufficed.

88. One wonders whether such a move might have found additional encouragement in the orthographic similarities of ת/ה and י/ו. Though these occur at the 'wrong' end of ירדת if one wants to read חרדו, such quibbles are frequently not persuasive for this translator, who practises a manoeuvre I call '2 [radicals] of 3 + dyslexia' to derive readings that diverge from the MT.

ὅταν ποιῇς τὰ ἔνδοξα, τρόμος λήμψεται ἀπὸ σοῦ ὄρη.

When you perform glorious (deeds), trembling from you[89] will seize
mountains.

Just as in prior verses, so here the idea of God's descent is avoided.
Either ירדת is once again translated as though from חרד and assigned
to the mountains (τρόμος. λήμψεται) with the subsequent non-translation of נזלו. Or, alternatively, נזלו generates τρόμος λήμψεται and
is moved forward in the verse, while ירדת is simply omitted.[90] In either
case, spectacular events are described in both texts, though *without
divine descent in the LXX.*

The explanation that I have been developing, which seeks to explain
the considerable LXX deviations in terms of conscious manipulation of
the text, may be supported by a similar move at Isa. 51.6. In the MT that
passage groups the heavens and the earth together with human beings as
perishable goods, over against the Lord's salvation and righteousness,
which will be eternal:

שְׂאוּ לשׁמים עיניכם והביטו אל־הארץ מתחת
כי־שׁמים כעשׁן נמלחו והארץ כבגד תבלה וישׁביה כמו־כן ימותון
וישׁועתי לעולם תהיה וצדקתי לא תחת

Lift up your eyes to the heavens, and look to the earth beneath; <u>for the
heavens will vanish like smoke</u>, and the earth will wear out like a
garment, and her inhabitants will die in the same way.[91] But my salvation will remain forever, and my righteousness will not be shattered.[92]

The LXX, by contrast, may not be equally pessimistic about the fate
of the heavens:

ἄρατε εἰς τὸν οὐρανὸν τοὺς ὀφθαλμοὺς ὑμῶν καὶ ἐμβλέψατε εἰς
τὴν γῆν κάτω, <u>ὅτι ὁ οὐρανὸς ὡς καπνὸς ἐστερεώθη</u>, ἡ δὲ[93] γῆ ὡς

89. Alternatively, 'trembling will seize mountains *because of you*'.
90. The latter option is *HR*'s preference, but I think mistakenly so in the light of
the LXX use of τρόμος and τρέμειν and in view of the fact that זלל never produces
either of these two Greek lexemes elsewhere.
91. Cf. the BHS apparatus, which proposes, following 1QIsaᵇ, כמובן (מובן
locusta).
92. Or 'dismayed', if the intention is to personify.
93. The postpositive particle δὲ is frequently given its adversative sense . If that
is the case here, the translator may be opposing the earth (which will grow old) with
heaven (which has been established, and is thus imperishable). Indeed, the
clustering of four occurrences of δὲ (each standing in for waw) is unusual for this

ἱμάτιον παλαιωθήσεται, οἱ δὲ κατοικοῦντες τὴν γῆν ὥσπερ ταῦτα ἀποθανοῦνται, τὸ δὲ σωτήριόν μου εἰς τὸν αἰῶνα ἔσται, ἡ δὲ δικαιοσύνη μου οὐ μὴ ἐκλίπῃ.

Raise your eyes towards heaven and look at the earth below, <u>for heaven has been established as smoke</u>, and the earth as a garment will grow old, and those who inhabit it will die just as these, but my salvation will remain forever, and my righteousness will not fail.

The translator appears to have substituted a creative word for the difficult verb מלל, which may refer to the *tearing apart* or *dissipation* of the heavens.[94] Thus, he has converted the destruction and disappearance of the heavens into their confirmation, strengthening, or solidification. This is apparent in his use—unique in the LXX—of στερεοῦν[95] for God's creative spreading out of the heavens in 45.12[96] and 48.13.[97]

It is possible that the translator, faced with a rare verb that was unknown to him, has simply reverted to vocabulary familiar to him with reference to the heavens. However, such an inadvertence seems unlikely in view of the complete reversal of the MT meaning that his translation effects. It is also brought into question by similar alterations elsewhere in LXX Isaiah.

For example, LXX Isa. 34.4 moves in the same direction while producing something less than a complete reversal. It accomplishes a similar result by means of a quite different technique. In this verse, three

translator and suggests that something more complex than simple copulative listing may be going on. However, granting an adversative meaning to δὲ renders it difficult to work out the logical relationship of the third, fourth and fifth components of the resulting list (οἱ δὲ κατοικοῦντες, τὸ δὲ σωτήριόν μου and ἡ δὲ δικαιοσύνη μου).

It is also tempting to find significance in the aorist ἐστερεώθη with reference to heaven, over against the future παλαιωθήσεται, used with reference to the earth. However, this may be nothing more than a standard translation of the Hebrew perfect and imperfect, respectively.

94. Verbal מלל appears only here in the Hebrew Bible. However, its cognate appears in Arabic, Ethiopic and Ugaritic, where it appears to mean *to tear away, to rip, to dismember, draw out*. An extension of these meanings, together with the context, is responsible for the meaning *to (be) dissipate(d), disperse(d)*, which is usually given for the verb in Isaiah; cf. BDB, KB.

95. LSJ: *to make firm or solid...strengthen...confirm*; passive, *to be firmly established*.

96. = נטה, a *hapax* equivalency.

97. = טפח, also a *hapax* equivalency.

things are asserted of the heavens or their host: (a) 'And all the host of heaven will rot away' (וְנָמַקּוּ כָל־צְבָא הַשָּׁמַיִם); (b) 'and the heavens will be rolled up like a scroll' (וְנָגֹלּוּ כַסֵּפֶר הַשָּׁמָיִם); and (c) 'and all their host will fall as a leaf falls withered from the vine' (וְכָל־צְבָאָם יִבּוֹל כִּנְבֹל עָלֶה מִגֶּפֶן).

There are textual uncertainties on the Hebrew side that may weaken the contribution of this verse to our discussion,[98] though it is not clear that these doubts are weighty. Furthermore, it may be possible to account for the LXX minus (וְנָמַקּוּ כָל־צְבָא הַשָּׁמַיִם has not been translated) by parablepsis, for both the first and second clauses begin with וَ… and end with הַשָּׁמַיִם. Still further, our translator often collapses a series of syntactical units, such as these three verbal clauses. However, this will more often than not involve the use of elements of each of the MT units, whereas in this case the first of the three has been cleanly omitted.

It is instructive to note that the most destructive of the references to heaven is the one that does not appear in the LXX, the one that promises that the host of heaven will decay, fester or rot. It is possible to imagine that the translator—though he could not skirt the claims of this verse altogether—found it possible to soften the impact by deleting the first of three clauses of his *Vorlage* (≈ MT). It is probably relevant that the action of rolling up a scroll need not be—in fact would not normally be—a violent or destructive one.

Possibly, then, LXX Isa. 34.4 makes its own unique contribution to our observation—which stands on its own apart from this verse—of the Isaiah translator's hesitance before the notion of heaven's demise.[99]

Isa. 40.22 produces what may be a related alteration at the hands of the LXX translator. In the MT of that verse, the prophet identifies the Lord as 'he who sits upon the vault (or circle) of the earth': הַיֹּשֵׁב עַל־חוּג הָאָרֶץ. When compared to the MT, the translator substitutes the notion of holding or sustaining for that of sitting. ὁ κατέχων τὸν

---

98. Cf. 1QIsa[a] and the BHS *propositum*.

99. Olofsson is sceptical with regard to the claims of Erwin and Fritsch that the LXX Psalms tone down God's destructive activities (*God Is my Rock*, 9-25). He is sympathetic to the opposite conclusion, agreeing with M. Flashar that 'Yahweh's destructive activities especially against his enemies, is [*sic*] in fact rather underlined than softened in the interpretation of the LXX Psalms', p. 21. Cf. Flashar, 'Exegetischen Studien zum LXX—Psalter', *ZAW* 32 (1912), pp. 81-116. The quotation registers Olofsson's words with regard to Flashar.

γῦρον τῆς γῆς. It is possible that the translator has divided the words differently from the MT. בעל חוג הארץ might well generate ὁ κατέχων τὸν γῦρον τῆς γῆς, especially if שׁ were conceived of as the late Hebrew relative particle.[100] Such an explanation is attractive, though it must concede its inability to account for יר.[101] This short-coming would be less serious if the act of reading בעל were a *choice*. In that event, the translator might have felt that he had done well to escape a threatening reading whilst leaving so little debris.

Whether this translation results from a conscious identification of בעל in the text, or is simply a paraphrastic rendering of the MT as we now have it, one suspects that it owes much to an attempt to deflect anthropomorphism. By allowing God to hold on to the earth's vault[102] rather than to sit on it, the translator effectively salvages not only the Lord's dignity, but that of his creation as well.

Still another example of the translator's beneficent feelings towards the creation occurs in LXX Isa. 54.9–10. In the MT, the Lord announces his goodwill towards Israel/Judah by referring to a comparable display of his mercy in the past: 'For these are like the days[103] of Noah to me...' The point of comparison is the endless duration of God's promises: 'Just as I swore that the waters of Noah would never again go over the earth, so I have sworn that I will not be angry with you.'

In 54.10, this point is strengthened by an antithetical comparison of mountains and hills—which, at least hypothetically, are *not* eternal—with the Lord's covenant and mercy, which *are*.[104] The LXX subverts the shape of this rhetoric by introducing into 54.10 the negative element of God's promises of self-restraint to Noah, pronounced in 54.9. Thus, the eternality of God's covenant with, and mercy towards, Israel/Judah are compared *synonymously* with the eternality of mountains and hills.[105] It may be that such geological protrusions are understood to be

100. The semantic overlap of בעל and κατέχειν is suggestive, though the equivalency does not occur in the LXX.

101. Unless the translator were to imagine something that might be represented as הֲ־יֵשׁ בעל.

102. Or, alternatively, to be the owner or master of it.

103. Or 'waters', which would hardly affect the meaning. The Hebrew text reads: כי־מי נח זאת לי (cf. BHS *propositum* כמי).

104. כי ההרים ימושו והגבעות תמוטנה חסדי מאתך לא־ימוש וברית שלומי לא תמוט אמר מרחמך יהוה.

105. Perhaps significantly for the question of nationalism, the LXX now makes these '*your* hills'.

among the beneficiaries of God's Noachic promise. Regardless, the LXX deflects the MT's assertion that mountains and hills *may* be shaken—or indeed, *will* be shaken—by stating that they, like divine promises, will certainly *not* suffer such a fate.[106]

The presence of such similar creation-preserving manoeuvres in LXX Isaiah encourages the view that the same motivation is present in Isa. 63.19(64.1). It seems likely that the translator has managed consciously to preserve the permanence of the heavens with the help of similar passages at 45.12 and 48.13, and that this manoeuvre illuminates his reticence to see the heavens torn open at 63.19(64.1).[107]

It is similarly instructive that TJ avoids the same two difficulties that are outflanked by the Greek translation at 63.19(64.1). As is frequently the case, TJ manifests the same modesties that are evident in the LXX text but expresses these by means of an altogether different strategy:

לא להון ארכינתא שמיא אתגליתא מן קדמך טוריא זעו

TJ has read MT לוא as the *plene* form of the negative particle.[108] This approach allows the meturgeman to insert להון as an ethical dative to affirm that it was not *for lawless Gentiles* (63.19) that the Lord moved the heavens.

Furthermore, in TJ God does not tear the heavens at all. Rather, the meturgeman has exploited the aural likeness of ק and כ in order to read

---

106. The relevant portion of the LXX now reads, καθότι ὤμοσα αὐτῷ ἐν τῷ χρόνῳ ἐκείνῳ τῇ γῇ μὴ θυμωθήσεσθαι ἐπὶ σοὶ ἔτι μηδὲ ἐν ἀπειλῇ σου τὰ ὄρη μεταστήσασθαι οὐδὲ οἱ βουνοί σου μετακινηθήσονται, οὕτως οὐδὲ τὸ παρ' ἐμοῦ σοι ἔλεος ἐκλείψει οὐδὲ ἡ διαθήκη τῆς εἰρήνης σου οὐ μὴ μεταστῇ. In the light of the fact that God's promise to Moses in the LXX committed him not to be angry with the earth (cf. MT, the waters of Noah will not go over the earth), the concern of the translator may be not only to sustain the earth's permanence, but also to avoid God's (by implication) cursing of it.

107. It is not clear exactly how he envisages smoke functioning as a simile for solidification or strengthening. It must be conceded that smoke does not intuitively suggest solidity. However, this translator is not working intuitively. Rather, he is translating a concrete text by means of a technique that allows relatively narrow parameters for the manipulation of it. Perhaps he imagines smoke as a coalescing solid over against clear blue sky. Regardless of the ambiguity of the details that he envisages, στερεοῦν is unambiguous in itself. Indeed, its meaning at 51.6 must be creative when its use elsewhere in LXX Isaiah is considered.

108. The meturgeman has *read* לוא but *written* לא. As Ziegler's second apparatus reports, the Revisers did the same.

the MT's לוא־קרעת as לא־כרעת.[109] He has taken the additional liberty of understanding קרעת in the causative sense normally reserved for the hiphil form of this verb. The word is then glossed by the Aramaic Aphel, ארכינתא.[110] Thus does Chilton arrive at the translation 'not for them did you incline the heavens and reveal yourself.'[111]

While it remains unclear exactly what the TJ text intends by this divine bending of the heavens, it certainly establishes a less destructive tone than the 'tearing' of the MT.[112] In this sense, it is conceptually similar to the LXX rendering of קרע by ἀνοίγειν.[113]

Furthermore, TJ joins LXX in removing all reference to a divine *descent*, though by different means. TJ's אתגליתא simply avoids any lexical or conceptual similarity to ירד,[114] reducing God's activity to the non-controversial act of self-revelation.[115]

---

109. קרע = *to tear (open)*; כרע = *to bend* or *bow*.

110. Aphel רכן = *to bend, incline*; cf. Jastrow, *Dictionary*, p. 1480.

111. Chilton, *Isaiah Targum*, p. 122. Cf. Stenning, *Targum*, p. 212: '[N]ot for them didst thou bow the heavens, *and* reveal thyself.'

112. It may even have an unalloyed positive connotation, linked as it is in the following clause with God's self-revelation. One thinks of the Isaianic language in which God *extends* (נטה) the heavens and wonders whether the Targum's divine and self-revealing *inclination* of the heavens might be creational rather than destructive. Although this is possible, it is probably *not* the case, since TJ elsewhere always uses תלא/תלי when the MT has God *stretch out* (נטה) the heavens (Isa. 40.22; 42.5; 44.24; 45.12; 51.3; Jer. 10.12; 51.15; Zech. 12.1). Furthermore, TJ has רכן at 2 Sam 22.10, when—as in the request of the prayer at Isa. 64.1—David attributes his rescue from enemies to the fact that God *bowed the heavens and came down*. However, even if TJ does not choose *creational* language to describe the action that the prayer urges upon God, it is decidedly less *destructive* than the MT's קרע.

113. Although the use of ἀνοίγειν suggests that the LXX translator did *not* see the possibility of reading MT קרע as כרע. Semantically, ἀνοίγειν is a much closer match for קרע. The Isa. translator's handling of this verb is idiosyncratic. Alone amid his fellow translators, he glosses it with διασχίζειν (twice) and ἀνοίγειν (once).

114. As well as to the various lexical bridges that might have facilitated the LXX translation: רתת (so Fischer), חרד and רעד(ה). Trembling does come in, but by the unremarkable glossing of נזלו (fr. זלל) with זעו (fr. זוע). For a satisfying discussion of Targumic אתגלי for BH ירד, cf. A. Chester, *Divine Revelation and Divine Titles in the Pentateuchal Targumim* (Texte und Studien zum antiken Judentum, 14; Tübingen: J.C.B. Mohr, 1986), pp. 100-27.

115. One which has no necessary *spatial* connotation, let alone anthropomorphic ones. Olofsson observes that the sensitivities that we observe in—*inter alia*—TJ

Thus, TJ—a work that displays frequent conceptual similarities with
LXX Isaiah—independently achieves the same results at 64.1 (MT
63.19) as those produced by the Greek text. This encourages the view
that the LXX manoeuvre is not a stumble, but rather an eloquent circum-
vention of ideas about God and his creation that might have proved
offensive in the *milieu* of the translator.

*Correlative Ameliorations or Clarifications of Cultic Vocabulary and/
or Religious Practice*
Isaiah 58.13-14. In Isa. 58.13-14, God extends lavish promises to Israel/
Judah if she will bring order and delight to her Sabbath observance. MT
58.14 reads,

אז תתענג על־יהוה והרכבתיך על־בָּמֳותֵי [במתי 'Q°re] ארץ
והאכלתיך נחלת יעקב אביך כי פי יהוה דבר

> Then you will delight in the Lord, and I will cause you to ride upon the
> high places of the land. And I will feed to you the inheritance of Jacob
> your father, for the mouth of the Lord has spoken.

The semantic residue of cultic infidelity that במה acquires in the
Hebrew Bible appears to be responsible for several paraphrastic renderings of this word in the LXX.[116] In this verse, the LXX glosses the
Hebrew expression with the less concrete but appropriately positive
phrase τὰ ἀγαθά. This appears to be a knowing allusion to Deut. 32.13.
In that verse, ירכבהו (במתי Q) על־במותי ארץ ויאכל תנובת שדי is
translated as ἀνεβίβασεν αὐτοὺς ἐπὶ τὴν ἰσχὺν τῆς γῆς, ἐψώμισεν
αὐτοὺς γενήματα αὐτῶν.

---

and the LXX may not be functions of either *Palestinian* or *Hellenistic* Judaism to the
exclusion of one or the other; cf. *God Is my Rock*, p. 17. Of 'the growing suspicion
of expressions which suggest that Yahweh could be seen by the ordinary Israelite or
leaders among the people or by cultic functionaries', Olofsson writes that this
suspicion 'may be part of a theological development which is manifest in both
Palestinian and Hellenistic Judaism, to emphasize the invisibility of God'. Indeed,
LXX Isaiah appears to be a work of *Hellenistic style* that shares a marked religious
affinity with protorabbinical and rabbinical works of Palestinian and Babylonian
origin.
   For a discussion of the *passivum divinum* in TJ Isaiah—and this with regard to a
nearly identical תתגל/ירד equivalency at 31.4—cf. van der Kooij, *Textzeugen*,
p. 176.
   116. Cf. Seeligmann, 'Problems', p. 223; Daniel, *Vocabulaire de culte*, pp. 40-
43.

The common usage of hiphil רכב and במות ארץ in the first part of the sentence, as well as hiphil אכל in the second, shows the Hebrew texts of Isa. 58.14 and the Deuteronomy passage to be cut from the same cloth. The Isaiah translator's use of ψωμίζειν—the only time he lays hold of this verb—may suggest that he was aware of the verse in Deuteronomy. Other translators are capable of using ψωμίζειν, though the Isaiah translator does not use it. The occurrences of the word in Exodus contexts might have attached to this lexeme a corresponding thematic resonance.[117] The suspicion that the translator's attention has fallen upon Deut. 32.13 is perhaps strengthened by the observation that both translators use ἀναβιβάζειν for רכב.[118]

However, this dual lexical similarity is not the only point at which his translation runs parallel to LXX Deut. 32.13. He has also adopted the same exegetical tool of paraphrasing במות by means of an abstract noun that places a positive value upon the במות without actually saying what they are. The Isaiah translator offers τὰ ἀγαθὰ τῆς γῆς where his predecessor in the Pentateuch prefers τὴν ἰσχὺν τῆς γῆς.[119] Against the proposal that this is a religiously motivated attempt to avoid connecting God to cultic high places, it might be argued that neither the Deuteronomy text nor the verse in Isaiah *refers* to high places in the first place. This is accurate. However, one would expect a 'naive' translation of the two texts to produce a Greek substantive[120] that denotes something that is physically 'high', perhaps ὕψος or ὑψηλός. The fact that it is *not* rendered in this way probably indicates that our

---

117. Num. 11.4, 18; Deut. 8.3, 16.

118. Although too much should not be made of this latter point. The employment of ἀναβιβάζειν for רכב does not *necessarily* require dependence upon Greek Deut. 32.13. Nevertheless, it is suggestive that ἀναβιβάζειν occurs only here for רכב in the Latter Prophets (though they do use ἀναβάτης for the substantive). It is far more a preference of the Pentateuch (the same equivalency occurs twice in Esther and once in Chronicles).

119. This methodology produces the opposite result in Ezek. 16.16 (εἴδωλα) and Mic. 1.5 (ἡ ἁμαρτία). An interesting antithetical example occurs at Exod. 3.17, where ואמר אעלה אתכם מעני מצרים = καὶ εἶπον Ἀναβιβάσω ὑμᾶς ἐκ τῆς κακώσεως τῶν Αἰγυπτίων εἰς τὴν γῆν τῶν Χαναναίων... One wonders whether the translator's mastery of Pentateuchal language and literature would have been such as to shape his translation of Isa. 58.14 in terms of a journey *from* one disagreeable reality and *to* a more positive one: τοῦ κακώσεως τῶν Αἰγυπτίων εἰς τὰ ἀγαθα τῆς γῆς Ισραηλ.

120. Or substantivized adjective.

When We All Go Home

two translators *are* ideologically motivated, for such a translation would simply mimic the strong LXX consensus that uses these adjectives as the standard representation of *cultic* high places.[121]

There is further evidence from within Isaiah that our translator is handling this Hebrew lexeme with sensitivity. The word does not occur frequently, but the translator appears to omit it when it can be associated with the Lord.[122] When it clearly refers to pagan cult, it is without embarrassment called a βωμός.[123]

It appears, then, that our translator has chosen and arranged his vocabulary at Isa. 58.14 so as to avoid cultic connotations. It may be that knowledge of (Greek?) Pentateuchal texts has facilitated this exegetical evasion.

There is yet another feature of 58.13 that shows the translator's attentiveness to matters of religious practice. In that verse, the poetic allusiveness with which cessation of normal activity on the sabbath is expressed might have appeared to require further explanation. It is not entirely clear what it means to turn one's foot from the sabbath. When placed beside the phrase that in the MT is pointed as (ו)(מְ)דַּבֵּר דָּבָר, the picture of silent immobility that it allows might have seemed far from the desired sabbatarian ethos.

The translator's solution comes in the form of a pair of exegetical clarifications. First, a phrase that has only the slightest attachment to the concrete features of the Hebrew text clarifies that it is *for work* that the

---

121. This, at least, would be true of the Isaiah translator. With regard to Deuteronomy, במות appear less commonly in the Pentateuch. When they are cultic, they are called στῆλαι.

122. In 14.14, the speaker is the king of Babylon. However, his intent to ascend to *God's* heights is taken seriously: אעלה על־במתי עב אדמה לעליון = ἀναβήσομαι ἐπάνω τῶν νεφελῶν ἔσομαι ὅμοιος τῷ ὑψίστῳ. Uncharacteristically, a large section of a verse is omitted at 36.7. This may be explicable upon broader text-critical grounds. However, it is remarkable that this unusual 'extended minus' includes a reference to *the Lord's* במה. The third example is 58.15 itself.

123. Of Dibon, 15.2; of Moab, 16.12. Van der Kooij employs a similar observation to discern that the translator approved of the Leontopolis altar, which he saw in the prophecy of Isa. 19.19. He calls it a θυσιαστήριον rather than a βωμός; cf. 'Servant of the Lord', p. 392.

The translator's habit of evaluating cultic practice and paraphernalia even as he translates the words that represent them is apparent as well in the unique equivalency at Isa. 17.8, where unorthodox incense altars (והאשרים והחמנים) are scorchingly sneered at as τὰ βδελύγματα αὐτῶν.

foot ought not to move: οὐκ ἀρεῖς τὸν πόδα σου ἐπ᾽ ἔργῳ. Second, for the translator, those words that ought not to be spoken are not just any words. Rather, they are angry ones: οὐδὲ λαλήσεις λόγον ἐν ὀργῇ ἐκ τοῦ στόματός σου. With these two unauthorized Greek additions, the translator appears to protect his reader from being misled by the economy of the Hebrew text into an absolutist interpretation of Sabbath observance.

Isaiah 61.3. Among the restorative promises that are granted to Zion's mourners in Isaiah 61 is the following change of name at 61.3a:

וקרא להם אילי הצדק מטע יהוה להתפאר

> And they will be called 'the mighty trees[124] of righteousness', 'the planting of the Lord' to display his glory.

Though the translator has elsewhere demonstrated his knowledge of איל as both 'mighty tree' and 'ram', he offers here the unprecedented expression καὶ κληθήσονται γενεαὶ δικαιοσύνης.[125] Assuming that the translator has sustained the horticultural context and not understood אילי as 'rams', his translation may reveal his unease with the aberrant cultic overtones of the אילים.

Already in 1.29 he has expressed a similar sentiment with unmistakable clarity. The prophetic verdict that 'you will be ashamed of the (cultic) trees in which you delighted'[126] is translated in such a manner as to leave no doubt about the nature of the shameful אילים. They are called εἴδωλα. Similarly, MT 57.5 identifies the practitioners of lustful cult amid large and leafy trees with the cultic slaughterers of their own children. Again, the trees in question are אילים. The translator knows them to be εἴδωλα.

Under these circumstances, it may have seemed faint praise to call Zion's liberated captives אילי הצדק, if indeed it was not an oxymoron. However, it is worth noting that his solution is not wholly creative, though it is ingenious. Rather than reverting to a euphemism of his own making, he seems to have utilized a feature of the following verse. Isa. 61.4 is closely linked to 61.3 in that its initial copula continues the description of Zion's mourners, now seen to be the builders who will

---

124. NRSV consistently translates this lexeme as 'oak(s)'. The standard lexica prefer to designate a *large* tree, but not a particular species.

125. 'And they will be called "generations of righteousness".'

126. <div dir="rtl">יבשו מאילים אשר חמדתם</div>.

rehabilitate deserted cities. The verse ends with these builders *renewing* towns that have lain desolate *from of old*: וחדשו ערי חרב שממות דור ודור. The translation is unremarkable except insofar as it renders the venerable expression דור ודור as εἰς γενεάς.

In the light of the translator's observable penchant for lexical levelling, it may be that he has exploited the lexeme γενεά—authorised in 61.4—as the means by which he can successfully evade the unseemly expression in 61.3. He may have read the equivalency דור/γενεά as the source of an agreeable equivalency איל/γενεά in the previous verse. Thus, the tainted expression אילי הצדק becomes the wholly attractive γενεαὶ δικαιοσύνης.

Isaiah 66.17.[127] The translation of Isa. 66.17 may allude to a wider tradition about temple abominations. The Hebrew text speaks of 'those who sanctify themselves and purify (themselves) to go into the gardens *after the one (who is) in the midst*'. The Hebrew expression אחר אחד בתוך [Q אחת] appears to refer to some aberrant ritual—or perhaps to its leader—although the details are unclear to modern eyes.

Indeed, the LXX translator may have known as little as we, for his gloss—καὶ ἐν τοῖς προθύροις—does little more than add a location for this defiled cultic procession that is parallel to the words 'into the gardens'. His choice of a destination is interesting, however, for it is the πρόθυρα that are the venue for such desecrations elsewhere, especially in LXX Ezekiel.

In Ezek. 8, and again in chs. 11 and 43, the πρόθυρον/α of the temple is/are associated with cultic desecrations, iniquity and failed leadership.[128] Indeed, the Ezekiel translator makes sustained use of this lexeme, finding it appropriate for rendering פתח, סף and מפתן *with regard to the temple forecourt(s)*, while using an array of other Greek lexemes when another referent is in mind.[129] It is possible that the

127. For a discussion of substantial deviations from the MT with regard to cultic vocabulary and activity in LXX Isa. 66.20 and 23, see Chapter 7.

128. As with restored princely leadership, purified cult and divine blessing in chs. 46–47.

129. Ezek. stands apart from LXX norms with regard to its preference for πρόθυρον. Only Jer. prefers it for פתח, only Judges for סף, and no other book for מפתן. In LXX Ezekiel it seems to become a *terminus technicus* of sorts. Thus, the fact that LXX Isaiah uses it in a related context in 66.17—and LXX Isaiah uses it nowhere else—may suggest that the translator knew a *Greek* Ezekiel. One alter-

Isaiah translator arrived at καὶ ἐν τοῖς προθύροις by noticing the conceptual parallels in Ezekiel, especially ch. 8, a linking of equivalent contexts that would work best if *Greek* Ezekiel were in mind.

The possibility of such an inner biblical link would have relevance for the task of outlining the translator's technique. However, it is just possible that it touches the matter of cultic amelioration as well. A hint in this direction may emerge from LXX Isa. 66.20. The discussion of that verse in Chapter 7, below, will suggest that the issue of access to the temple and to the Lord inside it mattered greatly to this translator. Indeed, it may well be that his translation of that verse—together with his treatment of a similar procession in ch. 2—excludes from the holiest places those who are not ethnically and cultically pure according to his definition.

The existence of such an exegetically nuanced approach in the same context that gives us the aberrant cult of 66.17 may justify what would otherwise be a solely speculative reading. That is, the translator may locate the abominations of 66.17 in the otherwise unauthorised πρόθυρα precisely in order to keep them out of the temple itself, where the re-turning Jews of 66.20 are shortly to present their legitimate sacrifices.[130]

Circumlocutions That Avoid Direct Speech about God
Isaiah 59.19, 21; 63.14. L.H. Brockington observed 'the tendency shown by both LXX and Targum to resolve a construct phrase in which God is the governed word. In the former the preposition παρὰ is frequently used...'[131] The same feature may be evident at LXX Isa. 59.19, where the רוח יהוה is rendered as ἡ ὀργὴ παρὰ κυρίου. At 59.21, the same idiom is used for the Lord's covenant: בריתי = ἡ παρ' ἐμοῦ διαθήκη. In 63.14, רוח יהוה is translated as the anarthrous πνεῦμα παρὰ κυρίου. In that context, it may refer to a commissioned (lesser) spirit rather than to God's own spirit.

---

native is that he read אחת (Q⁰re') as פתח, though LXX trends would not suggest πρόθυρον as an obvious choice for פתח.

130. As the Gentiles will present their mere *tribute* (cf. Chapter 7). It is conceivable that the curiously allusive אחר אחד בתוך may have suggested to the translator a procession *to the centre of the temple*, in which case his ἐν τοῖς προθύροις might have a polemical role to play.

131. 'Septuagint and Targum', pp. 80-86. Brockington cites Exod. 14.13 (ישועת יהוה //τὴν σωτηρίαν τὴν παρὰ τοῦ θεοῦ) and Gen. 15.4 (דבר יהוה = פתגמא מן יהוה קדם יהוה).

Summary and Conclusion

Just as we discovered to be the case with properly theological ameliorations, so in other areas the translator displays some of the same sensitivities that are apparent in other Jewish interpretative traditions. A
close study of LXX Isaiah suggests that the translator has utilized the
opportunities with which his text provides him in order to avoid
attributing personality to idols and celestial bodies, to soften sexually
explicit language, to mitigate the violence to which the Hebrew text
subjects the created world, and—in a few cases—to avoid speaking too
directly of God. In most instances, he appears to have sought licence
and facilitation from his source text itself for such transformations.
More rarely, a correlative amelioration will be carried out with little or
no authorization from the Hebrew text.

Chapter 6

NATIONALISM AND DIASPORA PERSPECTIVE IN LXX ISAIAH

LXX Isaiah appears to display a nationalistic bias that is largely absent from the Hebrew text. In this work, I use the term 'nationalism' according to a minimalist definition. I refer to the conviction that Jews were in some way superior to Gentiles and that their destiny was privileged over that of the nations. Since their prospects are usually understood to be wrapped up with those of Jerusalem, a focus upon Zion/Jerusalem will be included within this broad definition.

The Hebrew text of Isaiah is widely recognized to contain universalistic statements that are not entirely representative of the views maintained in other parts of the Hebrew Bible. It is often with respect to Hebrew Isaiah's most generous statements to and about the nations that the translator shows a reluctance that at points comes close to hostility.

This relatively negative view of the nations has as its corollary a positive view of Zion, even if this is not as easy to detect among the data that the Greek text affords us. Attempts to penetrate the psychology of the Jewish Diaspora of the period have produced contradictory evaluations. Seeligmann's viewpoint is representative of those scholars who place the *soul* of Diaspora Jewry back in Palestine:

> The tormenting realization of the Galuth was bound to deepen Jewish national feelings during the diaspora. These sentiments found a natural expression in over-emphatic veneration of the national symbols and in a constant yearning for liberation. Our translation contains several instances of this. National symbols *par excellence* are, to the Jews, Zion and Jerusalem... It is not easy to determine with certainty to what extent this ideal—the glorification of Zion and of Jerusalem—was inspired by a real, living desire for the restoration of Palestine as a national home.[1]

___

1. Cf. *LXX Version*, pp. 113-14. Further on this theme, Seeligmann writes: 'Even if the Isaiah translator did maintain a considerable measure of liberty in respect of the text before him, his translation was bound to allot a central position to

A mild statement from another point on the spectrum is to be found in the revised Schürer.[2]

> This (Deutero-Isaian) universalism was admittedly not wholly consistent in Judaism. Side by side with it went the view of Yahweh as the God peculiar to Israel, who had chosen *only* this people for redemption. The concurrence of both viewpoints gave rise to a tension in which now one, now the other prevailed. In theory, especially in Palestinian Judaism, particularistic thought undoubtedly predominated. In practice it was otherwise... However, it may be that in the diaspora the theory was more broadminded than among Palestinian Pharisees. The expansive tendencies of Judaism were probably stronger here than among the Palestinians.[3]

This description is of particular value in that it is made with reference to the same biblical text that is the focus of this volume. The assertion

---

the notion of God's intervention in the history and fate of Israel. Here, too, the translator's conceptions are *partly formed* by biblical data... Could it be that...[the translator's choice of words at 29.22]...is actually an echo of the Biblical belief in Israel being the chosen people?... Yet here too the Greek text contains transformations of the views put forward by the Hebrew text; partly on account of secularization of ideas, but mainly because God's Judgment, proclaimed by the prophet as an impending threat, was evidently looked upon by the translator as the actualized reality of Galuth, i.e. exile. A situation as complicated as that of living as a minority in alien—and soon hostile—surroundings evoked a set of reactions that are reflected in the translation. The Septuagint of Isaiah in particular—though not this translation alone—shows distinct traces of this kind of transformation; and, indeed, it gives one a striking insight into the Galuth psychology of Alexandrian Jewry' (*LXX Version*, pp.110-11 [emphasis mine]).

2.   *The History of the Jewish People in the Age of Jesus Christ (175 B.C.–A.D. 135)*, III.1. (A new English version, rev. and ed. G. Vermes, F. Millar and M. Goodman; Edinburgh: T. & T. Clark, 1986), pp. 159-60.

3.   With regard to the Septuagint as a window into Diaspora Judaism, studies that find evidence of a high degree of Hellenism and/or acculturation in certain LXX books appear to coincide loosely with the view that the Hellenised Judaism that produced such translations was neither Zion-centred nor strongly particularistic. For a fine example of two points on this particular compass, cf. Gerleman, *Proverbs*, a study that finds undeniable Stoic influence in LXX Proverbs, a non-Hebraic presence that makes clear 'the great differences between the Hebrew sage and the Hellenistic Stoic' (p. 54). In constant dialogue with Gerleman's assertion of the LXX Proverbs' 'Greek point of view' and 'religious-moralizing interpretation', Johann Cook's recent monograph carefully draws the discussion back in the direction of finding LXX Proverbs to be a 'fundamentally Jewish' work. Cf. *The Septuagint of Proverbs: Jewish and/or Hellenistic Colouring of LXX Proverbs* (VTSup, 69; Leiden: E.J. Brill, 1997), pp. 318, 322.

that Judaism's 'expansive tendencies' were likely to be stronger in the Diaspora than in Palestine goes beyond the bounds of the present study. However, I wish to contend that *LXX Isaiah* gives no indication that the translator shared such expansiveness. Indeed, just the opposite is the case.

Finally, it bears underlining—and this is an observation that is becoming widely recognized in scholarship—that Greek language and a strong attachment to what one might, for lack of a better term, call 'Palestinian theology' are not strange bedfellows. A fluent ease with the language of the Hellenistic cultural empire is not a certain indication that the speaker or writer displays a 'secularization' or 'Hellenization' of ideas. Indeed, a Diaspora Jew like the one whose translation lies before us is quite capable of exalting Zion and down-grading the nations in a Greek accent that might not have marked him off from his non-Jewish neighbour in the slightest degree.

The interrelationship of language and ideology is frequently fraught with surprises. A.R.C. Leaney has this to say of Jason of Cyrene, who shares the period in which LXX Isaiah is usually placed:

> In his presentation he reveals affinities with both chasidic piety and Hellenistic 'pathetic historiography'. His aim is to glorify Judaism above the Hellenism which he loathes but in doing so he uses Hellenistic terms... We are thus led to see some biblical literature in a truer perspective: it is the Greek additions to Esther which express a more strictly Jewish outlook than the original book... Add Esther seem to date to not much later than the Hebrew original and may represent the greater strictness of those reacting to a permissive Hellenism which they contrasted unfavourably with the original's own conscious assimilationist attitude in an oriental Diaspora.[4]

> We can see therefore that the authors of the place and time with which we are concerned who wrote in Greek either about or from within Judaism were related to 'Hellenism' in a great variety of ways...to write in Greek was perfectly consistent with a desire to maintain or reassert the Jewish claim to be unique and inviolable people of God.[5]

Leaney concludes after surveying Greek manuscripts from the Judaean desert:

4. 'Greek Manuscripts from the Judaean Desert', in J.K. Elliott (ed.), *Studies in New Testament Language and Text: Essays in Honour of George D. Kilpatrick on the Occasion of his Sixty-Fifth Birthday* (NovTSup, 44; Leiden: E.J. Brill, 1976), pp. 286-87.
5. Leaney, 'Greek Manuscripts', p. 287.

To summarize, the relevant history of Israel accustomed the nation to
Greek language and culture, and the use of the language was pervasive
enough to allow it to be used sometimes to inculcate stricter religious-
patriotic ideas; the Greek MSS found at Qumran and Wadi Khabra are
consistent in their text affiliation and vocabulary with the possibility that
they were written for members of the Qumran sect with its intense desire
to recreate a primitively innocent nation; and therefore that the sect
included members whose first language was Greek.[6]

In this chapter, we will sample representative nationalistic translations as these occur throughout LXX Isaiah, and then analyse those that
occur in chs. 56-66. Because the translational moves that correspond to
this are diverse in form and widely scattered, the categories surveyed in
the first section, below, do not correspond precisely to those which are
found in chs. 56-66 (Section II, below, pp. 226-32). Rather, the next
section is intended to show the spectrum of translational moves that
express nationalism and/or Diaspora sentiment. Section two then
analyses those instances that I have discerned in chs. 56-66.

Nationalistic Translations as a Feature of LXX Isaiah

Translations That Identify God Exclusively with Israel in LXX Isaiah
Isaiah 54.5. In the poignant poem of ch. 54, Israel is addressed as a
mother, abandoned with the passing of her youthful blush but surprised
late in life by new love and unexpected children.[7] The Lord himself is
her husband,[8] a point that is stressed in 54.5:

כי בֹעֲלַיִךְ עֹשַׂיִךְ יהוה צבאות שמו
וגֹאֲלֵךְ קדוֹשׁ ישׂראל אלהי כל־הארץ יקרא

> For your Maker is your husband, the Lord of hosts is his name;
> and the Holy One of Israel is your Redeemer, the God of the whole earth
> he is called.

The translator seems to have been put off by בֹעֲלַיִךְ. This may be for
reasons of the close association of the Lord with the term בַּעַל,[9] in

---

6.   Leaney, 'Greek Manuscripts', p. 300.
7.   54.1, 'Sing, O barren one who did not bear; burst into song and shout, you
who have not been in labour! For the children of the desolate woman will be more
than the children of her that is married.'
8.   54.6, 'For the Lord has called you like a wife forsaken and grieved in spirit,
like the wife of a man's youth when she is cast off.'
9.   Perhaps reading בַּעְלֵךְ or even בְּעֹלַיִךְ, which would more closely follow
the consonantal text (but cf. 1QIsa[a] בעלכי).

which the primary scandal might be described as religio-cultic. It is just as likely that the anthropomorphic description of God as Israel's husband—together with the paternity that this might be taken to imply—leads to the omission of בעליך in translation.[10] The LXX reconfigures the verse:

ὅτι κύριος ὁ ποιῶν σε κύριος σαβαωθ ὄνομα αὐτῷ καὶ ὁ ῥυσάμενός σε αὐτὸς[11] θεὸς Ισραηλ πάσῃ τῇ γῇ κληθήσεται.

For the Lord is the one who made you, the Lord of Hosts is his name, and the one who redeemed you is the very God of Israel. He will be called (so) in all the earth.[12]

It is the final phrase, (θεὸς Ισραηλ) πάσῃ τῇ γῇ κληθήσεται, that suggests that this verse may have undergone a nationalistic transformation. It is one thing for Israel's God to be called 'the God of the whole earth', as in the MT. This might well be restricted in its political implications to an affirmation that is voiced *within* Israel.[13] Indeed, it might even be universalistic in its intent. The Lord is not Israel's alone, the speaker might intend, but the God of the whole earth.

It is quite another for the translator to state that Israel's redeeming God will be called 'the God of Israel in the whole earth'. This rearticulation may concede to Israel a certain prominence that is absent in the MT. It is possible that it says more, for it may imply *Israel's* dominant presence *in all the earth*. Indeed, the language of enlargement in MT 54.2-3, with its promise that 'your descendants will possess the nations' might have seemed precedent enough for the apparently nationalistic retouching that the LXX translator has produced.[14]

10. Strictly speaking, Israel's children appear to be *adoptive* ones, for in 54.1 the gleeful mother has neither given birth nor suffered labour. However, targumists and translators are often just as concerned with improper conclusions that the reader might draw as they are with those that the author might have intended.

11. For αὐτὸς, Ziegler has ἅγιος by conjecture.

12. Or, perhaps, '...and the one who redeemed you is he. He will be called the God of Israel in all the earth.' Brenton wants to read the dative instrumentally, thus: '...and shall be called (so) *by* all the earth.' This is possible, as is the more local rendering, '...in all the *land*.' However, the phraseology of MT and LXX Isaiah suggest '...in all the earth', as above.

13. One thinks of Isa. 6.3, 'the whole earth is full of his glory'. This kind of affirmation is heard throughout the Isaiah text, and far beyond.

14. In LXX 43.15, a divine title is, somewhat similarly, transformed into an assertion of Israel's dominion over the nations; cf. Seeligmann, 'Problems', p. 227.

204 *When We All Go Home*

The probability that there are nationalistic dynamics at work in this verse is enhanced by the striking reversal in 54.6. In that verse, the imagery of Israel's temporary abandonment by the Lord (cf. 54.7) is denied by the bald provision of a negative. כי־כאשה עזובה ועצובת רוח קראך יהוה[15] becomes its opposite: οὐχ ὡς γυναῖκα καταλε-λειμμένην καὶ ὀλιγόψυχον κέκληκέν σε κύριος.[16]

Translations That Supply Pejorative References to Gentiles in LXX Isaiah
The Translation of זור *in LXX Isaiah 25.2, 5.* The Isaiah translator appears to harbour a low regard for the nations relative to the esteem in which he holds the children of Israel. It may be that his handling of זור allows us another glimpse of his willingness to circumvent the universalist message of the Hebrew book of Isaiah, especially as this occurs in the latter half of the book.

A similarity with the Greek Proverbs facilitates this insight. Affinities between the lexical choices made in LXX Isaiah and Proverbs suggest at the very least a shared linguistic style. In the verse at hand, the mutual terrain occurs rather in the area of content or, more specifically, in a shared manner of speaking about the foreigner.

זור is essentially an ethnic or national term. It need not imply that something is evil, though it often does. It need only state that it is foreign. Now in the nature of the case, what is *foreign* to the orthodoxies of the biblical writers will often be *evil* as well. However, it is important to observe that the Septuagint translators normally do not make explicit the pejorative reference of זור, even when the context makes it clear that the foreign thing is quite bad, or at least inappropriate and so inadmissible. Rather, they mimic their Hebrew source in utilizing words that denote only foreignness: principally ἀλλογενής, ἕτερος and ἀλλ-. If the context connotes evil as well, it must speak for itself.

For example, Exod. 30.9 forbids an unholy (so NRSV) incense (קטרת זרה = θυμίαμα ἕτερον). Num. 1.51 warns that any foreigner (הזר = ὁ

---

15. 'For as a wife who has been abandoned and grieved in spirit did the Lord call you...'
16. 'Not as a woman who has been abandoned nor (as) a faint-hearted (woman) has the Lord called you.' The negative conversion continues into the following clause, where waw is glossed by οὐδ'. In 54.7, the Lord does concede that he abandoned Israel (עזבתיך = κατέλιπόν σε); however, the fact that this was only for 'a brief moment' apparently is taken to mean that it was not *real* abandonment.

ἀλλογενής) who approaches the tabernacle must die. We read in Num. 3.4 that Nadab and Abihu died before the Lord when they offered illicit fire (זרה אֵשׁ = πῦρ ἀλλότριον). Even when alien oppressors are the foreign item, the same formalistic reserve applies. Jer. 5.19 consigns Israel to serve strangers (זרים = ἀλλοτρίοις) in a foreign land. Closer to home, Obad. 1.11 remembers the day that strangers (זרים = ἀλλογενῶν) carried off Jacob's wealth and—what is more—foreigners (נכרים = ἀλλότριοι) cast lots for Jerusalem. On none of these occasions—and there are many more like them—does the translator dare even to add a pejorative adjective, much less to translate with a substantive that would make explicit the wickedness of such foreign people or things. This is true even when the foreign thing is a strange *god*, as in Ps. 44(43).21.

Only Proverbs and Isaiah deviate from this pattern. The Greek Proverbs is profligate in its scattering of pejorative adjectives for foreign things. In 5.3, for example, the זרה is a γυνὴ πόρνη.[17] Prov. 6.1 casts the other as the ἐχθρός when it would seem the Hebrew writer merely meant someone other than oneself, in poetic parallel with 'your neighbour'. In Prov. 22.14, the זרה is an outright παράνομος. To these we might add two references that are questionable on textual grounds. Prov. 14.10 and 27.13 relate the זר to ὕβρις and ὑβριστής, respectively, though this may come about by way of a presumed relationship with זדון.

This is entirely in keeping with what the Hebrew *connotes*, for the proverbial foreign woman is meant to be avoided for her eclectic bed, not admired for her exotic accent. Nevertheless, in making explicit the evil of foreignness, the translator has distanced himself from the traditional reserve.

Only LXX Isaiah joins the Greek Proverbs in discarding the customary literalism and making the connoted evil explicit. The Isaiah translator is not shy about using ἀσεβής, a word that is exceedingly frequent in Proverbs, where it often translates רשע. Ἀσεβής also renders רשע seven times in Isaiah, a fact that indicates that it has not been evacuated of its essential meaning of 'evil' or 'impious'. However, it also represents זור four times, surpassing both the traditional ἀλλογενής and ἀλλότριος as the most used Greek word for זור in LXX Isaiah.

17. For a helpful appraisal of this term in LXX Proverbs, cf. J. Cook, 'אִשָּׁה זָרָה (*sic*) (Proverbs 1–9 Septuagint): A Metaphor for Foreign Wisdom?', *ZAW* 106 (1994), pp. 458-76. Cook answers the question that his title poses in the affirmative.

How then should this injection of a semantic element for evil into a word that nearly all LXX translators refuse to translate as anything other than 'foreign(er)' be explained? Possibly, it is simply one more datum linking the translation styles of the extremely daring translator of Proverbs with that of the more cautiously free translator of Isaiah. This explanation has a little to say about context-sensitive translation; it says nothing about the conceivable nationalism of the translator.

However, when one takes into account other indications that this son of the Diaspora—for we lack compelling reasons to abandon the consensus that he was an Egyptian Jew—shared neither Hebrew Isaiah's universalism nor its sympathy for the nations, a second option presents itself. Perhaps the linguistic indiscipline that permits a translator overtly to declare his disdain for the 'other' is best explained by disdain itself. If one-translator theories about the Greek Isaiah are correct, as I believe them essentially to be, then this is the translator who found the Servant's gathering of Israel in 49.6 to be not the 'small thing' of the MT next to the enlightenment of the Gentiles, but a 'great thing'. He is the same writer who found the Ethiopians of ch. 18 to be a people 'crushed and torn' rather than 'tall and polished'. He will consent to the nations entering Zion in ch. 66, so long as they are well-behaved σεβόμενοι.[18]

He may also have quietly signalled—by means of the four-time choice of ἀσέβης for זור—a certain nationalistic narrowness of vision when compared to the dangerously generous contract that lay before him.

Isaiah 26.11. The first verse of Isaiah 26 identifies the passage as a song that will one day be heard in a liberated Judah. Verses 26.10-11, however, envisages a moment when this liberation has not yet been made absolute, for the wicked (רשע) are still present and acting perversely in the 'land of uprightness'. Nevertheless, the song is largely about the

---

18. Indeed, one wonders whether the horizon-to-horizon vengeance wreaked upon the Gentiles in 59.18-19 is not determinative for the intriguing translation of 59.20, ובא לציון גואל ולשבי פשע ביעקב ('And a redeemer will come to Zion, and to those in Jacob who turn from transgression') is rendered by καὶ ἥξει ἕνεκεν Σιων ὁ ῥυόμενος καὶ ἀποστρέψει ἀσεβείας ἀπὸ Ιακωβ ('And the redeemer shall come *on Zion's behalf* and *he will turn irreligion from Jacob*'). The use of ἀσέβεια may indicate that the redeemer acts 'on Zion's behalf' by removing a particularly *Gentile* kind of irreligion, which would be a nationalistic subversion of the MT's urgings towards penitence.

accomplished salvation that will be celebrated 'on that day'. In describing such a new dawn, LXX Isa. 26.11 may depend upon LXX Zeph. 2.1. MT 26.11 reads:

יהוה רמה ידך בל־יחזיון
יחזו ויבשו קנאת־עם אף־אש צריך תאכלם

O Lord, your hand is lifted up. They do not see it. Let them see (your) zeal for (your) people, and be ashamed. Indeed, let the fire of your adversaries consume them.

In contrast to the probable meaning of the MT, LXX 26.11 understands the עם negatively:

Κύριε, ὑψηλός σου ὁ βραχίων, καὶ οὐκ ᾔδεισαν, γνόντες[19] δὲ αἰσχυνθήσονται· ζῆλος λήμψεται λαὸν ἀπαίδευτον, καὶ νῦν πῦρ τοὺς ὑπεναντίους ἔδεται.

O Lord, your arm is lifted high, but they have not known (it).[20] But when they realise (it), they will be ashamed. Zeal will take hold of a people uneducated, and fire will now consume the adversaries.

Two features of the LXX translation distinguish it from the meaning that the MT suggests. First, the עם of the MT appears to be the *beneficiary* of the Lord's zeal, whilst the LXX envisions its λαός as the *victim* of ζῆλος.[21] Second, the LXX describes this λαός as ἀπαί-

---

19. Seeligmann's observations (*LXX Version*, p. 40) about the translation of יחזיון and יחזו appear to underestimate the translator's dexterity. (BHS proposes the omission of יחזו ויבשו altogether.) While describing the translator's tendency not to follow standard equivalencies, but rather to translate the same word with different Greek lexemes, Seeligmann writes, 'In 26.11, the words ᾔδεισαν (sic) γνόντες as translation of יחזיון יחזו, are placed side by side in such a way as to almost make them appear like two alternatives to be read according to choice.' But the Greek pluperfect and aorist participle are not alternatives at all. Using the vocabulary available to him in the defective inventory of Greek verbs for knowing—for this is how he understands the sense of חזה here—the translator has nicely rendered the durative *failure to understand* with the pluperfect (= functional imperfect; cf. LSJ p. 350). He then captures the future *moment of perception* with the aorist participle and postpositive δὲ. There is no extraneous or alternative element to be found.

20. Or, '…was lifted high, but they did not know it.' There is no verb 'to be' in the first part of the first sentence. If one is supplied in English, its tense must be deduced from the context. Ἤδεισαν is a pluperfect form that usually has an imperfective meaning.

21. Although קנאת־עם is not expressly identified as *the Lord's* zeal, the

δευτο(ς), a word that has no explicit authorization in the Hebrew text.[22]

With regard to the negative identity of the λαός, it is easy enough to imagine how the translator might have understood the עַם to be a Gentile nation. The chapter deals with a future day when the Lord's salvation will have made of Judah a 'strong city' (26.1). The Lord will have merited Judah's trust by bringing low 'the dwellers in the height' (26.5). The clause that concerns us in 26.11 is bracketed by discussion of the intransigence of the wicked, just before, and then of their eventual consumption by fire, immediately after. Thus, the עַם could quite naturally have been taken as part of the fabric of this conversation about the wicked. It might have seemed to fit nicely in synonymous— rather than antithetical—parallelism with the final clause, אַף־אֵשׁ צָרֶיךָ תֹאכְלֵם.

The specific characterization of the λαός as ἀπαίδευτος would have been less spontaneous. Occurrences of ἀπαίδευτος and ἀπαιδευσία are concentrated in the sapiential books of the LXX. The Greek Proverbs have recourse to ἀπαίδευτος seven times, representing five characteristic idioms for fools.[23] In the Deutero-canonical books, it appears once in the Wisdom of Solomon and six times in Ben Sira.[24]

---

vocative יהוה at the beginning of the verse joins the frequency of the expression 'the zeal of the Lord' to create this presumption. Probably both the zeal and the people are intended to be understood as belonging to the Lord. Cf., for example, NRSV: 'your zeal for your people'; *Tanakh*: 'Your zeal for Your people'.

22. Ziegler, *Untersuchungen*, p. 67, limits himself to observing that 'die nämliche Wendung findet sich auch Soph 2,1 τὸ ἔθνος τὸ ἀπαίδευτον', but he neither comments upon whether this similarity is more than accidental nor explains how it may have come to be. I shall argue that it is not accidental at all; rather, it indicates that our translator has dealt with Isa. 26.11 *with the help of Greek Zephaniah*. With regard to the unauthorized λήμψεται, Ziegler helpfully remarks that our translator tends to translate בושׁ, חרד, and חיל with a noun + λήμψεται (*Untersuchungen*, pp. 39-40, 67). It appears to be significant that this slight expansion occurs when describing *negative* experiences. Clearly, it is this judgmental— rather than redemptive—aspect of קנאה that has captured the translator's imagination in this verse, in spite of what his *Vorlage* probably intended.

HUB is cryptically suggestive in the same direction as my argument will run: 'exeg; cf. Zeph 2¹G...' Ottley, *Isaiah*, II, p. 230, notes: 'λήμψεται, ἀπαίδευτον] These words are added by LXX., giving a new colour to the sentence.'

23. אֱוִיל and נָבָל, לוּץ, כְּסִיל, אֵין מוּסָר.

24. Of the four occurrences of the related word, ἀπαιδευσία, three occur in Ben Sira. The other is found at Hos. 7.16, where senseless Ephraim is seen to fall לְשׁוֹנָם מִזַּעַם = διὰ ἀπαιδευσίαν γλώσσης.

Outside of sapiential literature, only two LXX verses have ἀπαίδευτος: Isa. 26.11, where it is unauthorized by the Hebrew, and Zeph.
2.1, which reads as follows:

התקושׁשׁו וקושׁו הגוי לא נכסף

Gather together, gather, O shameless nation…

The LXX has:

Συνάχθητε καὶ συνδέθητε, τὸ ἔθνος τὸ ἀπαίδευτον

Gather together and unite, O nation uneducated.

The meaning of the final clause of the verse, נכסף לא, is not
transparent. BDB think the text is corrupt.[25] The translator of Zephaniah
has understood it to mean 'uneducated', either because the Hebrew term
was more familiar to him than it is to us or because this is the meaning
that the context suggested to him.[26] In order to express this, he has
chosen the rare word ἀπαίδευτος.

To at least some extent, then, ἀπαίδευτος must be considered an
authorized reading vis-à-vis the Hebrew text of Zephaniah.[27] On the
other hand, ἀπαίδευτον in Isa. 26.11 is *unauthorized*.

It seems doubtful that the Isaiah translator would have on his own
produced an adjective for עם (= λαός).[28] It is also probable that he had
external help in arriving at the notion of *lack of instruction* as the
defining characteristic of the people in question. That this description
should then have been achieved independently by use of the rare word
ἀπαίδευτος is not likely. The more persuasive explanation is that his
translation at 26.11 alludes to Zeph. 2.1.

---

25. Most modern translators appear to follow the etymological argument from
Arabic and NH that BDB dismiss, and thus to produce the notion of shamelessness
= *not to turn pale.*

26. Alternatively, cf. D.H. Ryou, *Zephaniah's Oracles against the Nations: A
Synchronic and Diachronic Study of Zephaniah 2:1–3:8* (Biblical Interpretation,
13; Leiden: E.J. Brill, 1995), pp. 21-22: 'The LXX reads ἀπαίδευτον (in passive,
'undisciplined,' a probable reading of נוֹסָר לא)…'

27. This is the case *maximally* if the translator understood נכסף לא to mean
'shameless' and expressed this with ἀπαίδευτος. It is the case *minimally* if he did
not understand נכסף לא but nonetheless felt himself constrained to translate it by
one means or another, even if this meant determining its meaning by the context.

28. He is much more likely to omit descriptive words when they do occur in MT
(≈ *Vorlage*) than to produce them when they do not.

Furthermore, the rarity of ἀπαίδευτος encourages the view that the translator's reference was to the *Greek* text of Zeph. 2.1, rather than the Hebrew. It is difficult to imagine that the Isaiah translator would have discerned a conceptual link between his text and MT Zeph. 2.1, recognised לֹא נִכְסָף as a synonym of 'uneducated', and then independently produced the same rare Greek translation as the translator of Zephaniah.

In addition to the lexical links I have described, there are broader contextual connections between Isaiah 26 and Zephaniah 1–2 that explain the translator's apparent decision to read the one in the light of the other.

Both passages locate their descriptions in some future *day*.[29] Both focus upon Jerusalem and Judah.[30] Both are particularly concerned with a place's *inhabitants*[31] and the Lord's *visitation*[32] of them.

However, the principal attraction of this verse for the Isaiah translator probably lay in the notion of the Lord's fiery zeal. In Zeph. 1.18—just one verse prior to 2.1—one reads:

...בְּיוֹם עֶבְרַת יְהוָה וּבְאֵשׁ קִנְאָתוֹ תֵּאָכֵל כָּל־הָאָרֶץ...

...on the day of the Lord's wrath; and in the fire of his passion the whole earth will be consumed.

...ἐν ἡμέρᾳ ὀργῆς κυρίου, καὶ ἐν πυρὶ ζήλους αὐτοῦ καταναλωθήσεται πᾶσα ἡ γῆ...

...in the day of the Lord's wrath, and in his fiery zeal will the whole earth be consumed...

One is immediately reminded of the similar language in Isa. 26.11, קִנְאַת־עָם אַף־אֵשׁ צָרֶיךָ תֹאכְלֵם. Once again, the features of the Greek text of Zephaniah enjoy specific authorization on the part of the Hebrew text, while several in LXX Isaiah do not. Thus, the evidence suggests

---

29. Isa. 26.1, בַּיּוֹם הַהוּא = Τῇ ἡμέρᾳ ἐκείνῃ; Zeph. 1.7, כִּי קָרוֹב יוֹם יְהוָה = διότι ἐγγὺς ἡμέρα κυρίου. At 1.8, BHS proposes the omission of וְהָיָה בְּיוֹם זֶבַח יְהוָה; however, the translator knew it and produced καὶ ἔσται ἐν ἡμέρᾳ θυσίας κυρίου. Cf. 1.9, 10, 12 for very similar cases. Cf. also Zeph. 1.14-16 קָרוֹב יוֹם־יְהוָה הַגָּדוֹל...קוֹל יוֹם יְהוָה מַר... . This emphasis on the Lord's wrathful day continues after 2.1.

30. Isa. 26.1 and verses earlier in the 'Isaiah Apocalypse': 24.23; 25.6-7; Zeph. 1.4, 10, 12.

31. Isa. 26.5, 9, 18, 21; Zeph. 1.4, 11, 18.

32. פָּקַד. Cf. Isa. 26.14, 16, 21; Zeph. 1.8, 9, 12; 2.7.

that the Isaiah translator is dependent upon Zephaniah—in one form or the other—rather than the reverse.

Nonetheless, the thesis that he is reading *Greek* Zephaniah does not find *absolute* confirmation, since LXX Isaiah does not duplicate καταναλωθήσεται, which is LXX Zephaniah's rendering of האכל. Rather, LXX Isaiah produces ἔδεται for האכלם. There is indeed clear evidence for allusion; but the relationship stops short of slavish dependence.

Several observations can now be made on the basis of the observable relationship between LXX Isa. 26.11 and Zeph. 2.1.

First, both general contextual features and specific lexical ones make it possible for the translator to have read Isaiah 26 as essentially contiguous with Zephaniah 1–2.

Second, the unauthorized appearance of ἀπαίδευτος in LXX Isa. 26.11 strongly suggests that the translator knew LXX Zeph. 2.1. Together with other indications of a late 'Isaiah project' that I have adduced, this points to a relative chronology of translation that places LXX Isaiah at or near the end of the prophets.[33] Its principal stylistic features are at home among the Greek translations of the Writings and the (mostly Greek) Deutero-canonical books.

Third, the rhetorical thrust of Zephaniah 1–2 may well have influenced the Isaiah translator's reading of עם as a *pejorative* reference. The Zephaniah passage appears to be a denunciation of disobedient Judah. The text promises a frightful 'day' on which 'in the fire of his passion the whole earth will be consumed; for a whole, a terrible, end he will make of all the inhabitants of the earth'. Once the Isaiah translator had brought his text into the conceptual universe of Zephaniah 1–2, it is easy to imagine how the language of zeal could be seen as judgmental—rather than redemptive—passion.

Finally, the translator appears to have retained certain discontinuities between the two passages. The Zephaniah passage delivers a merciless condemnation of Judah in ch. 1. LXX Isa. 26.11, in spite of the degree to

33. *Pace* such standard works as H. St John Thackeray, *A Grammar of the Old Testament in Greek According to the Septuagint* (Cambridge: Cambridge University Press, 1909; reprinted Hildesheim: George Olms, 1987), pp. viii-ix: 'We may conjecture that the Prophets made their appearance in a Greek dress in the second century B.C., Isaiah near the beginning of it, the group consisting of Jeremiah, Ezekiel and the Twelve (or large portions of this group) nearer the close...'

which it has become assimilated in tone and content to Zephaniah 1–2, continues to read like a celebration of Judah's deliverance over an *external* uneducated people.[34] If this reading is correct, the translator may have been influenced by his own positive pre-understanding of Judah's lot. On the other hand, Zephaniah 2 shifts its judgmental vigour from Judah to various surrounding nations.[35] It is conceivable that the Isaiah translator understood Greek Zephaniah's λαός ἀπαίδευτος as a cipher that looked forward to the Gentiles rather than backwards to Judah, and could be applied to each of the following doomed nations in its turn. As such, the phrase could have been imported into the Isaiah text without threatening the tranquillity of Judea.[36]

34. Alternatively, it is perhaps possible to read LXX Isa. 26 as a remnant's song. In this case, the adversaries—ὁ λαὸς ἀπαίδευτος—might well be fellow Judaeans. However, this does not seem to be the most natural reading.

Targum Jonathan dovetails with the reading I consider probable for LXX, in that it considers the wicked in this chapter to be Gentiles (cf. 26.12) who are still in the land. TJ reads קנאת־עם as a subjective genitive. It refers not to the Lord's zeal for his people, but rather the retribution of the people that will cover the adversaries.

For the intention of the MT to contrast righteous and delivered Judaeans with wicked and soon-to-be-conquered foreigners, cf. Gray, *Isaiah I–XXVIII*, pp. 398-99. O. Kaiser offers a slightly different picture: 'Eine Unterscheidung zwischen Juden und Nichtjuden wird dabei nicht getroffen, obwohl von dem Zusammenhang her die Jahwes Herrlichkeit und Herrschaft nicht anerkennenden Heiden im Vordergrund stehen dürften' (*Der Prophet Jesaja, Kapitel 13–29*, p. 170).

35. Cf. P.R. House, 'Dialogue in Zephaniah', in R.P. Gordon (ed.), *'The Place: Is Too Small for Us': The Israelite Prophets in Recent Scholarship* (Winona Lake, IN: Eisenbrauns, 1995), pp. 252-62 (260): 'Once a general notion of judgement is presented, the second major division of the book tells who will suffer with Judah in the great judgement (1:18–3:5). The prophet gives the first speech in this section, claiming that the 'shameful nation' Judah (2:1) will be joined in judgement by Philistia.'

36. Indeed, it is not indisputable that the גוי in Zeph. 2.1 is Judah. Cf. R.L. Smith, *Micah–Malachi* (WBC, 32; Waco, TX: Word Books, 1984), p. 132: 'The shameless nation is not identified in the pericope.' J.M.P. Smith identifies the nation as Philistia, in Smith *et al.*, *A Critical and Exegetical Commentary on Micah, Zephaniah, Nahum, Habakkuk, Obadiah and Joel* (Edinburgh: T. & T. Clark, 1912), p. 211. If the translator of Zephaniah understood the text in this way, that would bring him closer to LXX Isaiah.

At least one ancient interpreter understood the senseless nation to be Judah. Cf. TJ Zeph. 2.1: 'Assemble yourselves and come and draw near, O people of the generation which does not desire to return to the law...' Cf. Cathcart and Gordon, *The Targum of the Minor Prophets*, p. 168.

Translations That Elevate the Stature of Zion/Jerusalem/Israel in
LXX Isaiah

Isaiah 1.26-27. A poignant glimpse of Diaspora feelings toward the
mother city is to be glimpsed in LXX Isa. 1.26-27. A reworking of the
MT syntax yields a surprising reconfiguration of both the city and those
Jews who find themselves exiled from her. The Lord promises that,
following an exceedingly severe judgment,

ואשיבה שפטיך כבראשנה ויעציך כבתחלה
אחרי־כן יקרא לך עיר הצדק קריה נאמנה
(27) ציון במשפט תפדה ושביה בצדקה

> And I will restore your judges as (they were) at the first, and your sages
> as (they were) in the beginning. After this, you will be called 'The City
> of Righteousness', 'a faithful city'.[37] (27) Zion will be saved by justice,
> and her repentant ones by righteousness.

The LXX divides the verses differently:

> καὶ ἐπιστήσω τοὺς κριτάς σου ὡς τὸ πρότερον καὶ τοὺς
> συμβούλους σου ὡς τὸ ἀπ᾽ ἀρχῆς· καὶ μετὰ ταῦτα κληθήσῃ Πόλις
> δικαιοσύνης, μητρόπολις πιστὴ Σιων.[38] (27) μετὰ γὰρ κρίματος
> σωθήσεται ἡ αἰχμαλωσία αὐτῆς καὶ μετὰ ἐλεημοσύνης.

> And I will establish your judges as (at) the first, and your counsellors as
> from the beginning. And after these things you will be called 'The City
> of Righteousness', 'Zion the Faithful Mother City'. For with justice will
> her captive(s) be saved, and with mercy.

In the LXX the titles that Zion will receive include the rare word
μητρόπολις, a term that often connotes the centre to which the margins
relate.[39] Equally striking in this regard is the translation of וְשָׁבֶיהָ by ἡ

---

37. Alternatively, 'The Faithful City'.

38. The inclusion of Σιων, the first word of 1.27, with the syntax of the final
words of 1.26 (thus, μητρόπολις πιστὴ Σιων) has influenced the translation back
at 1.21. In that lament over the faithful city, now fallen into prostitution, קריה נאמנה
is translated as πόλις πιστὴ Σιων.

39. Cf. Seeligmann, *LXX Version*, pp. 113-14: 'In 1.26 אחרי כן יקרא לך עיר
הצדק קריה נאמנה is translated by καὶ μετὰ ταῦτα κληθήσῃ (sic) Πόλις
δικαιοσύνης μητρόπολις πιστή Σιων—the translator, splitting the verse in a
different way from that suggested by the Massoretic text; this calls to mind the
translation of Ps. 86(87).5: ולציון יאמר איש זה וזה ילד שם [So Seeligmann's quote;
but BHS, ילד בה...] μήτηρ Σιων ἐρεῖ (sic) ἄνθρωπος καὶ "Ανθρωπος ἐγενήθη
ἐν αὐτῇ... This usage may accordingly be considered to have been current among
Alexandrian Jewry.'

αἰχμαλωσία αὐτῆς.⁴⁰ While this may have resulted as an alternative vocalization (שְׁבְיָה or שְׁבִיָּה) of the available consonants, it is important to note that this would require the loss of the waw.⁴¹ Such a reading would also be obliged to erase an antithesis in the Hebrew text between the שָׁבִים—who are saved—and the פֹּשְׁעִים, the חַטָּאִים, and the עֹזְבֵי יהוה of 1.28, who meet their end.

It seems more likely that the translator has read out of the synonymous parallelism of his text (שְׁבֶיהָ//צִיּוֹן) two separate entities: Zion and *her* Diaspora captives. I shall suggest in Chapter 7⁴² that a similar reading of (synonymous) parallelism may have occurred at LXX Isa. 66.10, again creating two groups that are defined vis-à-vis Jerusalem/Zion. This may be an important glimpse of this translator's self-identity and his perception of Zion as the mother *from which* his community derives and the destination *to which* they hope to return. Presumably, his point of view would not have been unique among his Alexandrian brethren.

Isaiah 19.18, 23-25. Some of the most universalistic language of the entire Hebrew Bible occurs in Isa. 19.16-25, where Israel's paradigmatic enemies engage in Yahwistic worship.⁴³ There are subtle indications in vv. 23-25 that the translator has clung to Israelite prerogatives that the Hebrew text places in a more egalitarian perspective. Indeed, such hedging may have begun at an almost imperceptible level as early as 19.18. That verse anticipates a day when there will be five cities in the land of Egypt 'speaking the language of Canaan and swearing to the Lord of Hosts (וְנִשְׁבָּעוֹת לַ[יהוה] צְבָאוֹת...]).' The LXX has them swear 'by *the name* of the Lord [ὀμνύουσαι τῷ ὀνόματι

40. So also ς; cf. BHS apparatus.

41. Or, perhaps, its relocation. The waw from וּשְׁבֶיהָ may have been preserved in בִּצְדָקָה = καὶ μετὰ ἐλεημοσύνης.

It is also possible that the translator has read שְׁבֶיהָ as a plural participle of שׁוּב, with the MT, but has construed this in terms of *physical* return rather than as the MT's *moral* turning. Ἡ αἰχμαλωσία αὐτῆς would then be shorthand for those who will return, but have not yet done so. This explanation seems less likely than the one sketched out above.

42. Cf., below, 'Dismantled Parallelism', pp. 240-48.

43. Cf. W. Vogels, 'L'Égypte mon peuple—L'Universalisme d'Is 19,16-25', *Biblica* 57 (1976), pp. 494-514 (494): 'Tous les commentateurs d'Is 19,16-25 sont d'accord au moins sur un point: ce texte est d'une richesse exceptionnelle pour l'universalisme dans l'Ancien Testament. On a parlé d'un sommet religieux.'

κυρίου]', a change that could be dismissed as well within the bounds of standard translational license were it not for an identical Targum rendering at an equally sensitive ecumenical moment.[44]

In MT 19.23, where an international highway opens the way to ecumenical worship, the LXX deviation becomes clearer:

ביום ההוא תהיה מסלה ממצרים אשורה ובא־אשור
במצרים ומצרים באשור ועבדו מצרים את־אשור

> In that day there will be a highway from Egypt to Assyria, and Assyria will come to Egypt, and Egypt to Assyria, and Egypt will worship with Assyria.

Verses 19-22 make clear that this worship is Yahwistic. In 19.23, however, the translator stops short of such an affirmation. In the LXX,

---

44. Cf. Gordon, '*Terra Sancta*', p. 121: '...Naaman's professed intention of offering burnt offerings and sacrifices to the Lord when he returned to his native Syria appears with minimal alteration in TJ (2 Kgs v.17). The Targum, introducing its own brand of "Name Theology", simply substitutes "to the name of the Lord" for the MT's "to the Lord".' Cf. the rest of Gordon's paragraph for an evaluation of the importance of this subtle novelty.

If the insertion of ὄνομα represents the kind of exegetical nuance that I suggest, it would not be easily squared with van der Kooij's claim that the worship represented here is carried out by Jews in Egypt rather than by Egyptians; cf. 'Servant of the Lord', p. 392. Van der Kooij's assertion that ὁ λαός μου ἐν Αἰγύπτῳ καὶ ὁ ἐν Ασσυρίοις means 'my people *in* Egypt (not "among Egyptians") and *among* Assyrians' (the latter are understood to be invading Assyrians *in Egypt*) is probably compromised already by the observation that LXX Isaiah renders אשור almost exclusively by plural Ἀσσύριοι, whether in reference *to the place* or *to Assyrian people*. Of 44 occurrences of אשור, the only two exceptions are at 11.16, where מאשור = ἐν Αἰγύπτῳ, and 31.8, where the translator understands the reference to be to *an Assyrian man*. The translation of מצרים is marginally more helpful, since here the translator has recourse to Αἴγυπτος for the place and Αἰγύπτιοι for the people (Sing. Αἰγύπτιος does not occur). Still, the criteria that were decisive for the translator in each case are exceedingly difficult to ascertain, and often seem arbitrary (Cf., for example, ארץ מצרים = χώρα Αἰγυπτίων in 19.19 and χώρα Αἰγύπτου in 19.20).

Van der Kooij's argument seems virtually certain with regard to the LXX's reclaiming for Jews of the language 'my people Egypt/Assyria' in 19.25. He shows persuasive evidence of a particular interest in the Lord's (Jewish) people *in Egypt*. However, *pace* van der Kooij, it appears likely that the cultic activity carried out '*in the name* of the Lord' is understood by the translator to be that of Egyptians who approximate to, even if they do not actually achieve, fully Yahwistic worship.

καὶ δουλεύσουσιν οἱ Ἀιγύπτιοι τοῖς Ἀσσυρίους indicates that the
translator has read את as the accusative marker. This makes the
Assyrians the benefactors of Egyptian *service* rather than their co-
religionists in authentic Yahwistic cult, just as in TJ on the same verse.[45]
It would be perilous unflinchingly to call this conscious exegesis in the
light of this translator's difficulty in recognizing the preposition את.
Still, it does run contrary to the context, thus suggesting at least the
possibility that the translator is moving at cross-purposes with the
radical universalism of the Hebrew text and perhaps even quietly giving
voice to the tensions between Alexandria's Gentile and Jewish inhabitants that were seldom entirely absent.

Such an incipient trend—if it is that—is further developed in 19.24,
where the Hebrew text seems to drive home its universalistic intent by
the rhetorical extreme of subjugating Israel to the nations:

ביום ההוא יהיה ישראל שלישיה למצרים ולאשור ברכה
בקרב הארץ

> In that day, Israel will be third to Egypt and to Assyria, a blessing in the
> midst of the earth.

The LXX counters this sequence by the ambiguous placement of
Israel as third *among* the Assyrians and the Egyptians:

τῇ ἡμέρᾳ ἐκείνῃ ἔσται Ισραηλ τρίτος ἐν τοῖς Ἀσσυρίοις καὶ ἐν τοῖς
Ἀιγυπτίοις εὐλογημένος ἐν τῇ γῇ.

> In that day Israel will be third among the Assyrians and among the
> Egyptians, blessed in the land.

In addition to the possible subversion of the MT's sequential ordering
(Assyria, Egypt, then Israel), the LXX glosses the substantive ברכה
(blessing) with the passive participle εὐλογημένος (blessed). Any echo
of the notion found in Genesis 12 that Israel was to exist for the
blessing of the nations has been suppressed by the LXX. If that idea was
latent in the Hebrew text, it has been watered down by a functional
active-passive transformation that places Israel at the centre, where she
has become blessed—perhaps by Assyria and Egypt—rather than one
who blesses them.

If such a conversion is barely suggested by the details of 19.24, it is
probably confirmed in 19.25, where a reworking has been more widely

---

45. ויפל חון מצראי ית אתוראי.

recognized. The MT passage reaches its rhetorical climax there as the Lord applies to all three nations the descriptions usually reserved for Israel alone:

אֲשֶׁר בֵּרֲכוֹ יְהוָה צְבָאוֹת לֵאמֹר בָּרוּךְ עַמִּי מִצְרַיִם
וּמַעֲשֵׂה יָדִי אַשּׁוּר וְנַחֲלָתִי יִשְׂרָאֵל

> Whom the Lord of Hosts blessed, saying: 'Blessed are my people Egypt, and Assyria, the work of my hands, and Israel, my inheritance.'

It may be that both nationalism and the voice of Diaspora are to be heard in what appears to be the Septuagint's reclaiming of these titles for Israel herself, albeit in the places of her exile.

> ἣν εὐλόγησεν κύριος σαβαωθ λέγων εὐλογημένος ὁ λαός μου ὁ ἐν Αἰγύπτῳ καὶ ὁ ἐν Ἀσσυρίοις καὶ ἡ κληρονομία μου Ισραηλ.

> Whom the Lord of Hosts blessed, saying, 'Blessed are my people who are in Egypt and (my people) who are among the Assyrians and Israel, my inheritance.

The LXX achieves more economically an end similar to that which TJ reaches by exposition:

> …whom the Lord has blessed, saying, 'blessed are my people whom I brought forth from Egypt; because they sinned before me I exiled them to Assyria, and now that they repent they are called my people and my heritage, Israel.[46]

Isaiah 31.9. A fascinating reuse of available consonants in LXX Isa. 31.9 allows the translator to celebrate the blessings of Zionist genealogy with the same material that serves in the MT to describe the Lord's fiery zeal. At the end of a chapter that stresses the futility of relying upon Egypt and stresses that Assyria's downfall will be the work of a divine sword, MT 31.9b seals the oracle in this way:

נְאֻם־יְהוָה אֲשֶׁר־אוּר לוֹ בְּצִיּוֹן וְתַנּוּר לוֹ בִּירוּשָׁלָ͏ִם

Oracle of the Lord, who has a light[47]in Zion and a furnace in Jerusalem.

The LXX appears to view everything following נְאֻם־יְהוָה as the quoted oracle itself, a perspective that fits well with the chapter's insistence upon the city's inviolability:

---

46. Chilton, *Isaiah Targum*, p. 39.
47. NRSV and *Tanakh* have 'fire', which is probably correct in view of the parallel.

Τάδε[48] λέγει κύριος Μακάριος ὃς ἔχει ἐν Σιων σπέρμα καὶ οἰκείους ἐν Ιερουσαλημ.

The Lord says these things: 'Blessed is the one who has a seed in Zion and kinsmen in Jerusalem.'

Seeligmann notices the importance of this conversion. However, he apparently fails to observe that it is not so much a flight of the translator's fancy as a reconfiguration of the elements that the text itself provides.

> This loyalty to, and yearning for, Zion is clearly and strikingly expressed in the transposition of 31.9: the Hebrew text concludes a prophecy, warning the Jews against seeking the protection of Egypt, with the words...the translation transforms this into a blessing, heralding the supervening consequence... *This remarkable liberty taken by the translator* justifies the assumption that he sought to express an idea very prevalent among Alexandrian Jewry (emphasis added).[49]

In place of בציון לו אור־אשר, the translator has read זרע לו אשרי בציון. The alterations that this requires are attested elsewhere in MT/LXX Isaiah.[50] More difficult is the second portion of the parallelism, where one finds καὶ οἰκείους ἐν Ιερουσαλημ in the place of לו ותנור בירושלם. There seems to be no obvious way of generating καὶ οἰκείους from ותנור. Rather, it is most likely a translation *ad sensum* that testifies to the certainty of the translator that this is the statement that he wished to make.

As is so often the case, the details do not allow us to prove or to disprove intentionality on the part of the translator. Even short of affirming a conscious exploitation of the text's possibilities, however, one can observe that such a restatement of this Hebrew sentence is not likely to form itself in a mind that is, in terms of interpretational bias, a *tabula*

---

48. In the light of the plural τάδε, it may be that this formula refers back to the contents of vv. 1-9a, as in the MT. After all, the words that follow are really just *one* thing. In that case, 31.9b would then be an editorial comment occasioned by the entire picture of divine deliverance of Jerusalem. However, this seems unlikely in the light of this translator's use of τάδε λέγει as a stock translation of the formulaic נאם־יהוה.

49. *LXX Version*, p. 114.

50. ו/ז, ע/א (guttural interchange), 'dyslexic' reordering of consonants, and the addition of a yod. It is possible—though probably not necessary—that אשר was read as itself in addition to its reconfiguration as זרע. This would have facilitated the generation of the relative pronoun ὃς.

rasa. Thus, even if Seeligmann overestimates the translator's 'remark-able liberty', he seems well on target when he identifies in this Greek verse a 'loyalty to, and yearning for, Zion'.

Translations that Insert 'Zion', 'Jerusalem', 'Jacob', or 'Israel' in LXX Isaiah

It is not unusual to discover in TJ and LXX Isaiah a refined exegetical precision that specifies a protagonist that is either absent or only implicit in the source text.[51] Sometimes, this clarifying tendency inserts a reference to city and/or nation.

Isaiah 42.1. The polyvalent identity of the Lord's Servant[52] in Deutero-Isaiah has occasioned centuries of discussion, but the LXX translator was not party to any doubts about its corporate character.[53] When in 42.1 the Lord presents this figure and pledges divine support with the words הן עבדי אתמך־בו בחירי, the translator fills in the picture with details that he may have gleaned from the similar passages at 41.8, 44.1, 44.21 and 45.4,[54] [55] Ιακωβ ὁ παῖς μου, ἀντιλήμψομαι αὐτοῦ· Ισραηλ ὁ ἐκλεκτός μου...

The verb προσδέχεσθαι tends to appear in related passages where the Hebrew does not lead one to expect it, perhaps tying Servant passages

---

51. For example, 'priests': TJ 1.14 (10.32) and LXX 40.2; 'Gentiles': TJ 25.2, 28.2; 'Zion'/'Jerusalem': TJ 1.24, 4.6, 8.8, 10.32, 25.2, 33.14, 38.11, 49.19, 51.19, 54.1, 54.10, 54.15, 54.17, 56.9, 60.1 (w. LXX), 60.4, 60.12, 60.17, 61.10, 61.11(!), 66.6 and LXX 1.21, 1.26, 6.23 and 60.1; 'the parts of Judah': 8.23(LXX 9.1).

52. Throughout this discussion I will capitalize the word 'Servant' in recognition of the dramatic *persona* whose career is sketched out in the so-called 'Servant Songs'.

53. For a survey of the possible identities of the παῖς κυρίου in LXX Isaiah and the suggestion that it represents a 'priestly group of Onias' in Egypt, cf. van der Kooij, 'The Servant of the Lord', pp. 383-96.

54. Cf. 42.1, Ιακωβ ὁ παῖς μου, ἀντιλήμψομαι αὐτου· Ισραηλ ὁ ἐκλεκτός μου, where the national terms are absent from the Hebrew text, and 45.4, ἕνεκεν Ιακωβ τοῦ παιδός μου καὶ Ισραηλ τοῦ ἐκλεκτοῦ μου, where they are not. The language of 41.8, 44.1 and 44.21 is similar to that of 45.4. In every case except 42.1, the occurrences of 'Jacob' and 'Israel' are fully authorized by the Hebrew text. Cf. also 42.19, where the consonants that would produce MT עַבְדִּי are instead vocalized עֲבָדַי to produce οἱ παῖδές μου (in the same verse עבד = οἱ δοῦλοι).

55. *Pace* TJ, of which Chilton (*Isaiah Targum*, p. 81) says at this point: 'Although "servant" language has been used in respect of Israel (41.8), the present usage appears messianic...'

to those that speak clearly of return to Zion.[56] In 42.1, the Servant is referred to as בחירי רצתה נפשי. The LXX translates this phrase unremarkably as ὁ ἐκλεκτός μου, προσεδέξατο αὐτὸν ἡ ψυχή μου, utilizing a standard LXX equivalency (רצה//προσδεκ[χ]-). Both words appear frequently when sacrifice (or prayer) puts right some breach of communion.

Curiously, however, προσδέχεσθαι occurs in similar passages elsewhere where clear authorization from the Hebrew text is *not* forthcoming. Isa. 45.4, for example, is one of the verses that appears to motivate the provision of 'Jacob' and 'Israel' at 42.1, for these are equated there with the Servant and with God's 'chosen'. The LXX novelty at 45.4 is the provision of προσδέξομαί σε for אכנך (I betitle you). Two explanations suggest themselves: (a) the translator may have read אקוך;[57] or (b) when 42.1 *received* 'Jacob' and 'Israel' from 45.4, it may have also *given* προσδέχεσθαι to the later verse. Such cross-pollination is hardly uncommon in LXX Isaiah.

In either case, the two servant passages have become significantly more similar in the LXX than they are in the Hebrew text. This twofold interlocking of a verse that the Hebrew text does not make explicitly corporate with a similar passage that it *does* serves to interpret both in corporate, and perhaps national, terms.[58]

---

56. That is, because of the common presence of προσδέχεσθαι with various degrees of (non-)authorization. By means of the same approach, van der Kooij discovers the possibility that πόνος extends the Servant motif to passages where עבד (= παῖς/δοῦλος) does not appear; cf. 'The Servant of the Lord', p. 387.

57. From BDB I: 'I wait for you,' or BDB II: 'I gather you.' קוה does not generate προσδεκ(χ)- lexemes elsewhere in the LXX. However, several synonyms (שבר, קבל and יחל') do so. Furthermore, the translator understands the substantive קו at Isa. 28.10 as though it were from קוה and glosses it with προσδέχεσθαι.

58. One wonders as well whether the unparalleled use of προσδεχόμενοι ὑμᾶς for לפניכם in 55.12 might not extend the corporate servant motif still further, applying it where the word 'Servant' does not occur to people whom the LXX probably considered to be 'returnees'. In that verse, the going out and the coming back (LXX has going out and *being taught*) of the restored people (the context is resolutely plural) is to be greeted by the applause of the mountains and hills לפניכם (= προσδεχόμενοι ὑμᾶς). The attested use of προσδέχεσθαι for both the reception of foreign delegations and the acceptance of individuals into the citizenship of a city (cf. LSJ) is enticing with respect to a possible application of this verse to Diaspora expectation. Unfortunately, the evidence is too fragile to say more. The translator's remarkable choice of διδαχθήσεσθε for MT תובלון (hoph. יבל',

Isaiah 44.23. When in 44.23 the heavens and the various features of earth's landscape are urged to noisy celebration, the full explanation for the reason is curiously brief: כי־עשׂה יהוה. At the end of the verse, the Lord's deed is spelled out: 'For the Lord has redeemed Jacob, and will be glorified in Israel.' The translator, however, will not wait this long for the full story to be told. Rather, he chooses elements from the Isaianic stock-in-trade to gloss כי־עשׂה יהוה with the more explanatory ὅτι ἠλέησεν ὁ θεὸς τὸν Ισραηλ.

Translations That Make Exclusive and/or Expansive Territorial Claims
Isaiah 6.12. LXX Isa. 6.12 transforms the land's abandoned doom into a promise of the expulsion of certain men from it and the multiplication, in their place, of Israel's survivors. When the newly commissioned prophet asks the Lord how long his appalling career must last, the reply, in 6.11, is not encouraging: 'Until cities lie waste without inhabitant, and houses without people, and the land is utterly desolate...' MT 6.12 carries forward the theme of the land's judicially imposed abandonment:

ורחק יהוה את־האדם ורבה העזובה בקרב הארץ

...and (until) the Lord will have sent people far away,[59] and desolation will have multiplied in the centre of the land.

The LXX entirely reverses the contribution of this verse, marking it off from 6.11 by the stock transitional phrase μετὰ ταῦτα. It now refers to restoration rather than judgment. Those who are distanced from the land now appear to be Israel's oppressors rather than her own guilty exiles:

καὶ μετὰ ταῦτα μακρυνεῖ ὁ θεὸς τοὺς ἀνθρώπους, καὶ οἱ καταλειφθέντες πληθυνθήσονται ἐπὶ τῆς γῆς.

And after these things, God will remove the people far away, and the survivors will be multiplied on the land.

The translator has anticipated the reversal of this Hebrew verse that occurs in Isa. 49.19-20, rushing forward this happy dénouement into the far more gloomy early chapters.[60] The LXX text thus has something to

---

to be borne along; 1QIsa[a] תלכו) may have been facilitated by Aramaic ביל, *to study.*

59. Alternatively, 'For the Lord will send...' In either case, those who are sent far away are the judged citizens of Israel/Judah.

60. Cf. B.D. Sommer, 'Allusions and Illusions: The Unity of the Book of Isaiah

say not only about return from exile/Diaspora—a theme that is widely to be observed in the translation—but also about expulsion of those who have, meanwhile, occupied a place that does not belong to them. The LXX, like the Hebrew text, does not care further to define אדם/ τοὺς ἀνθρώπους, leaving to the context the same determining role that it had in the source text. It is possible that these were understood to be malicious compatriots, though the foreign occupier seems the more likely candidate.

Isaiah 27.12. MT Isa. 27.12 glimpses eschatological prosperity in the idiom of agricultural metaphor:

והיה ביום ההוא
יחבט יהוה משבלת הנהר עד־נחל מצרים[61]
ואתם תלקטו לאחד אחד בני ישראל

And in that day the Lord will thresh from the channel of the (Euphrates) River to the Wadi of Egypt, and you will be gathered, one by one, O children of Israel.

The translation displays a certain local colour in its rendering of נחל מצרים:

καὶ ἔσται ἐν τῇ ἡμέρᾳ ἐκείνῃ συμφράξει κύριος ἀπὸ τῆς διώρυγος τοῦ ποταμοῦ ἕως Ῥινοκουρούρων ὑμεῖς δὲ συναγάγετε τοὺς υἱοὺς Ισραηλ κατὰ ἕνα ἕνα.

And in that day the Lord will fence in (the territory) from the channel of the River to Rhinocolura. But (as for) you, gather the sons of Israel one by one.

The meaning of the MT threshing metaphor is not entirely clear.[62] It may be that the translator's use of συμφράσσειν (*to fence in/around*) for חבט is merely a demetaphorizing clarification of the metaphor.[63]

in Light of Deutero-Isaiah's Use of Prophetic Tradition', in R.F. Melugin and M.A. Sweeney (eds.), *New Visions of Isaiah* (JSOTSup, 214; Sheffield: Sheffield Academic Press, 1996), pp. 156-86 (160 n. 12). Cf. by the same author *A Prophet Reads Scripture: Allusion in Isaiah 40–66* (Stanford: Stanford University Press, 1998), p. 242.

61. For an elegantly concise summary of the difficulties of this second stich, cf. Williamson, *Book Called Isaiah*, p. 253.

62. Gray, *Isaiah I–XXVII*, pp. 461-62 surveys the history of its interpretation.

63. In this regard, cf. O. Kaiser, *Der Prophet Jesaja Kap 13–39* ([Göttingen: Vandenhoeck & Ruprecht: 1973] ET: *Isaiah 13–39* London: SCM Press, 1979), p. 231: 'By portraying Yahweh as threshing out the reaped ears of corn…within the

However, the LXX sounds remarkably similar to a tradition found in discussions of territorial boundaries in the Targums, whereby the age to come will find Israel living by itself, separated off from troublesome Gentiles.[64] Isa. 27.12 has such a discussion of expanded boundaries and a curious intrusion of separation language that may have been facilitated by reading חבש rather than MT חבם.[65]

The LXX goes on to render the final stich with reference to a subject that is not the children of Israel themselves. MT's passive וְאַתֶּם תְּלֻקְּטוּ (and you will be gathered) is rendered as the imperatival ὑμεῖς δὲ συναγάγετε, a translation that may derive from reading an active form[66] and imposing an imperatival sense upon the imperfect. If a conjecture is to be made about the identity of the ὑμεῖς—a guess that the LXX now forces upon the reader—one might begin with the Gentile couriers who accompany Jewish returnees to eschatological Zion elsewhere in this book.[67] The particle δέ of ὑμεῖς δὲ might then assume its mild adversative function, explaining how it is that fenced off Gentiles should find themselves—albeit temporarily—within the confines of the Land: 'But you...gather the children of Israel...'

Nationalistic Translations in LXX Isaiah 56–65

A series of far-reaching nationalistic translations in ch. 66 requires special discussion. Chapter 7 of this volume is dedicated to that end. The remainder of the present chapter treats of those nationalistic translations that occur in chs. 56–65. As noted at the beginning of this chapter, it is not possible to find every kind of nationalistic reading that is characteristic of LXX Isaiah in the last section of the book. For this reason, the subsections of this section ('Nationalistic Translations...') do not correspond exactly to those of the first section of this chapter.

boundaries of the original kingdom of David from the Euphrates to the Brook of Egypt, the wadi al 'arīš...he is actually referring, as the continuation shows, to the separation of Israelites and Gentiles. The Israelites will be carefully picked out... We are not told what happens to the Gentiles.'

64. Cf. Gordon, *'Terra Sancta'*, pp. 126-31, esp. the references to *separation* in TO Deut. 32.12 and TJ Mic. 7.14.

65. So Fischer, *Schrift*, p. 43. HUB rejects this. It appears quite possible, though not essential for an exclusivist explanation of the LXX.

66. E.g. qal תִּלְקְטוּ or piel תְּלַקְּטוּ.

67. Such a return is portrayed in the following verse, 27.13.

Nevertheless, the ideological continuity that stretches from the beginning to the end of LXX Isaiah remains unbroken.

*Translations That Elevate the Stature of Zion/Jerusalem in LXX Isaiah
56–65*
Isaiah 60.21. An alternative vocalization of נֵצֶר at 60.21 converts
Zion's people from being the *product* of divine viticulture, as in the MT,
to a sentinel keeping watch over the Lord's own vineyard. The MT says
to Zion:

ועמך כלם צדיקים לעולם יירשו ארץ

נֵצֶר מטעו [מטעי Qere] מעשה ידי להתפאר

> And (as for) your people, all of them will be righteous. They will inherit
> (the) land forever, the shoot of my planting, the work of my hands, for
> beautifying (myself).

The LXX reads:

καὶ ὁ λαός σου πᾶς δίκαιος καὶ δι᾽ αἰῶνος κληρονομήσουσιν τὴν
γῆν φυλάσσων τὸ φύτευμα ἔργα χειρῶν αὐτοῦ[68] εἰς δόξαν.

> And your entire people will be righteous, and they will inherit the earth
> (alternatively, land) forever, guarding the planting, the works of his
> hands for glory.

It is difficult to discern whether such a cooperation with God in his
labours would have seemed an improvement upon the already pleasant
picture of being 'the shoot of my planting, the work of my hands'. In
the LXX this description pertains to the land, of which Zion's people are
now the guardian. Clearly, however, it adds an element of collaboration
with God that the MT does not know.

This alternative is accomplished simply by reading נֹצֵר for the MT's
נֵצֶר. This kind of vocalic deviation cannot be assumed to have been a
conscious departure from the reading tradition that would become the
MT. However, the singling out of *Zion's* children, presumably to the
exclusion of others, and their stationing as the guardians of God's
vineyard might well have been amenable to the kind of nationalism that
leaves traces of itself in LXX Isaiah. Guards, after all, protect against
some external threat that seeks to make incursions upon the protected
space, a threat that comes from someone who does not belong.

---

68. The LXX is not alone in rendering features of this sentence in the third
person: 1QIsaᵃ מעשי ידיו מטעי יהוה; 1QIsaᵇ ידיו.

Isaiah 64.9(10). In a body of literature as preoccupied with the fate of Zion/Jerusalem as are the chapters under discussion, it is surprising to find in MT 64.9 reference to 'your holy *cities*', even if this is embedded in a lament that specifically mentions the names 'Zion' and 'Jerusalem':

עָרֵי קָדְשְׁךָ הָיוּ מִדְבָּר
צִיּוֹן מִדְבָּר הָיָתָה יְרוּשָׁלַ͏ִם שְׁמָמָה

> Your holy cities have become a desert. Zion has become a desert, Jerusalem a desolation.

Indeed, were it not for the plural הָיוּ later in the verse and for the absence of any textual evidence to support an emendation in favour of the singular, one well might wonder whether a scribe had absent-mindedly created עָרֵי from עִיר. However, the Hebrew text tradition refers with one voice to plural 'cities'.[69] The LXX translator, however, does not countenance more than one 'holy city'. LXX Isa. 64.10 has at the outset πόλις τοῦ ἁγίου σου ἐγενήθη ἔρημος. If the odd Greek title is to be construed as 'the city of your Holy One', the location would have appeared to be all the more restricted to Jerusalem. Zion reigns unchallenged.

Isaiah 65.9. It is possible that the curious syntax of LXX 65.9 witnesses to a kind of remnant theology that is absent from the MT. If such a theology is present, it is to be glimpsed in the determinate way that the Greek text refers to the 'seed'. In the aftermath of a judgment upon Zion's rebels in which the Lord, finally grown impatient, promises to pay back their provocations in full measure, he offers some hope: וְהוֹצֵאתִי מִיַּעֲקֹב זֶרַע וּמִיהוּדָה. The gloomy context—in which God promises not to destroy them all—as well as the anarthrous זֶרַע combine to create a chastened mood that reckons with the destruction of many and the survival of a relative few. The double *partitive mem*[70]—is ominous with respect to those who are left.

Here the LXX seems to diverge. It refers to a determinate body or perhaps to two: καὶ ἐξάξω τὸ ἐξ Ιακωβ σπέρμα καὶ τὸ ἐξ Ιουδα. The article seems to suggest a known entity, even though there has been no mention of a seed/descendancy thus far in the chapter. מִיַּעֲקֹב and מִיהוּדָה are now used attributively of the seed(s) rather than adverbially

---

69. Even TJ, from which one might have expected an exposition that maintains Jerusalem's uniqueness, has the plural קִרְוֵי קוּדְשָׁךְ הֲווֹ.

70. GKC §119w.

to localize God's 'bringing out'. This subtle shift may point to a kind of remnant/seed notion in the translator's interpretative tradition. It also deflects the ominous connotations of the Hebrew construction, although the text will not allow an undifferentiatedly rosy picture to be sustained (cf. esp. 65.12).

Translations That Enhance Israel's Stature vis-à-vis the Gentiles in LXX Isaiah 56–65
Isaiah 59.20. A slightly odd translation at Isa. 59.20 may signal that the intention of the Hebrew text has been substantially subverted in the Greek text. At the close of an oracle that describes the Divine Warrior's victory over the nations, MT 59.20 has the following:

ובא לציון גואל ולשבי פשע ביעקב נאם יהוה

> And he will come to Zion (as) a redeemer, to those in Jacob who turn (from) transgression—an oracle of the Lord.

Verses 18-19 sketch the victims of his wrath and those whom he leaves fear-struck in language that suggests that the battle has been against Gentiles:

> According to their deeds, so will he repay; wrath to his adversaries, requital to his enemies; *to the coastlands* he will render requital. So *those in the west* shall fear the name of the Lord, and *those in the east*, his glory; for he will come like a pent-up stream that the wind of the Lord drives on (NRSV, emphases added).

Thus, one can imagine how a reader might have anticipated in the words of 59.20 a simple redemption of Zion/Jacob over against the vanquishing of the nations. The words ולשבי פשע ביעקב appear to suggest the presence of transgression in Jacob itself, a dark reality from which some will *turn* and be redeemed while, presumably, others will not. Nevertheless, the structure of the entire oracle—with its elaborate portrayal of God's warfare against the nations and its brief climax in the redemption of Zion/Jacob—might have seemed, to the mind of a Jewish nationalist, to be an us-*versus*-them statement.

This, at any rate, may be the understanding that the LXX translator recorded in the Greek verse, which deviates significantly from that of the MT:

> καὶ ἥξει ἕνεκεν Σιων ὁ ῥυόμενος καὶ ἀποστρέψει ἀσεβείας ἀπὸ Ιακωβ.

> And the redeemer will come on Zion's behalf and he will turn back irreligion from Jacob.

It is noteworthy that, in the LXX, the redeemer comes *on Zion's behalf*. This motivation is fleshed out by his activity of turning back[71] ungodliness *from Jacob*. The Hebrew text—in which he comes to those in Jacob who themselves have turned—knows nothing of this activity at all.

In view of the preceding context, it is possible that the most natural reading of LXX 59.20 makes Zion/Jacob the virtuous benefactor of the Lord's military ejection of *Gentile* godlessness from their midst. It is difficult—though not impossible—to reconcile ἕνεκεν and ἀποστρέφειν ἀπό with any other view. If this is what the translator has intended, then we have in LXX 59.20 a glimpse of Diaspora hope not only of return to Zion, but also of the Warrior/Redeemer's cleansing of the mother city itself, perhaps from foreign occupation or influence.[72]

In spite of the considerably different meaning that attaches itself to the translated verse, the elements that facilitate such a conversion are present in the Hebrew text. The translator has handled the prepositions ל and ב unexpectedly, though not violently so.[73] The use of ἀποστρέφειν seems to require that he read ולשוב for ולשבי,[74] but this requires only a ו/י interchange and a 'dyslexic' reordering of the final two consonants. The possibility of a short series of useful accidents forces one to stop short of insisting upon a kind of midrashic *intention*, though the

---

71. One is tempted by the meaning *to send home*, which this verb sometimes carries; cf. LSJ, p. 220.

72. Though the translator is perfectly capable of using ασεβ- lexemes of unrighteous Jews, we saw earlier in this chapter his idiosyncratic use of the same word for the foreigner (זָר). This may offer some slight corroboration for the argument under development on the basis of the context of 59.20 and the vocabulary and syntax of its translation.

73. The proposition ל can have the meaning represented by ἕνεκεν, though the context and structure of this Hebrew verse would not normally suggest that meaning. It is not difficult to confuse ב and מ in the orthography of the period, and their respective meanings also overlap considerably; cf. N.M. Sarna, 'The Interchange of the Prepositions *Beth* and *Min* in Biblical Hebrew', *JBL* 78 (1959), pp. 310-16; L.H. Schiffman, 'The Interchange of the Prepositions *Bet* and *Mem* in the Texts from Qumran', *Textus* 10 (1982), pp. 37-43.

74. TJ's infinitive ולאתבא appears to reflect a reading of ולשבי similar to that of the LXX. However, the objects of the redeemer's turning, in TJ, are unambiguously מרודיא דבית יעקב (the rebels of the house of Jacob).

suspicion lingers. At the least, he has employed the features of his Hebrew text in the production of a quite distinct meaning. There is a kind of 'freedom' in this, but it is a liberty that is stubbornly conditioned by allegiance to the details of the Hebrew text.

Translations That Insert 'Zion', 'Jerusalem', 'Jacob' or 'Israel' in LXX Isaiah 56–65
Isaiah 60.1. The imperative expression that introduces ch. 60, קוּמִי אוֹרִי כִּי בָא אוֹרֵךְ וּכְבוֹד יְהוָה עָלַיִךְ זָרָח[75] is curiously vague about its intended audience. The context itself does not leave much doubt, however. Zion appears just two verses earlier, at 59.20. Similarly, the caravan of riches bound for a rebuilt city surely evokes parallel passages that do mention Zion, even if there is no mention of a city until 60.10 and no word about Zion herself until 60.14. The translator has not been equally content to let the context fill in the details. For קוּמִי אוֹרִי, he has Φωτίζου φωτίζου, Ιερουσαλημ...

Translations That reflect Diaspora Experience in LXX Isaiah 56–65
Isaiah 61.7. It is possible that a unique Hebrew–Greek equivalency in 61.7 evidences a reading of the Hebrew text from the perspective of Diaspora longing. The LXX omits the quite negative first stich of the verse, which occurs within a context that is overwhelmingly positive for Zion's rebuilders. The Hebrew is not only negative in tone, but also difficult to understand.[76]

תחת בשתכם משנה וכלמה ירנו חלקם
לכן בארצם משנה יירשו שמחת עולם תהיה להם

> Instead of your shame (which was double), and dishonour was cried aloud to be their lot—therefore, they will inherit in their land a double portion. Eternal joy will be theirs.

75. 'Arise! Shine! For your light has come and the glory of the Lord has broken out upon you.' The verbs themselves are unambiguously feminine, which would imply that they correspond to a *place*. The unpointed suffixes on the nouns, however, could just as well be masculine if they were approached atomistically.

76. TJ also seems to struggle with the Hebrew text as it now stands, with its problematic reference to 'your shame' (בשתכם). Chilton translates (*Isaiah Targum*, pp. 118-19): 'Instead of your being ashamed and confounded, two for one the benefits I promised you I will bring you, *and the Gentiles will be ashamed*, who were boasting *in their lot*' (emphases added).

The LXX omission is plain to see, but our focus will fall upon its rendering of מִשְׁנֶה:

οὕτως ἐκ δευτέρας κληρονομήσουσι τὴν γῆν, καὶ εὐφροσύνη αἰώνιος ὑπὲρ κεφαλῆς αὐτῶν.

Thus they will inherit the land a second time, and eternal joy will be upon their head.

The translator has either dismissed or failed to understand portions of his text. That his gaze has wandered is evident in that the simple phrase שִׂמְחַת עוֹלָם תִּהְיֶה לָהֶם has been translated under the influence of phraseology from 35.10 and 51.11, where both the Hebrew and the Greek texts place 'eternal joy upon their heads'. It appears that the first stich was too difficult to understand or, alternatively, that its identification of shame and disgrace as Zion's lot could not be made to fit.

More to the point, מִשְׁנֶה—which in the MT refers to the *bounty* of the returnees' inheritance—has been made to speak in the MT of its resumption after interruption. Outside Isa. 61.7, ἐκ δευτέρου/ας occurs ten times. It always means 'a second time' and, in the translated books, it always derives from שֵׁנִית (עוֹד) or תִּנְינוּת, its Aramaic equivalent.[77] The Isaiah translator understood מִשְׁנֶה in accordance with this standard equivalency, though he appears to have made a concession to grammatical gender by rendering it as a feminine.[78]

Though I do not think a conscious deviation from the Hebrew meaning *double portion* can be proved, it does appear that the translator has understood the expression to speak of the *return* of Zion's children to an inheritance that once was theirs but of which they had since become dispossessed. It is likely that he understood this to be the return under Cyrus, preceding his own era as this did by centuries. If, however, the omitted first stich owes anything to conscious alteration of a distasteful message, this increases the chance that the verse has been carefully exegeted. In such a case, ἐκ δευτέρας might have had a special resonance for those who hoped for another kind of return,[79] this time not to a land abandoned, but rather to joyful reunion

---

77. Compare Targumic תַּרְתֵּין זִמְנִין (twice), an expression that is not without relevance for the dating of Targum traditions. Cf. R.P. Gordon, *Studies in the Targum to the Twelve Prophets* (VTSup, 51; Leiden: E.J. Brill, 1994), pp. 41-42.

78. Elsewhere it is masculine.

79. Cf. the discussion of pilgrimage to Zion in Chapter 7.

with the 'brethren' (cf. 66.20) who already know the goodness of the place.

Summary and Conclusion

LXX Isaiah appears to display a nationalistic tendency towards disdain of the Gentiles and an exaltation of Israel/Judah and Jerusalem/Zion. This particularistic sentiment—which at the same time evidences a palpable Diaspora perspective—is expressed in Hellenistic idiom that displays little of the Hebraistic style that characterizes the more literally translated books of the Septuagint.

Although not every one of these types is apparent in chs. 56–65, this nationalistic bias comes to expression in translations that identify God exclusively with Israel, in pejorative references to Gentiles, in an enhanced stature for Zion and/or Israel, in the clarifying provision of words like 'Israel' or 'Jerusalem' where this is merely implicit in the source text, in exclusive and/or expansive territorial claims, and in translations that embellish Israel's standing vis-à-vis the nations.

In consequence, the Greek text of Isaiah maintains prerogatives for Jews that the universalism of the Hebrew text gives away. Several striking instances of such nationalism in Isaiah ch. 66 will be analysed in the following chapter.

Chapter 7

NATIONALISM AND DIASPORA PERSPECTIVE IN LXX ISAIAH 66

It is widely held that Trito-Isaiah in general—and ch. 66 in particular—
shows evidence of distinct and mutually combative Jewish groups in
postexilic Palestine.[1] The issue of diversity among the Second Temple
constituencies that scholars attempt to reconstruct with the help of the
Hebrew text has generated a substantial scholarly literature. The same is
not true with regard to relationships *between Jews and Gentiles* as these
can be glimpsed behind the Isaiah text or as they are projected by the
author into a Zion-centred future. These lines, it would appear, are
rather more clearly drawn.

The situation with regard to the *Greek* text of ch. 66 appears to be
quite the opposite. In this chapter, the burning issue seems to concern
relationships between Jews, on the one hand, and Gentiles, on the other.
Whatever fissures can be traced within the Judaism that is contemporary with the Hebrew text—for example, between pro-Temple and
anti-Temple groups—have virtually been sealed in the Greek edition. In
66.5, for example, the ugly picture of strife between (Jewish) brethren
appears to have been replaced by the image of a besieged community
living under the contemptuous glare of outsiders.[2] The contemporizing
reading of the text that the translator carries out has silenced intramural
Jewish debate in favour of an agenda that occupies itself instead with
'the Gentile question'.

---

1.   For the identification of pro- and anti-Temple partisans, together with the
placement of the postexilic prophets within their presumed camps, cf. J. Lindblom,
Prophecy in Ancient Israel (Oxford: Basil Blackwell, 1962), pp. 406-407. P.D.
Hanson's, *Dawn of Apocalyptic* has become a standard-bearer among those who are
confident enough to attempt daring social reconstructions on the basis of such texts
as Trito-Isaiah. Cf. also J.D. Levenson, *Theology of the Program of Restoration of
Ezekiel 40–48* (Missoula, MT: Scholars Press, 1976).
2.   Cf. Chapter 3, 'Isaiah 57.16', pp. 63-64.

Gentile God-Fearers in LXX Isaiah 66.14

The LXX divergence
Throughout the Greek translation of the second half of the book of
Isaiah, the Lord's Servant has been understood to refer in the first
instance to Israel[3] or to some portion of that nation.[4] One is surprised,
then, upon reaching LXX 66.14, to find the Lord's servants glossed as οἱ
σεβόμενοι,[5] a word that during the Graeco-Roman era had become at
least a semi-technical term for Gentile God-fearers.[6] This appears to be
the first of several rearrangements of the Jewish and Gentile assign-
ments and opportunities which are to be found in LXX 66 vis-à-vis the
Hebrew text traditions.

That the Hebrew Bible offers differing views of exactly how Zion's
'restoration programme' will embrace non-Israelites has long been a
matter of record.[7] It may now be possible to affirm that LXX Isaiah
occupies a nuanced mediating position between, say, Ezekiel's exclu-
sivistic posture and the rather more inclusive one found in the Hebrew
text of Isaiah.

---

3.   So W. Zimmerli and J. Jeremias, *The Servant of God* (SBT, 20; London:
SCM Press, 1965), pp. 42-44, though not exclusive of messianic reference to an
individual.

4.   Cf. van der Kooij, 'The Servant of the Lord', pp. 388, 394-95. Cf. also
Oswalt on the 'servants of the Lord' and 'his enemies' (*The Book of Isaiah: Chapters 40–66* [Grand Rapids: Eerdmans, 1998]), pp. 679-80: 'As the book of Malachi
shows, the sense that there was not a clear enough distinction between these two
groups became a major problem in the post-exilic era.'

5.   Or οἱ φοβούμενοι. See below.

6.   In spite of calling this the translator's identification, I am aware of the possibility that this is a Christian interpolation. Such a notion approaches plausibility
when one considers the evidence that the vocabulary of LXX Isa. 66 varies from the
standards employed in chs. 1–65. One explanation might involve a late (Christian?)
reworking of an earlier translation. For the fourth-century tension between Cyril's
interpretation of 'Jerusalem' in LXX Isa. 66.10 as the city itself—rejoicing at the
Resurrection—and that of Eusebius, who considered this Jerusalem to be the holy
people—in his day, the Church—cf. P.W.L. Walker, *Holy City, Holy Places?*
(Oxford, 1990), pp. 322-24. Walker notes Eusebius's reference to God's θεοσεβὲς
πολίτευμα. For further instances of alleged Christian interpolations in LXX Isaiah,
cf. Seeligmann, *LXX Version*, pp. 24-30.

7.   E.g., recently, S.L. Cook, 'Inner Biblical Interpretation in Ezekiel 44 and the
History of Israel's Priesthood', *JBL* 114 (1995), pp. 207-208, where reference is
made to 'the uniquely positive Isaianic view of foreigners'.

The Term σεβόμενοι/φοβούμενοι. Two observations about the Hebrew text of Isa. 66.10-17 and its interpretation are easily made. First, the precise relationships of ideas in this section and its surrounding context in ch. 66 are difficult to determine. This opaqueness may have allowed for more than one synthesis of the distinct syntactical units found in this context.

Second, this pericope is widely viewed as a call *to Jews* to rejoice over Jerusalem's final prosperity. Scholars have made no suggestion that the Hebrew text summons to revelry anyone but Jews, for it is they who will benefit from the Lord's intervention.[8]

---

8. Cf., for example, Skinner, *Isaiah*, II, p. 242: 'The connexion of ideas is frequently extremely difficult to trace...'; p. 243, vv. 5-17 are 'marked by unusual and perplexing disconnectedness of subject', vv. 10-14 are 'an invitation *to all true-hearted Israelites* to rejoice in her felicity, and share in her consolation' (emphasis added); McKenzie (*Second Isaiah*, p. 208), among others, translates: 'Rejoice, Jerusalem' with the LXX at v. 10, thus clarifying who is being summoned to joy; p. 208, 'the unity of the poem is not strict'; p. 209, 'the saving act means the appearance of a large number of true Israelites'; Whitehouse, *Isaiah*, II, p. 333 n. 1: 'Those who are to rejoice are the *inhabitants* of the city, and not those who lived outside the borders of Judah'; G. Fohrer, *Das Buch Jesaja. 3. Band Kapitel 40–66* (Zürcher Bibelkommentare; Zürich: Zwingli-Verlag, 1964), pp. 280-81; Watts, *Isaiah 34–66*, p. 360: 'אֵת "with" is used with שִׂמְחָה only here' (BDB, p. 970); E. Achtemeier, *The Community and Message of Isaiah 56–66: A Theological Commentary* (Minneapolis: Augsburg, 1982), pp. 144-45 (apparently); Kissane, *Isaiah*, II, p. 325: 'Those *who love* Jerusalem and *who mourn* over it...are the faithful remnant, as opposed to the apostates who have "forgotten Sion"'; E.W. Conrad, *Reading Isaiah: Overtures to Biblical Theology* (Minneapolis: Fortress Press, 1991), p. 147; P.-E. Bonnard, *Le Second Isaïe: Son disciple et leurs éditeurs. Isaiah 40–66.* (Paris: Librairie Lecoffre, 1972), p. 489 n. 11: 'Les serviteurs opposés en Israël aux impies'; G.A.F. Knight, *The New Israel: A Commentary on the Book of Isaiah 56–66* (Edinburgh: Handsel, 1985), p. 111, apparently; A. Dillman, *Der Prophet Jesaia* (Leipzig: S. Hirzel, 1890), p. 538: '...Gott...Gericht über seine Feinde hält, *bes.* über die Sünder u. Abtrünnigen in *Isr.*' (emphasis added). Dillmann may open the door to Gentile participation in the *positive* aspects of v. 14; G.W. Wade, *The Book of the Prophet Isaiah, with Introduction and Notes* (London: Methuen, 2nd edn, 1929), p. 416; C.C. Torrey, *The Second Isaiah: A New Interpretation* (Edinburgh: T. & T. Clark, 1928), p. 473; I.W. Slotki, *Isaiah: Hebrew Text and English Translation* (Hindhead, Surrey: Soncino, 1957), p. 323; E.J. Young, *The Book of Isaiah: The English Text, with Introduction, Exposition, and Notes*. III. *Chapters 40 through 66* (Grand Rapids: Eerdmans, 1972), p. 525.

However, it appears that the LXX translator saw things differently, for in v. 14 we find an LXX divergence from the Hebrew text, the importance of which is concealed by its low profile:

The MT reads:

וראיתם ושש לבכם ועצמותיכם כדשא תפרחנה
ונודעה יד־יהוה את־עבדיו וזעם את־איביו

> And you will look, and your heart will rejoice and your bones will blossom like the grass. And the hand of the Lord will be made known to his servants, but he will be indignant with his enemies.

The Septuagint reads as follows:

καὶ ὄψεσθε, καὶ χαρήσεται ὑμῶν ἡ καρδία, καὶ τὸ ὀστᾶ ὑμῶν ὡς βοτάνη ἀνατελεῖ· καὶ γνωσθήσεται ἡ χεὶρ κυρίου τοῖς σεβομένοις αὐτόν, καὶ ἀπειλήσει τοῖς ἀπειθοῦσιν.

> And you will look, and your heart will rejoice and your bones will spring up like greenery. And the hand of the Lord will be made known to those who reverence him but he will threaten the unbelievers.

The identification of the Lord's servants as his σεβόμενοι is striking. Indeed, this identification is not wholly certain, for many manuscripts have τοῖς φοβουμένοις.[9] In 1934 Ziegler indicated that he favoured τοῖς φοβουμένοις,[10] whereas his critical edition—first published in 1939—includes τοῖς σεβομένοις as his preferred reading.[11]

Nevertheless, this uncertainty as to the original LXX reading does not bear the negative consequences for this study that might at first appear to be involved, since both lexemes share two remarkable characteristics. First, these terms had acquired a special sense within Hellenistic Judaism. They were technical terminology for Gentile God-fearers, people whose attraction to Judaism produced an identification with the Jewish community but did not lead to circumcision and full conversion.[12] The

---

9.   Among which are represented Ziegler's Origenic and Lucianic (the whole) groups, as well as a number of his mixed codices. Perhaps his support of the τοῖς σεβομένοις reading in the *editio* is owing to his high regard for the Alexandrian group in LXX Isaiah.

10.   *Untersuchungen*, p. 43.

11.   *Editio*, p. 368.

12.   Cf. Schürer, *Jewish People*, III.1, pp. 166-69. The evidence gathered in the revised Schürer for the expression φοβούμενοι/σεβόμενοι τὸν θεόν and θεοσεβεῖς as referring to a formal group of Gentile God-fearers comes from (a) Josephus, (b) the Acts of the Apostles and (c) a variety of inscriptions. This volume recognises

recent study of Reynolds and Tannenbaum concludes that a God-fearer is:

> ...someone who is attracted enough to what he has heard in Judaism to come to the synagogue to learn more; who is, after a time, willing, as a result, to imitate the Jewish way of life in whatever way and to whatever degree he wishes (up to and including membership in community associations, where that includes legal study and prayer); who may have had held out to him various short codes of moral behaviour to follow, but does not seem to have been required to follow any one; who may follow the exclusive monotheism of the Jews and give up his ancestral gods, but need not do so; who can, if he wishes, take the ultimate step and convert, but need not do so, and is, whether he does or not, promised a share in the resurrection for his pains.[13]

While much of the evidence for identifying this terminology as *technical* rests upon evidence that is later than the LXX period, it appears that such terminology had already come into use by the time the Greek translation was in process, and that the LXX usage is best understood as an early stage of a continuum that extends into the New Testament period and beyond. This is essentially the view of Reynolds and Tannenbaum. They find 'the earliest evidence' in LXX 2 Chron. 5.6. However, it is possible, in my view, that the evidence from LXX Isaiah 66 is contemporary or even earlier.

Second, σεβόμενοι and φοβούμενοι are highly unusual renderings of an עבד lexeme. Nowhere else in the Isaiah translator's 61 encounters with עבד does he render it with either σέβειν or φοβεῖν. Indeed, nowhere else in the entire LXX does עבד generate either of these two Greek words. In the light of the more than 1,300 occurrences of עבד lexemes in the Hebrew Bible, the two Greek equivalencies attested in this verse are remarkable.

Indeed, the fact that precisely these two readings are to be found in LXX manuscripts is probably significant. If a scribe or copyist were to

---

objections to viewing the term as referring to a fixed group, but finally rejects such doubts.

In the course of their analysis of a third-century BCE inscription, J. Reynolds and R. Tannenbaum produce a thorough discussion of the usage of θεοσεβής, σεβόμενος, and φοβούμενος. Cf. *Jews and God-Fearers at Aphrodisias: Greek Inscriptions with Commentary* (Cambridge: Philological Society, 1987), pp. 47-67. Their cautious and well-stated conclusions are consonant with those of the revised Schürer.

13. *Jews and God-Fearers*, p. 65.

alter either of these two readings, such a change would almost certainly be in the direction of τοῖς δούλοις or τοῖς παισί(ν), the two common LXX equivalencies for עבד־, or perhaps even towards one of the less common renderings that appear in Isaiah.[14] The circumstance that the manuscripts vacillate between two translations of עבד־ that are *hapax* equivalencies, and that precisely these two terms appear interchangeably with a very specific meaning in Hellenistic literature, is telling. The person responsible for this change may well have understood that both terms are acceptable, since together—and uniquely—they denote Gentile God-fearers. But in his particular *milieu*, one of the two may have come to seem preferable. Thus, a decision was made in favour of one or the other, but without taking recourse to the much more common renderings of עבד־ that would have led the reader outside the conceptual realm of Gentile God-fearers.

It appears, then, that the LXX translator has signalled his recognition of Gentiles within the restored Jerusalem of this passage. Furthermore, the tradents responsible for the alteration between σεβομένοις and φοβουμένοις—regardless of the direction of the change—have followed this peculiar interpretation. They are merely quibbling over which of the two terms fits more appropriately.

While Vermes and his colleagues have presented the extrabiblical evidence that supports the use of these words to designate a discrete community of Gentiles who were attached to the Jewish communities of their day, the LXX use of σεβόμενος is also instructive in this regard. Outside Isa. 66.14, the word appears only three times where the LXX is translating the Hebrew Bible.

In the first case, Job 1.9, the Satan says of Job—manifestly a non-Israelite—Μὴ δωρεὰν σέβεται Ἰωβ τὸν θεόν;[15] In the second, Jon. 1.9, the seaborne prophet finds himself explaining his Hebrew identity to his shipmates: δοῦλος κυρίου ἐγώ εἰμι καὶ τὸν κύριον θεὸν τοῦ οὐρανοῦ ἐγὼ σέβομαι ὃς ἐποίησεν τὴν θάλασσαν καὶ τὴν ξηράν.[16] The third case, Isa. 29.13, is part of the Lament over Ariel. Though

---

14. E.g. τοῖς οἰκέταις, τοῖς θεραπεύουσι.

15. The interrogative ה is rendered by μὴ + the indicative, which expects a negative reply. This is one of many cases in the LXX, as indeed in any translation, where a formally converse translation that substitutes a negative-for-positive (or vice versa) is in fact a materially unchanged one.

16. According to the MT, his initial description says עברי אנכי. The LXX translates this δοῦλος κυρίου ἐγώ εἰμι, as witnessed with only minor variations by all manuscripts.

speaking of Jerusalemites, it rhetorically questions their status as the Lord's people by referring to them as הזה העם (= ὁ λαὸς οὗτος) instead of the stereotypical עמי (= ὁ λαός μου). The LXX goes on to say μάτην δὲ σέβονταί με.

Each of these three occurrences of σέβομαι translates the verb ירא, which is also the standard source of LXX φοβεῖν translations. This is, of course, not the case in Isa. 66.14. Furthermore, all of them are dealing with foreigners, albeit in a different way each time. Job is a non-Israelite worshipper of the Lord. Jonah describes his religious loyalty in the language that Jews would have used with foreigners.[17] The Isaiah text describes Yahwistic worship on the part of those who have forfeited their claim to be the Lord's people.[18]

The cumulative weight of this evidence encourages the view that we should read σεβομένοις/φοβουμένοις in LXX Isa. 66.14 as a reference to Gentile God-fearers.

Dismantled Parallelism. How are we to explain such an interpolation of non-Israelites into a discussion that students of the *Hebrew* text uniformly view as a Jewish matter?

The answer probably lies at the convergence of two paths. The first is the *Sitz im Leben* of the translator. The likelihood that the Alexandrian Jewish community enjoyed the express sympathy of some non-Jews is strong. Probably, the translator and his community were cognizant of this sympathetic Gentile presence in a way that the author and tradents responsible for the Hebrew Isaiah texts did not contemplate.

The second path is a text-interpretative one. This aspect of the discussion takes into account both the translation technique that the translator applies to the Isaiah text itself and his interaction with non-Isaiah texts.

17. However, Greek-speaking Jonah avoids using the Greek participle, which the MT's participle might have encouraged. He says ἐγὼ σέβομαι (τὸν κύριον), not ἐγὼ σεβόμενός εἰμι τοῦ κυρίου.

18. The use of σέβομαι with a Gentile referent is also embedded in the New Testament evidence. The Gospels use the verb twice (Mt. 15.9, Mk 7.7). Both are quotations of LXX Isa. 66.14 with only minor variations of word order. In Acts, the verb occurs eight times (13.43, 50; 16.14; 17.4, 17; 18.7, 13; 19.27 (of Artemis). In each case, the context establishes a Gentile subject, sometimes in direct contradistinction to Jews who are also present. The remaining occurrence appears in Rom. 1.25, where the context treats knowledge of God that is unmediated by Torah, thus urging a Gentile referent as well.

It is to be observed that a lexical, grammatical or syntactical problem will sometimes 'destabilize' this translator so that a thorny difficulty creates a snowball effect on the following clauses or verses. He frequently fails to respect the structures of parallelism that the Hebrew text presents to him. Frequently, he collapses parallelisms according to an instinct for abbreviation that converts clear synonymous or antithetical relationships into a mixed statement from which one general point can usually be salvaged.[19] At other times, he expands such parallelisms. Regardless of the precise move, the common feature is his failure to honour the relationships established by the Hebrew text.[20]

We noted at the beginning of this discussion that the relationships between syntactical units in this chapter are difficult. This fact, coupled with the difficulties that the translator encounters in rendering Hebrew parallelism, may have set the scene for the σεβομένοις reading at 66.14.

At 66.10, the MT reads:

שִׂמְחוּ אֶת־יְרוּשָׁלַ͏ִם וְגִילוּ בָהּ כָּל־אֹהֲבֶיהָ
שִׂישׂוּ אִתָּהּ מָשׂוֹשׂ כָּל־הַמִּתְאַבְּלִים עָלֶיהָ

Be glad with Jerusalem and shout for joy in her,[21] all you who love her.
Be exceedingly joyful with her, all you who mourn over her.

This verse contains an intricate kind of parallelism. Two verbal clauses are linked to one vocative expression in the first stich. All three of these features are qualified by phrases that relate to Zion.[22] The stich is rounded off by the vocative expression.

---

19. M. Sokoloff uses the term 'telescoping' to refer to a similar tendency in the Qumran Targum to Job: 'A recurring characteristic of the translator is his telescoping of two phrases which appear in the H text in *parallelismus membrorum*. The translator combined the parallel words or phrases into one unit, thus destroying the poetic character of the original, but gaining compactness in style' (*The Targum to Job from Qumran Cave XI* [Jerusalem: Ahva, 1974], p. 8). Nevertheless, the Isaiah translator's inventory of transmutations is far more diverse than that which Sokoloff finds in the material he investigated.

20. The Septuagint translator of Isaiah is not the only one among his peers who treats parallelism in a way that diverges from the MT. Cf., for example, Ps. 11(10) 5, which not only divides the parallelism differently than does the MT, but also includes a subject-object inversion. However, the frequency with which this occurs in LXX Isaiah sets its translator apart.

21. Alternatively, with NRSV: '...and be glad *for her*' (emphasis added).

22. 'with Jerusalem', 'in her', 'who love her'.

In the second stich, there is just one verbal clause, again qualified by a prepositional phrase relating to Zion.[23] However, it is elongated—perhaps by way of compensation for the 'missing' second verb—by a noun that is cognate to the verb (שִׂישׂוּ/מְשׂושׂ). The closing clause of the second stich (כל־המתאבלים עליה/כל־אהביה) then matches the similar vocative expression that finished off the first stich.

It seems quite natural to read the Hebrew according to the following structure:

(a) The first two verbs answer to the first vocative clause. The third verb answers to the final vocative clause.

(b) The following features are synonymously parallel with their congeners: (1) all three verbal clauses; (2) both vocative clauses; and (3) both stichs.

(c) The syntactic differentiation between 'Jerusalem' and those who experience certain emotions with regard to her is a literary ploy rather than a distinction between two distinct referents in the real world. It distinguishes between an abstract entity (the city) and the inhabitants of that city. At the same time, the verse both personifies and refuses to personify the city, so that Jerusalemites can rejoice and be glad *with her and in her at the same time.*[24] However, the imagery does not remove the discussion beyond the bounds of those who are already intimately associated with Jerusalem.

The LXX reads as follows:

εὐφράνθητι, Ιερουσαλημ, καὶ πανηγυρίσατε ἐν αὐτῇ, πάντες οἱ ἀγαπῶντες αὐτήν, χάρητε χαρᾷ, πάντες ὅσοι πενθεῖτε ἐπ᾽ αὐτῆς

Rejoice, O Jerusalem, and have a feast in her, all you who love her;
Be exceedingly joyful, all you who mourn over her.

Several modifications are at once apparent. The LXX ignores the preposition את in both the first and second stich. This disturbs the Hebrew parallelism by no longer reading את־ירושלם as a prepositional phrase functioning adverbially upon שׂמחו and parallel to בה. Rather, את־ירושלם is read as a vocative clause still linked to שׂמחו but now parallel to כל־אהביה (= πάντες οἱ ἀγαπῶντες αὐτήν). Instead of summoning some distinct group of people to rejoice 'with Jerusalem',

---

23. 'with her'.

24. The first verbal clause personifies the city. The second and third, in which the city is viewed as an inhabited *place*, do not. The participial clauses which close each stich are ambiguous with regard to the issue of personification.

the city itself is now called to rejoice. The same conversion occurs in the second colon, where שִׂישׂוּ אִתָּהּ מָשׂוֹשׂ becomes χάρητε χαρᾷ.[25]

The MT has the preposition (אֶת־(יְרוּשָׁלַ͏ִם, a lexeme that the Isaiah translator fails to recognize on a number of occasions. Though his tendency would have been to read אֵת as the *nota accusativi*, he would have found it difficult to make sense of that particle here.[26] Thus, he probably ignored אֵת and made what he could of the phrase without it.[27]

We are then left with a first colon that is susceptible to being read in some manner other than as synonymous parallelism. In the first clause of this colon, an imperative is directed at Jerusalem. In the second, a distinct imperative is directed at 'those who love her'.

It may be possible that the translator read an intended synonymous parallelism in his *Vorlage* and (mis)understood it as referring to two different entities: Jerusalem and those who love Jerusalem.[28] Indeed, we

25. Other notable features of the LXX text are the unique provision of πανηγυρίσατε and the translation of הַמִּתְאַבְּלִים by the second plural πενθεῖτε. This latter rendering is probably no more than an allocation of the second plural referent of שׂישׂוּ to two points in the Greek phrase rather than one: χάρητε and πενθεῖτε. It is probably due to the exigencies of Greek style—one nominative plural participle had just been used and our translator has an aversion to redundancy—and of little or no interpretative value.

26. Cf. BDB, p. 853. There is considerable evidence that the Isaiah translator struggled with the preposition אֵת. Of the 34 occurrences of this preposition in its simple form, he produces a clear sense of accompaniment or proximity (cf. BDB, p. 854) less than half the time. Misunderstanding of this preposition may have played a role in the translations at 14.20, 28.18b, 30.8, 36.16, 37.9, 40.14, 41.4, 43.2, 45.9 (twice), 49.25, 50.8, 53.9, 54.15, 57.15, 62.11, 63.11, 66.10 and 66.16. It is possible that the translator was completely ignorant of this word and that his cases of—in our eyes—appropriate translation were the fortunate by-product of guessing according to the context.

27. Alternatively, he may have read both of these occurrences as *nominative* אֵת, though this seems unlikely. Cf. GKC §117i; J. MacDonald, 'The Particle אֵת in Classical Hebrew: Some New Data on its Use with the Nominative', *VT* 14 (1964), pp. 264-75; P.P. Saydon, 'Meanings and Uses of the Particle אֵת', *VT* 14 (1964), pp. 192-210.

28. Cf. Chapter 6, 'Isaiah 1.26-27', pp. 215-16, for discussion of a similar reading of synonymous parallelism with regard to Zion/Jerusalem in 1.26. Furthermore, a fascinating and complicated *relecture* at Isa. 10.5-6 produces results that are strikingly similar to the scenario I am proposing for 66.10. The MT declaims Assyria's failure to recognize that she is (merely) 'the rod of my anger and a staff in their hand, my indignation...' The Lord deploys his Assyrian rod temporarily to punish Judah, who is described ironically in terms normally reserved for pejorative

have already seen that 66.12 is translated in such a way as to articulate the special intimacy with the Lord that will be the lot of Jerusalem's children and also to describe the Lord's overwhelming the hubris of nations.[29] The latter thought, at least, is absent from the Hebrew text.

If Gentile God-fearers are a feature of the translator's *milieu*—and if they are as much on his mind as our analysis of this chapter suggests— then one might even conjecture that the terms in question are now ethnic/religious groupings: 'Jerusalem' as the Jews; 'those who love her' as Gentile God-fearers.[30] Such a conception might allow some Gentiles a certain affinity for, and relationship with, 'Jerusalem' without including them among those (Jews) who *fully* belong.

The rest of this chapter describes a bifurcated humanity, but the primary division does not lie between Jews and Gentiles. It falls, rather,

---

reference to Gentiles: בגוי חנף **אשלחנו ועל־עם** עברתי אצונו לשלל שלל שלל...
Though space does not allow exploration of the many details of this text that the translator has altered, one observes simply that he has converted the *synonymous* parallelism that describes Judah into a nationalistic *antithesis* that describes, first, a Gentile nation (Assyria) and, then, a newly favoured Judah: εἰς ἔθνος ἄνομον ἀποστελῶ καὶ τῷ ἐμῷ λαῷ συντάξω ποιῆσαι σκῦλα... The 'people of my wrath' has become the covenantally coloured 'my people', the plundered become the plunderer. It is important to approach the admittedly opaque details of 66.10 with this kind of precedent in mind.

Gerleman and Cook agree that LXX Proverbs—a work that shares affinities with LXX Isaiah—tends to sharpen the contrasts of its parent text and to replace synonymous parallelism with antithesis. Cf. Gerleman, *Proverbs*, pp. 18, 26-27, and Cook, *Septuagint of Proverbs*, pp. 86-87. In LXX Isaiah, the phenomenon of 'corrected ellipsis' accomplishes the first of these in some measure. It is possible that the verse in question exemplifies the second, although this tendency is not as widespread in LXX Isaiah as Gerleman and Cook recognize it to be in the Greek Proverbs.

29. Cf. Chapter 3, 'Isaiah 66.9-12', pp. 81-83. Although we will not return to the details of that verse here, the argument presented in Chapter 3 is important to the thesis that the translator sustains a preoccupation with Gentiles not merely in isolated instances in ch. 66, but rather as a recurring motif that shapes his treatment of the entire eschatological vision.

30. If such an analysis is plausible, the translator has read the imperatives as directed at three literary *personae* instead of just two: Jerusalem, all those who love her and all those who mourn over her. How he identified the third *persona* (the mourners) is a matter of conjecture. Nowhere else does the Hebrew Bible speak of mourning (אבל) over (על) Jerusalem, though it does use the expression for ten other occasions of mourning. LXX Isa. 66.10 uses πενθέω + ἐπί, as do the majority of the verses. Its use of the genitive (αὐτῆς) after ἐπί, however, is unique among the ten.

between those who are the beneficiaries of God's future actions, and those who suffer its consequences. There is, however, a *secondary* division among those who are the beneficiaries of God's blessing: it falls between blessed Jews and blessed Gentiles.[31] Though this particular preoccupation does not emerge explicitly in this chapter until v. 18, it has been introduced previously in the book.[32] Furthermore, when it does come to the fore in 66.18, the 'exaltation' of the righteous Gentiles that takes place is remarkably unrestrained.[33] Perhaps our translator has simply advanced the dénouement by some eight verses.[34]

In sum, contextual features are present that might have caused a translator who was inexpert in the intricacies of Hebrew parallelism and at the same time unsettled by the relationship of Jew and Gentile to find not one but two groups in 66.10a, one of them being Gentiles 'who love Jerusalem'. Perhaps these are his σεβόμενοι.

The particular phrase 'those who love Jerusalem' remains to be considered. There are only a few passages in the Hebrew Bible that refer to people who love (= אהב) Jerusalem or Zion.[35] Ps 122.6, 'Pray for the peace of Jerusalem! May they prosper who love you!' gives no indication of a Gentile reference.[36] However, Ps. 129.5 offers us the interesting statement, 'May all who hate Zion be put to shame and turned backward!'[37] Interestingly, this wish is prefaced by the introductory phrase, 'Let Israel now say...' Thus, the literary context pits

31. Since this chapter seems to describe heterodox Jews as well, there is probably also a secondary division between judged Jews and Gentiles, though the text makes little of this.

32. E.g. 2.1-4; 56.3-8.

33. Perhaps including even the selection of some Gentiles as priests and Levites, 66.21.

34. It is remarkable that even when the Gentiles are introduced in this chapter, it is in contradistinction to wicked *Jews*. 'For I know *their* works...' in v. 18 refers back, in the present form of the chapter, to the abominators of v. 17, who are presumably Jewish. The verse continues '...and I am coming to gather all *nations*...' The dual-ethnic nature of the people to whom God relates at the end of this chapter is pronounced, and might well have been the conceptual background to the transformation I am suggesting at LXX 66.10. The translator may give evidence that he is struggling with the precise composition of a *new Israel*.

35. Three verses speak of *God's* love for Zion: Mal. 2.11, Ps. 78.68 and Ps 87.2.

36. שַׁאֲלוּ שְׁלוֹם יְרוּשָׁלָ͏ִם יִשְׁלָיוּ אֹהֲבָיִךְ = ἐρωτήσατε δὲ τὰ εἰς εἰρήνην τὴν Ιερουσαλημ καὶ εὐθηνία τοῖς ἀγαπῶσίν σε.

37. יֵבֹשׁוּ וְיִסֹּגוּ אָחוֹר כֹּל שֹׂנְאֵי צִיּוֹן = αἰσχυνθήτωσαν καὶ ἀποστραφήτωσαν εἰς τὰ ὀπίσω πάντες οἱ μισοῦντες Σιων.

Israel against 'all who hate Zion' and nearly demands that the referent be a Gentile group. This is the only reference that the Hebrew Bible makes to people hating (= שׂנא) Zion or Jerusalem.

It would not be unusual for the Isaiah translator to display awareness of exegetical tradition embedded in the Greek Psalms. Perhaps a conceptual category of Gentiles who *hate* Zion is the corollary of the notion of non-Jews who *love* her. It is just possible that the appearance of rare emotive language about relating to Jerusalem has reinforced a predisposition to sighting Gentiles 'too early' in this chapter, even as early as v. 10.[38]

Surprising support for this possibility may come from the 'eschatological psalm' of the Greek text of Tobit 13, a passage that offers— among other striking similarities to LXX Isaiah 66—a picture of Gentiles bringing eschatological tribute (δῶρα!) to Jerusalem.[39] Immediately following the arrival of Gentile tributaries in Jerusalem, the psalm offers these remarkable words in 13.14-16:

ἐπικατάρατοι πάντες οἱ μισοῦντές σε·
εὐλογημένοι ἔσονται πάντες οἱ ἀγαπῶντές σε εἰς τὸν αἰῶνα...
μακάριοι ὅσοι ἐλυπήθησαν ἐπὶ πάσαις ταῖς μάστιξίν σου ...

Cursed be all those who hate you.
Forever blessed shall be all those who love you...
Blessed those who grieved over all your scourges...

The longer and probably earlier text tradition represented by Codex Sinaiticus differs considerably in a fascinating direction. Where the tradition cited above refers to an implicitly Gentile group identified as 'those who hate you (i.e. Jerusalem)', the parallel textual tradition offers an extensive and explicit description of Jerusalem's destroyers that can only have a *Gentile* (and Babylonian) referent.[40]

---

38. In Lam 1.2 (LXX τῶν ἀγαπώντων αὐτήν) and 1.19 (τοὺς ἐραστάς μου), Zion mourns surrounded by her treacherous (former) lovers. These appear to represent various nations. This is not without interest for the current discussion, though their status as hostile entities would appear to distance this passage somewhat from the possible use of אהב to speak of Gentiles who are well-disposed towards Jerusalem.

39. Cf. 13.13: ἔθνη πολλὰ μακρόθεν ἥξει (S: καὶ κάτοικοι πάντων τῶν ἐσχάτων τῆς γῆς) πρὸς τὸ ὄνομα κυρίου τοῦ θεοῦ δῶρα ἐν χερσὶν ἔχοντες καὶ δῶρα τῷ βασιλεῖ τοῦ οὐρανοῦ.

40. ἐπικατάρατοι πάντες, οἳ ἐροῦσιν λόγον σκληρόν, ἐπικατάρατοι ἔσονται πάντες οἱ καθαιροῦντές σε καὶ κατασπῶντες τὰ τείχη σου καὶ

Then, when the text cited above moves to the parallel expression οἱ ἀγαπῶντές σε,[41] Sinaiticus labels these apparently Gentile lovers of Jerusalem as οἱ φοβούμενοί σε! It may not be possible to conclude without doubt that *God-fearers* and *Jerusalem-fearers* are the same people, yet the probability is considerable. The context and terminology of Tobit 13 suggest that the same kind of two-track dealing with good Gentiles and bad Gentiles that I am suggesting for LXX Isaiah 66 has influenced that Greek text as well. Indeed, a recent study of Tobit mentions that the final stich of the text cited above (μακάριοι ὅσοι ἐλυπήθησαν ἐπὶ πάσαις ταῖς μάστιξίν σου) 'is very reminiscent of Isa. 66.10...([r]ejoice with her in joy, all you who mourn over her).'[42] Though the fragmentary nature of the Qumran evidence for Tobit's Semitic *Vorlage* necessarily conditions such conclusions,[43] it appears that the editors of Tobit's Greek recensions have utilized the language of *loving, hating, grieving over*, and even *fearing* Jerusalem to exegete their eschatological psalm in a way that takes account of Gentile sympathizers. The similarities between the Greek passages of Tobit and Isaiah strengthen the suggestion that the Isaiah translator—at 66.10, 66.14 and elsewhere—has done the same.

Gentiles Earlier and Lowlier. My intention has not been to provide a detailed exegesis of LXX Isa. 66.10. Rather, I have wished to account for the appearance of σεβόμενοι in 66.14.

πάντες οἱ ἀνατρέποντες τοὺς πύργους σου καὶ ἐμπυρίζοντες τὰς οἰκήσεις σου.

C.A. Moore notices the Gentile referent of the 'abbreviated' expression οἱ μισοῦντές σε in the 'G¹' text, then comments that its brevity has been explained vis-à-vis the longer 'G²' text as 'the Greek editor's desire not to offend needlessly his Roman readers, who would not have appreciated the strong, negative feelings of *Codex Sinaiticus* toward those who did not revere the Holy City'; cf. *Tobit: A New Translation with Introduction and Commentary* (AB, 40A; New York: Doubleday, 1996), p. 281.

41. Only two published Semitic texts contain portions of the Tob 13.14-16. Of these, only one (4QpapTobᵃ ar) is relevant to the argument under development. Where both Greek recensions have [ὦ] μακάριοι οἱ ἀγαπῶντές σε, this text produces טובי כל רחמיכי. Cf. M. Broshi et al., *Qumran Cave 4, XIV. Parabiblical Texts, Part 2*. DJD XIX (Oxford: Clarendon, 1995), p. 29.

42. Moore, *Tobit*, p. 281.

43. Cf. F. García Martínez, *The Dead Sea Scrolls Translated: The Qumran Texts in English* (Leiden: E.J. Brill, 1994), pp. 293-99.

Irrespective of whether the obvious difficulties at 66.10 have favoured an encounter with Gentiles there and at 66.14, they surface as the object of God's humbling fury in 66.12. Then, by the time we get to v. 14, foreigners under the rubric of οἱ σεβόμενοι have arrived in the flesh. There, in v. 14c-d, we find an example of parallelism that, this time, is clearly antithetical:

ונודעה יד־יהוה את־עבדיו וזעם[44] את־איביו

...and the hand of the Lord will be made known with regard to his servants, but he will be indignant with his enemies.

This verse, in the LXX, appears to function not as an antithesis between the primary cognitive division of the chapter—the righteous and the wicked—but between one side of the secondary division: righteous Gentiles and wicked Gentiles.[45]

καὶ γνωθήσεται ἡ χεὶρ κυρίου τοῖς σεβομένοις αὐτόν, καὶ ἀπειλήσει τοῖς ἀπειθοῦσιν.

And the hand of the Lord will be made known to those who reverence him, and he will threaten those who disobey.

We may now be in a position to understand this verse as follows: '...and the hand of the Lord will be made known to those Gentiles who reverence him, and his indignation shall be against those (Gentiles?) who do not.'

Ironically, the LXX translation of this chapter appears to be more *and* less eager to deal generously with Gentile God-fearers. *More*, because its preoccupation with their fate is arguably closer to the surface and its approach to it more rapid than in the Hebrew texts. *Less*, for, although the Septuagint wants them in, we shall see that it balks at their full equality with the eschatological Jews.[46] 'Welcome to Jerusalem...',

---

44. BHS *propositum* וְזַעְמוֹ.

45. Or perhaps 'righteous Gentiles and wicked Jews and Gentiles'.

46. In arguing, *pace* G. Gerleman, that LXX Proverbs is not a Hellenistic but a *Jewish*-Hellenistic document, J. Cook writes, 'Because of the inherent dangers in Hellenism, the translator actually went out of his way to avoid all possible misunderstanding. Consequently, on these points the Septuagint is in a certain sense *a more conservative text than the* MT' (emphasis added); 'The Septuagint Proverbs as a Jewish–Hellenistic Document', in L. Greenspoon and O. Munnich (eds.), *VIII Congress of the International Organization for Septuagint and Cognate Studies, Paris 1992* (Atlanta, Scholars 1995), pp. 349-65 (360). The burden of Cook's argument in this article as in his other works is that Hellenistic thought is, in that

the plot seems to run, 'The Gentile dining hall is just down those stairs…'[47]

Place Assignments in the Eschatological Pilgrimage to Zion

As the climactic event of the book of Isaiah, the Lord sends some of the Gentile survivors of his eschatological vengeance off to the nations to tell of his glory and to bring back the Israelites who reside there. The Hebrew text of 66.20 seems to present a straightforward comparison: these emissaries will bring back the readers' brethren from the nations upon various means of transport. Furthermore, they will present these brethren to the Lord as an offering. This offering is analogous to the

---

translator's mind, the specific evil to be feared. This analysis is not so far removed from my own contention that non-Jewish Hellenists were on the Isaiah translator's mind, and that his translation is more conservative than his source text with regard to the nature and fate of such foreigners.

We have, in a later body of literature that, in spite of the intervening period of time, is not wholly removed from Second Temple literature like LXX Isaiah, an example of how the events surrounding early Judaism influence the attention that Jews give to the nature and destiny of Gentiles. In *Paul and Palestinian Judaism*, p. 210, E.P. Sanders writes of Rabbinical literature: 'The question of the fate of the Gentiles was obviously a serious issue in the minds of those who witnessed the destruction of the Temple… In any case, there is no one view of the situation of Gentiles which prevailed throughout the Tannaitic period. The general impression is that the Rabbis were not ungenerous except when special circumstances moved them to view Gentiles with bitterness.'

47. In evaluating the possibility of a begrudging attitude on the part of Diaspora Jews towards Gentile participants in Jerusalem's future glory, it is helpful to be reminded of just how much was at stake. Cf. M. Hengel, 'Jerusalem als jüdische *und* hellenistische Stadt', in B. Funck (ed.), *Hellenismus. Beiträge zur Erforschung von Akkulturation und politischer Ordnung in den Staaten des hellenistischen Zeitalters: Akten des Internationalen Hellenismus-Kolloquiums 9.–14. März in Berlin* (Tübingen: J.C.B. Mohr [Paul Siebeck], 1996), p. 300: 'Eine weitere große und wieder nicht sehr homogene Gruppe stellten die Rückwanderer aus der Diaspora dar. Auch hier werden je nach Herkunft erhebliche Unterschiede bestanden haben… Auch die Motivation der Rückkehr mag recht verschieden gewesen sein. Für die einen war diese durch das Heiligtum und den Kultus begründet, für andere durch Jerusalem als Ort der Ankunft des Messias und die Erwartung der Auferstehung. Die einen mögen mehr durch das priesterliche Ideal, die andern stärker durch die eschatologische Hoffnung bestimmt gewesen sein. Eine dritte Möglichkeit war die Anziehungskraft der Heiligen Stadt als Zentrum des Tora-studiums, geht doch nach Jes 2,3 "vom Zion die Tora aus".'

מנחה that the Israelites present—and presumably have presented for some time—to the Lord, in a clean vessel.

The LXX translator, however, graces this parade with a more elaborate offering, a dual assemblage of worshippers, and a distinct liturgy. By doing so, he appears to drive a wedge between the Jewish and Gentile contingents of the eschatological pilgrimage to Jerusalem, reserving for the latter only second-class privileges.

The MT reads:

והביאו את־כל־אחיכם מכל־הגוים מנחה ליהוה בסוסים
וברכב ובצבים ובפרדים ובכרכרות על הר קדשי ירושלם
אמר יהוה כאשר יביאו בני ישראל את־המנחה
בכלי טהור בית יהוה

And they shall bring all your brothers from all the nations as an offering to the Lord, on horses, and in chariot(s), and in litters, and on mules, and on dromedaries, up to my holy mountain Jerusalem, says the Lord, just as the Israelites bring a grain offering in a clean vessel to the house of the Lord.[48]

48. I am unaware of any Bible translation or scholar who reads the Hebrew in a way that departs from the scholarly consensus on three points: (1) ב = instrumental (vehicular) *beth* in each case; (2) כאשר יביאו = a comparison with present or past Israelite cult; and (3) בכלי טהור refers to the *Israelite* מנחה, not the Gentile one. Two Bible translations relegate the Israelite מנחה to the past: *The Berkeley Version in Modern English* (Grand Rapids: Zondervan, 1959) reads '…just as the Israelites used to bring their cereal offerings.' B. Boothroyd's translation (London: Partridge and Oakey, 1853) reads, '…as the sons of Israel brought their offering.' T.K. Cheyne, *Isaiah*, II, p. 131, discusses both the past and present alternatives as functions of theories about the book's composition. The *New Jerusalem Bible* slightly distances this מנחה from observable practice: '…like Israelites bringing offerings.' These changes are not material for our study, in that they continue to represent a simple comparison of the future Gentile מנחה to the known—whether present or past—Israelite מנחה.

There is, however, an interesting note in the interpretation found in TJ Isaiah, the verb of which does not differ aspectually from the verb in the MT (דייתון בני ישראל). Stenning (*Targum*, p. 222) translates as above: '…as the children of Israel bring an offering.' Chilton, however, renders the second half of the verse '*with* horses and *with* chariots, and *with* mules, and *with* songs, upon my holy mountain, to Jerusalem, says the LORD, just as the sons of Israel *will bring* an offering…' (emphasis added) (*Isaiah Targum*, p. 128). Though he is translating a text that remains formally quite similar to the MT, his translation diverges from the consensus outlined above on points 1 and 2. Unfortunately, Chilton does not comment on this part of his translation.

248 *When We All Go Home*

The Septuagint reads as follows:

καὶ ἄξουσιν τοὺς ἀδελφοὺς ὑμῶν ἐκ πάντων τῶν ἐθνῶν δῶρον κυρίῳ μεθ' ἵππων καὶ ἁρμάτων ἐν λαμπήναις ἡμιόνων μετὰ σκιαδίων εἰς τὴν ἁγίαν πόλιν Ιερουσαλημ, εἶπεν κύριος, ὡς ἂν ἐνέγκαισαν οἱ υἱοὶ Ισραηλ ἐμοὶ τὰς θυσίας αὐτῶν μετὰ ψαλμῶν εἰς τὸν οἶκον κυρίου.

And they shall bring your brothers from all the nations as tribute to the Lord—together with horses and chariots—in covered mule-drawn carts with sunshades into the holy city, Jerusalem—for the Lord has said (it) —when[49] the sons of Israel bring me their sacrifices with psalms into the house of the Lord.

A More Elaborate Offering
While for the MT the brethren transported back from the Diaspora are themselves the gift to the Lord, the LXX agglomerates the *means* upon which they are transported to the *gift* itself.[50] In the Hebrew text, the returnees are carried 'upon horses, upon chariots, upon litters, upon mules and upon dromedaries'.[51] The LXX, on the other hand, singles out covered mule wagons as the vehicles by which the emissaries accomplish their mission, while the horses and chariots become a part of the procession that is to be offered to the Lord *along with* the returnees from Diaspora.[52]

49. Or 'just as'. See discussion below.
50. One wonders whether omission of the first כל (את־כל־אחיכם) = τοὺς ἀδελφοὺς ὑμῶν) betrays embarrassment over the continued presence of a Jewish diaspora in Alexandria. To drop כל in order to recognize the continued presence of Jews outside Jerusalem would appear to fit within this translator's willingness to update his text. It would of course not be a necessary alteration if he viewed the whole of this chapter as pointing towards a moment that was still in the translator's own future. However, if he understood it as referring at least in part to the return from Persian exile, a motivation would not be lacking.
It remains impossible to determine whether this omission is intentional and motivated by disappointment that not *all* the brethren have returned to Jerusalem, for כל is omitted with some regularity throughout the text in the absence of evidence for intentionality. While πᾶς, πανταχοῦ, ὅλος and οὐδέν account for the vast majority of the occurrences of כל in Isaiah, the word is left untranslated on at least 38 occasions. Thus, while one may suspect an actualizing motive for its omission at 66.20, it is not possible to prove this.
51. ב + the article is repeated before each of the five nouns.
52. The preposition ἐν in the phrase ἐν λαμπήναις ἡμιόνων appears to be marked off from other listed items as the truly vehicular ἐν by the use of μετά (of

Though this might at first appear a culpable misjudgment on the part of the translator, it is possible to understand why he translated as he did, for כ prefixed to a beast of burden is not the most common way for the Hebrew Bible to speak of mounts.[53] Rather, we more often find that a person rides upon (על־) a beast or vehicle, or that he simply rides (רכב) an animal. [54]

Furthermore, there are examples of כ + a beast or vehicle where the idea is manifestly one of exchange or accompaniment, the latter of which corresponds to the LXX translator's understanding in the verse under consideration.[55] Additionally, there are several passages where some combination of beasts, chariots and carts was indeed part of a list of gifts presented as a מנחה or קרבן, again matching the LXX interpretation of our verse.[56]

All these factors might have conspired to prepare the translator to consider some of the listed items of 66.20 not as transport, but rather as items of tribute. This conversion is accomplished in the Greek text by breaking down the monotonous chain of Hebrew prepositions + articles into two types of prepositional phrases: μετά + genitive for the accompanying gifts; and ἐν + dative for the vehicular mode.

accompaniment) for those other items. For the Hebraistic translation of כ by ἐν to designate accompaniment, cf. Gehman, 'Hebraisms of the Old Greek Version of Genesis', *VT* 3 (1953), pp. 141-48 (143).

Alternatively, it may just be possible that horses and chariots merely *accompany* the Jewish returnees and their Gentile porters rather than that they comprise part of the tribute package. However, it seems to me that the text supports the view elaborated above.

53. It occurs of chariots at 2 Kgs 9.21, 24 (?), 10.16, Jer. 17.25, 27.4 and of animals in Jer. 17.25, 22.4, 1 Chron. 12.40 and Est. 8.10.

54. For על־ + a substantive (or pronoun with antecedent animal- or vehicle-substantive, cf. Judg. 4.15, 2 Sam. 13.29, 18.9, 1 Kgs 20.20, 2 Kgs 14.20, Isa. 30.16, 31.1, 36.8, Jer. 6.23, 50.42, Hos. 14.4, Eccl. 10.7 and 2 Chron. 25.28 and 35.24. For רכב על־ specifically, cf. Isa. 36.8, Hab. 3.8, Zech. 1.8 and Est. 6.8, 9. For רכב + a direct object, cf. 2 Kgs 7.14, 9.18 and 2 Kgs 9.19. For כ + a substantive, Isa. 66.20, Jer. 17.25, 22.4, Ezek. 23.6, 12, 23, 38.15, Amos 2.15 and Est. 8.10.

55. Exchange (GKC §119p, *beth pretii*): Gen. 47.17. Accompaniment (GK §119n): Exod. 15.19, 2 Kgs 5.9, Isa. 22.6, Ezek. 26.7 (translated μεθ᾽ ἵππων, as Isa. 66.20), where the plurals make it impossible that this was vehicular beth. Other instrumental uses: 2 Kgs 29.23 (K), Hos. 1.7 and Dan. 11.40.

56. Num. 7.3, 1 Kgs 10.25 and 2 Chron. 9.24.

Table 1. *Accompanying modes of transport and/or tribute*

	MT		LXX	
1st member	בסוסים	on horses	μεθ᾽ ἵππων	with horses
2nd member	וברכב	and on chariotry	καὶ ἀρμάτων	and (with) chariots
3rd member	ובצבים	and on covered wagons	ἐν λαμπήναις	in covered wagons
4th member	ובפרדים	and on mules	ἡμιόνων	linked adjectivally to third member (i.e. covered mule-drawn wagons)
5th member	ובכרכרות	and on she-camels	μετὰ σκιαδίων[57]	with sunshades

This prepositional variety is not the only way in which the translator destabilizes the regularity of the Hebrew syntax in question. He also combines the third and fourth members, converting covered wagons and mules into covered mule wagons. This 'collapsing' of various listed items is consonant with the Isaiah translator's normal handling of lists.

Finally, כרכרות[58] is omitted, or, more likely, its 'slot' is filled by the quaint ornamentation that is added to the covered mule wagons in the place of the fifth member: sunshades to assure the returnees the comfort and dignity that the occasion merits. It has long been known that the Isaiah translator's mastery of Hebrew vocabulary often falls short of the text before him, and that, when this occurs, he appears to provide whatever Greek rendering he can glean from the context. However, μετὰ σκιαδίων should not be seen as a desperate guess. Rather, it is the

---

57. Daniel believes ובכרכרות is rendered by μετὰ ψαλμῶν, which appears in the second half of the verse because 'le traducteur ne mettait pas ce complément sur le m(e)me plan que les précédents', p. 213 n. 37. This agrees with TJ, which renders ובכרכרות with בתושבחן = 'with songs'. Μετὰ σκιαδίων, for her, is not a translation of ובכרכרות, but 'une sort de remplissage, destiné à reproduire apparemment le nombre des compléments circonstanciels du verbe'. However, this reconstruction leaves the LXX with no rendering of בכלי טהור and deprives the text of an adequate explanation for the rather colourful μετὰ σκιάδων. Thus, Daniel's reconstruction—though admirably venturous—allows for improvement.

Nevertheless, there remains one alluring aspect of her suggestion that μετὰ ψαλμῶν refers to MT ובכרכרות, though Daniel appears not to have noticed it. It is the possibility that ובכרכרות has been read as ובכנ(ו)רות and then translated not as the *instrument*, but as the *songs produced by the instrument*: μετὰ ψαλμῶν.

58. A *hapax legomenon*. 1QIsa[a] reads ובכורכובות.

product of thoughtful reflection on what this pilgrimage means.

In the Septuagint, σκια- lexemes sometimes refer to the physical phenomenon of the shadow. However, the majority of uses—those which interest us—are metaphorical. Of these, there is roughly an even distribution into positive and negative references. The positive group, to which our instance belongs, refers to protection and provision, usually divine.[59]

This Greek lexeme translates five distinct Hebrew words in the Exodus and Wilderness texts of the Greek Pentateuch.[60] That is, the LXX provides a standardized rendering for a concept that, though found in diverse Pentateuchal texts, has no common Hebrew vocabulary in those texts.

After the Pentateuch, virtually all LXX occurrences of σκια- correspond to צל, a word that occurs only once in the Pentateuch.[61] These instances are not clear allusions to the Pentateuchal texts, except for two instances that occur in Isa. 4.5-6. In these two verses, we find transparent Exodus terminology applied to an oracle about Zion's future restoration. Curiously, our translator interpolates σκιάσει in 4.5, where the MT speaks of the 'cloud by day' but has no Hebrew verb that corresponds to σκιάσει. That is, he introduces a Greek verb that has acquired Exodus resonances where the Hebrew text on its own would not have generated it. This probably indicates the translator's familiarity with the word's Exodus associations and his desire to apply these to the context of Isaiah 4.

Returning to 66.20, we find a similar interpolation of a different σκια- lexeme when the translator hits upon the difficult ובכרכרות. It may be that the translator did not know this word, and fell back upon the context for assistance.[62] However, his thinking seems to have been

59. The negative group speaks of gloom, terror, or the unenduring nature of something.

60. פרש: Exod. 37.9(38.8) (the cherubim); שׁכן: Num. 9.18, 22 (the cloud); נוח: Num. 10.36 (the cloud [implicit in MT]); נטה: Num. 24.6 (probably date palms, but read by LXX as valleys); חפף: Deut. 33.12 (the Lord *encompasses* his beloved [Benjamin]).

61. צל occurs in the Pentateuch only at Gen. 19.8. In the rest of the LXX, σκια- translates צל 30 times with only 5 scattered exceptions. Σκια- often translates צלמות, which I include for the purposes of this discussion as a form of צל.

62. An alternative possibility—that ובכרכרות is omitted because she-camels would not have been an appropriate animal for Israelite processions—should probably not be discarded altogether. However, it is weakened by the motley connection

somewhat more profound than the simple notion that every covered mule wagon needs a set of sunshades. By selecting μετὰ σκιαδίων, he suggests to us that he read this pilgrimage to Zion in the light of Isa. 4.2-6. He seems to have considered the application of Exodus motifs to *that* Zion passage as authorization for application of the same to *this* one, even if it lacked them[63] in the Hebrew text before him.[64]

For the Septuagint translator, the Gentiles' offering is many-faceted. It includes not only that striking gift of returned Jews, but horses and chariots as well. This is not merely cult. It is amassed tribute. As we shall soon see, the Greek vocabulary itself will underline this point.

A dual Assemblage of Worshippers

The presentation of the returnees in Jerusalem by the Gentile emissaries is compared, in the Hebrew text, to another offering that is familiar to the readers: the מנחה that the Israelites present in the same location.

The description is a straightforward comparison of a future, unrealized event with an activity that is both realized and familiar to the readers.[65] Both the grammar (כאשר יביאו for comparison with an ongoing action) and the context (the מנחה-offering) unite to provide a context

of animals and vehicles that *are* allowed to remain, as well as by the fact that this is not a truly thoroughbred *Israelite* procession at all. *Their* role is to serve as well-borne tribute to the Lord.

63. But cf. Hugenberger, 'Second Moses', p. 125: 'Finally, a passage such as 51.9-11 demonstrates that the second exodus was to reflect the pattern of the original in a pilgrimage/triumphal procession to God's holy mountain (cf. 41.17-20...66.20-23).'

64. Since כרכר and σκιάδιον are *hapax legomena,* one might entertain the notion, proposed by A. Schenker ('Gewollt dunkel Wiedergaben in LXX? Am Beispiel von Ps 28 (29), 6', *Biblica* 75 [1994], pp. 546-55), that some LXX translators considered themselves under the obligation to avoid clarifying an ambiguous Hebrew passage, even if they felt they understood its 'hidden' meaning. If my analysis is correct, the translator did not know כרכר and his 'substitute' translation was influenced by the composite Exodus and Zion motifs of ch. 4. One wonders, however, if there might have been a way to express the same thought of sunshades by some use of the very common σκία or σκιάζων, rather than resorting to the otherwise unattested σκιάδιον. If Schenker's proposal obtains here, the translator may have communicated his best understanding of the text via a translation that was not the most transparent one available to him. On the other hand, perhaps every perspiring Alexandrian knew what a σκιάδιον was.

65. If not in contemporary practice in Jerusalem, then at least as a constituent feature of traditional Yahwistic cult.

for describing the 'new thing'. It is announced in terms of its formal similarity to an old thing, which is to say the well-known practice of the מנחה-offering.

It is true, the Gentile worshippers in Jerusalem and the human offering that they will present are a radical departure from Torah norms. Nevertheless, both can be comprehended by the points of contact that they share: the goodness of the Israelite practice of offering the מנחה and the care—a clean vessel—with which it is practised.

The Septuagint text disrupts the familiarity that makes this comparison work. It takes the surprising path of translating כאשר יביאו as ὡς ἂν ἐνέγκαισαν. The combination of ὡς with the conditional particle and the aorist optative verb might be suspected of removing the activity from the realm of comparison—for which it would have to refer to a realized, familiar activity—and of thrusting it into the realm of an unrealised and perhaps not-yet-experienced action.[66]

If it does so, it raises two crucial questions: (1) What is the function of the grammar and syntax? That is, to what action do they jointly refer? And (2), who are the 'Israelites' who perform this activity? For if the optative has its classical function of denoting an unreal situation, these 'Israelites' would appear no longer to be ancestors or contemporaries of the readers of LXX Isaiah, nor are their liturgical habits necessarily known to them. Rather, the optative might now speak of a practice which is contrary to present reality.

Several possibilities suggest themselves already: 'as the Israelites (will) present their offerings to me'; 'so that the Israelites might present their offerings to me';[67] 'in the same way as Israelites might present

66. For the decline of the optative mood in Hellenistic Greek, cf. BDF §65(2) and C. Cox, 'Job's Concluding Soliloquy: Chh. 29–31' in *VII Congress of the International Organization for Septuagint and Cognate Studies, Leuven 1989* (Atlanta: Scholars Press, 1991), pp. 332-33. It is surprising, in the light of the oft-cited news of its demise, that the optative occurs more than 500 times in the Septuagint. Thackeray (*Grammar*, §15.2) observes helpfully that it is still common in the LXX *in wishes*. However, uses such as the one in LXX Isa. 66.20 *are* rare.

67. This is the translation offered by Ottley (*Isaiah*, I , p. 327). Cf. Smyth, *Greek Grammar*, §1824 c: 'The potential optative with ἄν is also used in…purpose clauses…'; §2202: 'ὡς ἄν and ὅπως ἄν with the optative occur very rarely in Attic prose (in Xenophon especially), and more frequently after secondary than after primary tenses. ἔδωκε χρήματα Ἀνταλκίδᾳ ὅπως ἂν πληρωθέντος ναυτικοῦ…οἵ τε Ἀθηναῖοι…μᾶλλον τῆς εἰρήνης προσδέοιντο *he gave money to Antalcidas in order that, if a fleet were manned, the Athenians might be more*

their offerings to me';[68] 'as though the Israelites (had) presented their offerings to me'; and 'when the Israelites present their offerings to me'.[69]

This matter is best approached from two distinct angles:

First, one must survey those passages in the *Hebrew* text where כאשׁר is followed closely by a verb in the imperfect aspect. We will observe how the LXX handles these cases. This approach promises to illuminate *the inventory of meanings for the Hebrew* that were available to the Isaiah translator.

Second, it is necessary to analyse those passages in which the Septuagint form is similar to our Greek construction in 66.20[70] even when it is translating a *different* Hebrew construction. This line of

---

disposed to peace X.H.4.8.16.' Cf. §2278 for similar uses of the 'consecutive optative'. The rarity of this form is reflected in the LXX. I am unable to locate a single Septuagint clause that unites ὡς + a conditional particle + an optative verb and functions as a purpose or result clause.

68. Cf. Smyth, *Greek Grammar*, §1766a: 'So with ὡς ἄν, ὥσπερ ἄν ει...παρὴν ὁ Γαδάτας δῶρα πολλὰ φέρων, ὡς ἄν (*scil.* φέροι τίς) ἐξ οἴκου μεγάλου *Gadatas came with many gifts, such as one might offer from large means* X.C.5.4.29, φοβούμενος ὥσπερ ἄν εἰ παῖς *fearing like a child* (ὥσπερ ἄν ἐφοβεῖτο, εἰ παῖς ἦν) P.G.479a.'

Smyth's examples are very close in several respects to the phrase under study in LXX Isa. 66.20. However, they appear in a section entitled 'ἄν without a Verb', which somewhat reduces their comparability. The words in parentheses are supplied by Smyth in order to clarify the meaning of the sentence.

69. Cf. Smyth, *Greek Grammar*, §1824: 'The potential optative with ἄν states a future possibility, propriety, or likelihood as an *opinion* of the speaker; and may be translated by *may, might, can* (especially with a negative), *must, would, should* (rarely *will, shall*).'

However, similar forms can also function in future temporal clauses without the restraint of the speaker's opinion: §2405: 'The optative with ἄν (κέ) in Homer, where Attic would have the simple optative is potential or virtually equivalent to a future. Thus, αὐτίκα γάρ με κατακτείνειεν Ἀχιλλεύς...ἐπὴν γόου ἐξ ἔρον εἴην *for let Achilles slay me forthwith, when I have satisfied my desire for lamentation.*' Cf. §2406: 'The potential optative or indicative (with ἄν) having its proper force may appear in temporal clauses...φυλάξας...τὸν χειμῶν' ἐπιχειρεῖ, ἡνίκ' ἄν ἡμεῖς μὴ δυναίμεθ' ἐκεῖσ' ἀφικέσθαι *by watching for winter* to set in *he begins his operations when we are unable* (he thinks) *to reach the spot* D.4.31.'

If ἡνίκ' ἄν is functionally similar to ὡς ἄν in our passage, then this example might hold particular relevance. Cf. LXX Deut. 27.3, where ὡς ἄν διαβῆτε τὸν Ιορδάνην is parallel to ἡνίκα ἐὰν εἰσέλθητε εἰς τὴν γῆν; also Prov. 6.22.

70. I.e., ὡς ἄν + a verb in the subjunctive or optative moods.

approach complements the former one. It will bring to light other examples of the Greek construction at hand that might be missed if we were to restrict our view to the Hebrew form that produced LXX Isa. 66.20.

On the basis of the evidence yielded by these two glances at panoramic LXX usage, we will return to LXX Isa. 66.20 to see what can safely be concluded about the picture the translator had in mind. It is essential to distinguish between two tasks. On the one hand, one must develop the broader background material, based on pan-LXX phenomena. On the other hand, one must also analyse how *this particular translator* manages the appearances of our Hebrew construction and employs Greek constructions like the one he has utilized at 66.20. The Isaiah translator displays an independent character that must not be sacrificed to 'general LXX tendencies'. Nonetheless, those broader patterns will help us to define what our particular translator might have been thinking when he handed us this complex translation.

The Hebrew Construction: כַּאֲשֶׁר *Followed by an Imperfect Verb.* I have endeavoured to create a typology of LXX renderings of this construction.[71] It is important to be clear that my focus falls upon what the LXX translators attempted to make of the phrase, not upon its intended meaning by its Hebrew author.[72] I have attempted to discern the intention of the LXX authors in each case on grammatical, syntactical and contextual grounds.[73]

---

71. In those cases where כַּאֲשֶׁר is followed by two or more verbal clauses that are dependent upon it, I have examined only the first. The second and following clauses sometimes acquire a semi-independent status vis-à-vis כַּאֲשֶׁר, which makes their value for this analysis open to question.

72. The two will often be alike, of course, but this should not be assumed in advance.

73. I am aware of a certain circularity that could be alleged against this methodology, in that I have utilized some of the grammatical and syntactical evidence to discern the *meaning* that the translators intended. I have then returned to categorize that same evidence in terms of its meaning. However, I believe contextual considerations act as a control and effectively safeguard the method, in that with their aid it is possible to make a preliminary determination of meaning that is not *solely* dependent upon the grammatical and syntactical evidence alone. These contextual considerations reside largely in the LXX text, but the Hebrew text will necessarily come into play, since it will often assist us to discern what the LXX translator could reasonably have intended to state.

In the Septuagint, this Hebrew construction is interpreted according to four referents which are logically distinguishable:

(1) *A potential, unrealized or indefinite event.* Events in this category may be only potential in that it is not certain that they will ever occur (i.e. *'If "a" should occur*, then "b" '). Or they may be unrealized in that while they are expected to occur at some time, the timing of that future occurrence is unknown to the speaker (i.e. *'When you do "a",* then "b" '). This is sometimes expressed in terms of casuistic law. Finally, they may be indefinite in that, while they will certainly occur, the precise circumstances of the occurrence are unknown (i.e. 'Do "a" *as much as you like*').

(2) *A 'distanced' event.* This is used when the speaker describes or compares two items of which he does not wish to speak too familiarly. Consequently, he inserts a barrier of 'reserve' between himself and straightforward description. That is, ' "a" may appear *as if* it were "b";' but this is to say less than ' "a" is like "b" ', and much less than ' "a" is "b".'

(3) *A realised event.* In this category, one event is compared with another that is known because it has occurred.

(4) *Comparison with a habitual practice or naturally recurring event.* This is by far the most common understanding of כאשר + the imperfect verb in the LXX. It appears frequently when a hypothetical event is described in terms of a known event or process. 'Unrealised "a" will be like realized and known "b".' This is a kind of straightforward comparison.[74]

A Potential, Unrealised or Indefinite Event. If this is what the translator intended to convey, we might understand the meaning in this manner: '…as/when the Israelites might present the מנחה', leaving open the circumstances under which this might occur. Or, alternatively, '…should the Israelites present the מנחה'. Or again, '…as/when the Israelites present the מנחה', assuming that they will at some point do so, but not defining when this might occur. It will be appreciated that these alternatives assume various degrees of certainty, but all of them refer to an event that does not occur regularly and that, from the speaker's perspective, is regarded as unrealized.

74. This is the way Bible translators and commentators have uniformly read the construction in MT Isa. 66.20, as far as I am aware.

7. *Nationalism and Diaspora Perspective*   257

A *'Distanced' Event*. Turning to the next category of meanings that the LXX authors found in our Hebrew construction, we encounter the phenomenon of 'distancing language'. This mode of discourse is common in the Hebrew Bible in theophany contexts, where a human being is called upon to describe for his peers a vision of the divine. This is accomplished by surrounding the components of description with language that reserves judgment on the actual nature of the things described.[75]

It is likely that this phenomenon, when it is related to descriptions of the deity, is a reverential *refusal to describe*, an attempt to preserve the boundaries of religious propriety. But that is not its sole use, for it also comes into play to express 'secular' politeness between human beings.

It is not surprising that the LXX has its own version of this linguistic manoeuvre. Indeed, it seems to contribute its own reverential tastes even in moments when the MT does not call for this. For example, in Exod. 33.11 the Hebrew text seems to report simply that 'the Lord used to speak to Moses face to face, *as a man speaks to his friend*'. The Hebrew construction, formally, is like the one we are analysing: כאשר ידבד איש אל־רעהו. The LXX seems to wish to qualify this report by removing it one step from reality, thus ὡς εἰ τις λαλήσει πρὸς τὸν ἑαυτοῦ φίλον. The insertion of the particles ὡς εἰ produces an 'as though' connotation. Moreover, the selection of the future indicative verb—an unusual choice—further separates this daring conversation from those that a man might undertake with his friend.

If this is the intention we are to infer in LXX Isa. 66.20, then the meaning will be that the Gentile emissaries will make their offering *in a way that is somehow comparable with the way in which the Israelites present their* מנחה. It would fall to the context to define in what ways the two presentations are alike, and in what ways they are distinct. This, then, is the second category of the LXX authors' semantic inventory with which to render כאשר + the imperfect verb.

A *Realised Event*. We proceed now to a category of passages where כאשר + the imperfect verb seems required by the context to denote a reference to past, realized events.

In Exod. 1.12, for example, we read וכאשר יענו אתו כן ירבה = καθότι δὲ αὐτοὺς ἐταπείνουν τοσούτῳ πλείους ἐγίνοντο. The

---

75. Cf. Chapter 4, 'Isaiah 66.15', pp. 119-22, for this use of the language in Ezek. 1.

coordinated Hebrew imperfects denote an act that was repeated over time.[76] The Greek translator had no difficulty with this slightly unusual use of the imperfect, producing a translation with none of the characteristic indications of an unrealized situation (e.g. conditional particles, subjunctive or optative moods).[77]

In 1 Sam. 24.14, the Hebrew imperfect apparently envisages a proverb that *continually* speaks. Again, the LXX suffers no difficulty in rendering this as a realized—though continuing—event.

What is to be noticed, however, is that none of these Greek readings employs the characteristics of unreality that we have cited above. It is a simple task, then, for the LXX to understand כאשר + the imperfect as referring to a past or present realized event and to communicate this without any of the conditional elements found in LXX Isa. 66.20. It is unlikely, therefore, that the LXX translator of Isaiah is glancing back at the temple practice of generations past, or that he is looking from Egypt towards contemporary Palestinian practice in order to compare the future Gentile offering with these. He has coined too elegant and oblique a phrase for that to be the case.

A Habitual or Naturally Recurring Activity. We come now to the fourth and final category of renderings of the same Hebrew construction, those that refer to a habitual or naturally repeated activity. This shares with the previous category a time frame in the realized present, and so there is considerable overlap between them. Still, this fourth class of translations extends further into the unrealized future in that it refers to a repeated activity that may be already partially realized but which is understood to continue on as well. While the prior category shifted its attention subtly toward the *realized aspect* of a continuing activity, here the focus lies with equal subtlety on its *unrealized* aspect.

---

76. Cf. GKC §107(e). See Exod. 17.11 for the same phenomenon. Cf. also A. Marx, *Les offrandes végétales dans l'Ancien Testament: Du tribut d'hommage au repas eschatologique* (VTSup, 57; Leiden: E.J. Brill, 1994), p. 18: 'Ce n'est en fait qu'au cours de la période exilique que l'offrande d'une minḥāh indépendamment de tout sacrifice sanglant semble être devenue habituelle. De telles offrandes y sont en tout cas suffisamment répandues pour que le prophète puisse utiliser, pour décrire le retour des exilés, l'image de la minḥāh apportée au Temple dans des vases purs par les enfants d'Israël (Es. lxvi 20).' Cf. also p. 88.

77. In Exod. 8.23, the translator seems to have misrepresented a reference to future divine revelation with a past command. There כאשר יאמר אלינו = καθάπερ εἶπεν ἡμῖν.

If this is the picture that our translator had in mind, then we might understand that the Gentile offering will take place 'as when the Israelites offer the מנחה', leaving unexpressed the timing and all non-essential circumstances of this occurrence. This is by far the largest category of readings.

It is now possible to summarize the information that emerges from the assignment of all translations of כאשר followed by an imperfect verb to the semantic types outlined above. First, this Hebrew construction produces four distinguishable meanings in the LXX. Second, we find that the Greek subjunctive is the most commonly utilized verbal mood. The optative appears once with the conditional particle to mark a distancing phrase, and five times—always without the conditional particle—to render a comparison with a habitual or naturally recurring event. Third, the LXX Isa. 66.20 translation would find *nearly identical* formal corroboration as a distancing phrase and *similar* formal corroboration as a comparison with a realized event.[78] There are also numerous examples of comparison with a potential, unrealized or indefinite event that are *nearly identical* and *similar*, except that the verbal mood is subjunctive rather than optative. I have suggested that, in post-classical Greek, this distinction has eroded to the point that our reading might line up with this category as well.

Thus, the evidence reaped when one begins from the Hebrew form is inconclusive. We find no Greek translations of this Hebrew construction that *exactly* mimic the form at Isa. 66.20. However, we do find *similar* Greek forms. While isolation of these forms presents us with a menu of ways in which our translator *could have understood* the Hebrew phrase, it does not help us to narrow down the possible meanings of 66.20, since these include no less than three of the four different meanings of our typology.

The Greek Construction: ὡς ἂν *Followed by a Subjunctive or Optative verb.*[79] As stated above, the purpose of this section is to approach the

---

78. In Judg. 16.9, the adverb—ὃν τρόπον—differs, and the c.p does not appear. In four other cases, the adverb is ὡς (twice) or ὡσεὶ, but the c.p. does not appear.

79. Cf. Thackeray, *Grammar*, §15.2: 'As regards the *moods*, the optative, which is defunct in the modern language, is still commonly used (in the LXX) to express a wish: other uses viz. with a[n in principal sentences (questions etc.) to express possibility and in subordinate clauses (conditional, final etc.) are rare except in the literary essay known as 4 Maccabees, which uses it freely.'

problem of the Isa. 66.20 rendering from the other side, that is, from the angle of Septuagintal use of the same *Greek* phrase independent of the underlying Hebrew.[80]

This time, the results are suggestive. When ὡς ἄν is followed by a syntactically related subjunctive or optative verb in the LXX,[81] all but two represent temporal clauses; that is, they refer to an action in the future whose precise moment of fulfilment is not known.[82]

Of these, the majority represent a single expected action in the future. For example, Lev. 14.34 is representative of what becomes a stock LXX reference to the imminent conquest of Canaan: ὡς ἄν εἰσέλθητε εἰς τὴν γῆν τῶν Χαναναίων ἣν ἐγὼ δίδωμι ὑμῖν ἐν κτήσει...[83] A minority of these seem to indicate a repeated action in the future. Once again, the details of its realization do not fall within the horizon of the speaker. It is to be assumed that the action will take place more than once, even if this iterative phenomenon is expressed by a representative singular.[84]

For the purposes of understanding the ὡς ἄν clause at LXX Isa.

---

80. LSJ (pp. 2038-2039) attest several useful occurrences of ὡς ἄν: 'as much as can be', μαχομένους ὡς ἄν δυνώμεθα κρατιστα, Xenophon. *Anabasis* 3.2.6 (v/iv BCE); 'however (in whatever way)', ὡς ἄν ποήσῃς, Sophocles' *Ajax* 1369 (v BCE); 'when', ὡς ἄν c.subj, *Zenon Papyri* 251 (iii BCE), τὰ δὲ λοιπὰ ὡς ἄν ἔλθω διατάξομαι, *1 Cor.* 11.34!; ὡς ἄν αὐτὸς ἥλιος...αἴρη, Sophocles. *Philoctetes* 1330 (v BCE); 'that, in order that'... 'in this sense ὡς and ὡς ἄν...are used with the subj. after the primary tenses of the indic., and with the optative after the past tenses' (Isa. 66.20 uses the optative after the *future* tense. This may have been the kind of usage that prompted Ottley's translation); to mark a wish, 'oh that!', ὡς ἄν ἔπειτ᾽ ἀπὸ σεῖο οὐκ ἐθέλοιμι λείπεσθαι, *Iliad* 9.444 (This occurrence bears the most exact formal likeness to our clause of those mentioned. It corresponds semantically to my category 'wishful exclamation' below).

81. LXX Isa. 66.20 represents the only LXX occurrence of ὡς ἄν + *optative*. The other 36 examples have ὡς ἄν + *subjunctive*.

82. Ezra 10.3 is ambiguous: καὶ νῦν διαθώμεθα διαθήκην τῷ θεῷ ἡμῶν ἐκβαλεῖν πάσας τὰς γυναῖκας καὶ τὰ γενόμενα ἐξ αὐτῶν ὡς ἄν βούλῃ...; 1 Macc. 3.60 uses the expression to define a reality of which the details are inaccessible to the speaker: ὡς δ᾽ ἄν θέλημα ἐν οὐρανῷ οὕτως ποιήσει.

83. These 'single-event' references are Gen. 12.12, Exod. 9.29, 13.11, Lev. 14.34, Deut. 27.3, 27.4, 28.1, Josh. 2.14, 3.8, 3.13, 6.5, 8.5, 8.6, Judg. 21.21, 1 Kgdms 9.13, 10.2, 10.5, 2 Kgdms 13.28, 3 Kgdms 1.21, 4 Kgdms 5.6, 6.32, Judith 11.15, 1 Macc. 15.9.

84. Cf. Gen. 30.38, Exod. 28.43, Lev. 22.27, Deut. 30.1, 3 Kgdms 8.38, 2 Paralip 6.30, Prov. 1.27, 6.22, 18.17, Isa. 8.21.

66.20, it is important to recall that it stands slightly apart from these references in terms of verbal mood. It alone has ὡς ἄν + a verb in the *optative* mood. One suspects that at this late point in the language, this feature should not be overworked. The overwhelming use of ὡς ἄν + the subjunctive as a *temporal* clause favours the view that the example at Isa. 66.20 is temporal also.

If the above analysis is correct, it can be concluded that the most common function of the above Greek construction—which is identical to that found at LXX Isa. 66.20, except that the verb is in the subjunctive mood—is to denote an action that is understood to relate to some undefined point in the future. [85] *It is striking that nowhere does it render a comparison with a realised event.*

Conclusions on the Worshippers and Their Context. What, now, can we conclude about the phrase ὡς ἄν ἐνέγκαισαν οἱ υἱοὶ Ἰσραηλ? Initially, we saw that this Hebrew construction can be translated according to a wide variety of meanings in the LXX. Following this, we looked at our clause from the point of view of the Greek construction. This time, the data became more instructive. We found a preponderance of examples where this Greek form denoted an unrealized action, and none where it rendered a comparison with a wholly or partially realized event.

It appears, then, that our translator has received a simple Hebrew comparison of unknown-to-known, unrealized-to-realized, and transformed it into a temporal reference to a future, unrealized event. It appears to mean, 'And they shall bring all your brethren…(together with the accompanying gifts)…to my holy city Jerusalem, says the Lord, *when the Israelites present to me their sacrifices*…'

If so, this is a reference to an eschatological מנחה that will coincide with the (full?) return of the Diaspora Jews. It suggests that the translator understood the בני ישראל not as those who inhabited the *history* of his people, but rather as a *future*, honoured, body of Israelites. These appear to enjoy a certain pre-eminence at the eschatological festival, since the moment at which the Gentile emissaries present their tribute is

---

85. The New Testament evidence supports this conclusion. All three New Testament occurrences of ὡς ἄν + a *subjunctive* verb mean 'when…' (Rom. 15.24; 1 Cor. 11.34; Phil. 2.23). This construction does not appear in the New Testament with an optative verb.

known as the time when the Israelites present their מנחה.⁸⁶ If this is so, we have fallen upon a trace of nationalism of the kind that preserves for Israel a nuanced distinctiveness even when revered texts and contexts do not so stipulate. The MT *comparison* of two presentations—Gentile and Israelite offerings—has been broken down into something different. The sentence now serves *to locate temporally* the Gentile pilgrimage *at the time when the sons of Israel shall offer their (eschatological) offering.*

This is, from a modern perspective, an invention, a product of the Greek and not the Hebrew text. It may, however, point to an exegetical tradition of which it is merely a detail.

A Distinct Liturgy
There is a further nationalistic hint in the distinct translations of the two מנחות of this verse. It, too, contributes to the dualistic nature of the eschatological worshippers. The latter מנחה, that of the sons of Israel, is called a θυσία by the translator. This is the standard LXX rendering of both מנחה and זבח in the vast majority of contexts where these are cultic offerings.⁸⁷ When they are *not* cultic offerings, however, but rather gifts that one is obligated to present by political or military circumstances, the LXX normally uses δῶρα, in the plural.⁸⁸

86. The plural τὰς θυσίας αὐτῶν for singular את־מנחתה is interesting, though not problematic. Especially in the Pentateuchal literature, the representative singular מנחה is frequently translated by the plural θυσίας, in this way indicating nothing more than that the translators understood the ongoing sacrificial practice to which the Hebrew singular makes reference. Perhaps here one is to think not of one great eschatological sacrifice, but rather of the *restoration* or *inauguration of a new phase* of Israelite θυσίαι at some future moment.

87. For a careful analysis of the difficulties which the Septuagint translators of the Pentateuch threw up for their successors by their decision to utilize θυσία for both of these Hebrew words, cf. Daniel, *Vocabulaire du culte*, pp. 201-204. Cf. also Marx, *Offrandes végétales*, pp. 5, 12, 15.

88. Cf. nearly all the Genesis occurrences; Judg. 3.15, 17, 18 (twice); 1 Kgdms 10.27; 3 Kgdms 10.25; Isa. 39.1; Pss. 39(40).7; 71(72).10; 1 Chron. 18.2, 6; 2 Chron. 9.24; 17. 5, 11; 26.8. Daniel explains the plural dw'ra for the singular מנחה for secular tribute as an attempt to make explicit (a) the collective nature of the Hebrew singular and the emphatic nuance, 'en accord avec la splendeur nécessaire de la minḥâh'; (*Vocabulaire du culte*, p. 203). Isa. 66.20 is the only place in the entire LXX where מנחה—either singular or plural—is rendered by singular δῶρον, which violates the standard rendering of tribute that Daniel has pointed out. This is not the only occurrence of unexpected singulars in Isa. 66. It may suggest, along

Daniel discusses two verses, both of them in Chronicles, that do not at first glance appear to adhere to this standard.[89] In 2 Chronicles 32, one reads of the deliverance of Hezekiah and the inhabitants of Jerusalem from the king of Assyria, following which God 'gave them rest on every side'.[90] The verse immediately following, 32.23, reads:

ורבים מביאים מנחה ליהוה לירושלם ומגדנות ליחזקיהו מלך
יהודה וינשׂא לעיני כל־הגוים מאחרי־כן.

The first half of this verse provides the kind of parallelism that might have produced a clear lexical distinction in Greek. That is, מנחה ליהוה...ומגדנות ליחזקיהו might well have produced θυσία τῷ θεῷ...δόματα τῷ Εζεκια. Instead, we find δῶρα...δόματα. Daniel notices that the translator has read both the first and second stich of the parallelism as tribute, rather than cultic offering.[91] In this she is probably correct, given (a) the fairly steady adherence to his own translational standards that the translator of Chronicles displays,[92] and (b) the unelaborated רבים who bring this double tribute.

Though it is not transparent in the MT that these 'many' are Gentiles rather than the inhabitants of Judah and Jerusalem, the translator seizes his prerogative to find an antecedent for רבים. He chooses the nations in whose sight Hezekiah was elevated (32.23b) rather than the arguably plausible alternative, the subjects of Hezekiah whose presence has occupied the context for several verses.[93]

lines first hinted at by Ziegler (*Untersuchungen*, pp. 42-44), that an older and more literal Greek translation has been (incompletely) reworked by the translator of LXX Isaiah.

89. *Vocabulaire du culte*, p. 212.

90. 2 Chron. 32.22.

91. 'Le parallélisme avec מגדנות invitait assurément à ne pas entendre ici *minḥâh* au sens proprement sacrificiel, et à se représenter ces peuples, convenant de la fortune du roi de Juda et la puissance de la Divinité que le protégeait, et leur portant simplement, à l'un comme à l'autre, une sorte de présent d'hommage, presque un tribut' (*Vocabulaire du culte*, p. 212).

92. A trait that makes reading exegetical nuance out of lexical choice a more confident exercise here than in LXX Isaiah, generally speaking.

93. Most scholars seem to agree with the LXX that רבים refers to Gentiles. So S. Japhet, *The Ideology of the Book of Chronicles and its Place in Biblical Thought* (Bern: Peter Lang, 1989), p. 197; also *idem*, *I and II Chronicles: A Commentary* (OTL; London: SCM Press, 1993), p. 991: 'This turn of events also has political and religious ramifications: "many brought gifts to the Lord...and precious things to Hezekiah"'; H.G.M. Williamson, *Israel in the Book of Chronicles* (Cambridge: Cambridge University Press, 1977), pp. 122-23: '(R.) Mosis (*Untersuchungen zur*

In addition to the mention of the nations in the surrounding context, he may have been drawn towards this choice by the relatively common biblical idioms עמים רבים and גוים רבים and others like them.[94] Moreover, the relatively few cases where רבים appears absolutely, as here, tend towards a pejorative meaning, often designating those outside the circle of the pious individual or community.[95] Perhaps, then, it was familiarity with this biblical phraseology that moved the Chronicler's Greek translator to see in the bearers of this מנחה Hezekiah's Gentile neighbours rather than his Judahite subjects. The reference to the nations in the final clause of the verse, which Daniel sees as the determining factor, would then fall into place as confirmation of the translator's exegesis.

For our purposes, the relevant fact is that the translator signalled to us his interpretation of the verse not by explicitly qualifying the רבים, but rather by rendering מנחה as δῶρα.

The second unusual translation of apparently cultic מנחה by δῶρα occurs in 1 Chron. 16.28-29, a pair of verses that may shed additional

Theologie des chronistische Geschichtswerk, Freiburg, 1973), thinks that...the Chronicler has anticipated the prophetic hope of the pilgrimage of the nations to Jerusalem... Whether or not Mosis has correctly understood the Chronicler's intention here, it must at least be taken in connection with 2 Chr 32.23'; also *idem, I and II Chronicles* (NCB; London: Marshall, Morgan & Scott, 1982), p. 385; P.R. Ackroyd, *I and II Chronicles, Ezra, Nehemiah: Introduction and Commentary* (London: SCM Press, 1973), p. 194; R.B. Dillard, *2 Chronicles* (WBC, 15; Waco, TX: Word Books, 1987), p. 253: 'Many *came* bringing offerings...' C.F. Keil, *Chronik, Esra, Nehemia und Esther* (Leipzig, 1870; reprinted Basel: Brunnen Verlag, 1990), p. 360, sees both Judahites and Gentiles here: 'Bei רַבִּים hat man nicht blos [sic] an Israeliten, sondern wol [sic] hauptsächlich an Nachbarvölker zu denken...' Two authors are ambiguous: R.J. Coggins, *The First and Second Books of the Chronicles* (Cambridge Bible Commentary on the New English Bible; Cambridge: Cambridge University Press, 1976), p. 283: '...Hezekiah was duly rewarded by the honour in which all now held him'; and Jacob M. Myers, *II Chronicles* (AB, 13; New York: Doubleday, 1965), p. 190.

94. For עמים רבים, cf. Ezek. 32.9, 38.8, 9, 15; גוים רבים, Jer. 27.7; מלכים רבים, Jer. 27.41; Cf. also Deut. 7.17, Ezek. 26.7, Zech. 8.20-22(!), Dan. 11.10, 40.

95. Exod. 28.2; Mal. 2.6, 8 (?); Pss. 3.3; 4.7; 55.19; 56.3; 71.7. Cf. also 1 Kgs 18.25; Isa. 8.7; Ezek. 33.24, Nah. 1.12; Pss. 37.16; 119.157. The expression in these latter verses is not identical with the absolute substantive of the first group, yet the use of רבים retains the same pejorative sense. In Daniel, an enigmatic and oracular use of רבים prevails. It at once conceals the identity of the referents and leads one to think in Gentilic terms, i.e. of quantities of *nations*.

light on LXX Isa. 66.20. In this passage, an Asaphite hymn summons Israel to declare the Lord's glory 'among the nations...among...all peoples.' Then, as the gods of these nations are debunked, the call goes out to their worshippers to turn instead to the Lord. In this context we read:

> Ascribe to the LORD, O families of the peoples,
> ascribe to the LORD glory and strength!
> Ascribe to the LORD the glory due his name;
> bring an offering (מנחה), and come before him!

Again, the LXX translator provides δῶρα for מנחה, prompting Daniel to observe:

> Therefore one begins to wonder whether the translator of Chronicles has displayed a certain reluctance to extend to foreigners the consecration of true sacrifices, the Temple cult being in his eyes a privilege of Israel.[96]

We have, then, two examples in an LXX book that shares affinities with LXX Isaiah[97] of Gentile pilgrimage *to Jerusalem* and cultic participation there, together with a withholding of *full* cultic privileges. In the first, their gift is downgraded when its presentation is described. In the second, Gentiles are invited to present an already downgraded gift.

Returning to Isa. 66.20, we note that the two מנחות of the Hebrew text are pressed into the service of a new exegetical precision in the LXX. The Septuagint translator will not have these Gentiles presenting a θυσία.[98] That prerogative, it seems, is reserved for Jews, not to mention the detail that horses and chariots[99] have no place as *cultic* offerings to the Lord. Thus, he avails himself of a time-honoured Septuagint tradition of lexically defining *what kind of* מנחה is under discussion. Our translator will allow the Gentiles to present only a δῶρον. As we have seen, this is probably not so much tribute *which is like the Israelite*

---

96. 'On en vient donc à se demander si le traducteur des Chroniques ne manifestait pas une certain répugnance à prêter à des étrangers la consécration de véritables sacrifices, le culte dans le Temple étant à ses yeux un privilège d'Israël, « *Vocabulaire du Culte* », p. 212.

97. I have indicated elsewhere that the lexical choices of LXX Isaiah are similar to those made by, *inter alia*, Chronicles and Proverbs.

98. Marx implicitly recognizes this distinction by his inclusion of 66.20a in his list under 'Les emplois génériques' and 66.20b under 'Les emplois spécialisés' (*Offrandes végétales*, pp. 12, 15).

99. As we have seen, for the translator these are no longer *means of travel* but *items of tribute*.

offering as it is a subordinate gift presented on a certain occasion: when the Israelites offer their מנחה.[100]

Furthermore, the precise destination of these מנחות is curiously specified in the LXX.[101] The Gentile tribute in the MT is to be presented על הר קדשׁי ירושׁלם. In the LXX this becomes εἰς τὴν ἁγίαν πόλιν Ιερουσαλημ. This conversion—from הר to עיר—may represent a downgrading of access for the Gentiles. The *city* is one thing, the translator may feel, but the *holy mountain* itself might be taken to represent out-of-bounds Temple precincts.

The LXX can be read as though translating אל עיר קדשׁי ירושׁלם. The alteration of הר to עיר by way of orthographic or phonological confusion is possible to imagine,[102] and אל/על confusion is evident throughout the Hebrew text tradition.[103] It is the *conjunction* of two otherwise unremarkable conversions—together with the appearance of

---

100. Daniel seems to suggest that the dual translations at Isa. 66.20 denote tribute—not cult—without recognizing the nationalistic import of this change (*Vocabulaire du culte*, pp. 202, 212-13). She suggests that such a מנחה is a 'véritable cadeau qu'on fait au sanctuaire ou aux prêtes' but not 'une offrande proprement cultuelle'. Pace Daniel as I understand her, it is not so much *what is given* or *the place where it is deposited* that makes the first (Gentile) מנחה a δῶρον, but rather *who is giving it*.

101. In his concern for the *content* of tribute/worship and now for the *place*, the translator may echo the twofold preoccupation of TJ at Mal. 1.11. Cf. Gordon, 'Terra Sancta', p. 122: 'For the targumist there is no question of Gentile worship being acceptable to God, nor can he allow the unique cultic status of Jerusalem to be compromised.' As we have seen, the translator alters his text in the translation process not principally because he is 'free', but rather because he is constrained by some of the same theological commitments that motivate other tradents of the Hebrew Bible.

102. Although it never happens in any of the 57 occurrences of הר in Isaiah. It is also exceedingly rare elsewhere. In spite of 570 occurrences of הר, one finds only Job 15.10, הר־יערים = πόλιν Ιαριμ; 2 Kgs 23.16, בהר = ἐν τῇ πόλει; and 2 Chron. 21.11 בהרי יהודה = ἐν πόλεσιν Ιουδα.

Further against an accidental confusion of עיר/הר, the Isaiah translator handles הר קדשׁי without difficulty in the other six appearances of this phrase in Isaiah.

Against any attribution of the change at 66.20 to nationalistic ideology, one must be careful to balance 56.7, where Yahwistic foreigners are indeed granted cultic access אל־הר־קדשׁי, which is parallel to 'my house of prayer' and 'my altar'. In that passage—and perhaps not in 66.20—the sincere conversion and orthodox practice of such Gentiles is emphatically stated.

103. Indeed, the MT differs on this very point with 1QIsaᵃ, which has אל.

a twofold LXX plus—that suggests exegetical intent at this point.[104]

The plus comes with reference to the Israelite מנחה. The phrase כַּאֲשֶׁר יָבִיאוּ is made more specific with a dative pronoun referring to the Lord: ὡς ἂν ἐνέγκαισαν...ἐμοί. At the same time, the Israelite מנחה is specified as τὰς θυσίας αὐτῶν.

It may well be that both these unauthorized pronouns set the Israelite offering over against the Gentile tribute. In the first case, the clarification would specify that the former comes directly *to the Lord*, while the unexpected εἰς τὴν ἁγίαν πόλιν allowed the Gentiles and their tribute to enter only as far as the city. In the second instance, αὐτῶν—a word that does not seem strictly necessary in the absence of an antithetical offering with which their sacrifices are being contrasted—would nicely accentuate the dualism that the entire text has appeared to develop.

A fascinating LXX expansion at Isa. 2.2 may strengthen the case for such a nationalistic reading of double destinations—rather than just one—at Isa. 66.20. Isaiah 2 also presents its own eschatological pilgrimage that brings Gentiles to Jerusalem. Where the MT has
והיה באחרית הימים נכון יהיה הַר בית־יהוה בראש ההרים ונשׂא מגבעות ונהרו אֵלָיו כל־הגוים, the LXX offers ὅτι ἔσται ἐν ταῖς ἐσχάταις ἡμέραις ἐμφανὲς <u>τὸ ὄρος κυρίου καὶ ὁ οἶκος τοῦ θεοῦ</u> ἐπ᾽ ἄκρων τῶν ὀρέων καὶ ὑψωθήσεται ὑπεράνω τῶν βουνῶν καὶ ἥξουσιν ἐπ᾽ <u>αὐτὸ</u> πάντα τὰ ἔθνη.

The translator has somewhat uncharacteristically dismantled the construct chain הַר בית־יהוה and introduced *two* destinations into his translated text: τὸ ὄρος κυρίου *and* ὁ οἶκος τοῦ θεοῦ.[105] This

---

104. Fischer notices the possibilities for variation with such a frequent phrase, and then suggests that 'es ist m., daß אֶל עֶזְ[רָ]ךְ schon in LXX-V gestanden hat' (*Schrift*, p. 68). Cf. also pp. 81 and 84. Such an observation is undoubtedly accurate concerning what *might have been*, but it merely relocates the problem of MT–LXX disagreement without attempting to solve it.

105. This transformation requires that a copula be added and—in addition—a second divine appellative, in this case τοῦ θεοῦ. Some degree of influence may have been exercised by 2.3, where the Gentiles animate one another to go up אֶל־הַר־יהוה...אֶל־בית אלהי יעקב. The Septuagint inserts καὶ at that point as well.

The well-known parallel passage at Mic. 4 has only <u>τὸ ὄρος</u> τοῦ κυρίου...καὶ σπεύσουσι πρὸς <u>αὐτὸ</u> λαοί.

It is just conceivable that the verb in הַר יְהְיֶה in 2.2 has been understood as the Tetragrammaton and is responsible for the presence of two divine names, so that

expansion might go unnoticed—or perhaps be dismissable as only a levelling with the similar dual phrase at 2.3—were it not for the fact that the resumptive prepositional phrase אליו is translated by ἐπ' αὐτό.[106] It is this component of the text that stipulates the destination to which 'all the Gentiles' process. Under normal circumstances, grammatical exigencies would require that the neuter gender of ἐπ' αὐτό refer back to an antecedent of the same gender. Contextually, there appear to be three possible antecedents: (a) the neuter τὸ ὄρος κυρίου, (b) the masculine antecedent ὁ οἶκος τοῦ θεοῦ, and (c) a combination of the two. Only the first provides the expected agreement in gender and number.

Significantly, the translator has not said that the Gentiles will come ἐπ' αὐτόν/αὐτῷ, which would suggest that their destination was 'the house of God'. Nor has he written ἐπ' αὐτούς/αὐτοῖς, which would use the masculine pronoun as 'gender-inclusive', with both 'mountain' and 'house' as its antecedent.[107] Rather, his use of the neuter ἐπὶ αὐτό almost certainly refers back to the only neuter antecedent, the ὄρος κυρίου.[108] It would appear, then that the LXX or its *Vorlage* has altered the text by dividing a single referent into two—הר בית־יהוה into τὸ ὄρος κυρίου καὶ ὁ οἶκος τοῦ θεοῦ—and then referring back only to the second of these when speaking of the destination of the Gentiles.

This observation must be balanced against the enthusiasm of the Gentiles in Isa. 2.3, where they fully intend that their pilgrimage will end in the house of the God of Jacob itself.[109] Nevertheless, the fact that the translator—whether unconsciously or not—has allowed the

---

יהיה הר בית־יהוה = τὸ ὄρος τοῦ κυρίου καὶ ὁ οἶκος τοῦ θεοῦ. Though the translation of divine names and titles in LXX Isaiah makes this plausible, it seems unlikely.

106. Cf. the variants αυτον and αυτω, which Ziegler records but does not prefer. Were one of these to be the original—which does not appear likely—then my use of 2.2 to support the argument for dual destinations would apply only to the scribe who inserted αὐτό.

107. It is possible to imagine the neuter ἐπ' αὐτά/αὐταῖς exercising this function also, but the translator has not chosen this option either.

108. The only alternative explanation that I can conceive of is that αὐτό refers back comprehensively to τὸ ὄρος τοῦ κυρίου καὶ ὁ οἶκος τοῦ θεοῦ, taken as a hendiadys. But it is difficult to explain why the Hebrew construction would have been expanded in the first place if the only result is to create a hendiadys.

109. Might the translator have suspected that Zion's guests were reaching for more than would be theirs?

alterations that we have observed at 2.2 may provide some independent corroboration for the nationalism that appears in a similar context at 66.20.

One further transformation awaits our attention. It concerns the manner in which one or both of these offerings is to be made.

In the Hebrew text, an offering is carried out 'with a clean vessel' (בכלי טהור). In the Greek text, it is performed 'with psalms' (μετὰ ψαλμῶν).[110] In the MT, the description probably applies to the Israelite מנחה, not to the Gentile presentation of the Israelite brethren.[111] This is suggested by the word order and, particularly, by the parallelism of על הר קדשׁי with בית יהוה, each phrase marking the end of its respective descriptive clause.[112]

110. The possibility that this phrase was directly borrowed from another biblical text seems to be obviated by the fact that μετὰ ψαλμῶν occurs nowhere else in the LXX. One wonders, however, whether Zech. 14—a chapter that shares several prominent features with the final verses of Isa. 66—might have influenced LXX Isa. 66.20 at a conceptual level. In Zech. 14.20-21, one reads of the time of Zion's exaltation that everything in Jerusalem will then be holy. This blanket consecration will extend even to such mundane articles as the bells (TJ 'blankets'?; cf. Cathcart and Gordon, *Targum of the Minor Prophets*, p. 226 n. 50.) of the horses. Indeed, '...the cooking pots (סיר = λέβης) in the house of the LORD shall be as holy as the bowls in front of the altar; and every cooking pot in Jerusalem and Judah shall be sacred to the LORD of hosts.'

If the Isaiah translator had this text in mind, it might have seemed obvious that one ought not to single out any particular cultic bowl as a כלי טהור. Under such conditions, worship μετὰ ψαλμῶν might represent an agreeable harmonisation. Cf. also R.P. Gordon, 'Inscribed Pots and Zechariah XIV 20–1', *VT* 42 (1992), pp. 120-23.

If one is to grant the possibility that the final pilgrimage of Zech. 14 has exercised an influence upon the similar scene in Isa. 66, then one further point arouses interest. We have seen that LXX Isa. 66.20 can be read—over against the MT—to disallow the Gentiles access to the *mountain* of the Lord, restricting them to the *city*. Zechariah ends with a prediction that is meant to be reassuring, one which would resonate with this reading of LXX 66.20: ולא־יהיה כנעני עוד בבית־יהוה צבאות ביום ההוא.

111. But cf. F. Delitzsch, *Jesaja* (Leipzig: Dörflin u. Franke, 1879; reprinted from the 5th edn, Basel: Brunnen-Verlag, 1984), p. 683: 'Die Mincha ist die Diaspora Israels und dem reinen Gefäß entsprechen die zu Gefäßen der Ehre gewordenen Heiden...'

112. Not to mention the difficulty of presenting a large number of human beings in a clean vessel, unless the possibility of metaphorization is stretched to its limits and, probably, beyond.

When We All Go Home

Nowhere in the Torah is it prescribed that a כלי טהור is the proper vessel for the מנחה.[113] There *is* discussion of כלים for which one is to be careful to maintain ritual purity.[114] However, these articles are not specifically connected with the מנחה.

Cultic instruments are sometimes called טהור,[115] or are said to be made of material that is טהור.[116] Furthermore, after Nehemiah evicts Tobiah from the Lord's house, he gives orders for the chambers to be cleaned (טהר) and then immediately brings back the כלים that belonged there, 'along with the cereal offering and the frankincense'.[117] Similarly, the Chronicler reports that part of Hezekiah's cultic reform implied the cleansing (טהר) of the 'house of the Lord, the altar of burnt offering and all its utensils' (כליו).[118] It is to this general concern for cultic purity—and not to any specific מנחה practice—that the Hebrew text of Isa. 66.20 most probably refers.

How, then, are we to explain the Greek text? Given the translator's habit of re-arranging Hebrew poetic structures, it is *a priori* possible that the neat parallelisms that I have sketched out above for the Hebrew text are no longer *en vigueur* in the LXX translation. Indeed, there are some indications in the text that μετὰ ψαλμῶν may indeed have come to describe the *Gentile* offering.

One avenue of approach that teases even if it fails to convince is that which posits an inner-Greek development. It is worth noting that טהור is commonly translated with καθαρός. Now a lyre is a κιθάρα, which is consonantally identical as well as alike in one or more vowels, depending upon the particulars of the case. A כלי can be a *musical instrument*,[119] and it is just possible to imagine a scribe whose mind was

113. Cf. Marx, *Offrandes végétales*, p. 74: 'L'offrande de farine est présenté aux prêtes dans un récipient: si les princes, au moment de la consécration de l'autel, apportent leur offrande dans de bols, qe'ārāh, d'argent et dans des coupes, mizrāq, d'argent (Nb. vii 13 et passim), les Israélites ordinaires ont dû se contenter de la présenter dans des récipients purs, *kelî ṭahôr* (voir Es. lxvi 20).'

114. Cf. Lev. 11.32; 13.58-9; Num. 19.18.

115. The Menorah, Exod. 31.8; 39.37.

116. The Menorah, Exod. 25.39; 37.24; the table vessels, plates, incense dishes, bowls and flagons for libations, Exod. 37.16.

117. את־המנחה והלבונה.

118. 2 Chron. 29.18.

119. Cf. Ps. 71(72).22. Ziegler makes this particular observation as well, in dismissing prior claims that μετὰ ψαλμῶν results from orthographic confusion: 'Es ist nicht anzunehmen, daß der Übers. hier in מִזְמוֹר (Scholz 40), תּוֹדָה (Ottley II

on temple worship understanding ἐν σκεύει καθαρῷ as ἐν σκεύει κιθάρας, and then paraphrasing by μετὰ ψαλμῶν.[120]

Indeed, Ps. 71(70).22 comes startlingly close to this:

גם־אני אודך בכלי־נבל אמתך אלהי

אזמרה לך בכנור קדוש ישראל

καὶ γὰρ ἐγὼ ἐξομολογήσομαί σοι ἐν σκεύει ψαλμοῦ τὴν ἀλήθειάν σου ὁ θεός ψαλῶ σοι ἐν κιθάρᾳ ὁ ἅγιος τοῦ Ισραηλ

However, while such an accidental development is theoretically possible, there are two claims against it: (1) the number and scope of incidents of mental indiscipline that would need to have occurred; (2) the unanimity of the Greek manuscript tradition in favour of the text as it now stands, with no evidence of intervening stages.

If, however, one leaves behind the notion of *accidental* error and considers the possibility that the translator has delivered up a conscious exegetical treatment of the text, there may well be room for the dynamics outlined above to have produced the text as we now have it.

Koenig, in his *tour de force* against the 'empiricist' tradition of Septuagint studies, argues that the translator of LXX Isaiah was in possession of a systematic hermeneutic by verbal analogy. This fact went unappreciated by those who saw the translator as a neutral, passive tradent:

---

388), שִׁיר (Fischer 68) verlesen hat. Die obigen Beispiele legen nahe, daß er einfach das hebr. "reines Gefäß" zu deuten versuchte, nachdem öfters כלי ein Musikinstrument bezeichnet, vgl. Am 6, 5; 1 Par 16,5;2 Par 34.12; besonders Ps 70(71), 22 (ἐν σκεύει ψαλμοῦ = MT)' (*Untersuchungen*, p. 84).

LXX Amos 6.5 does not recognize כלי as an instrument. Ziegler might also have mentioned Neh. 12.36; 1 Chron. 15.16, 16.42 and 23.5; and 2 Chron. 5.13, 7.6, 23.13, 29.26-27 and 30.21. In Neh. 12.36, בכלי־שיר דויד = (αἰνεῖν) ἐν ᾠδαῖς Δαυιδ. Apart from LXX Isa. 66.20, this is the only place in the LXX where the translation provides an abstract-for-concrete (in this case, songs-for-instruments) translation.

Ziegler does not attempt to explain what would motivate the not inconsequential move from *on a pure musical instrument* to *with psalms*.

120. A strikingly similar conversion from the instrument that produces music to the music that is produced occurs in Neh. 12.36. This verse reports that a number of musicians entered the temple in procession *with the musical instruments of David, the man of God* (בכלי־שיר דויד איש האלהים). The LXX regards them as having entered *to praise by means of the odes of David, the man of God*, αἰνεῖν ἐν ᾠδαῖς Δαυιδ ἀνθρώπου τοῦ θεοῦ.

Thus, the achievements of the analogical hermeneutic remain un-appreciated and are confused with accidental or empirical modifications. The result is that their methodological inspiration has not been identified. The hermeneutical facts have been purely and simply confused with those of accidental corruption, whether by (the translator's) failure to perceive or by alterations freely introduced into the text.[121]

The method of scriptural analogies established the relationship with the base text by means of the idea of a *reciprocal participation of texts* belonging to a single literary corpus, established upon sovereign authority. The method of verbal analogies establishes the relationship by means of the idea of a *reciprocal participation of words*, thus supplying a formal kinship that is *independent of any semantic connection* (final emphasis added).[122]

Koenig's work is based specifically upon alleged hermeneutical moves practised by the Isaiah translator upon the *Hebrew* text and dependent upon the interplay of formally similar *Hebrew* words. These hermeneutical manoeuvres are now embedded for us in the Greek witness to them. However, there seems to be no *a priori* reason for excluding the possibility that the same formal techniques might been employed upon the *Greek* text at the same time. While the evidence for a *haphazard* change of the kind I have suggested above is not strong, there *is* reason to suspect an intentional, interpretative move that produced μετὰ ψαλμῶν.[123]

When once this possibility has been set out, it is interesting to observe another point of agreement between Ps. 71(72).22 and Isaiah,

<hr>

121. 'Les faits d'herméneutique analogique restent donc invisibles et ils se con-fondent avec les altérations accidentelles ou empiriques, tant que leur inspiration méthodique n'a pas été identifiée. C'est bien ce qui s'est produit en critique. Les faits herméneutiques ont été purement et simplement confondus avec les faits de dégradations par accidents, par méconnaissance du sens ou par modification librement introduite dans le texte'. *L'herméneutique analogique*, p. 195. Koenig's most sinister villains are Ziegler and Ottley.

122. La méthode des analogies scripturaires assure la relation avec le texte de base par l'idée d'une *participation réciproque des textes* d'un même corpus érigé en autorité souveraine. La méthode des analogies verbales assure la relation par l'idée d'une *participation réciproque des termes* offrant une parenté de formé, *indépendamment d'un rapport sémantique'* (final emphasis added), Koenig, *L'herméneutique analogique*, p. 197.

123. There is one other tantalizing instance of an abstract-for-concrete translation of כלים: in Num. 4.17, Eleazar is given oversight 'of the sanctuary and its vessels' = πᾶσι τοῖς ἔργοις.

namely the divine appellative קְדוֹשׁ יִשְׂרָאֵל. As is widely understood, this title is so characteristic of Isaiah as to be nearly his private property. Of 32 such designations in the Hebrew Bible, only 6 do not belong to Isaiah. If a wide-ranging intertextual dynamic lies behind the translator's work, it might be the case that his attention was drawn specially to a psalm that shared this important—and otherwise unusual—divine title.

Another text tradition converges slightly with Isaiah's adaptation of this verse. TJ reads:

וייתון ית כל אחיכון מכל עממיא קרבנא קדם יוי בסוסוון
וברתכין וברחילון ובכודנון ובתשבחן על טורא דקודשי
לירושלם אמר יוי כמא דייתון בני ישראל ית קרבנא במן
דכי לבית מקדשא דיוי

> And they shall bring all your brethren from all the Gentiles as an offering before the Lord, with horses and with chariots, and with ewes, and with mules, and with songs, upon my holy mountain, to Jerusalem, says the Lord, just as the sons of Israel will bring an offering in a clean vessel to the sanctuary of the Lord.[124]

The Targum mirrors the five-unit syntactical chain of the MT when speaking of the modes of transport for the return from Diaspora. However, in place of the difficult Hebrew *hapax legomenon* in the fifth slot, TJ reads ובתשבחן (= 'with songs of praise'). Since the dating of the Targumic sources is notoriously difficult, it will not be easy to associate this reading with the LXX text.[125] However, the Targum shows some promise of attesting a similar and *textually independent* statement that the return from Diaspora is to occur 'with songs of praise'. Contrary to the LXX, however, TJ's songs do not derive from כלי טהור. In spite of its fascinating similarity to μετὰ ψαλμῶν, TJ's music actually occurs in a different section of the verse. Indeed, Targum has a rendering of כלי טהור that is quite prosaic and unsurprising.[126]

124. So Chilton, *Isaiah Targum*, p. 128.

125. Two Targumists recently advise against making facile connections between tendencies shared by the Targums and the ancient versions: 'Of the readings and interpretations which *Tg.* Minor Prophets has in common with the other major versions of antiquity (LXX, Syr, Vg), little need be said here in view of the fact that such points of correspondence are as often as not attributable to common tradition, or even coincidence, as to direct influence by one version upon another' (Cathcart and Gordon, *Targum of the Minor Prophets*, p. 11).

126. TJ's potential parallel with the LXX in this verse must be limited to the

Regardless of whether the solutions outlined above are wholly satisfactory for explaining the move from כלי טהור to μετὰ ψαλμῶν, it behoves us to suggest a *motive* for such a transformation. We have already seen that, when confronted with two מנחות, our translator allows the sons of Israel a full θυσία, while restricting the Gentile pilgrims to mere δῶρα. The case of μετὰ ψαλμῶν may present us with an analogous restriction of cultic privilege.

It is possible to read μετὰ ψαλμῶν as qualifying the presentation of the *Gentile* offering. Indeed, v. 19 and the major part of v. 20 have been a wordy description of what *Gentiles* will do, interrupted only by the parenthetical comparison that begins with כאשר. Verse 21 may resume the description of what Gentiles will do.[127] I have argued above that the

conceptual level and not applied to the handling of specific phrases. The appearance of TJ's ובתשבחן in what appears to be the location corresponding to the MT's ובכרכרות is not exceedingly surprising, since the Targums have a strong predisposition to employy שבח lexemes on religious and/or joyous occasions. Cf., for example, Cathcart and Gordon, *Targum of the Minor Prophets*, p. 201 n. 10, on משבחין, 'singing praises', in Jerusalem's open squares: 'For MT "playing"; BH śḥq is normally rendered by "praise" (e.g. 2 Sam. 6.5; Jer 15.17), doubtless considered more circumspect in a context like the present one. (*Tg.* also uses "praise" for the dervish-like activities of the "sons of the prophets" in 1 Sam. 10.5-13; 19.18-24.)'

The translation of MT ובכרכרות by this lexeme is probably explained by comparison with the Targum of 2 Sam. 6.14. There, David's awkwardly exuberant dancing is narrated like this: ודוד מכרכר בכל־עז לפני יהוה. The Targum translates decorously with משבב. It is highly likely that TJ Isa. 66.20 understands ובכרכרות to be related to מכרכר of TJ 2 Sam. 6.14—whether as an intentionally exegetical move or not—and translates accordingly.

127. If, that is, the new Levites are to be understood as taken from among the Gentile pilgrims. So, for example, Dillman, *Jesaia*, p. 542; Cheyne, *Isaiah*, II, p. 131, both Jews and Gentiles; Westermann, *Jesaja 40–66*, p. 426; Delitzsch, *Jesaja*, p. 683; C. von Orelli, *Die Propheten Jesaja und Jeremia* (Munich: C.H. Beck'sche, 2nd edn, 1891), p. 213; P.D. Miscall, *Isaiah: Readings* (Sheffield: JSOT Press, 1993), p. 148, both Jews and Gentiles; A.S. Herbert, *The Book of the Prophet Isaiah, Chapters 40–66* (Cambridge: Cambridge University Press, 1975), p. 197; R.N. Whybray, *Isaiah 40–66* (NCB; London: Oliphants, 1975), p. 291, probably; Young, *Isaiah*, III, p. 535. Young supports the unusual interpretation of "your brethren" in v. 20 as Gentile converts. Thus, it is Jews who present Gentiles as a מנחה, whereas all other commentators propose just the opposite; Achtemeier, *Isaiah 56–66*, pp. 148-49; T.R. Birks, *Commentary on the Book of Isaiah, Critical, Historical, and Prophetical* (London: Rivingtons, 1871), p. 331.

For the idea that מהם refers to Israelites, cf. Duhm, *Jesaia*, pp. 488-89; K. Marti, *Das Buch Jesaja* (Tübingen: J.C.B. Mohr, 1900), p. 413; Watts, *Isaiah 34–66*,

most natural way to read MT 66.20 is to begin the parenthetical statement at באשר and to end it after the final word of v. 20. However, it is possible to end the parenthetical statement after את־המנחה, leaving the final words of the verse—כלי טהור בית יהוה—to resume the theme of Gentile worship.

If this is how the translator understood the syntax, we might suspect that he simply could not envisage Gentile hands on sacred vessels.[128] This might well have motivated the fascinating transformation—whatever its precise mechanics—that turns a bowl into songs.

It appears that LXX Isa. 66.20 is moving its text in a direction that is at once eschatologizing, actualizing and nationalistic. It is eschatologizing because it relocates the Israelite θυσίαι to a future time. It is actualizing because it is struggling with the text in the light of a contemporary concern—the precise role of Gentile converts—that did

p. 365 (apparently); Wade, *Isaiah*, pp. 420-21; Slotki, *Isaiah*, p. 325, probably; A. Penna, *Isaia: La Sacra Bibbia. Volgata Latina e traduzione Italiana dai test originali illustrate con note critiche e commentate* (Torino: Marietti, 1964), p. 629, probably (commenting on Vulgate text).

Admittedly, this reconstruction embraces a certain tension between restricted privileges offered to Gentiles and the seemingly fuller cultic functions required of a Levite.

128. Cf., for example, Whybray, *Isaiah 40–66*, p. 291: 'As can be seen from the Priestly Code, everything connected with sacrifices had to be ceremonially clean. These Gentiles are therefore compared to a clean vessel... This is a striking reversal of the general attitude towards foreigners, who were regarded as *ipso facto* טמא, "unclean"...' The translator may have found this 'striking reversal' too harsh to bear. Note that for Whybray and others who comment on the Hebrew text, the connection between the Gentile worshippers and the phrase כלי טהור is somewhat distant: it consists of a simile that compares the Gentiles, in their function as transportation, to a pure vessel. It is still the *Israelites* who present their offering in this vessel. I am suggesting a slightly different reading on the part of the LXX, that is, that the translator understood כלי טהור to refer adverbially all the way back to the initial word of v. 20. This proposal brings the edges of cleanness and uncleanness closer together than in the consensus reading of the MT.

It must be conceded that this reading of the syntax allows the Gentiles access εἰς τὸν οἶκον κυρίου. This is perhaps an argument against attributing μετὰ ψαλμῶν to Gentile cult, in the light of my earlier argument that allowing them into the עיר rather than upon the הר itself belies a nationalistic Jewish bias. If indeed the final clause of this verse is to be attributed to the Israelite מנחה, then the argument from Zech. 14 for a universal (rather than restricted) state of holiness in eschatological Zion once again raises its head.

not receive the same attention in the original composition. It is nationalistic, because it retains a marginally higher prominence for the Israelites in the eschatological moment that it describes: down-grading the
Gentile מנחה to δῶρα, possibly removing their access to the holy
vessel(s), and identifying that very event as the time 'when the Israelites offer the מנחה.'

Summary and Conclusion

The Hebrew text of Isaiah 66 addresses twin evils, that of apostate
Jewish brethren as well as the ubiquity of the nations. The Greek text of
this chapter, on the other hand, knows nothing of a divided Jewish
community. Rather, it gives evidence of intense concern with regard to
the fate of the Gentiles vis-à-vis Zion's true children, a preoccupation
that brings non-Jews onto the scene earlier in the Greek chapter than in
its Hebrew source. Whatever sympathy the translator felt for god-
fearing Gentiles—who were presumably well-disposed towards their
would-be Jewish co-religionists—is counterbalanced by his inability or
unwillingness to allow them full rights as paid-up Yahwists in the
Lord's restored Jerusalem. They will participate in that city's final
glories, but only as tribute-bearers who remain in the moral shadow of
those returned Jews who offer eschatological sacrifice to the Lord
himself in his own house.

Chapter 8

SUMMARY AND CONCLUSIONS

The primary purpose of this book has been to describe the motivations of the translator of LXX Isaiah as these come to expression in chs. 56–66. Building upon the studies of Ziegler, Seeligmann, van der Kooij, Koenig and others, I have argued upon the grounds of lexical and grammatical-syntactical analysis that the translator displays recurrent—and therefore identifiable—*tendencies*. I have taken the Hebrew text as our *Ausgangspunkt*, attempting to treat seriously the basic fact that LXX Isaiah is *a translation*, rather than an independent literary creation. At the same time, with van der Kooij, I have been persuaded that the Greek text has its own inner coherence that makes atomistic analysis of particular verses unfruitful.

The results of this study concur with Orlinsky and the Scandinavian school that theological exegesis is to be identified only after careful study of the translator's wider technique and the linguistic options available. However, I have argued against the scepticism with regard to discovering the translator's theological 'fingerprints' that characterizes the 'Orlinsky school'.

Theological *Tendenz* and homiletical motivation can be discerned, although these are not expressed upon every available opportunity. The translator, as we have seen, has not provided a systematic interpretation of his source text. Remaining closer to the details of his Hebrew *Vorlage* than has been widely recognized, he has—by a combination of mishap and complex exegetical manoeuvre—produced a translation that differs from his source in tone and detail. Deviations between the generally similar extant Hebrew texts (MT and Qumran) and the LXX translation are not to be explained by a single process (accident or exegesis). The evidence, rather, is both diverse and ambiguous. The explanation of it must take into account instances of error, of unconscious amelioration and of fully aware theological exegesis.

Using a highly inductive approach, we have catalogued the translator's normal procedures with the Hebrew lexemes and grammatical-
syntactical constructions that he meets in Hebrew Isaiah. We have then
paid special attention to exceptions to those norms, for it is here that his
own contribution is most easily to be seen.

In Chapter 1 we surveyed the history of LXX Isaiah studies. We
accepted the consensus that the LXX *Vorlage* approximates to known
Hebrew texts. It was suggested that 'freedom' is not an adequate description of the translator's method, especially if this connotes a loose and/or
arbitrary relationship with his source text. Rather, the translator seldom
strays from his Hebrew text for more than two or three words. In this
respect, his approach is quite 'conservative'. We also suggested that his
work is to be seen in contiguity with that of wider scribal and exegetical
practice in ancient Judaism. His membership in that loose guild is a
further limitation to his alleged 'freedom'.

In Chapters 2 and 3 we attempted to develop Seeligmann's views
with regard to the 'homiletical' purpose in LXX Isaiah. Whereas Seeligmann reached his conclusions on the basis of the actualizing *content* of
the Greek text, the argument in the present work was founded upon two
grammatical and syntactical observations. In the first place, the translator frequently 'personalizes' his text by turning third-person references
into first- and second-person statements (Chapter 2). We examined and
then dismissed the possible objection that such alterations may be the
result of non-ideological grammatical 'levelling', principally because
the move is far more often in a 'personalized' direction than in its
opposite.

In Chapter 3, we noted the translator's habit of 'imperativization'.
Declarative statements are with considerable regularity turned into
commands and, with less frequency, into cohortative or 'jussive' statements. Noting parallels in the New Testament, I argued that both these
transformations serve homiletical ends and that the translator was
creating a 'preached text'.

In Chapters 4 and 5 our attention turned to 'ameliorative readings', in
which a statement about God (Chapter 4) or about some other delicate
matter (Chapter 5) was toned down or otherwise diverted from its scan-
dal-making potential. Interacting with scholars who reject such intentions (e.g. Orlinsky, Soffer)—as well as with those who affirm such
theological exegesis but with inadequate attention to the counter-
evidence (e.g. Fritsch)—we concluded that a modest but persistent

tendency to create toned down translations does indeed characterize the Isaiah translator. This is fully in line with the targumic tendency. Indeed, the Isaiah translator shares a number of religious sensibilities with the creators of the Targums. Repeatedly, the two works evade the same problems in the Hebrew text, though usually by independent means.

In Chapters 6 and 7 it was argued that the translator displays both Jewish nationalism and Diaspora sentiment. He appears not to be fully in accord with the Hebrew text's generosity towards the nations. Whereas elsewhere in LXX Isaiah this bias is more clearly evident, in chs. 56–66 it is expressed more subtly. The translator's presumed situation in the Alexandrian Diaspora does not reduce his estimation of Jerusalem, the Metropolis. On the contrary, his Hellenistic style is employed to express Zion-centred sentiment. Even if we were obligated to question Seeligmann's attribution of an inferiority complex to the Diaspora psyche, our study affirms the identification of a particular concern with Diaspora Judaism in LXX Isaiah that has been developed upon other grounds by Seeligmann, van der Kooij and Koenig.

Throughout this investigation, conclusions were reached inductively. Close comparison of the Hebrew and Greek texts sought to identify all possible deviations, only a small number of which were discussed in this volume. Frequent recurrence of certain kinds of divergences was taken as evidence of the translator's methodological *Tendenz*. The procedure has been to seek to explain the Greek text in terms of the details of its Hebrew source. On a number of occasions, the results were compared with Targum Jonathan and other representative texts of ancient Judaism.

A disputation of these results, then, might take one of three paths. First, it might attempt to prove a looser link between the Hebrew and Greek texts than this presentation has demonstrated, claiming for the translator more liberty as an independent author than this study has seen fit to allow. Such an explanation would then need to account for the wide-ranging similarities between the two texts.

Alternatively, my thesis could be contested by claiming a closer link between the two texts. This would require that apparent LXX deviations be explained as unremarkable and adequate renderings of the Hebrew text (so, generally, Orlinsky). Any such response would necessarily account for the failure of the Isaiah translator to follow the more literalistic precedents established by the Pentateuchal and other translators, as well as for the accumulation of oddly non-straightforward translations that seem to reflect the same anxieties (for example, the reluctance to have God 'come down').

Finally, a response to my conclusions might accept the deviations that have been identified and allow for the possibility of theological motivation for them, while adducing different ideological reasons for their existence. In any case, one would need to begin with the Hebrew/Greek deviations that constitute the primary empirical evidence.

If the arguments presented here are deemed persuasive, they link up with several related areas of research and suggest a number of avenues for further study.

First, in the course of developing my arguments, I have repeatedly observed that a Zion-centred, nationalistic agenda has been articulated in the language of fluent Hellenistic Greek. Indeed, the general theological inclination of the Isaiah translator, we have seen, resembles that which comes to later expression in Jewish literature like the Targumim, which are sometimes considered the antithesis of Jewish universalism. This study would appear to corroborate the decoupling with regard to ancient Diaspora Judaism of language and other cultural accoutrements from the theological tenets that were once presumed to accompany them. This is a development that is often associated with the name of Martin Hengel, though it is increasingly being brought into direct relationship with LXX translation technique, for example, in the work of Johann Cook.

There is far more theological exegesis in LXX Isaiah than it has been possible to present in this short work. Indeed, the survey of Chapter 1 has suggested already that analysis of this and related phenomena has been carried out only piecemeal thus far. Such a study promises to be particularly enriching if it is carried out in constant dialogue with Targums and targumists (not to exclude later rabbinical literature and its modern interpreters). One thinks, for example, of the work already done by D.W. Gooding, in which features of 3 Reigns are compared with later rabbinic treatment of certain biblical characters.

Second, the language of LXX Isaiah is exceedingly creative when compared with that of the Greek Pentateuch and Prophets (including here the Former Prophets/Historical Books). Though this translator seems not to wish to *appear* creative—he routinely uses one Greek word for multiple Hebrew synonyms in a given context—his inventory of vocabulary is almost astonishing. Paradoxically, lexical levelling within a certain context appears side by side with the production of a very high number of instances where a given Hebrew lexeme is rendered by a Greek equivalent that represents that Hebrew word in the LXX nowhere else ('*hapax* equivalency'). What is more, a large number of Greek words that appear in LXX Isaiah do so nowhere else in the Septuagint in the place of *any* Hebrew source ('*hapax legomenon*').

This situation suggests that the translator had a large and diverse vocabulary that far exceeds the breadth that one is accustomed to finding in other LXX books. At the same time, he seems not to have considered it important to demonstrate this, if a particular Greek word seemed adequate for the translation of a passage that used numerous Hebrew synonyms.

Though space has not permitted exploration of this matter in this work, it appears possible to find considerable overlap between the language of LXX Isaiah and that of LXX Proverbs, Job and the originally Greek books of this corpus. It is also possible that a reading of LXX Isaiah that is attentive to extrabiblical (Egyptian) Koiné of the period will further refine matters of the translator's geographical, linguistic and social location. Ziegler's identification of linguistic local colour in this book appears to invite further development.

Third—and not unrelated to the former point—the burgeoning interest in the study of the ancient Jewish Diaspora can only be enhanced by contributions from Septuagintalists who have a chastened willingness to ferret out the translator's own interpretative contribution to the biblical text he has produced. There is much to be done in the way of bringing together the increased possibility of historical description of the Jewish Diaspora near the turn of the era, on the one hand, and linguistic-exegetical analysis of LXX books, on the other. Although students of LXX Isaiah like van der Kooij have reminded their peers that a control of the period's history is essential for interpretation of the LXX, such an approach has been more often called for than rigorously practised. One thinks especially of the research into the rise of the synagogue phenomenon and suggestions regarding the liturgical genesis of the LXX that were being made already at the turn of this century. Much remains to be done in tying together these disparate threads where the evidence suggests that they might justifiably be joined.

This study has sought to remind its readers of the conservative features of the LXX text vis-à-vis its presumed *Vorlage*, this in the face of wide-ranging scholarly appreciation of its obvious liberties. In closing, however, one recognizes that LXX Isaiah is particularly fertile ground precisely because—with all the limitations underlined in these chapters—the translator so eagerly invests his own interpretative energies in the formidable project he carries out. It is remarkable that, after a century of modern examination of these 66 chapters of Greek verse and prose, there remains so much room for exploration of the ambitious mind that gave them to us.

BIBLIOGRAPHY

Achtemeier, Elizabeth, *The Community and Message of Isaiah 56–66: A Theological Commentary* (Minneapolis: Augsburg, 1982).

Ackroyd, Peter R., *I and II Chronicles, Ezra, Nehemiah: Introduction and Commentary* (London: SCM Press, 1973).

—*Exile and Restoration. A Study of Hebrew Thought of the Sixth Century BC* (London: SCM Press, 1968).

Aejmelaeus, Anneli, *On the Trail of the Septuagint Translators: Collected Essays* (Kampen: Kok, 1993).

Barr, James, *The Typology of Literalism in ancient biblical translations*. Mitteilungen des Septuaginta-Unternehmens (MSU) 15 (Göttingen: Vandenhoeck und Ruprecht, 1979).

—*Comparative Philology and the Text of the Old Testament, with Additions and Corrections* (Oxford: Oxford University Press, 1968) (reprinted with additions and corrections, Winona Lake, IN: Eisenbrauns, 1987).

Barthélemy, Dominique, *Les devanciers d'Aquila: Première publication intégrale du texte des fragments du Dodécaprophéton* (VTSup, 10; Leiden: E.J. Brill, 1963).

—*Critique textuelle de l'Ancien Testament*. II. *Isaïe, Jérémie, Lamentations* (OBO, 50.2; Göttingen: Vandenhoeck & Ruprecht, 1986).

Berlin, Adele, *The Dynamics of Biblical Parallelism* (Bloomington: Indiana University Press, 1985).

Bettiolo, P. *et al.*, *Ascensio Isaiae, Textus* (Corpus Christianorum, Series Apocryphorum, 7; Turnhout: Brepols, 1995).

Birks, T.R., *Commentary on the Book of Isaiah, Critical, Historical, and Prophetical* (London: Rivingtons, 1871).

Blenkinsopp, Joseph, 'The "Servants of the Lord" in Third Isaiah. Profile of a Pietistic Group in the Persian Epoch', *Proceedings of the Irish Biblical Association* 7 (1983), pp. 1-23 (reprinted in Gordon (ed.), *'The Place Is Too Small for Us'*, pp. 392-412).

Bonnard, P.-E., *Le Second Isaïe: Son disciple et leurs éditeurs. Isaiah 40–66* (Etudes Bibliques; Paris: Librairie Lecoffre, 1972).

Boothroyd, B., *The Holy Bible, containing the Old and New Testaments* (London: Partridge & Oakey, 1853).

Brenton, Lancelot C.L., *The Septuagint with Apocrypha: Greek and English* (London: Samuel Bagster, 1851) (reprinted in Peabody, MA: Hendrickson, 1986).

Brock, Sebastian, 'The Phenomenon of Biblical Translation in Antiquity', in Jellicoe (ed.), *Studies in the Septuagint*, pp. 541-71.

Brockington, L.H., 'Septuagint and Targum', *ZAW* 66 (1954), pp. 80-86.

Broshi, M. *et al.*, *Qumran Cave 4, XIV: Parabiblical Texts, Part 2* (DJD, 19; Oxford: Clarendon Press, 1995).

Broyles, Craig C. and Craig A. Evans (eds.), *Writing and Reading the Scroll of Isaiah: Studies of an Interpretative Tradition*, I (VTSup, 70; Leiden: E.J. Brill, 1997).

Burrows, Millar (ed.), *The Dead Sea Scrolls of St. Mark's Monastery*. I. *The Isaiah Manuscript and the Habakkuk Commentary* (Cambridge, MA: American Schools of Oriental Research, 1950).

Cathcart, Kevin J. and Robert P. Gordon, *The Targum of the Minor Prophets: Translated, with a Critical Introduction, Apparatus, and Notes* (The Aramaic Bible, 14; Edinburgh: T. & T. Clark, 1989).

Chester, Andrew, *Divine Revelation and Divine Titles in the Pentateuchal Targumim* (Texte und Studien zum antiken Judentum, 14; Tübingen: J.C.B. Mohr, 1986).

Cheyne, T.K., *The Prophecies of Isaiah: A New Translation with Commentary and Appendices* (2 vols.; London: Kegan Paul, Trench & Co., rev. 5th edn, 1889).

Chilton, Bruce D., *The Glory of Israel: The Theology and Provenience of the Isaiah Targum* (JSOT Sup, 23; Sheffield: JSOT, 1983).

—*The Isaiah Targum: Introduction, Apparatus and Notes* (Aramaic Bible, 11; Edinburgh: T. & T. Clark, 1987).

Coggins, R.J., *The First and Second Books of the Chronicles* (Cambridge Bible Commentary on the New English Bible; Cambridge: Cambridge University Press, 1976).

Conrad, Edgar W., *Reading Isaiah* (Overtures to Biblical Theology; Philadelphia: Fortress Press, 1991).

Cook, Johann, 'אִשָּׁה זָרָה (Proverbs 1–9 Septuagint): A Metaphor for Foreign Wisdom?', *ZAW* 106 (1994), pp. 458-76.

—*The Septuagint of Proverbs: Jewish and/or Hellenistic Colouring of LXX Proverbs* (VTSup, 69; Leiden: E.J. Brill, 1997).

Cox, Claude, 'Job's Concluding Soliloquy: Chs. 29–31', in Cox (ed.), *VII Congress*, pp. 325-39.

Cross, Frank Moore Cross, David Noel Freedman and James A. Sanders (eds.), *Three Scrolls from Qumran: The Great Isaiah Scroll, the Order of the Community, the Pesher to Habakkuk* (Jerusalem: Albright Institute of Archaeological Research and Shrine of the Book, 1972).

Daniel, Suzanne, *Recherches sur le vocabulaire du culte dans la Septante* (Etudes et Commentaires, 61; Paris: Librairie C. Klincksieck, 1966).

Delitzsch, Franz, *Jesaja* (Leipzig: Dörflin u. Franke, 1879) (reprinted from the 5th edn, Basel: Brunnen-Verlag, 1984).

Dillard, Raymond B., *2 Chronicles* (WBC, 15; Waco, TX: Word Books, 1987).

Dillman, August, *Der Prophet Jesaia* (Kurzgefasstes exegetisches Handbuch zum Alten Testament; Leipzig: S. Hirzel, 1890).

Duhm, Bernhard, *Das Buch Jesaia* (Göttinger Handkommentar zum Alten Testament; Göttingen: Vandenhoeck & Ruprecht, 1922).

Emerton, J.A., 'A Note on the Alleged Septuagintal Evidence for the Restoration of the Hebrew Text of Isaiah 34:11-12', *Eretz-Israel* 16 (1982, Harry M. Orlinsky Volume), pp. 34-36.

Emerton, J.A., and Stefan C. Reif (eds.), *Interpreting the Hebrew Bible: Essays in Honour of E.I.J. Rosenthal* (Cambridge: Cambridge University Press, 1982).

Erwin, H.M., 'Theological Aspects of the Septuagint of the Book of Psalms' (unpublished dissertation, Princeton Theological Seminary, 1966).

Fischer, Johann, *In welcher Schrift lag das Buch Isaias den LXX vor?* (BZAW, 56; Giessen: Alfred Töpelman, 1930).

Flashar, M., 'Exegetischen Studien zum LXX–Psalter', *ZAW* 32 (1912), pp. 81-116.

Flint, P.W., 'The Septuagint Version of Isaiah 23:1-14 and the Massoretic Text', *BIOSCS* 21 (1988), pp. 35-54.

Fohrer, Georg, *Das Buch Jesaja. 3. Band, Kapitel 40–66* (Zürcher Bibelkommentare: Zürich: Zwingli-Verlag, 1964).

Fritsch, Charles T., 'The Concept of God in the Greek Translation of Isaiah', in J.M. Myers, O. Reimherr and H.N. Bream (eds.), *Biblical Studies in Memory of H.C. Alleman* (Locust Valley, NY: J.J. Augustin, 1960), pp. 155-69.

—'Studies in the Theology of the Greek Psalter', in B.Z. Luria (ed.), זר לגבורות. *Zalman Shazar Jubilee Volume* (Jerusalem: Kiryat Sefer, 1973).

Funck, Bernd (ed.), *Hellenismus: Beiträge zur Erforschung von Akkulturation und politischer Ordnung in den Staaten des hellenistischen Zeitalters. Akten des Internationalen Hellenismus-Kolloquiums 9.–14. März in Berlin* (Tübingen: J.C.B. Mohr [Paul Siebeck], 1996).

García Martínez, Florentino, *The Dead Sea Scrolls Translated: The Qumran Texts in English* (Leiden: E.J. Brill, 1994).

Gehman, Henry. S., 'Hebraisms of the Old Greek Version of Genesis', *VT* 3 (1953), pp. 141-48.

Gerleman, Gillis, *Studies in the Septuagint. III. Proverbs* (Lund: Gleerup, 1956).

Gibson, J.C.L., *Davidson's Introductory Hebrew Grammar~Syntax* (Edinburgh: T. & T. Clark, 1994).

Gordon, R.P., 'The Targumists as Eschatologists', in J.A. Emerton (ed.), *Congress Volume, Göttingen, 1977* (VTSup, 29; Leiden: E.J. Brill, 1978), pp. 113-30.

—'*Terra Sancta* and the Territorial Doctrine of the Targum to the Prophets', in J.A. Emerton and Stefan C. Reif (eds.), *Interpreting the Hebrew Bible: Essays in Honour of E.I.J. Rosenthal* (Cambridge: Cambridge University Press, 1982), pp. 119-31.

—'Inscribed Pots and Zechariah XIV 20–1', *VT* 42 (1992), pp. 120-23.

—*Studies in the Targum to the Twelve Prophets: From Nahum to Malachi* (VTSup, 51; Leiden: E.J. Brill, 1994).

—' "Converse Translation" in the Targums and Beyond', *JSP* 19 (1999), pp. 3-21.

Gordon, Robert P. (ed.), *'The Place Is Too Small for Us': The Israelite Prophets in Recent Scholarship* (Winona Lake, USA: Eisenbrauns, 1995).

Goshen-Gottstein, M.H., 'Theory and Practice of Textual Criticism: The Text-Critical Use of the Septuagint', *Textus* 3 (1963), pp. 130-58.

Gottstein, M.H., 'Die Jesaia-Rolle im Lichte von Peschitta und Targum', *Biblica* 35 (1954), pp. 51-71.

—'Die Jesaiah-Rolle und das Problem der hebräischen Bibelhandschriften', *Biblica* 35 (1954), pp. 429-42.

Gray, George Buchanan, *A Critical and Exegetical Commentary on the Book of Isaiah I–XXVII* (title page, *I–XXXIX*). 1. *Introduction and Commentary on I–XXVII* (ICC; Edinburgh: T. & T. Clark, 1912).

Hanson, Paul D., *The Dawn of Apocalyptic* (Philadelphia: Fortress Press, 1975).

—*Isaiah 40–66: Interpretation* (Atlanta: John Knox Press, 1995).

Hayward, Robert, *The Targum of Jeremiah: Translated, with a Critical Introduction, Apparatus, and Notes* (Aramaic Bible, 12; Edinburgh: T. & T. Clark, 1987).

Hengel, Martin, 'Jerusalem als jüdische *und* hellenistische Stadt', in Funck (ed.), *Hellenismus.*

Herbert, A.S., *The Book of the Prophet Isaiah, Chapters 40–66* (Cambridge Bible Commentary on the New English Bible; Cambridge: Cambridge University Press, 1975).

House, Paul R., 'Dialogue in Zephaniah', in Gordon (ed.), *'The Place Is Too Small for Us'*, pp. 252-62.

Hugenberger, G.P., 'The Servant of the Lord in the "Servant Songs" of Isaiah: A Second Moses Figure', in Satterthwaite, Hess, and Wenham (eds.), *The Lord's Anointed*, pp. 105-140

Hurwitz, Marshall, 'The Septuagint of Isaiah 36–39 in Relation to that of 1–35, 40–66', *HUCA* 28 (1957), pp. 75-83.

Japhet, Sara, *The Ideology of the Book of Chronicles and its Place in Biblical Thought* (Beiträge zur Erforschung des Alten Testaments und des Antiken Judentums, 9; Bern: Peter Lang, 1989).

—*I and II Chronicles. A Commentary* (OTL; London: SCM Press, 1993).

Jastrow, Marcus, *A Dictionary of the Targumim, the Talmud Babli and Yerushalmi, and the Midrashic Literature* (New York: Pardes, 1950) (reprinted New York: Judaica Press, 1996).

Jellicoe, Sidney, *The Septuagint and Modern Study* (Oxford: Oxford University Press, 1968).

Jellicoe, Sidney (ed.), *Studies in the Septuagint: Origins, Recensions, and Interpretations. Selected Essays with a Prolegomenon by Sidney Jellicoe* (New York: Ktav, 1974).

Jobes, Karen H., *The Alpha-Text of Esther: Its Character and Relationship to the Masoretic Text* (SBLDS, 153; Missoula, MT: SBL, 1996).

Kaiser, Otto, *Der Prophet Jesaja, Kapitel 13–39* (Das Alte Testament Deutsch, 18; Göttingen: Vandenhoeck & Ruprecht, 1973).

Keil, Carl Friedrich, *Chronik, Esra, Nehemia und Esther* (Leipzig, 1870, reprinted Basel: Brunnen Verlag, 1990).

Kissane, Edward J., *The Book of Isaiah: Translated from a Critically Revised Hebrew Text with Commentary. II. XL–LXVI* (Dublin: Richview Press, 1943).

Klein, M.L, 'Converse Translation: A Targumic Technique', *Biblica* 57 (1976), pp. 515-37.

—'Associative and Complementary Translation in the Targumim', *Eretz-Israel* 16 (1982, Harry M. Orlinsky volume), pp. 134-40.

Knight, George A.F., *The New Israel: A Commentary on the Book of Isaiah 56–66* (International Theological Commentary; Edinburgh: Handsel, 1985).

Koenig, Jean, *L'herméneutique analogique du judaïsme antique d'après les témoins textuels d'Isaïe* (VTSup, 33; Leiden: E.J. Brill, 1982).

Kooij, Arie van der, 'Die Septuaginta Jesajas als Dokument Jüdischer Exegese.—Einige Notizen zu LXX-Jes. 7', in *Übersetzung und Deutung: Studien zu dem Alten Testament und seiner Umwelt ALEXANDER REINARD HULST gewidmet von Freunden und Kollegen* [no editor listed] (Nijkerk: G.F. Callenbach, 1977), pp. 91-102.

—*Die alten Textzeugen des Jesajabuches: Ein Beitrag zur Textgeschichte des Alten Testaments* (OBO, 35; Göttingen: Vandenhoeck & Ruprecht, 1981).

—'A Short Commentary on Some Verses of the Old Greek of Isaiah 23', *BIOSCS* 15 (1982), pp. 36-50.

—'Accident or Method? On "Analogical" Interpretation in the Old Greek of Isaiah and in 1QIs^a', *BO* 43 (1986), pp. 366-76.

—'The Old Greek of Isaiah 19:16-25', in Cox (ed.), *VI Congress*, pp. 127-66.

—'The Old Greek of Isaiah in Relation to the Qumran Texts of Isaiah: Some General Comments', in George J. Brooke and Barnabas Lindars (eds.), *Septuagint, Scrolls and Cognate Writings: Papers Presented to the International Symposium on the Septuagint and its Relations to the Dead Sea Scrolls and Other Writings, Manchester, 1990* (SBLSCS, 33; Atlanta: Scholars Press, 1992), pp. 195-213.

—'Isaiah in the Septuagint', in Broyles and Evans (eds.), *Writing and Reading the Scroll of Isaiah*, pp. 513-29.

—' "The Servant of the Lord": A Particular Group of Jews in Egypt According to the Old Greek of Isaiah. Some Comments on LXX Isa 49,1-6 and Related Passages', in Ruiten and Vervenne (eds.), *Studies in the Book of Isaiah*, pp. 383-96.

—*The Oracle of Tyre: The Septuagint of Isaiah XXIII as Version and Vision* (VT Sup, 71; Leiden: E.J. Brill, 1998).

Lampe, G.W.H., *A Patristic Greek Lexicon* (Oxford: Oxford University Press, 1961).

Laubscher, Frans du T., 'Epiphany and Sun Mythology in Zechariah 14', *JNSL* 20 (1994), pp. 125-38.

Leaney, A.R.C., 'Greek Manuscripts from the Judaean Desert', in J.K. Elliott (ed.), *Studies in New Testament Language and Text: Essays in Honour of George D. Kilpatrick on the Occasion of his Sixty-Fifth Birthday* (NovTSup, 44; Leiden: E.J. Brill, 1976), pp. 283-300.

Lentzen-Deis, Fritzleo, *Die Taufe Jesu nach den Synoptikern: Literarkritische und gattungsgeschichtliche Untersuchungen* (Frankfurter Theologische Studien, 4; Frankfurt: Josef Knecht, 1970).

Levenson, Jon Douglas Levenson, *Theology of the Program of Restoration of Ezekiel 40–48* (Missoula, MT: Scholars Press, 1976).

Lindblom, J., *Prophecy in Ancient Israel* (Oxford: Basil Blackwell, 1962).

Lust, J., E. Eynikel, and K. Hauspie, *A Greek–English Lexicon of the Septuagint, Part II. K–Ω* (Stuttgart: Deutsche Bibelgesellschaft, 1992).

Lust, J., 'The Demonic Character of Jahweh and the Septuagint of Isaiah', *Bijdragen* 40 (1979), pp. 2-14.

Macintosh, A.A., *Isaiah xxi: A Palimpsest* (Cambridge: Cambridge University Press, 1980).

—*Hosea* (ICC; Edinburgh: T. & T. Clark, 1997).

Marti, Karl, *Das Buch Jesaja* (Kurzer Handkommentar zum Alten Testament; Tübingen: J.C.B. Mohr, 1900).

MacDonald, John, 'The Particle את in Classical Hebrew: Some New Data on its Use with the Nominative', *VT* 14 (1964), pp. 264-75.

Martin, Ralph A., *Syntactical Evidence of Semitic Sources in Greek Documents* (SCS, 3; Missoula, MT: SBL, 1974).

Marx, Alfred, *Les offrandes végétales dans l'Ancien Testament: Du tribut d'hommage au repas eschatologique* (VTSup, 57; Leiden: E.J. Brill, 1994).

McCarter, Jr., P. Kyle, *Textual Criticism: Recovering the Text of the Hebrew Bible* (Philadelphia: Fortress Press, 1986).

McCarthy, Carmel, *The Tiqqune Sopherim and Other Theological Corrections in the Masoretic Text of the Old Testament* (OBO, 36; Göttingen: Vandenhoeck & Ruprecht, 1981).

McKenzie, John L., *Second Isaiah: Introduction, Translation, and Notes* (AB; New York: Doubleday, 1968).

Mekilta de-Rabbi Ishmael (trans. by Jacob Z. Lauterbach; 3 vols.; Philadelphia: Jewish Publication Society of America, 1933).

Melugin, Roy F., and Marvin A. Sweeney (eds.), *New Visions of Isaiah* (JSOTSup, 214; Sheffield: Sheffield Academic Press, 1996).

Menken, Maarten J.J., *Old Testament Quotations in the Fourth Gospel: Studies in Textual Form* (Kampen: Kok, 1996).

Miscall, Peter D., *Isaiah. Readings: A New Biblical Commentary* (Sheffield: JSOT Press, 1993).

Moore, Carey A., *Tobit: A New Translation with Introduction and Commentary* (AB, 40A; New York: Doubleday, 1996).

Motyer, J.A., *The Prophecy of Isaiah* (Leicester: Inter-Varsity Press, 1993).

Mulder, Martin Jan (ed.), *Mikra. Text, Translation, Reading and Interpretation of the Hebrew Bible in Ancient Judaism and Early Christianity* (Compendia Rerum Iudaicarum ad Novum Testamentum, 1; Assen: Van Gorcum, 1990).

Muraoka, T., 'Hebrew Hapax Legomena and Septuagint Lexicography', in Claude E. Cox (ed.), *VII Congress of the International Organization for Septuagint and Cognate Studies, Leuven 1989* (SCS, 31; Atlanta: Scholars Press, 1991), pp. 205-222.

Myers, Jacob M., *II Chronicles, Translation and Notes* (AB; New York: Doubleday, 1965).

North, Christopher R., *The Second Isaiah: Introduction, Translation and Commentary to Chapters XL–LV* (Oxford: Oxford University Press, 1964).

O'Brien, D.P., '"Is this the Time to Accept...?" (2 Kings V 26B): Simply Moralizing (LXX) or an Ominous Foreboding of Yahweh's Rejection of Israel (MT)?', *VT* 46 (1996), pp. 448-57.

Oesterley, W.O.E., *The Psalms: Translated with Text-Critical and Exegetical Notes* (London: SPCK, 1953).

Olley, J.W., *'Righteousness' in the Septuagint of Isaiah: A Conceptual Study* (SCS, 8; Missoula, MT: Scholars Press, 1979).

—'The Translator of the Septuagint of Isaiah and "Righteousness"', *BIOSCS* 13 (1980), pp. 58-74.

Olofsson, Staffan, *God Is my Rock: A Study of Translation Technique and Theological Exegesis in the Septuagint* (Stockholm: Almqvist & Wiksell International, 1990).

Orelli, C. von, *Die Propheten Jesaja und Jeremia* (Munich: C.H. Beck'sche, 1891).

Orlinsky, Harry M., 'The Treatment of Anthropomorphisms and Anthropopathisms in the Septuagint of Isaiah', *HUCA* 27 (1956), pp. 193-200.

—'The Septuagint as Holy Writ and the Philosophy of the Translators', *HUCA* 46 (1975), pp. 89-114.

Oswalt, John N., *The Book of Isaiah: Chapters 40–66* (Grand Rapids: Eerdmans, 1998).

Ottley, R.R., *The Book of Isaiah According to the LXX (Codex Alexandrinus). I. Introduction and Translation with a Parallel Version from the Hebrew* (Cambridge: Cambridge University Press, 2nd edn, 1909).

—*The Book of Isaiah According to the Septuagint (Codex Alexandrinus). II. Text and Notes* (Cambridge: Cambridge University Press, 1906).

—*A Handbook to the Septuagint* (London: Methuen, 1920).

Penna, Angelo, *Isaia: La Sacra Bibbia. Volgata Latina e Traduzione Italiana dai Test Originali Illustrate con Note Critiche e Commentate* (Torino: Marietti, 1964).

Perrot, Charles, 'The Reading of the Bible in the Ancient Synagogue', in Mulder (ed.), *Mikra*, pp. 161-88.

Peters, Melvin K.H., 'Septuagint', *ABD*, V, pp. 1093-104.

Porter, Stanley E. and Brook W.R. Pearson, 'Isaiah through Greek Eyes: The Septuagint of Isaiah', in Broyles and Evans (eds.), *Writing and Reading the Scroll of Isaiah*, pp. 531-46.

Rahlfs, Alfred, *Septuaginta: Id est Vetus Testamentum graece iuxta LXX interpretes, edidit Alfred Rahlfs* (Stuttgart: Deutsche Bibelgesellschaft Stuttgart, 1935, 1979).

Redpath, H.A., 'A Contribution towards Settling the Dates of the Translation of the Various Books of the Septuagint', *JTS* 7 (1906), pp. 606-15.

Rowland, Christopher, *The Open Heaven: A Study of Apocalyptic in Judaism and Early Christianity* (London: SPCK, 1982).

Ruiten, J. van, and M. Vervenne (eds.), *Studies in the Book of Isaiah* (Festschrift Willem A.M. Beuken; BETL, 132; Leuven: Peeters, 1997).

Ryou, Daniel Hojoon, *Zephaniah's Oracles against the Nations: A Synchronic and Diachronic Study of Zephaniah 2:1–3.8* (Biblical Interpretation Series, 13; Leiden: E.J. Brill, 1995).

Sanders, E.P., *Paul and Palestinian Judaism: A Comparison of Patterns of Religion* (London: SCM Press, 1977).

Sarna, Nahum M., 'The Interchange of the Prepositions *Beth* and *Min* in Biblical Hebrew', *JBL* 78 (1959), pp. 310-16.

Satterthwaite, Philip E., Richard S. Hess, and Gordon J. Wenham (eds.), *The Lord's Anointed: Interpretation of Old Testament Messianic Texts* (Carlisle: Paternoster, 1995).

Saydon, P.P., 'Meanings and Uses of the Particle אֵת', *VT* 14 (1964), pp. 192-210.

Schaper, Joachim, *Eschatology in the Greek Psalter* (WUNT, 2.76; Tübingen: J.C.B. Mohr [Paul Siebeck], 1995).

Schenker, A., 'Gewollt dunkel Wiedergaben in LXX? Am Beispiel von Ps 28 (29), 6', *Bib* 75 (1994), pp. 546-55.

Schiffman, Lawrence H., 'The Interchange of the Prepositions *Bet* and *Mem* in the Texts from Qumran', *Textus* 10 (1982), pp. 37-43.

Schleusner, Joh. Fried., *Novus Thesaurus Philologico-Criticus: Sive, Lexicon in LXX. et Reliquos Interpretes Græcos, ac Scriptores Apocryphos Veteris Testaementi. Editio Altera, Recensita et Locupletata* (3 vols.; London: Jacobi Duncan, 1929).

Scholz, Anton, *Die alexandrinische Uebersetzung des Buches Jesaias* (Würzburg: Leo Woerl, 1880).

Schürer, Emil, *The History of the Jewish People in the Age of Jesus Christ (175 B.C.–A.D. 135)*, III.1 (new English version, rev. and ed. Geza Vermes, Fergus Millar and Martin Goodman; Edinburgh: T. & T. Clark, 1986).

Seeligmann, I.L, *The LXX Version of Isaiah: A Discussion of its Problems* Mededelingen en Verhandelingen No. 9 van het Vooraziatisch-Egyptisch Genootschap 'Ex Oriente Lux' (Leiden: E.J. Brill, 1948).

—'Problems and Perspectives in Modern Septuagint Research', *Textus* 15 (1990), pp. 169-232.

—מקרים בתולדות נוסחת המקרא ('Researches into the Criticism of the Masoretic Text of the Bible'), *Tarbiz* 25 (1955–56), pp. 118-39.

Shenkel, James Donald, *Chronology and Recensional Development in the Greek Text of Kings* (Cambridge, MA: Harvard University Press, 1968).

Skinner, J., *The Book of the Prophet Isaiah, XL–LXVI* (Cambridge Bible for Schools and Colleges; Cambridge: Cambridge University Press, 1917).

Slotki, I.W., *Isaiah. Hebrew Text and English Translation with an Introduction and Commentary* (Hindhead, Surrey: Soncino, 1957).

Smith, John Merlin Powis, William Hayes Ward and Julius A. Bewer, *A Critical and Exegetical Commentary on Micah, Zephaniah, Nahum, Habakkuk, Obadiah and Joel* (ICC; Edinburgh: T. & T. Clark, 1912).

Smith, P.A., *Rhetoric and Redaction in Trito-Isaiah: The Structure, Growth and Authorship of Isaiah 56–66* (VTSup, 62; Leiden: E.J. Brill, 1995).

Smith, Ralph L., *Micah–Malachi* (WBC, 32; Waco, TX: Word Books, 1984).

Smyth, Herbert Weir, *Greek Grammar* (rev. Gordon M. Messing; Cambridge, MA: Harvard University Press, 1956).

Soffer, Arthur, 'The Treatment of Anthropomorphisms and Anthropopathisms in the Septuagint of Psalms', *HUCA* 38 (1957), pp. 85-107; reprinted in Sidney Jellicoe (ed.), *Studies in the Septuagint: Origins, Recensions, and Interpretations. Selected Essays with a Prolegomenon by Sidney Jellicoe* (New York: Ktav, 1974), pp. 395-417.

Soisalon-Soininen, Ilmari, *Studien zur Septuaginta-Syntax. Zu seinem 70. Geburtstag am 4 Juni 1987*. in A. Aejmelaeus and R. Sollamo (Series eds.), Annales Academiæ Scientiarum Fennicæ B 237 (Helsinki: Suomalainen Tiedeakatemia, 1979).

Sokoloff, Michael, *A Dictionary of Jewish Palestinian Aramaic of the Byzantine Period* (Ramat-Gan: Bar Ilan University Press, 1990).

Sollamo, Raija, *Repetition of the Possessive Pronouns in the Septuagint* (SCS, 40; Atlanta: Scholars Press, 1995).

Sommer, Benjamin D., 'Allusions and Illusions: The Unity of the Book of Isaiah in Light of Deutero-Isaiah's Use of Prophetic Tradition', in Melugin and Sweeney (eds.), *New Visions of Isaiah*, pp. 156-86.

—*A Prophet Reads Scripture: Allusion in Isaiah 40–66* (Stanford: Stanford University Press, 1998).

Sperber, Alexander, *The Latter Prophets According to Targum Jonathan* (The Bible in Aramaic, 3; Leiden: E.J. Brill, 1962).

Stenning, J.F., *The Targum of Isaiah* (Oxford: Oxford University Press, 1949).

Swete, Henry Barclay, *An Introduction to the Old Testament in Greek* (Cambridge: Cambridge University Press, 1914).

Taylor, J. Glen, *Yahweh and the Sun: Biblical and Archaeological Evidence for Sun Worship in Ancient Israel* (JSOTSup, 111; Sheffield: JSOT Press, 1993).

Tcherikover, Victor A. (ed.), *Corpus Papyrorum Judaicarum*. I (Cambridge, MA: Harvard University Press, 1957).

Thackeray, H. St J., 'The Greek Translators of the Prophetical Books', *JTS* 4 (1903), pp. 578-85.

—*A Grammar of the Old Testament in Greek According to the Septuagint* (Cambridge: Cambridge University Press, 1909) (reprinted as Henry St John Thackeray, *A Grammar of the Old Testament According to the Septuagint* [Hildesheim: George Olms, 1987]).

—'Primitive Lectionary Notes in the Psalm of Habakkuk', *JTS* 12 (1910/11), pp. 191-213.

—*The Septuagint and Jewish Worship. A Study in Origins*. The Schweich Lectures, 1920 (London: Oxford University Press, 1921).

Torrey, Charles Cutler, *The Second Isaiah: A New Interpretation* (Edinburgh: T. & T. Clark, 1928).

Tov, Emanuel, *The Greek Minor Prophets Scroll from Naḥal Ḥever (8evXIIgr)* (DJD, 8; Oxford: Oxford University Press, 1990).

—*Textual Criticism of the Hebrew Bible* (Assen: Van Gorcum, 1992).

—*The Text-Critical Use of the Septuagint in Biblical Research* (Jerusalem: Simor, 2nd edn, rev. and enlarged, 1997).

Troxel, Ronald L., 'ESCATOS and Eschatology in LXX–Isaiah', BIOSCS 25 (1992), pp. 18-27.

Verkuyl, Gerrit (ed.), *The Holy Bible: The Berkeley Version in Modern English* (Grand Rapids: Zondervan, 1959).

Vogels, W., 'L'Égypte mon peuple—l'universalisme d'Is 19,16-25', *Bib* 57 (1976), pp. 494-514.

Wade, G.W., *The Book of the Prophet Isaiah, with Introduction and Notes* (London: Methuen, 2nd edn, 1929).

Waltke, Bruce K. and M. O'Connor, *An Introduction to Biblical Hebrew Syntax* (Winona Lake, IN: Eisenbrauns, 1990).

Watts, John D.W., *Isaiah 34–66* (WBC, 25; Waco, TX: Word Books, 1987).

Westermann, Claus, *Das Buch Jesaja, Kapitel 40–66* (ATD, 19; Göttingen: Vandenhoeck & Ruprecht, 1966).

Wevers, John William, *Notes on the Greek Text of Exodus* (SBLSCS, 30; Missoula, MT: SBL, 1990).

Whitehouse, O.C., *Isaiah XL–LXVI* (Century Bible; Edinburgh: T. & T. Clark, 1905).

Whybray, R.N., *Isaiah 40–66* (New Century Bible; London: Oliphants, 1975).

Williamson, H.G.M., *Israel in the Book of Chronicles* (Cambridge: Cambridge University Press, 1977).

—*I and II Chronicles* (NCB; London: Marshall, Morgan & Scott, 1982).

—'Isaiah 1.11 and the Septuagint of Isaiah', in A. Graeme Auld (ed.), *Understanding Poets and Prophets: Essays in Honour of George Wishart Anderson* (JSOTSup, 152; Sheffield: JSOT Press, 1993), pp. 401-12.

Williamson, H.G.M., *The Book Called Isaiah: Deutero-Isaiah's Role in Composition and Redaction* (Oxford: Oxford University Press, 1994).

Wutz, Franz, *Die Transkriptionen von der Septuaginta bis zu Hieronymus: Beiträge zur Wissenschaft vom Alten Testament*, II (Stuttgart: W. Kohlhammer, 1925).

Young, Edward J., *The Book of Isaiah: The English Text, with Introduction, Exposition, and Notes*. III. *Chapters 40 through 66* (Grand Rapids: Eerdmans, 1972).

Ziegler, Joseph, *Untersuchungen zur LXX des Buches Isaias: Alttestamentliche Abhandlungen*, XII.3 (Münster: Aschendorff, 1934).

—*Isaias: Septuaginta Vetus Testamentum Graecum, Auctoritate Academiae Scientiarum Gottingensis editum*, XIV (Göttingen: Vandenhoeck & Ruprecht, 3rd edn, 1983).

Zillessen, Alfred, 'Bemerkungen zur alexandrinischen Übersetzung des Jesaja (c. 40–66)', *ZAW* 22 (1902), pp. 238-63.

Zimmerli, Walther, and Joachim Jeremias, *The Servant of God* (SBT, 20; London: SCM Press, 1965).

INDEXES

INDEX OF REFERENCES

OLD TESTAMENT

INDEX OF AUTHORS